ANCIENT TEXTILES SERIES VOL. 9

WAR AND WORSHIP
Textiles from 3rd to 4th-century AD Weapon Deposits in Denmark and Northern Germany

WAR AND WORSHIP
Textiles from 3rd to 4th-century AD Weapon Deposits
in Denmark and Northern Germany

Susan Möller-Wiering

with a contribution by
Lise Ræder Knudsen

Oxbow Books
Oxford and Oakville

ANCIENT TEXTILES SERIES VOL. 9

Published by
Oxbow Books, Oxford, UK

© Oxbow Books and the individual authors, 2011

ISBN 978-1-84217-428-9

This book is *available* direct from

Oxbow Books, Oxford, UK
(Phone: 01865-241249; Fax: 01865-794449)

and

The David Brown Book Company
PO Box 511, Oakville, CT 06779, USA
(Phone: 860-945-9329; Fax: 860-945-9468)

or from our website
www.oxbowbooks.com

A CIP record is available for this book from the British Library

Library of Congress Cataloging-in-Publication Data

Möller-Wiering, Susan.
  War and worship : textiles from 3rd to 4th-century ad weapon deposits in Denmark and northern Germany / Susan Möller-Wiering.
       p. cm. -- (Ancient textiles series vol. 9)
  Includes bibliographical references.
  ISBN 978-1-84217-428-9
 1. Thorsberg Site (Germany) 2. Textile fabrics, Ancient--Schleswig (Germany and Denmark) 3. Water-saturated sites (Archaeology)--Schleswig (Germany and Denmark) 4. Excavations (Archaeology)--Schleswig (Germany and Denmark) 5. Schleswig (Germany and Denmark)--Antiquities. I. Title.
  NK8907.3.M65 2011
  677.00943'512--dc22
                            2011011462

Front cover: Shield boss XFN from Illerup Ådal, with two layers of different textiles. Photo: Susan Möller-Wiering.
Back cover: Drawing by Catrin Ueker. © Susan Möller-Wiering.

Ancient Textiles Series Editorial Comitee:
Eva Andersson Strand, Margarita Gleba, Ulla Mannering
and Marie-Louise Nosch

Printed in Great Britain by
Short Run Press, Exeter

CONTENTS

List of figures ... ix
List of tables ... xi
Acknowledgements ... xii
Glossary ... xiii

Part 1

1. Introduction ... 1
   Consecrated war booty ... 1
   Textiles ... 2
   Chronology ... 2
   Method ... 3

2. Illerup Ådal ... 4
   2.1. Introduction ... 4
     Site and research history ... 4
     Chronology ... 4
     Origin of non-textile finds ... 5
     Textiles ... 5
   2.2. Technical aspects of the textiles: comparative overview ... 6
     Material ... 6
     Weaving types ... 6
     Edges and tablet weaves ... 8
     Patterns and colours ... 9
     Napping ... 7
     Textile quality ... 10
     Fur ... 12
   2.3. Technical details, context and functions ... 12
     Description according to find clusters ... 12
     Primary functions ... 25
     Intentional damage ... 25
     Wrapping ... 26
     Intended selection? ... 28
     Spatial context ... 30

3. Vimose ... 31
   3.1. Introduction ... 31
     Site and research history ... 31
     Chronology ... 31
     Origin of non-textile finds ... 31
     Textiles ... 32
   3.2. Technical aspects of the textiles ... 32
     Material ... 32
     Weaving types ... 32
     Textile quality ... 34

Contents

- 3.3. Context and functions ... 34
  - Cloth bundle ... 34
  - Other weapons ... 35
  - Primary functions ... 37
  - Wrapping and intentional damage ... 38
  - Intended selection? ... 38
  - Spatial context ... 38
  - Chronological context ... 38

4. Thorsberg ... 40
- 4.1. Introduction ... 40
  - Site and research history ... 40
  - Chronology and origin of non-textile finds ... 40
  - Textiles ... 41
- 4.2. Technical and functional aspects of the textiles ... 41
  - 4.2.1 Description according to find numbers ... 41
  - 4.2.2 Technical aspects: comparative overview ... 67
    - Material ... 67
    - Weaving types ... 67
    - Edges ... 68
    - Looms ... 72
  - 4.2.3 Context and functions: comparative overview ... 74
    - Cloaks ... 75
    - Tunic and trousers ... 76
    - The sacrifice ... 77
    - Spatial context ... 77
    - Isotope analyses ... 78

5. Nydam ... 81
- 5.1. Introduction ... 81
  - Site and research history ... 81
  - Chronology ... 81
  - Textiles ... 82
- 5.2. Technical aspects of the textiles ... 82
  - Material ... 82
  - 5.2.1 Weapons ... 83
    - Weaving types ... 83
    - Textile quality ... 84
  - 5.2.2 Clasps ... 84
    - Weaving types and textile quality ... 84
  - 5.2.3 Caulking material ... 85
    - Weaving types ... 85
    - Textile quality ... 85
  - 5.2.4 Others ... 87
- 5.3. Context and functions ... 87
  - 5.3.1 Weapons ... 87
    - Weapons in pit VI ... 87
    - Other weapons ... 89
    - Primary functions ... 89

		The sacrifice	89
		Chronological context	90
		Origin of weapons	90
	5.3.2	Clasps	90
		Primary functions	90
		Spatial context and sacrifice	91
		Nydam IV	93
		Chronological context and origin of clasps	93
	5.3.3	Caulking material	93
		Structural context	93
		Functional context	94
		Chronological context and origin of the Nydam boat	94
	5.3.4	Others	94
5.4.	Comparisons within the Nydam material		95
	5.4.1	Technical aspects of the textiles	95
		Weaving types	95
		Textile quality	96
	5.4.2	Context and functions	96
		Primary functions	96
		The sacrifice	96
		Origin of non-textile finds	97
		Chronological context	97
		Clasps vs. caulking material	97

6. Gremersdorf-Techelwitz 99

7. Comparisons 100

7.1. Comparisons of the sites 100

7.1.1 Technical aspects 100

Material 100

Weaving types and textile quality 100

Edges 102

7.1.2 Context and functions 103

Primary functions 103

The sacrifice 105

Chronological context 107

7.2. Comparisons with other material 107

Technical aspects 108

Tunics 108

Trousers 113

Cloaks 117

Caulking material 120

Consecrated textiles 121

Textiles in graves 122

Textiles in settlements 124

8. Summary and Conclusion 127

Illerup Ådal 127

Vimose 128

Thorsberg 128

    Nydam 130
    Specific aspects in comparison 130
    Textiles from other sources 131
    Origin 132
    Textiles for war 133
    War and worship 133

9. Zusammenfassung und Ergebnisse 135
    Illerup Ådal 135
    Vimose 136
    Thorsberg 137
    Nydam 138
    Spezielle Aspekte im Vergleich 139
    Textilien aus anderen Quellen 140
    Herkunft 141
    Textilien für den Krieg 142
    Krieg und Kult 142

10. Bibliography 145

11. Appendix 151
   11.1. Illerup Ådal: list of textiles 154
   11.2. Vimose: list of textiles 155
   11.3. Thorsberg: list of textiles 156
   11.4. Nydam: list of textiles 158
   11.5. Nydam: list of examined weapons stored at Archäologisches Landesmuseum
        Schloss Gottorf, Schleswig 161

Part 2

12. Tablet-woven textiles from 3rd to 4th-century AD weapon deposits in Denmark and northern Germany 163
Lise Ræder Knudsen

12.1 Introduction 163
12.2 Description of the finds 163
    Illerup 163
    Nydam 165
    Thorsberg 168
    Vimose 176
12.3 The interpretation and comparison of different technical details concerning tablet-woven borders found in weapon deposits 177
    Independent bands versus integrated bands 177
12.4 The large cloak from Thorsberg F.S. 3686 "Prachtmantel 1" 184
12.5 Conclusions 191

LIST OF FIGURES

All photos and drawings by the individual authors unless stated otherwise in captions.

1.1. Illerup Ådal, thread counts of tabbies 7
1.2. Illerup Ådal, thread counts of diagonal twills in z/z 7
1.3. Illerup Ådal, thread counts of diamond twills in z/z 8
1.4. Illerup Ådal, thread counts of diagonal twills in z/s 8
1.5. Illerup Ådal, thread counts of diamond twills in z/s 9
1.6. Illerup Ådal, thread counts of spin-patterned twills 9
1.7. Illerup Ådal, indications of napping on lancehead RBO 11
1.8. Illerup Ådal, sewn fur on shield boss RBB 14
1.9. Illerup Ådal, find cluster 85/85, sketch of weapons with textiles, not to scale 19
1.10. Illerup Ådal, microstratigraphy in the vicinity of shield boss IWR 21
1.11. Illerup Ådal, section of find cluster 111/100 24
1.12. Illerup Ådal, shield boss STA with linear damages 26
1.13. Illerup Ådal, coiled up rope UAU in find cluster 79/104 29
1.14. Vimose, thread counts 33
1.15. Vimose, thread counts of the textiles in the "cloth bundle" 34
1.16. Vimose, wrapping according to the axes on lancehead 24756 36
1.17. Vimose, wrapping laid double on lancehead 24721 36
1.18. Thorsberg, edge of the tunic (3683) with starting border and selvedge 44
1.19. Thorsberg, edged hole on the tunic (3683) 44
1.20. Sketch of the "Thorsberg seam", not to scale 45
1.21. Thorsberg, open seam along the side of the tunic (3683) 45
1.22. Thorsberg, open seam along the side of the tunic (3683) 46
1.23. Thorsberg, seam in the left sleeve of the tunic (3683) 46
1.24. Thorsberg, beginning of the slits at the lower end of the sleeve (3683) 47
1.25. Thorsberg, faded outside and partly red threads along a cut on the tunic (3683) 47
1.26. Thorsberg, upper edge on the right hip of trousers 3684 50
1.27. Thorsberg, cords along the open seam on the lower leg of trousers 3684 50
1.28. Thorsberg, heel with gore and hemmed "Thorsberg seams" on trousers 3684 51
1.29. Thorsberg, pair of trousers 3685 52
1.30. Thorsberg, cut upper edge of trousers 3685 53
1.31. Thorsberg, starting edge on cloak 3687 56
1.32. Thorsberg, transition from ground weave to fringes along the finishing border on cloak 3687 56
1.33. Thorsberg, cloak 3687 56
1.34. Thorsberg, cloak 3688 with cuts 57
1.35. Thorsberg, 3697, finishing border 61
1.36. Thorsberg, weaving mistakes on 3699 62
1.37. Thorsberg, 3700 with woolly and smooth stripes 64
1.38. Thorsberg, 24824a with trimmed edge 64

1.39.	Thorsberg, thread counts	68
1.40.	Thorsberg, cloak 3686, starting edge	70
1.41.	Thorsberg, cloak 3688 and 24823a/b, two variations of border, not to scale	71
1.42.	Thorsberg, cloak 3688, warp ends turned over with extending threads inserted	71
1.43.	Hypothetical warping method for tablet weaves with outermost securing cord	73
1.44.	Nydam, thread counts	83
1.45.	Nydam, hook of a pair of clasps (7093)	86
1.46.	Nydam, caulking material on plank 5780 (lower right)	86
1.47.	Gremersdorf-Techelwitz, shield boss 11392d	99
1.48.	All sites, average thread counts of tabbies	102
1.49.	All sites, average thread counts of plain 2/2 twills in z/z and s/s	103
1.50.	All sites, average thread counts of plain 2/2 twills in z/s and spin patterned	104
1.51.	All sites, average thread counts of broken and diamond twills in z/z and z/s	104
1.52.	Hjemsted, Sievern and Flögeln-Voßbarg, thread counts	123
2.1.	Cat. no. 01, Illerup. Imprint of tablet-woven border	166
2.2.	Cat. no. 02, Illerup. Imprint of tablet-woven border	166
2.3.	Cat. no. 03, Illerup. Imprint of tablet-woven border	166
2.4.	Cat. no. 04, Illerup. A tablet-woven border preserved on a lancehead	166
2.5.	Cat. no. 05, Illerup. A tablet-woven border and twill fabric preserved on the surface of a shieldboss	166
2.6.	Cat. no. 05, Illerup.	166
2.7.	Cat. no. 06, Illerup. A lancehead on which a twill fabric is preserved	167
2.8.	Cat. no. 07, Nydam. A tablet-woven border preserved in the corrosion of a nail	167
2.9.	Cat. no. 08, Nydam. A twill fabric edged with an integrated border	167
2.10.	Cat. no. 09, Nydam. An imprint on wood of a tablet-woven border	167
2.11.	Cat. no. 10, Thorsberg. A thick border of at least 56 tablets of different threading	167
2.12.	Cat. no. 11, Thorsberg. A coarse twill fabric edged by a border of at least 12 tablets	167
2.13.	Cat. no. 12, Thorsberg. Tabby edges made by four tablets	170
2.14.	Cat. no. 13a, Thorsberg. The tablet-woven edge of the Thorberg tunic with edging cord	170
2.15.	Cross-section representing the four threads in each tablet, and the weft of the tablet border	170
2.16.	Cat. no. 13b, Thorsberg. Tablet-woven border with pattern sewn onto the sleeves of the tunic	170
2.17.	Cat. no. 14a, Thorsberg. Drawing of the finishing border of the large cloak	170
2.18.	Cat. no. 14a, Thorsberg. Tablet-woven finishing border of the large cloak	171
2.19.	Cat. no. 14b, Thorsberg. Tablet-woven border opposite the finishing border of the large cloak	171
2.20.	Cat. no. 14c, Thorsberg. Remaining fringes of the large cloak	174
2.21.	Cat. no. 14d, Thorsberg. The tablet-woven left side border	174
2.22.	Method of weaving border F.S. 3688	174
2.23.	Cat. No. 15, Thorsberg. A tablet-woven border edging a twill fabric	175
2.24.	Cat. No. 16a, Thorsberg. A large twill fabric edged by a tablet-woven border	175
2.25.	Cat. No. 16b, Thorsberg	175
2.26.	Cat. No. 17, Thorsberg. A fine, light brown, twill fabric edged by a tablet-woven border	175
2.27.	Drawing showing the appearance of an edge of a border	175
2.28.	Cat. no. 18. Thorsberg. A leg wrap edged by tablet-woven borders	178
2.29.	Cat. no. 20, Thorsberg. A twill fabric edged by a tablet-woven border	178
2.30.	Cat. no. 21, Thorsberg. A very fine tablet-woven border with elaborated fringes	178
2.31.	Cat. no. 22, Thorsberg. A diamond-twill fabric edged by a tablet-woven border of three tablets	178

List of Figures and Tables

2.32.	Cat. no. 23, Thorsberg. Finishing border of a twill fabric	178
2.33.	Cat. no. 24, Thorsberg. Side border of 12 tablets	178
2.34.	Cat. no. 25, Vimose. Lancehead on which a preserved tablet-woven border is seen	179
2.35.	Cat. no. 26. Vimose. Fragment of a tablet-woven border preserved in the corrosion of a spearhead	179
2.36.	Cat179. no. 27, Vimose. Shield boss with fringes and a fragment of tablet-woven border	179
2.37.	Cat. no. 29, Vimose. A weak imprint of a tablet border on the blade of a lancehead	179
2.38.	Warp from Tegle in Norway, where tablet-woven side borders are prepared	179
2.39.	A leg wrapper from Thorsberg	183
2.40.	The large cloak from Thorsberg F.S. 3686	186
2.41.	The lower edge of the finishing border of the large cloak F.S. 3686	187
2.42.	Making a tablet-woven starting border with two balls of yarn	187
2.43.	Making a tablet-woven border after the fabric was taken off the loom	187
2.44.	Two z-spun single threads cross each other	190
2.45.	When the threads are allowed to twist they refuse	190
2.46.	A z-spun and an s-spun thread are joined in a cross	190
2.47.	When the threads are allowed to twist they do!	190
2.48.	Left side border of the large cloak F.S. 3686 from Thorsberg	190
2.49.	Schlabow's drawing of the cloak as it is mounted	192
2.50.	Schalbow's drawing computer manipulated	193
2.51.	A coarse twill fabric from Thorsberg with interlinking loops at the edge	194

LIST OF TABLES

1.1.	Illerup Ådal, size of pattern units in diamond twills	12
1.2.	All sites, average thread counts of all weaving types	102
1.3.	All sites, features characterising the sacrifice	107
1.4.	Characteristic features of tunics compared to Thorsberg	112
1.5.	Weaves and thread counts of cloaks	118
2.1.	Number of tablets pr. cm used to make the borders from Illerup, Nydam, Thorsberg and Vimose	164
2.2.	The distribution of integrated and independent borders from weapon deposits	180
2.3.	Tablet-woven borders in weapon deposits	195

ACKNOWLEDGEMENTS

The present study describes the results of the research project "Textiles for War". It would never have been successful without the generous support of many people and institutions – providing material, information, comments and, above all, financing for the entire project. I am most grateful to, in alphabetical order:

Eva Andersson Strand, Centre for Textile Research, Copenhagen, Denmark
Archäologisches Landesmuseum Schloss Gottorf, Stiftung Schleswig-Holsteinische Landesmuseen, Schleswig, Germany
Marie-Louise Bech Nosch, Centre for Textile Research, Copenhagen, Denmark
Lise Bender Jørgensen, Norges Teknisk-Naturvitenskapelige Universitet, Trondheim, Norway
Ruth Blankenfeldt, Archäologisches Landesmuseum Schloss Gottorf, Schleswig, Germany
Marianne Bloch Hansen, Centre for Textile Research, Copenhagen, Denmark
Carlsberg Foundation, Copenhagen, Denmark
Centre for Textile Research, The Danish National Research Foundation's Centre for Textile Research, University of Copenhagen, Denmark
Claus von Carnap-Bornheim, Archäologisches Landesmuseum Schloss Gottorf, Schleswig, Germany
Martin Ciszuk, Högskolan i Borås, Borås, Sweden
Joanne Cutler, Institute of Archaeology, University College, London, United Kingdom
DressID, a project financed by the EU
Carol van Driel-Murray, University of Amsterdam, Amsterdam, The Netherlands
Forskningsrådet for Kultur og Kommunikation, Forsknings- og Innovationsstyrelsen, Copenhagen, Denmark
Roberto Fortuna, Nationalmuseet, Copenhagen, Denmark
Karin Frei, Centre for Textile Research, Copenhagen, Denmark
Margarita Gleba, Centre for Textile Research, Copenhagen, Denmark
Karin Göbel, Archäologisches Landesmuseum Schloss Gottorf, Schleswig, Germany
Lena Hammarlund, Högskolan i Borås, Borås, Sweden
Jørgen Ilkjær, Moesgård Museum, Moesgård, Denmark
Iron Age in Northern Europe, a project financed by the Carlsberg Foundation
Nina Lau, Archäologisches Landesmuseum Schloss Gottorf, Schleswig, Germany
Ulla Mannering, Centre for Textile Research, Copenhagen, Denmark
Vibe Maria Martens, Centre for Textile Research, Copenhagen, Denmark
Suzana Matešić, Archäologisches Landesmuseum Schloss Gottorf, Schleswig, Germany
Moesgård Museum, Moesgård, Denmark
Cherine Munkholt, Centre for Textile Research, Copenhagen, Denmark
Nationalmuseet, The National Museum of Denmark, Copenhagen, Denmark
Anna Nørgaard, Vikingeskibsmuseet, Roskilde, Denmark
Xenia Pauli Jensen, Nationalmuseet, Copenhagen, Denmark
Lise Ræder Knudsen, Center for Bevaring af Kulturarven, Vejle, Denmark
Andreas Rau, Archäologisches Landesmuseum Schloss Gottorf, Schleswig, Germany
Flemming Rieck, Vikingeskibsmuseet, Roskilde, Denmark
Irene Skals, Nationalmuseet, Copenhagen, Denmark
Julian Subbert, Universität Hamburg, Germany
Ingrid Ulbricht, Archäologisches Landesmuseum Schloss Gottorf, Schleswig, Germany
Jürgen Wiering, punctum saliens, Rendsburg, Germany
Gabriele Zink, Archäologisches Landesmuseum Schloss Gottorf, Schleswig, Germany

GLOSSARY

The glossary encompasses textile-related terms mentioned in chapters 1, 7 and 8.

2/2 twill: see *twill*.

Balanced: the *thread count* of the *warp* is rather similar to that of the *weft*, e.g. 18 × 14 threads per cm.

Basket weave: *weaving type* like *tabby*, but with two parallelly used *threads* instead of one both in *warp* and *weft*.

Braid: at least three strands of *fibres* or other flexible material are intertwined into a rather long, but relatively thin structure.

Breeches: here *trousers* reaching only to the knees (not necessarily as a riding-garment).

Broken twill: see *twill*.

Cashmere: very fine *wool* of the Kashmir goat.

Chevron twill: see *twill*.

Clasp: fastening device for clothing consisting of two parts, here of hook and eye.

Cloak: loose, sleeveless outer garment worn around the shoulders.

Cord: here several *threads* twined together and used as one.

Cuff: end of a sleeve around the wrist.

Diagonal twill: see *twill*.

Diamond twill: see *twill*.

Fabric: here a woven piece of *textile*.

Fibre: the smallest unit in a *thread* and thus in a *textile*. Here most often a single *hair*.

Finishing border: border at the end or bottom of a *fabric*, fastening the loose *warp* threads by plaiting or *tablet weaving*; typical on fabrics woven on the *warp-weighted loom*.

Gold tinsel: here *thread* made of a gold strip wound around a core of other *fibres*.

Goose-eye twill: see *twill*.

Grain: lines or pattern visible in a *fabric*, based on the *weaving type*.

Gusset: triangular insertion into e.g. a *tunic* in order to enlarge or widen a certain part of it.

Hair: here in general the *fibres* growing on the skin of animals; in particular, rather thick animal fibres while the thin ones are called *wool*.

Half basket weave: *weaving type* like *tabby*, but with two parallelly used *threads* instead of one in either *warp* or *weft*.

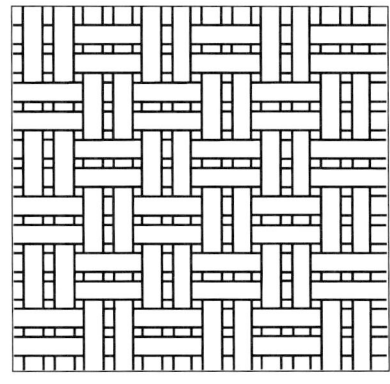

Basket weave

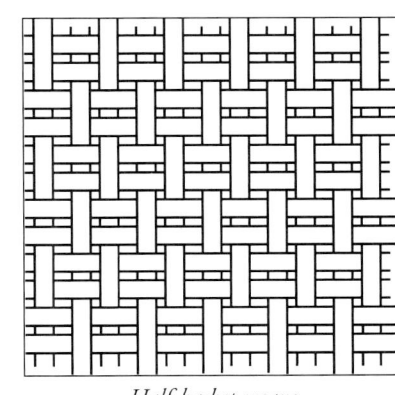

Half-basket weave

Hem: edge of a fabric fastened by folding and stitching, e.g. as the lower end of a shirt.

Leg wrap: here long, broad strip of *fabric* to be wound around the lower leg as part of the leg clothing.

Legging: here long, more or less tubular piece of clothing for only one leg, fastened e.g. to a belt, usually used in pairs and worn above *trousers*.

Napping: special finishing for a wool *fabric*, pulling out and cutting ends of *fibres*, resulting in a soft surface like very short-haired fur.

Pattern unit: number of *threads* in *warp* and *weft* (respectively) of a quarter rhombus or square making up the pattern in a *diamond twill*.

Plain twill: see *twill*.

Prachtmantel: magnificent *cloak*, defined by Karl Schlabow (1976, 66) as edged with a broad, polychrome *tablet weave* woven with over 100 tablets.

Quality: often only referring to categories of *thread count*; in a strict sense, however, the term refers to a combination of elements characterising a *fabric* or a piece of clothing including selection, preparation and fineness of *fibres*, eveness of spinning and diameter of *threads*, type and evenness of the weave, thread count, colour and – in given cases – care spent on final steps like sewing, hemming, *napping* and decorations.

Reps: variant of *tabby* in which the *warp* covers the *weft* or vice versa.

S-spinning: see *spinning direction*.

Seam: line along which two edges of *fabric* are sewn together.

  Thorsberg seam: variant of a seam found in Roman Iron Age clothing, see Fig. 1.20.

Selvedge: edge of a *fabric* parallel to the *warp*, created by the *weft* reaching the edge, turning by 180° and running back into the fabric.

Spin pattern: see *spinning direction*.

Spinning direction: *fibres* are spun into a *thread* by twisting them either clockwise or anti-clockwise; when looking onto the length of the thread, the twist results in a diagonal arrangement of the fibres.

  S-spinning: fibres running in a thread apparently from top left to bottom right, like the middle part of the letter "S".

  Z-spinning: fibres running in a thread apparently from top right to bottom left, like the middle part of the letter "Z".

  spin pattern: alternating (groups of) threads spun in s- and z-direction in the *warp* and/or the *weft* of a *fabric*.

S- and z-spinning

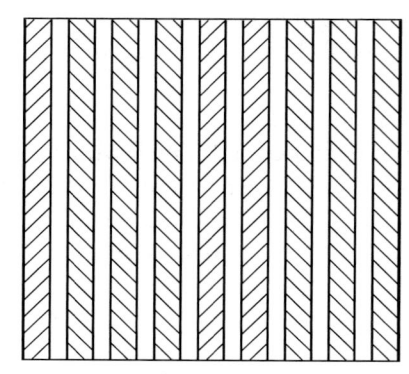

Spin pattern

Starting border: strong, band-like, woven border to be fastened to a *warp-weighted loom* and from which the *warp threads* of the future *fabric* protrude; often made as *tablet weave*.

Starting cord: cord used instead of a *starting border*.

Tabby: a basic *weaving type*, the simplest one; each *warp thread* runs alternating over and under subsequent *weft threads* and vice versa.

Tablet weave: band-like weave using thin tablets (usually square with a hole in each corner) for arranging the *warp*; for further details, see Ræder Knudsen (this volume).

Textile: flexible structure based on *fibres*; can be linear (*thread*) or two- or three-dimensional (*fabric*, sprang, knitting, felt and others).

Tabby

Thorsberg seam: see *seam*.

Thread: linear structure made from spun *fibres*; here = yarn.

Thread count: number of *threads* per cm in *warp* and/or *weft* of a *fabric*; = tpc.

Tpc: see *thread count*.

Trousers: two-legged garment reaching from about the waist to the ankles.

Tubular edge: variant of *selvedge* in which the outermost warp threads form a tube.

Tubular warping: *warp* on a vertical, two- (or three-) beamed loom (i.e. the warp is stretched vertically between the horizontal beams, without weights), turning the continuous warp thread again and again around a horizontal thread that marks the beginning as well as the end of the weave, thus resulting in a tubular *fabric*; the tube can be converted into a flat fabric by removing that particular thread.

Tunic: here shirt to be pulled over the head, with or without sleeves.

Twill: a basic *weaving type*; here only present as 2/2 twill in a number of variants; the *grain* of a twill is characterised by diagonal lines.

2/2 twill: each *warp thread* lies on top of two *weft threads*, then passes under the next two weft threads, then again above the next two and so on; the neighbouring warp thread repeats the pattern, but shifted by one weft thread, thus creating the diagonal lines.

Chevron twill

broken twill: here a 2/2 twill with an occasional change in the direction of the diagonal lines, probably due to a weaving mistake.

chevron twill: here a 2/2 twill with a regular change in the direction of the diagonal lines, but restricted to changes in either warp or weft, resulting in a zig-zag-pattern.

diagonal twill: a 2/2 twill with continuous diagonal lines running obliquely across the whole fabric; here = plain twill.

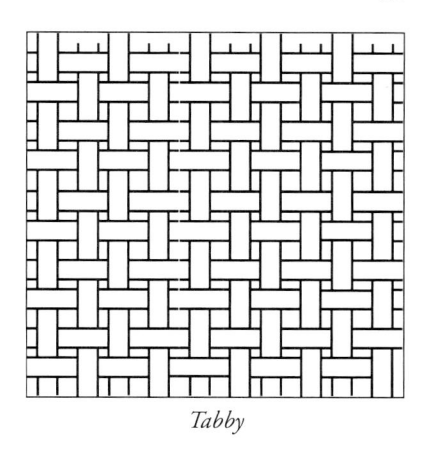

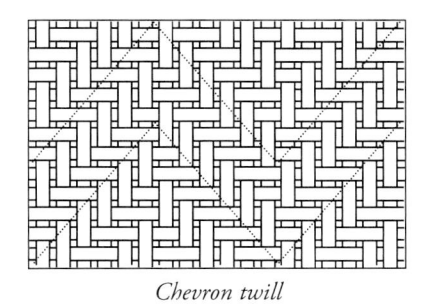

Diagonal twill

diamond twill: a 2/2 twill with a regular change in the direction of the diagonal lines both in warp and weft, resulting in a pattern of squares or more often rhombi with a distinct arrangement of threads along the lines of change.

goose-eye twill: a 2/2 twill similar to the diamond twill, but with a different arrangement of threads along the lines of change; apparently often a weaving mistake.

plain twill: see *diagonal twill*.

Warp: entirety of as well as single *threads* making up the length of a *fabric*; fastened to the loom and stretched before starting to weave and remaining passive during the process of weaving (↔ weft).

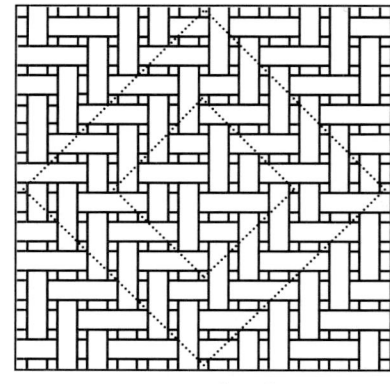

Diamond twill

Warp-weighted loom: almost vertical loom on which the *warp* protrudes from a *starting border* fastened to one horizontal beam at the top, being stretched by weights at the bottom.

Weaving type: structure of a *fabric* as determined by the arrangement of the *warp* and the process of inserting the *weft*; two basic weaving types are relevant here: *tabby* and 2/2 *twill*.

Weft: (theoretically) continuous *thread* making up the width of a *fabric*; inserted into the *warp* during weaving, thus representing the active part in process of weaving (↔ warp).

Weft-dominated: *fabric* in which the *weft* covers the *warp* to a great extent.

Wool: here in general soft *hair* of animals like sheep and goat, assigned for *textiles*; in particular the fine ones.

Yarn: see *thread*.

Z-spinning: see *spinning direction*.

PART 1

1. INTRODUCTION

Until 150 years ago, bogs or fens characterised the landscapes of Denmark and northern Germany. Many of them once consisted of swampy areas as well as open lakes. In the course of time, the lakes disappeared due to natural processes and – later – as a result of human intervention. For archaeologists, many of these bogs prove to be a highly valuable source. This book focuses on the four bog sites of Thorsberg in Germany, and Nydam, Vimose and Illerup Ådal in Denmark.[1] All four sites are well-known for containing a substantial amount of archaeological materials, particularly weapons. They also shed light on the Roman Iron Age in the Barbaricum and continue to generate new research questions and results. They are not by far the only weapon deposits, but they are amongst the largest ones known to date. Weapon deposits of the first five or six centuries AD were discovered at about 30 sites, primarily in Denmark but also in southern Sweden and northernmost Germany (von Carnap-Bornheim and Ilkjær 2008, 10, Abb. 1). One of the smallest assemblages was found in Gremersdorf-Techelwitz in Schleswig-Holstein and is briefly included in this study.

CONSECRATED WAR BOOTY

Archaeological research into the bogs and their weapons began about 150 years ago. One of its pioneers was the Danish archaeologist Conrad Engelhardt (1825–1881) who excavated parts of Thorsberg, Nydam and Vimose as well as Kragehul.[2] His publications on these sites appeared in 1863, 1865, 1869 and 1867, respectively. The idea that the weapons could have been consecrated to deities emerged already in this early period. Jens Jacob Asmussen Worsaae (1821–1885) proposed this hypothesis in 1865 and Conrad Engelhardt supported it in his book on Kragehul in 1867 (pp. 16–17). To date, a lively scholarly debate has ensued over the identity of the people whose belongings were sacrificed, the question of who the aggressors were, the areas where the battles may have taken place, and many others issues. Recent contributions to this discussion may be followed in publications such as *Sejrens Triumf* (2003),[3] Abegg-Wigg and Rau (2008) and the PhD thesis of Xenia Pauli Jensen (2008) and are not repeated here in any detail. On a more general level, sacrifices in the Roman Iron Age have been evaluated by Wolf-Rüdiger Teegen (1999).

The hypothesis of sacrificed war booty is supported by written evidence, of for example, Caesar, Strabo, Diodor, and Orosius. These sources were already cited by Worsaae and Beauvois in the 1860s, and then by Engelhardt (1867, 16–17) and still continue to be the subject of discussion (e.g. Ilkjær 1975, 151; Grane 2003). They report on a custom of the Gauls who dedicated some of the potential booty already before the battle, and who after the battle consigned gold and silver into lakes. They further report on similar habits amongst the Germanic tribes, namely the Cimbri and Teutons, who, after a battle against the Romans in the late 2nd century BC, destroyed their booty (including clothes) in fury before casting it into a river.

The majority of archaeological war booty assemblages testify to damage which precede their immersion in the bogs. Conrad Engelhardt surmised that much of this damage did not originate in the battles themselves, but was due to the subsequent rituals (1869, 5). This has been confirmed by modern research (e.g. Petersen 1995, 24).

TEXTILES

Following Claus von Carnap-Bornheim and Jørgen Ilkjær's interpretation of the situation in Illerup Ådal (1996a, 16), which represents the currently held view on the weapon deposits (Carnap-Bornheim and Ilkjær 2008, 9), the point of departure for the present investigation is the hypothesis that the materials were sacrificed by the people living in the neighbourhood or region of the bog in question, and that the weapons and personal belongings were once owned by foreign warriors. It was not assumed, however, that this also applied to the textiles which might have been taken from local resources. Von Carnap-Bornheim and Ilkjær (ibid.,15) proposed that the items had been collected in sacks. Güde Bemmann and Jan Bemmann too argued that some fabrics, which had been discovered in Nydam as a closed find together with spearheads, represented a sack (1998 vol. 2, 229). Sacking material would probably rather indicate local additions than foreign material. On the other hand, Jørgen Ilkjær also considered the possibility that the textiles might have been garments belonging to the warriors (1993a, 16). Since clearly identifiable pieces of clothing were excavated in Thorsberg, this hypothesis seems valid. The possibility that the fabrics represent bags hanging from the belt and containing personal belongings (ibid., 123) may only be a minor one.

While the clothes found in Thorsberg attracted much attention from the very outset, the textiles from other sites remain relatively unknown to date. The literature related to the various deposits is cited below in the relevant chapters. With the exception of Thorsberg, publications dealing particularly with textiles from weapon deposits are almost non-existent, apart from the preliminary results of the present research (Möller-Wiering 2008; 2000; forthcoming b).

CHRONOLOGY

In recent decades, the rapidly growing knowledge of the weapon deposits have resulted – amongst other issues – in the identification and definition of single deposits on the large sites and thus in a detailed chronology. Much of this work was undertaken by Jørgen Ilkjær, who provided information pertaining to about 17 sites correlated in a table (2003, 46, fig. 2). Of the four sites relevant here, the sacrifices first began in Vimose, followed by Illerup, Thorsberg and Nydam. In the case of Vimose, an even more refined chronology was developed by Xenia Pauli Jensen (2008, 34–40) demonstrating that, the first weapons had already been deposited by the first century AD (Vimose 0). Yet, since all four sites contain more than one deposit, some chronological overlapping exists in the later phases. On the other hand, textiles are not preserved from every single deposit. The oldest large group of weaves proves to be the material from Illerup Ådal. Therefore, Illerup was chosen as the first site to be described here, followed by Vimose, Thorsberg and finally Nydam. More information about each site is given below.

METHOD

Due to different preservation conditions in Illerup Ådal, Vimose, Thorsberg and Nydam, the textile materials and thus the possibilities for their evaluation vary from site to site. This results in separate descriptions, interpretations and lists for each site. Yet, it is self evident that in each case, the investigation begins with an examination of the technical details of the fabrics including microstratigraphy. The inspection was focused on those items which were recognised as textiles from the outset. Moreover, certain amounts of weapons were examined in order to identify possible additional textile material. It was impossible – and did not seem reasonable – however, to check the entire corpus of material comprising tens of thousands of metal items. Based on these fundamental data, the textiles from each site are then compared to one another and described as a unit characterising the particular site. Yet, the evaluation is not restricted to technical aspects. In order to answer questions e.g. about the textiles' functions before and within the sacrifice, the correlation between weave and non-textile artefact as well as their spatial distributions need to be analysed wherever possible. Having interpreted the material from each site from various perspectives, comparisons are drawn between Illerup, Vimose, Thorsberg and Nydam. Again, the evaluation not only includes technical features but emphasises the overall context. Finally, textiles from other sites and even other regional and chronological contexts are taken into account for comparison.

Notes

1. As the names do not refer to settlements but to landscape elements – a hill (Thorsberg), a pond (Nydam), a bog (Vimose) and a valley (Illerup Ådal) – it might be correct to use them together with an article, i.e. "the Vimose" etc. Yet, since the article is usually left out in the literature, this will be done here as well.
2. Kragehul is situated about 30 km southwest of Odense on the island of Fyn. This site, however, was not included in this project.
3. An English edition, *The Spoils of Victory: The North in the Shadow of the Roman Empire* and a German one, *Sieg und Triumpf: der Norden im Schatten des Römischen Reiches*, both edited by L. Jørgensen, B. Storgaard and L. G. Thomsen, were published in 2003 by the National Museum of Denmark.

2. ILLERUP ÅDAL

2.1. INTRODUCTION

Site and research history

The valley of Illerup Ådal is situated in the Jutland Peninsula, about 25 km southwest of Århus. Earlier, a lake had covered the valley bottom. The prehistoric site was discovered in 1950 (Ilkjær 1990a, 15–16) and excavations were begun the same year. However, the major fieldwork was conducted between 1975 and 1985. Subsequently, Jørgen Ilkjær has played a salient role in the research pertaining to this site. Although only c. 40% of the area has been excavated, more than 15,000 objects have come to light (ibid., 24). A recent overview of the site's history, its material and interpretation was given by Ilkjær in 2006 (published 2008). Detailed results have been issued in a series of twelve volumes to date. They deal with different categories of materials, i.e. lances and spears (Ilkjær 1990a, 1990b), belts and personal belongings (Ilkjær 1993a, 1993b), luxury sets of weapons and horse-riding equipment (von Carnap-Bornheim and Ilkjær 1996a, 1996b, 1996c, 1996d), shields (Ilkjær 2001a, 2001b) and swords (Biborski and Ilkjær 2006a, 2006b). Among these, vol. 8 (von Carnap-Bornheim and Ilkjær 1996d) is of particular interest as it contains the complete set of site maps in a scale of 1:10, 1:5 and 1:2. Three brief reports on some textiles had been submitted by Lise Bender Jørgensen 30 years ago,[1] but remain unpublished to date.

The basic chemical composition of the ground in Illerup Ådal was favourable to the preservation of metals. Moreover, substantial amounts of items crafted of wood, bone and antler were found. However, the chemicals were not conducive to the preservation of wool and leather. Yet, some textiles did survive, primarily preserved by iron oxides from shield bosses, lanceheads and spearheads, swords, arrows and axes. Moreover, pieces of cordage as well as complete ropes came to light. The finds were not distributed evenly in the bog but were encountered in certain areas, i.e. within more than 40 "find clusters". Such a cluster ("Fundkonzentration") is defined as an assemblage in which the finds lay so closely that they must have been deposited together (Ilkjær 1993a, 16). These artefacts are stored at Moesgård Museum near Århus.

Chronology

As far as is excavated to date, the weapon deposit of Illerup Ådal consists of four depositions, "Platz" A–D. Platz A covered most of the former lake while B and C encompassed smaller areas stretching from the southern shore out into the lake. Platz D was restricted to a small spot in the very northeast (Ilkjær 1990a, 25, Abb. 14). Both Platz A and B belong to period C1b, Platz A being dated to c. AD 200, Platz B to the years around AD 230 (Ilkjær 2003a, 46, fig. 2; Biborski and Ilkjær 2006a, 13). The deposition of Platz C was created in period D1 or c. AD 375. The material of Platz D is even younger, belonging to the later part of period D1 (Ilkjær 1993a, 16).

All textiles belong to Platz A. This is confirmed for most of the relevant clusters in the description of the shields (Ilkjær 2001a). In four cases, i.e. find clusters 70/114, 123/114, 129/105 and 151/119, no such hints are given in that context. Yet, a comparison between a map showing the location of the various clusters (von Carnap-Bornheim and Ilkjær 1996a, 20, Abb. 1) and another map giving the extensions of Platz B–D (Ilkjær 1990a, 25, Abb. 14) supports this view, since those four clusters are located north and east of Platz B and C while Platz D is situated still further northeast.

Origin of non-textile finds
According to Jørgen Ilkjær's research, it is rather the personal belongings of the warriors than their weapons that are able to illuminate the provenance of the materials found in Illerup and the other sites (1993a, 374–386). As far as Platz A in Illerup is concerned, lighters and combs and thus their owners are claimed to be of Scandinavian origin, particularly from south and west Norway and west Sweden including Västergötland (ibid., 378–380).

Textiles
Although the number of textile finds from Illerup Ådal – c. 100 – is rather small in comparison to the thousands of metal objects recovered from the site, this material has to be considered one of *the* major Roman Iron Age textile assemblages in Denmark. The present investigation encompasses a total of 102 find numbers with textiles and/or fur (1 item being without an official number): 53 shield bosses, 1 hand brace, 2 pieces from shield rims, 20 lanceheads, 9 spearheads, 3 swords, 3 axes, 1 knife, 1 rivet, 1 belt buckle, 1 piece of wire and 2 pieces of shafts. Lise Bender Jørgensen's examinations (1978–1980) of in total 18 finds were incorporated in this research, particularly for finds HBD, HBE, IXK, IXU, IYE and IYK, either due to their unavailability for the present investigation or as no textiles remained on the iron. In these cases, her results appear in the list and are marked as such. A few weapons displayed in the exhibition at Moesgård Museum near Århus were mounted and could therefore only be inspected on one side and then only without a microscope, e.g. shield bosses MBL and VFB. Other pieces, such as spearhead AAII and axe AAMC, are currently covered in textile only on one side although the fabrics seemingly reached around to the back; it may be surmised that, the textile was removed on the back in order to make the metal visible. It was impossible to ascertain the kind of objects to which five find numbers had belonged. Three very small fragments were rejected because they are kept in liquid and the containers were unopened (LKU, MAE, without number [IMP?]). Five finds were in such a poor condition that they could not be included. In another five cases (FNZ, GHZ, MQU [MQV?], VEE, ZML), no textiles could be identified. In some instances, traces or imprints of textiles were observed in the ground during the excavations, but could not be saved (Ilkjær 1993a, 16). Such traces are known from clusters without preserved textiles, e.g. 166/121 (ibid., 112), as well as from spots with surviving weaves. Examples of the latter are find clusters -6/60 and 85/85. In the last mentioned case, some textile seems to have lain partly on top of knife LFS – from which no textiles are recorded; but this patch also extended to a large area all around the knife (ibid., 25–26, 78).

On a few artefacts, more than one fabric was preserved. In other cases, textile remnants belonging to a particular weapon are partly preserved on the iron, partly as loose fragments of fabric. Additionally, some find numbers include more than one box with loose woven pieces, but no corresponding metal object. In the majority of cases, the examination included the entire range of features – when possible, while for 24 loose fragments only the main characteristics were studied. One item (TEX) consists of unwoven yarn. On ULW and RBB, fur was preserved in combination with textile.

In sum, the following amounts constitute the basis for the further description: 101 well-documented[2] woven textiles (belonging to a fewer number of cloths), some of them including tablet weave; 1 tablet weave without other weave, 1 × fringes, 1 × yarn, 8 × incomplete sets of data.

2.2. TECHNICAL ASPECTS OF THE TEXTILES: COMPARATIVE OVERVIEW

The documentation of the finds from Illerup Ådal is of an excellent quality, allowing for a very detailed interpretation of the technical results within the context of each item, e.g. identifying how textile fragments from different weapons belong to one cloth. Therefore only an overview is provided in this section and more detailed information on single items can be found in the following section elucidating the textiles in their immediate context.

Material

The bulk of the textile material from Illerup is preserved on the iron objects and has undergone conservation together with them. Several fragments, however, were removed from the metal finds and are stored unconserved. Often, the structure of the fibres is lost due to mineralisation or a poor state of preservation or hidden as an effect of conservation. However, some textiles on iron finds as well as those loose fragments clearly indicate that they are made of animal hair. No further investigation was carried out on the fibres, but it is highly likely that, it is all sheep wool except for an obviously vegetal s-spun cord connected to a wooden shaft (TEX).

Weaving types

Two different basic weaving types are present amongst the 101 well-documented textiles from Illerup: tabby and 2/2 twill. There are only 12 tabbies, all made up of z-spun yarns in both thread systems (1/1 z/z). Besides these fabrics, tabby structure in z/s occurs in tubular selvedges (see below) belonging to z/s twills. The lowest thread count per cm measured within this group (selvedges not included) is 8–9 × 7 (item YSW), the highest 20 × 13–14 (ADDP) and 18–20 × 11–16 (TYF) (Fig. 1.1). Often, threads of clearly different diameter were used side by side.

The twills are much more numerous and varied although the basic binding is always 2/2. There are 89 well-documented pieces of twill.[3] About 9% are spin patterned (see below), but otherwise simple, diagonal twills. About 31% are woven solely from z-spun yarn (2/2 z/z) while 60% have "z" in one system combined with "s" in the other (2/2 z/s). Both these variations occur as diagonal twills and as diamond twills. In some cases of either small or poorly preserved fragments, a change of direction of the twill lines could be verified only for one system. Thus, these pieces are possibly broken twills without diamonds; but since no larger pieces of broken twill were registered, it seems more likely that they represent sections of diamond twill. In all, five subgroups were identified among the twills: z/z diagonal (19 ×), z/s diagonal (15 ×), z/z diamond (9 ×), z/s diamond (38 ×) and spin-patterned diagonal (8 ×).

The diagonal twills in z/z (2/2 z/z) have thread counts of between 11 × 9–10 and 20 × 20–21 threads per cm² (Fig. 1.2). They are more common than the diamond variation in z/z. Theoretically, the diagonal twills could be sections of diamonds, however, in most cases their size is large enough to exclude this in all probability. An exception might be the twill on the small belt buckle QLC which could perhaps belong to the diamond twill on axe QPA. The thread counts in the diamond twills in z/z (2/2 z/z diamond) tend to be a little higher, between 14 × 11–12 and 22–23 × 19 threads

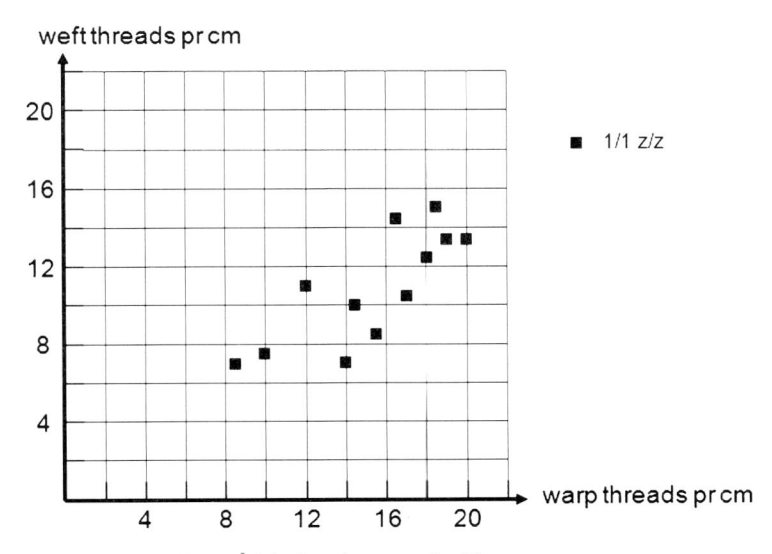

Fig. 1.1. Illerup Ådal, thread counts of tabbies

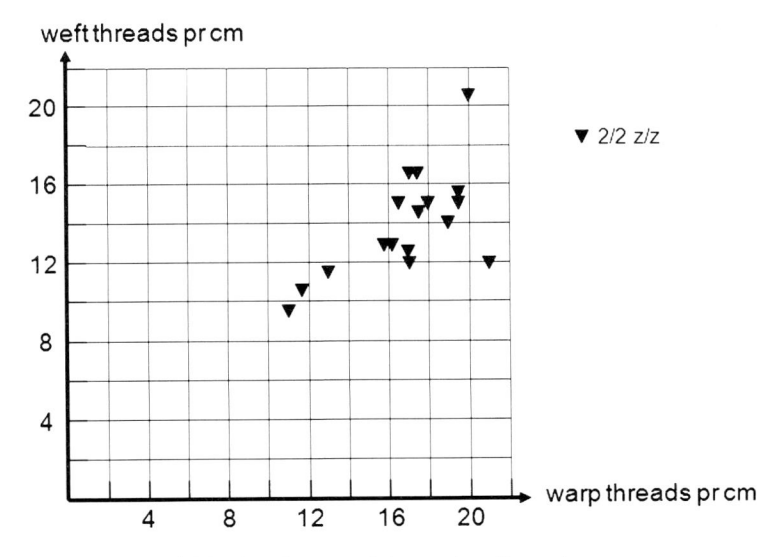

Fig. 1.2. Illerup Ådal, thread counts of diagonal twills in z/z

per cm (= tpc) (Fig. 1.3). In z/s, the thread count for the diagonal twills (2/2 z/s) lies between only 7 × 9 and 15 × 18 tpc, sometimes with more threads per cm in the weft than in the warp (Fig. 1.4). Again, it is higher in the diamond twills (2/2 z/s diamond): between 11 × 12 and 22–23 × 18–20 tpc (Fig. 1.5). And finally the spin-patterned twills have thread counts of between 16–17 × 12 and 20–22 × 16 threads per cm² (Fig. 1.6). In this respect, the spin-patterned fabrics – although woven as plain twill – are closer to the diamond twills than to the other diagonal twills.

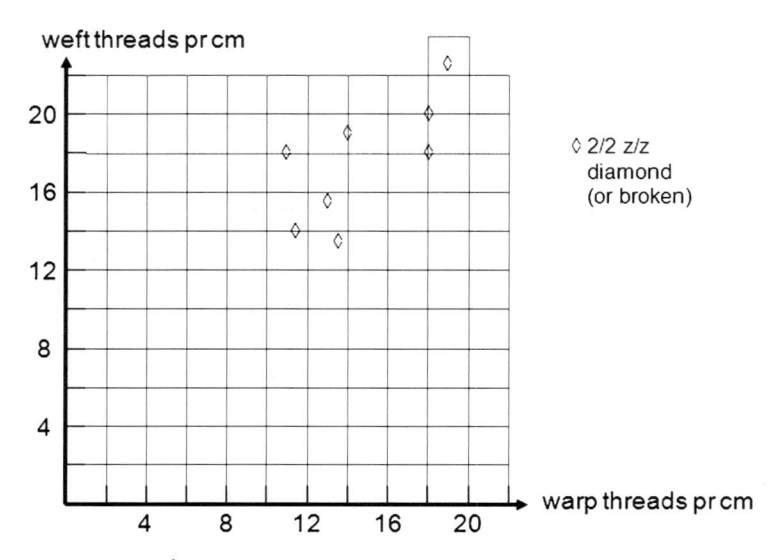

Fig. 1.3. Illerup Ådal, thread counts of diamond twills in z/z

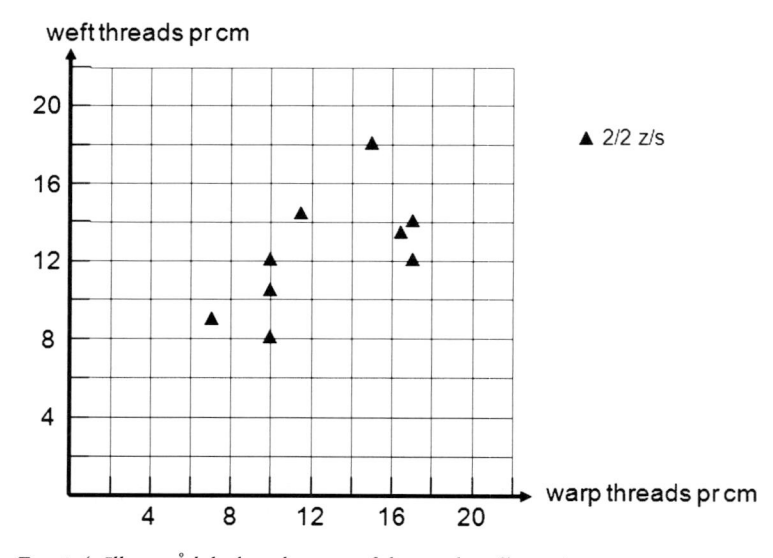

Fig. 1.4. Illerup Ådal, thread counts of diagonal twills in z/s

Edges and tablet weaves

Tablet weaves are registered for 6 pieces (QPC, VFD, UNK, IXK, IXL and IYF). This group is described by Lise Ræder Knudsen (this volume). Only in a few cases, have edges other than tablet weave been preserved (HAS, STA, TXC?, IWR, IYK). They all belong to the same type: tubular selvedges which are connected to diamond twills in z/s.

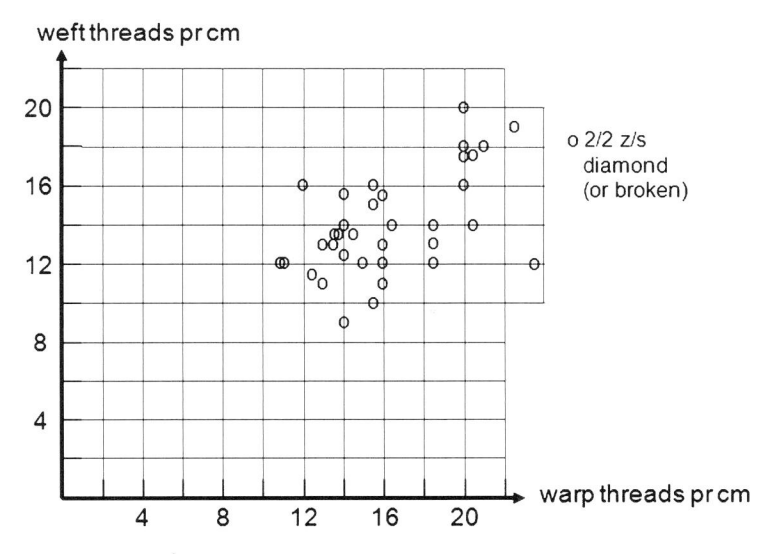

Fig. 1.5. Illerup Ådal, thread counts of diamond twills in z/s

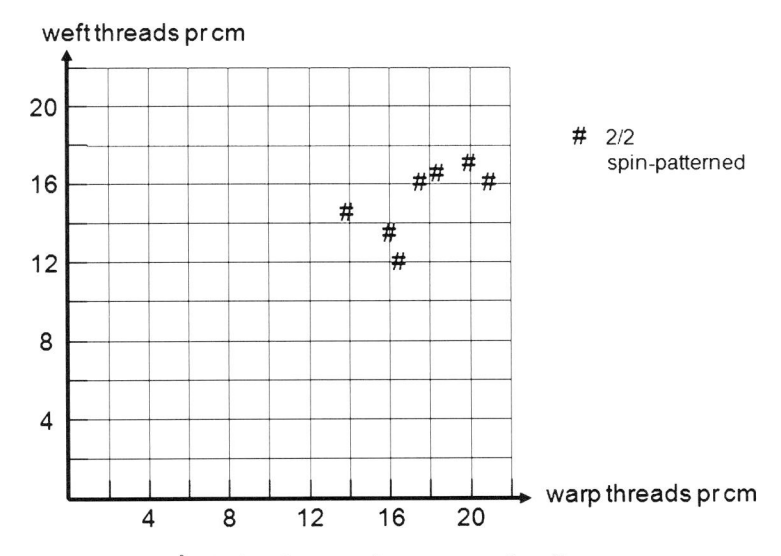

Fig. 1.6. Illerup Ådal, thread counts of spin-patterned twills

Patterns and colours

As mentioned above, 49 textiles (55%) were woven as diamond twill and 8 pieces (9%) were spin-patterned. Both these types do not need colour to provide a visual effect. Moreover, it is open to question whether colours – either natural or dyed – had been used in creating patterns in the material from Illerup Ådal.

The majority of textiles still adhering to the metal finds do not provide any hint as to their original colour. Some well-preserved but currently reddish brown fabrics include a few distinctly dark fibres, thus suggesting that the wool as a whole was not dark but originally white. It is impossible to say how many of these textiles were dyed. No unambiguous dyestuff was observed in the textile material on the iron objects, but loose fragments belonging to 12 find numbers, perhaps even 14, are clearly red. In one of these cases (VFD), the same fabric is still preserved on the metal, although without any noticeable dyestuff there. Other colours have not been found. Yet, as about 50% of the non-conserved material still show traces of dyeing, it seems probable that the majority of fabrics were originally dyed.

In order to describe the size of the diamonds, usually the "repetition" is given, i.e. the number of threads after which the weaving direction both in warp and weft has changed twice and the diamond is completed. However, after having counted the number of threads wherever possible, it emerged that even the four quarters of a single diamond often differ from one another. Therefore, such a quarter of a diamond is preferred here as a pattern unit, i.e. the number of threads between each change of weaving direction in warp and weft.

The spin patterns found in Illerup Ådal are characterised by changes between z- and s-spun threads in warp and weft, thus creating checks. In some cases, also twined yarns had been used. The size of these checks can either follow a strict system of small units (AAII, AAKA, AAOI) or be highly variable (MBL, UFF, UFN).

Napping

At least 17 textiles seem to have been napped. This signifies that after weaving, fibres were partly pulled out from the threads, resulting in a pile on the surface and concealing the weave. Usually, this interpretation is based on hairs preserved on the metal, between the iron and the cloth (Fig. 1.7). This feature was encountered on z/z diagonal twills (4 out of 19), z/z diamond twills (3 out of 9), z/s diamond twills (8 out of 38) and spin-patterned twills (2 out of 8). This constitutes c. 20–33% within each group. Indications of napping were neither found on tabbies (12 items) nor on z/s diagonal twills (15 items).

Textile quality

The textiles are of good quality. There are no low quality products. Generally, as far as may be ascertained, the wool fibres had been prepared carefully. The spinning had been conducted with care, only amongst the tabbies were clearly variable diameters registered. There are only few weaving mistakes. The fabrics are mostly medium to fine in terms of threads per cm (according to Tidow 2000, 108).[4] Only three pieces – one tabby and two diagonal twills in z/z – may be called coarse while 14 examples of various twill variations were measured as being very fine.

Apart from tablet weaves, the use of twined yarn for weaving is rare within this material. It appeared in two twills, found once each on AAII, AAKA, AAMX and AAOI (find cluster 111/100) and also on ZBP (solitary find). At first sight, they may be considered a sign of poor quality, as if the weaver merely used whatever was at hand. Yet, the opposite seems to be the case. The twined yarns were used as an integral part of the spin patterning. No indications of napping were found which signifies that the patterns remained visible. The thread count of approximately 18.5 × 16.5 tpc in the case of AAII, for example, is rather high. On ZBP, it is lower (14 × 14.5 tpc) but cannot at all be regarded as poor quality. Perhaps, the stripes of twined yarn material were intended to resemble tablet weaves.

Fig. 1.7. Illerup Ådal, indications of napping on lancehead RBO

Another qualitative aspect is the evenness of the diamond patterns. However, there is no common definition or scale for regularity, and the small size of the fragments results in a small data basis and accordingly reduced possibilities for evaluation. Frequently, however, the number of threads per pattern unit varies from unit to unit, shifting around a certain value. Only in very rare cases, do several identical units follow immediately in a row, three identical units occurring twice (TYH, UNK), and four units only once (STA). All in all, 90 units could be determined; the various sizes are presented in Table 1.1. In the first row, the total numbers for each size are given. Below, these numbers are split up according to z/z versus z/s, and to napped versus others. The latter signifies that, although, indications of napping are absent, it should not necessarily be excluded, as it is not possible to ascertain if they had never been napped or if the napping had disappeared. Some results are as follows:

- The sizes of the pattern units are more variable than might be expected.
- The most common unit consists of nine threads (25 ×), followed by ten threads (16 ×), i.e. about 46% belong to these two categories.
- These figures suggest some standardization which, however, is far from indicating that the weavers themselves found this a priority.
- Another frequent occurrence is at 18 threads (7 ×).
- Generally, odd (46 ×) and even (40 ×) numbers per unit occur in comparable frequencies (the four examples of units larger than 20 are not included since their true size is unknown).
- Assuming that in z/s fabrics, the z-spun system is typically the warp, the s-spun system the weft, more information may be derived:

Table 1.1. Illerup Ådal, size of pattern units in diamond twills

	all	def. < 6	6	7	8	9	10	11	12	13	14	15	16	17	18	19	> 20
all measurements	90	1		1	5	7	25	16	7	4	6	5			1	7	1	4
z/z all	23			1		1	8	7	2			2						2
z/s all	67	1			5	6	17	9	5	4	6	3			1	7	1	2
z/z napped	4						2		1			1						
z/s napped	25				2	2	8	3	4	2	1				1	1		1
z/z others	19		1		1		6	7	1			1						2
z/s others	42	1 (prob. mistake)			3	4	9	6	1	2	5	3			1	6		1 (prob. napped)

- Amongst the fabrics of this group, it appears that despite all variability, the pattern units in the z-system most often consist of even numbers combined with odd numbers in the s-system.
- The most common number in the z-system is 10, followed by 18. In the s-system, the probable weft, 9 occurs most often, followed by 13.
- The identical numbers occur in the z/z diamond twills. Based on this observation, the system with primarily even pattern units may be regarded as probable warp, that with prevailing odd numbers as the probable weft.
- The latter refers to three items (XFN, STA, KAT). In these cases, the weft defined here is more closely woven than the warp. As a consequence, the system with the highest number of threads per cm² is also regarded as weft in WZO, IUK and ZAR.
- Pattern units of 18 should not be regarded as a doubled unit of 9 threads.
- All units larger than 14 threads were observed in the probable warp.
- No general differences between napped fabrics and others seem to be evident.

Napping should be interpreted as a finish resulting in a more valuable cloth. It may rather be expected on clothing than e.g. on packing material. If it were clothing, it is impossible to determine whether the napped surface was worn inside or outside. In this context, it is worth reiterating that this feature was observed on several diamond twills as well as on two pieces of spin-patterned twill (UFF and UFN) because the napping hides the patterning effect. This may signify that napping was chosen for the inside in order to leave the patterning visible. On the other hand, the patterns of UFF and UFN are highly variable and thus possibly less suitable for display. Thus, it might well be that in this case – the fragments probably belong to one cloth – the patterning was of minor importance and the napping possibly worn on the outside.

Fur

Remnants of fur were found at least twice, on shield bosses RBB and ULW. In both cases, it was preserved in combination with textile, and in both instances, the hairy side was in contact with the iron. The type of fur could not be determined.

2.3. TECHNICAL DETAILS, CONTEXT AND FUNCTIONS

Description according to find clusters

During the excavation, it became evident that the artefacts were not evenly distributed but often clustered in numerous smaller areas. Apparently, within these clusters, the combination of materials was not accidental but seemed to be arranged systematically (von Carnap-Bornheim and Ilkjær 1996a, 15). While individual parts of e.g. one and the same shield were often discovered within different clusters,[5] the combination of e.g. horse-riding equipment, sword belt and shield including valuable metals suggests that the equipment of one particular warrior was laid down as a set (ibid., 32), at least in the case of the officers. Furthermore, seemingly the entire or almost entire equipment won in the battle was subsequently consigned to the lake (ibid., 17). Fortunately, the detailed documentation of the clusters was published as one of the volumes in the Illerup series (von Carnap-Bornheim and Ilkjær 1996d). However, only some of them – still? – contained textiles. These clusters and their corresponding site maps are chosen here as a basis for both a more detailed description of the textiles' characteristic features and their immediate context. The clusters are named according to their location on the site, i.e. their co-ordinates. Pattern units of diamond twills are provided wherever possible.

-6/60

Find cluster -6/60 is one of the largest assemblages, containing more than 500 find numbers (Ilkjær 1993a, 23). Yet, only six textile finds were registered. No tabby was found amongst these, but all five variations of twill were recovered. The loose fragment MDC, a diagonal twill in z/z (2/2 z/z), was dyed red. The textile on lancehead LHH was identified as 2/2 z/s; thus, it might belong to the fabric of shield boss LCW. Yet due to its tiny size of less than 1 cm², although in more than one layer, it is also possible that it is a part of a diamond twill. In that case, it might be connected to lancehead MII (2/2 z/s diamond). Two layers of textile were also observed on shield boss MBL. This fabric is characterised by spin patterning which was identified as follows:

system A: ≥ 6 × s, 76 × z, ≥ 11 × s
system B: ≥ 23 × z, 16 × s, 16 × z, 16 × s, 14 × z, 16 × s, ≥ 83 × z

The maps of this cluster include further textile signatures. Sometimes, they even have find numbers of their own (LMF, LMP). LMF was recorded on the sediment besides other finds. LMP as well as other textiles or imprints lay on top or below items such as knives, shield bosses or ropes (Ilkjær 1993a, 25).

1/68

Four textile finds originate from find cluster 1/68 and at least three different fabrics are present here. The preserved area of the z/z twill on the little belt buckle QLC is so small that it could be a section of a diamond twill. However, there is no doubt about the z/s twill on sword QMZ and the z/s diamond twill on axe QPA. Some hairs were observed on the metal of QPA, close to the preserved cloth fragment. It is highly likely that they are remnants of a napped surface of the fabric. Both weapons were wrapped in the corresponding fabric in at least two layers. Only some of the features of the twill on lancehead QPC could be identified. It is, nevertheless, noteworthy because first, the fibres are rather coarse and second, there is hair between the metal and the fabric. Since the diameter of the hair seems to match that of the tissue fibres, it is likely that this fabric was napped. Furthermore, there is a tablet weave (see Ræder Knudsen, this volume).

25/66

Within this cluster, four weaving types, related to nine non-textile finds were preserved. One of the somewhat few objects with two different textiles is shield boss RGZ. Next to the metal, a tabby was found (1/1 z/z) on both the outside of the dome as well as on its inside. Due to a fold, it makes up two layers on the inside. The measured thread counts are 19 × 11 tpc and 15 × 11 tpc. On top of

Fig. 1.8. Illerup Ådal, sewn fur on shield boss RBB

this, again on both sides, a diagonal z/z twill (2/2 z/z), possibly with fringes, follows. It is marked by many linear cuts. Close to RGZ and overlapping it partly, lay RCX, the separate top of a shield boss. Here again, a tabby with a thread count of 14–15 × 10 tpc was observed (1/1 z/z). It is highly likely that both pieces belong to the same fabric. Whether the boss and the separate top too originally constituted a unit, is unknown. In any case, they were unconnected when they were wrapped in textile, possibly both first in tabby and then in z/z twill, although the twill was not found on the top. Neither fabric was preserved on any other item within this cluster.

Shield boss RBB is another piece with two different organic fragments. Some fur was preserved directly on the boss, with a piece of textile on top of it. The hair, the length of which could not be measured, is closest to the metal, thus demonstrating that the shield boss was placed on the hairy side of a possible fur garment. The fur is characterised by a seam (Fig. 1.8). It combines two similar pieces by top sewing back and forth on the non-hairy, inner side, using the same stitching holes for both directions and thus creating a row of crosses. The crosses are 4.5–7 mm long and 5–6 mm wide. The yarn is z-spun, not twined, 1.2 mm thick and seemingly of hair. The stitching holes were driven from the hairy outer side to the inner side. The textile on top of it has z-spun threads in both systems, woven as chevron or diamond twill (2/2 z/z chevron or diamond): a break was found only for one thread system, but the area with identifiable threads is very small. Moreover, since no clear chevron twill was found in Illerup but diamond twills are widely attested, it seems more likely that it is in fact a diamond twill. The same applies to the fragments from shield boss QZA which were preserved in two layers and which seem to have been dyed red.

Fragments of z/s twill were observed on four items. Although the textile remnants on shield boss QZE are not particularly small, their condition is such that it is impossible to determine if it is a diamond twill or perhaps rather a chevron twill. The diamond twill on sword RCC, lying c. 1 m away from QZE, was composed of similar threads. The thread count is somewhat higher but within a range indicating that both fabrics might represent the same fabric. The diamond twill on lancehead RBO possesses a little lower thread count and the yarns are thicker. Some hairs found between the metal and the fabric, may indicate napping. The same applies to shield boss RBA where it is possible to examine the area between the iron and the fabric: this side of the tissue is very hairy in contrast to the other side which is smooth. Furthermore, it was possible to trace the pattern units of the diamonds to some extent: they are irregular, containing 7, 9, 11 and 19 ends in the z-system, and ≥ 7, 9 and ≥ 10 picks in the s-system (each number found once). In some areas, there are two layers of fabric. The fabric QAT found together with an arrow shaft is very poorly preserved. It is a z/s twill, possibly woven as diamond twill.

41/73

41/73 constitutes one of the largest find clusters (von Carnap-Bornheim and Ilkjær 1996a, 80), in terms of textiles as well as in general. The textiles, which were preserved on 16 metal objects, may be grouped into at least four types.

Tabby in z/z (1/1 z/z) was observed on lancehead XBZ and on shield boss VZT. However, according to the thread count which differs widely in both thread systems, these two tabby fragments – located about 60 cm away from one another – do not derive from the same fabric. On shield boss VZT, the yarns of one system are destroyed to a great extent, leaving the threads of the other system in parallel rows.

Diagonal twill in z/z (2/2 z/z) is widespread. According to the co-ordinates (Ilkjær 2001b, Liste 1), shield bosses XAZ and XBK seem to have lain partly on top of each other. Yet, it cannot be said with certainty whether both were wrapped in the same twill, since the thread count on XAZ is 20 × 21 tpc, while on XBK, it is 20 × 14–15 tpc. However, some hair was observed on XAZ, partly between the iron and the lower layer of textile, partly on top of the upper layer of textile. The identical situation applies to XBK where it is evident that the fabric was napped. Thus it is highly likely that the same cloth – laid double – was used for wrapping both shield bosses. Whether it constituted one package or two, remains open to debate.

Due to its tiny size, no thread count was recorded on the loose fragment from rivet plate WYO, which lay near the above mentioned shield bosses XAZ and XBK. It may belong to the textile from the bosses or represent a part of a diamond twill. Two other examples of diagonal 2/2 z/z were found on shield bosses VRL and WME, c. 2 and 3 m distant from XBK to the northwest and northeast, respectively. They are both similar to the twill on XBK in thread count but there are no signs of napping. On VRL, there are two layers of textile, the upper of which possesses two straight-cut edges. On WME, three layers of fabric and a weaving mistake were found, resembling a break but without a change in the direction of the twill line.

Diamond twill in z/z was found on two shield bosses, WZO (outside and perhaps inside) and XFN, lying c. 50 cm away from each other. The thread count is 20 × 18 threads per cm on WZO compared to 11.5 × 14 on XFN. On WZO, the fabric is preserved in two layers, with hair in between. Thus, this textile might have been napped while no hair was observed in connection with XFN. On XFN, the following pattern was counted: in system A, the direction changed three times after 10 threads, once after 11 threads. In system B, pattern units of 9 threads were observed twice, while in another area, no change occurred within 30 threads.

On shield boss XFN, on top of the 2/2 z/z diamond, another twill, a diamond twill in z/s (2/2 z/s diamond) was preserved. Apart from the opposite spinning direction in one thread system, it is of similar quality. Within the s-spun system, pattern units of only 7 picks were observed twice, while in the other direction, no break was found within 10 threads. Next to XFN lay shield boss WYX whose flange lay on top of that of XFN. The diamonds there are more elongated, due to 24 × 12 tpc and thus probably represent a different fabric. In the z-spun system, only one pattern unit of 10 threads was observed, while two others were much bigger than this but could not be determined with certainty. In the other system, units of again 10 threads occurred twice, along with a unit of 13 threads. A weaving mistake may be discerned, where the z-spun warp runs across three picks in the weft. Hair is preserved on the metal, particularly close to the rim, sometimes making up tiny strands. This indication for napping is again a feature which distinguishes this shield boss from XFN.

Only a few centimetres away from XFN and WYX, another shield boss with a z/s diamond twill, XNW, was found. The thread count could not be measured but hairs were found between the iron and the two layers of fabric, indicating napping. Thus, it may have belonged to WYX. A little further north, on shield boss XBV, yet a different diamond twill in z/s came to light. It is rather coarse with only 10 × 8 tpc. And finally, c. 2 metres to the southwest, a diamond twill in z/s with 16 × 11 tpc was preserved on lancehead VSG. On this, there is a pattern unit of 17 threads in the warp before the direction changes, compared to 9 in the weft; both of which numbers were measured once.

Shield boss WYR was found very close to the above-mentioned bosses XAZ and XBK with their diagonal twills. What is left on this object, are Z-twined threads, possibly representing fringes. The situation on shield boss XBW and on spearhead VVB too is highly ambiguous. No textile details can be determined on VVB, but it is worth mentioning that there is hair between the fabric and the iron. The hairs seem to make up a little strand and seem to be thicker than the fibres in the woven part; yet, the possibility that it is a napped fabric should not be excluded. No textile is left on XBW; a few imprints possibly indicate a diamond twill.

46/119

There are only two relevant textile finds from find cluster 46/119. The first one is a possible tabby on ZHL, a hand brace of a shield. Regrettably, the state of preservation is so poor that no further details could be determined. The other textile is a common z/z twill on axe ZKI. The twill was found both on the blade and on the top, suggesting that the weapon was wrapped in the cloth.

56/78

Four textile items representing at least two cloths are known from the central part of this cluster. The fabric on shield boss HAS is listed as an item of its own, termed HAT. It is a common z/s diamond twill, although rather coarse, with 14 × 14 tpc.[6] The twill is preserved together with its tubular woven side edge. Circa 0.8 cm before the edge, the twill turns into a rep-like tabby which runs as a fold back to the main weave. The warp covers the weft totally. It is impossible to count the warp ends within the edge; however, there seem to be at least around 30 threads making up the tubular edge. It was also impossible to ascertain the number of weft picks per shed within the edge. Since there are c. 5 weft units per cm in the edge compared to 13–14 weft picks per cm in the fabric, there may be three weft threads within each shed in the selvedge. Twill and tubular edge are comparable to IWR and IYK in find cluster 85/85.

Lancehead HAK was found on top of shield boss HAS. The fabric on HAK could not be identified more precisely than as possibly being twill. Although it would seem likely, whether or not it belonged to HAT cannot be determined.

According to the site map, HBD is the iron rim of a shield and HBE a separate find number for a textile belonging to HBD. Lise Bender Jørgensen analysed two pieces of textile labelled HBD and HBE. They are both diagonal twills in z/s.

57/90

Textiles from six shield bosses and five lanceheads[7] originate from this find cluster along with two loose fragments that cannot be connected to any metal find. They were recovered within an area of c. 1.5 m × 1.5 m. The range of weaving types comprises 1/1 z/z, 2/2 z/z with and without diamonds plus 2/2 z/s, again with and without diamonds. The only attestation to tabby belongs to shield boss TYF, in at least two layers and overlaid by a twill (see below).

The three diagonal twills in z/z (2/2 z/z) may well belong to one, relatively coarse fabric. They were observed on shield boss SQE (at least two layers) and on lanceheads VFD and TWT. On both latter objects, this textile is combined with a chevron or diamond twill in z/s. Regarding VFD, it may be stated that the diagonal, plain twill lies on top of the diamond twill, and the same is most probably true for TWT, although here, the diamonds could not be confirmed. A fragment on shield boss STA too is in z/z, but with clearly more threads per cm and woven as a diamond twill. The thickness of the yarns is unusually variable. The pattern units in system B were determined as 8 (1 ×) and 9 threads (4 ×). Only one unit of 10 threads was detectable in the other direction. The fabric was dyed red as can be seen on some loose, non-conserved fragments also labelled STA which are stored together with sediment.

Other loose fragments belonging to STA consist of a red-dyed diamond twill in z/s (2/2 z/s diamond). This diamond twill in z/s was attested again on top of the above described z/z twill on shield boss STA, although the red colour is no longer visible here. Traces of a tubular side edge most probably belong to this fabric. Although no direct connection between the twill and the rep-like edge was observed, the technical details in combination with the orientation of the edge suggest their correspondence.

Diamond twills in z/s constitute the largest group within this find cluster as well as in general. Here in 57/90, most of them have thread counts of around 12 × 12 tpc: on shield bosses STA, TYF (possibly chevron) and TYH, on lanceheads TXC, TWT (could be chevron) and VFD, and in the loose fragment TYR. The latter – in two layers – as well as a loose, non-conserved piece from VFD are dyed red. The pattern units were only followed on TYH, they are variable and rather large: in the warp, it is 13 (1 ×), ≥ 14 (1 ×) and 18 (3 ×); in the weft it is ≥ 8, 9, 12 and ≥ 16 (each found once). A weaving mistake – an incorrect change of the twill line – was observed on TYH.

The diamond twill on lancehead TXB is the only one with a higher thread count in warp and weft: 16–18 × 14–16 tpc. The pattern units could be measured only sporadically: ≥ 7, 9 and ≥ 9 in the warp, ≥ 7 and 9 in the weft (each counted once); generally, the units seem to be rather small. Two layers of fabric were observed. On lancehead TXC, the diamond twill is combined with rep of nearly 1 cm width, seemingly a tubular side edge. However, the twill is present along both sides of this feature, thus it probably represents another layer or perhaps a seam.

The z/s twills from shield boss VFI, from the very top of shield boss VFB and in a loose, red-dyed fragment from VFI could either be diagonal ones or rather diamond twills. It has been mentioned above that on lanceheads TWT and VFD as well as on shield boss STA, a z/z diagonal twill is combined with a z/s diamond twill, the first overlaying the second. Between them, a tablet weave is preserved on VFD (see Ræder Knudsen, this volume). Furthermore, on one spot on VFD, there are single hairs on the metal, below the diamond twill. They appear coarser than the fibres in the twill and do not seem to belong to the textile. Lancehead TWU was wrapped in a twill with z-spun yarn in one system. Other details were not registered.

70/114

The only textile from find cluster 70/114 is a typical z/s diamond twill on the socket of spearhead YYA. The pattern units in the warp were determined as 8 (2 ×) and ≥ 8 threads (1 ×), in the weft ≥ 4 and ≥ 7 (once each). The fabric was wrapped around the iron spearhead in at least two layers.

79/104

Although only four metal items with textiles are preserved from this find cluster (shield bosses UFF, UFN, ULW and UNK), there are three different types of weave and fur. The latter is found on ULW, directly on the iron. The hair is about 2 cm long and lies in lightly curved locks. On top of it, two layers of tabby (1/1 z/z) were identified.

At least three layers of a z/s diamond twill can be observed on UNK. The pattern units in the warp are 10, 12 and 18 (each appearing once), while in the weft, a unit of 9 threads was found four times and units of 7, 11 and 13 once each. Parallel to the s-system, a broad tablet-woven edge accompanies the twill.

UFF and UFN were found very close to each other. On both, there are twills with a chequered appearance due to spin patterning and it is highly likely that these two shield bosses were once wrapped in the same cloth. The pattern was followed in two areas on UFN. In one case, units of ≥ 9 × z, 12 × s and ≥ 10 × z were observed in one system, combined with ≥ 34, but probably over 50 × s in the other direction. In the other area, ≥ 62 × s and ≥ 12 × z in one direction is supplemented by ≥ 22 × s, 9 × z, 8 × s and ≥ 10 × z in the other direction. From these figures, it can only be concluded that the width of the stripes and thus the size of the checks are highly variable and no specific pattern was seemingly achieved. However, in this case it is even open to question whether the pattern showed up at all since the surface is rough wherever it is protected rather than exposed. Therefore, it is possible that the fabric was napped, thus concealing the effect of the spin patterning. Indications of napping were also found on UFF.

85/85

Among the material presented here, 85/85 constitutes the most complex find cluster, with 15 items from c. 1 m² and another one from some distance (Fig. 1.9). Four types of weaving as well as tablet weave are represented. A tabby (1/1 z/z) is known from shield boss IXY where it is preserved directly on the metal, beneath a z/s twill (see below). A loose rivet packed together with the boss possesses

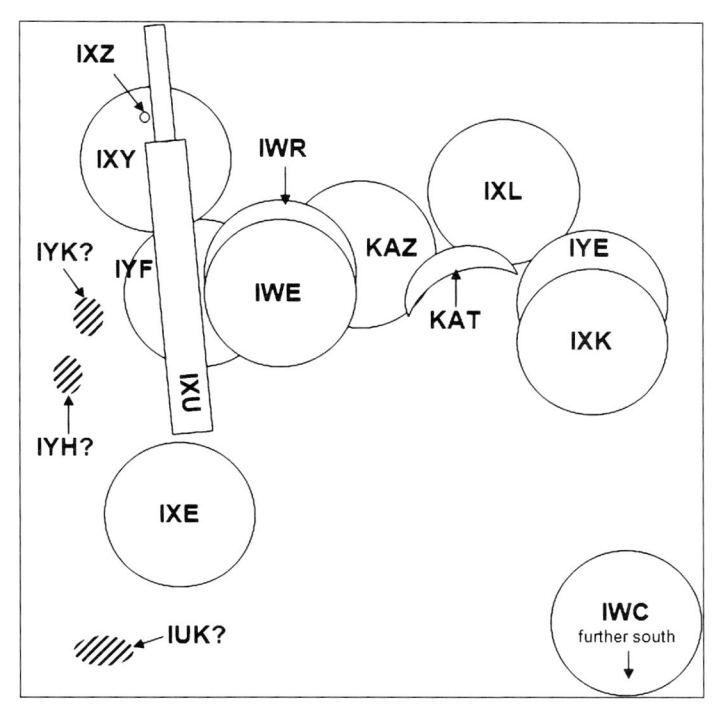

Fig. 1.9. Illerup Ådal, find cluster 85/85, sketch of weapons with textiles, not to scale

traces of this tabby on the top as well as along the shaft but with a gap between both sections. If the rivet sat in a hole of the boss while being excavated, it signifies that the tabby originally covered both sides of the boss – i.e. the shield boss was wrapped in it. Sword IXU, to which wire IXZ belongs, was found on top of boss IXY. The wire lay directly above the shield boss and shows fragments of the same tabby while the sword is associated with a twill.

Immediately beside shield boss IXY and also below sword IXU, another shield boss, IYF was found. On it, a twill in z/z and a tablet weave are visible (see Ræder Knudsen, this volume). Two layers of the tablet weave, dyed red, are preserved as a loose fragment. The 2/2 z/z can be perceived on the outside as well as on the inner rim of the shield boss, which might be interpreted as wrapping. Seemingly the same diagonal twill may be reported from yet another shield boss, IXE, found a few centimetres away, at the end of the sword.

A diamond twill in z/z was observed in at least two layers on the fragment of shield boss KAT. The measurements of pattern units in system A are 10 (2 ×), in system B ≥ 14 and ≥ 18 (once each). On one spot, a small brush of fibres can be perceived on the iron. A comparable and possibly identical twill comes from spearhead IUK which probably lay about half a meter away, close to the above-mentioned shield boss IXE. The pattern units are ≥ 11 and 14 in system A (each once), while in system B, 9 threads (2 ×) and ≥ 9 threads (1 ×) were measured. Short hairs indicate napping. The spearhead was wrapped in this diamond twill woven cloth of which two layers are preserved.

Shield boss IXY was mentioned earlier in connection with the tabby. On top of the tabby, a diagonal twill in z/s (2/2 z/s) was found. No break suggesting a chevron or diamond twill was observed but the state of preservation is poor. The thread count is rather low, 11.5 × 13 tpc. Loose fragments of a similar fabric, with 10 × 12 tpc (measured by Lise Bender Jørgensen), come from shield boss IXK, about half a meter distant from IXY. Furthermore, Bender Jørgensen reported on a tablet-woven band of more than 3 cm width, belonging to IXK. Lise Ræder Knudsen examined corresponding remnants on the shield boss (this volume). It is possible that they should be seen in connection with the red-dyed tablet weave on shield boss IXL. In the case of IYF, it is unclear as to which twill – diagonal in z/z or diamond in z/s – the red-dyed tablet weave belonged. Ræder Knudsen regards it as an independent band, possibly sewn to a cloak (ibid.).

The largest group of textiles within this find cluster – as in several others – again constitutes the diamond twills in z/s. They were observed on sword IXU and on or together with seven shield bosses (IWC, IWE, IWR, IXY, IYE, IYF and KAZ), supplemented by two loose fragments (IYH, IYK). It is uncertain as to how many different varieties are represented in this group – but it is not impossible that they all originate from the same fabric. Their only distinguishing features are the thread count and the pattern units. Regrettably, the latter could be calculated only for six finds, generally due to the tiny size of the fragments or to their poor state of preservation.

Taking into account the figures for these six items, it seems that there might be two different fabrics: one with at least 20 × 15 tpc and pattern units of most often around 13 threads (IWC[8], IWE[9], IXU[10] and IYF[11]), and another with c. 16 × 13 tpc and a very irregular pattern unit (IWR[12] and IYK[13], although IWR was possibly napped while indications of napping were not recorded for IYK). Amongst the rest of the fragments with unknown pattern units, IYH and parts of IWR seem to match the first group with a higher thread count while IYE might belong to the second, somewhat coarser group with irregular pattern units. Two cases (IXY and KAZ) remain unclear.

Shield boss IWR requires yet a closer examination. Five measurements were taken in total: two indicate the group of diamond twills with lower thread count and very variable pattern units, two other spots have thread counts which match the finer diamond twill, but no pattern units were recorded there; the fifth measurement of thread count lies in between. The fragments with a high thread count are dyed red and are preserved in up to four layers. They are now loose but are bent as if they once covered the rim of the flange. Whether or not all layers represent the same quality, or if perhaps a finer fabric lies on top of the slightly coarser variant cannot be determined. The coarser and seemingly napped twill was observed on top of the boss, probably also on its inner side and on a loose fragment. Thus it might well be that the shield boss was first wrapped in the coarser twill and then in the finer one. Regarding the coarser remnants, a fold with stitching holes as well as a tubular edge have to be reported. At first sight, the latter resembles a rep band, the typical appearance of such an edge; however, it is clearly round woven.

Lise Bender Jørgensen mentioned a "repsbort", i.e. a rep woven section, along the edge of the diamond twill found on the inside of shield boss IYK. This piece did not comprise part of the present investigation, but it is most likely that this again is in fact a tubular edge. The connected diamond twill described by Bender Jørgensen is one of the rather coarse type described above which is also preserved as a loose fragment. In the latter case, the pattern units are c. 13, ≥ 17 and ≥ 21 threads in the z-system combined with c. 11 threads in the s-system (all numbers observed once). Thus it is an example of the coarser, irregular-patterned type of diamond twill as on boss IWR with its tubular edge. There is little doubt that these two items belong together.

Moreover, it must be noted that the stratigraphy remains somewhat uncertain for shield boss IYF. What is preserved on the metal is the plain 2/2 z/z, inside and outside. The shape of a loose fragment

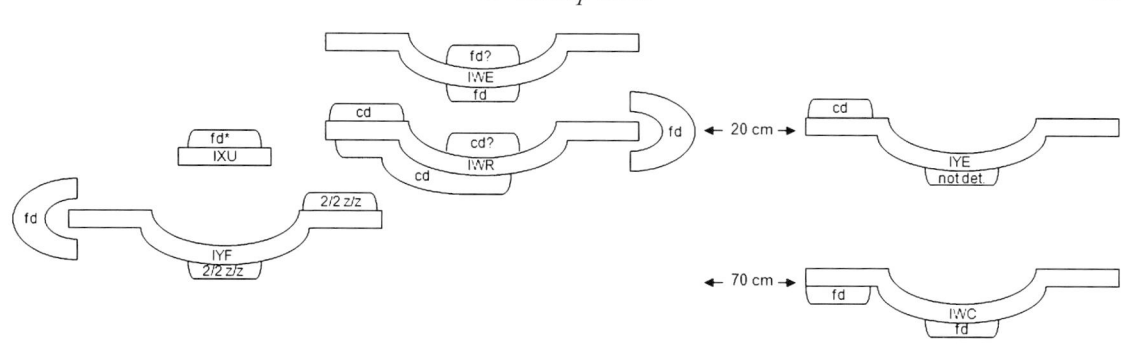

Fig. 1.10. Illerup Ådal, microstratigraphy in the vicinity of shield boss IWR. fd = finer variant of diamond twill, cd = coarser variant of diamond twill. * = unknown whether on top or beneath the blade

of the 2/2 z/s diamond twill is indicative of its original position around the rim of the boss, and, according to Lise Bender Jørgensen, this twill was also found on both sides. It seems likely that the two fabrics at least overlapped. Since the plain diagonal twill is somewhat spread widely on the boss, it seems highly likely that this plain twill was the fabric in which the shield boss was first wrapped and that the diamond twill was to be found on the outside of the package.

Finally, the location of the diamond twills relatively to each other is described, following the principles of microstratigraphy as established by Inga Hägg (1974, 1989) (Fig. 1.10). Three items preserving the finer diamond twill lay very close to one another. Lowest was shield boss IYF with a plain twill on the metal and the finer variant of diamond twill as – probably – the outer layer. Above IYF, sword IXU was found with another piece of the finer diamond, but it is uncertain as to whether it was on the upper side of the blade or below it. The third item with this twill is shield boss IWR. On the site map, it is drawn right beside sword IXU and above the boss IYF. As on IYF, the finer twill on IWR seemingly made up an outer cover, reaching around the rim of the flange. This is in close accordance with the observations made on shield boss IWE, which was stuck in IWR and on which the finer diamond twill is visible on the outside of the dome and probably on its inside as well. This combination of bosses with fine fabric between them makes it evident that the finer diamond twill cannot simply make up the outer cover for a number of weapons lying loosely within it, but that it was used for individual wrapping. Moreover, a loose outer cover had probably only little chance of survival.

The coarser variant of the diamond twill was found on the outside of the dome and flange of shield boss IWR. Furthermore, it was preserved on the inner side of the flange and possibly the dome of the same weapon. According to Lise Bender Jørgensen's documentation, it was also observed below shield boss IYE, while IYK could not be located.

87/89
Shield boss MNH once carried the textile MNL, a now loose piece of z/s diamond twill possibly dyed red. Within the warp, the recorded pattern units encompass 8 (2 ×) and 10 threads (3 ×), while in the weft, the figures are ≥ 7, ≥ 9 (once each) and 9 (2 ×). Probably the same diamond twill covers lancehead MML found in the vicinity. Here the pattern units in the warp are ≥ 7 and ≥ 11, in the weft ≥ 7 and ≥ 10 (once each).

88/109
A tabby (1/1 z/z) is preserved on the inner flange of shield boss YSW, thus suggesting that the boss had been removed from the shield boards. The tabby is made from unusually thick threads with only 8–9 × 7 tpc. The two spearheads YME and YPL as well as lancehead YWN were each wrapped separately in pieces of cloth. Nevertheless it seems likely that the diagonal twills in z/z (2/2 z/z) on YME and YPL originate from the same fabric. Although the thread count is measured as 17 × 12.5 tpc on the first and 17 × 16.5 tpc on the latter, they share another feature: short hairs preserved directly on the iron which may be due to napping. For lancehead YWN, a chevron or rather possibly a diamond twill in z/s was used for the wrapping. According to the hairs found on the metal, this textile seems to have been napped as well.

89/74
Knife FMH is the only object with textiles in this find cluster and the knife was clearly wrapped individually. The fabric used for this purpose was a z/s diamond twill with a pattern unit of ≥ 13 threads in the warp (1 ×) and ≥ 9 in the weft (2 ×). There is a clear mark between the blade and the tang, as if the handle was still in place when the wrapped knife was consigned to the lake. Yet, the textile extends a little bit beyond this mark.

91/84
A tiny fragment of 0.2 × 0.3 cm might have been textile but no specific traits could be distinguished. It is uncertain if this now loose piece once belonged to MQU (a shield boss with leather) or to MQV (a spearhead).

92/97
Again, only one textile is attested in this find cluster: a z/s diagonal twill preserved not on metal but on sediment (MYP). The red-dyed threads are uncommonly thick, possibly as a secondary effect, resulting in a thread count of currently only 7 × 9 tpc.

95/110
Once again only one preserved textile per find cluster is to be reported from 95/110. It is a diamond twill in z/z (2/2 z/z diamond), preserved on shield boss ZAR. The pattern units determined in one system are 6 (1 ×), ≥ 9 (1 ×), 10 (1 ×), ≥ 12 (1 ×) and 14 (1 ×). In the other system, only one break was found, separating a highly fragmentarily preserved group of ≥ 3 threads from a large homogeneous section of ≥ 48 threads creating a somewhat chevron type appearance instead of diamonds. The fabric covers parts of the outside of the boss. It stretches from the uppermost portion of the dome to the rim of the flange, leaving out the transition from dome to flange.

111/100
Among the ten relevant items from find cluster 111/100, at least four different weaving types are present. A tabby (1/1 z/z) was found on shield boss AAME (Fig. 1.11). Partly on top of it rested lancehead AALZ. The latter was wrapped into a diagonal twill in z/z (2/2 z/z) with 21 × 12 tpc. Also wrapped in a diagonal twill in z/z was axe AAMC, only c. 10 cm away from lancehead AALZ and immediately beside shield boss AAME. The thread count was measured as 18 × 15 tpc. AAMD, the fragment of a shield boss, was found between the lancehead and the axe. Again, it carries a diagonal

twill in z/z, with 19.5 × 15 tpc. It is very likely that all three twills once belonged to the same fabric. However, the fact that at least the lancehead and the axe have textiles on both sides demonstrates that they were individually wrapped in textile.

AAIH is a red-dyed textile found together with spearhead AAIB, about 1 metre away from the above mentioned items. It is a z/s diamond twill which stands alone in this context, i.e. this weaving type is not as widely attested here as in many other clusters.

A little further north, shield bosses AAOI and AAMX came to light along with lancehead AAKA and spearhead AAII. Fragments of a spin-patterned twill are preserved on all four items. On spearhead AAII, there are two layers on one side while the back is free of textile, yet it seems as if the cloth might have gone around the spearhead. The pattern in system B is as follows:
≥ 2 × z, 4 × zS, 10 × z, 4 × zS, 4 × z, 12 × zS, 4 × z, 4 × zS, 10 × z, 4 or 5 × zS, 4 × z, ≥ 8 × zS. In system A, the pattern is similar in principle but without twined yarns, i.e. the pattern is made up of z- and s-spun threads. Lancehead AAKA was clearly wrapped in this cloth. Moreover, this fabric was identified on the outer side of shield boss AAOI, while this is uncertain for some undetermined material on its inner side. Finally, a loose fragment from shield boss AAMX is preserved. The exact pattern was not recorded but since spin patterns are rare, it is likely that it belongs to this same group.

123/114
Lanceheads ADDP and ADDQ were found on top of each other, orientated along the same axis. The same kind of tabby (1/1 z/z) was found on both, most likely representing the same cloth. However, they were not merely placed together and then wrapped at once in a textile (together with spearhead ADDO and possibly other items), since the fabric was found on both sides of each spearhead, on ADDQ in at least two layers. This signifies that, as also attested in cluster 111/100, the weapons were either wrapped individually in merely a fragment of the cloth, or one after the other in a more or less complete piece of cloth or clothing. On ADDP, the fabric is damaged by linear cuts.

127/114
The only textile from this find cluster was observed on shield boss AAYN. It is a diamond twill in z/s. No further details could be determined.

129/105
Again only one textile is attested in find cluster 129/105. A diamond twill in z/s was wrapped around lancehead ADBZ, preserved in up to four layers and lying in folds. The determinable pattern units in the warp are 10 (2 ×) and ≥ 10 (1 ×), in the weft 9 (2 ×) and ≥ 10 (1 ×). Moreover, signatures of textiles are recorded below the nearby knife AASW as well as on top of knife AARU which lay further away (Ilkjær 1993a, 106–107).

151/119
Two lanceheads with textiles, AAVU and AAVW belong to this find cluster. The twill on AAVU could not be determined in any detail, while that on AAVW is clearly a diamond twill in z/s. Its pattern units (each counted once) are 9 or 10 and ≥ 8 in the warp compared to ≥ 6 and ≥ 8 in the weft.

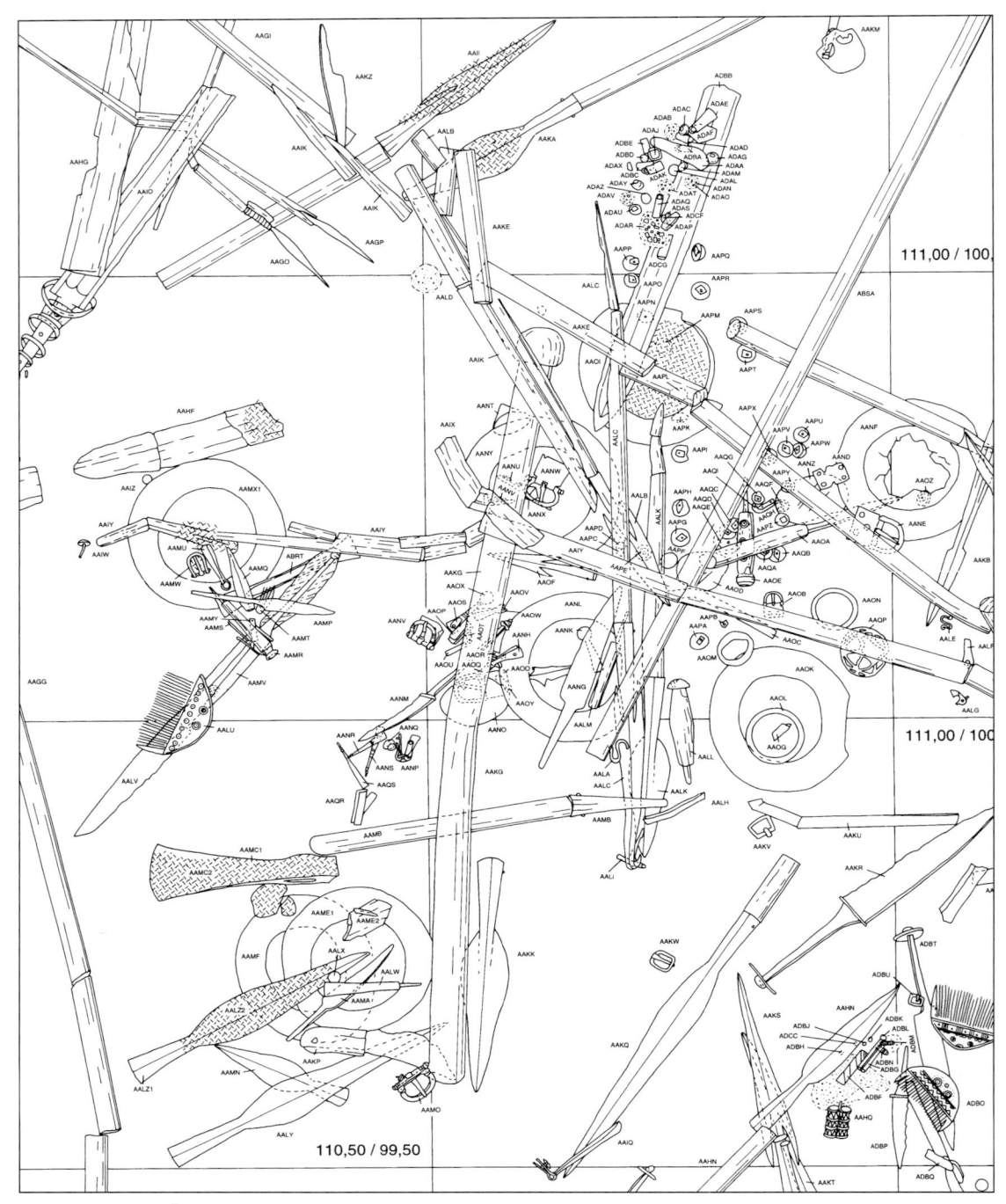

Fig. 1.11. Illerup Ådal, section of find cluster 111/100. Shield boss AAME to the lower left, not to scale (© Jørgen Ilkjær)

Unknown provenance or beyond the find clusters

Spearhead ZBP was found as a single item lying apart from the find clusters. The textile on it is a spin-patterned twill with a thread count of c. 14 × 14 tpc. In one yarn system, z- and s-spun yarns were found while in the other, z-spun and then S-twined threads were combined with groups of s-spun yarns. Thus, it resembles the spin-patterned fabric encountered in cluster 111/100 but there, the S-twined yarns alternate with groups of z-spun threads.

Furthermore, some distance away from the clusters, a fragment of a shield boss labelled ZML came to light. On its surface, no textile, but rather some single short hairs were observed. As on other objects, these hairs probably indicate a napped cloth in which the item was wrapped.

The exact location of find TEX could not be reconstructed. It is a piece of a coarse, obviously vegetal, yarn, spun in an s-direction. A final item that must be mentioned is a diagonal twill in z/s without a find number.

Primary functions

One of the main characteristic features of the textile material from Illerup is the small size of the fragments. No traces of sewing or tailoring can be perceived, except for a seam made on fur (on shield boss RBB). The absence of such features may indicate that the fragments primarily originate from non-tailored textiles. Broad tablet weaves as with UNK (see Lise Ræder Knudsen, this volume) and IXK may be interpreted as a primarily decorative and high quality feature suggestive of clothing. Moreover, the quality of the regular weaves may provide further hints. It was emphasised above that the quality is generally high in terms of both homogeneity of the material as well as of thread counts. Indications of napping occurred in several instances and napped textiles were most likely intended for clothing. Since the quality of napped and non-napped weaves is otherwise almost identical, the latter group may provisionally also be regarded as clothing. A further aspect is discussed in the passage below on damages.

Finally, some non-textile finds, i.e. small buckles are considered here as they shed some light on the costumes. Some of them belong to baldrics and horse-riding equipment and within this group, iron is rather insignificant (Ilkjær 1993a, 158). Among those buckles interpreted as personal belongings of the warriors, one out of 7 or 8 is made of bronze while the vast majority comprise iron buckles. In the present context, the difference may be interpreted as a question of – besides affordability – visibility. Baldrics and horse-riding equipment belong to the higher echelons of the army and were visible when worn. The simplicity of the small belt buckles, particularly those of iron, on the other hand, seems to imply that these were worn invisibly, i.e. under a tunic, in contrast to some broad luxury belts. Thus, the small buckles may be interpreted as an accessory belonging to trousers.

Intentional damage

Strokes or blows from swords, axes or other weapons occur on many weapons. On the shield bosses, they result in linear damage or holes, depending on the item which had been used to inflict the damage. It was mentioned above that some marks may have originated in the battle while many others were subsequently inflicted as part of a ritual performance. To mention just one example from the material under investigation, shield boss XBK was hit with a hammer and thus broken into several pieces, characterising the destruction as secondary (Ilkjær 2001a, 61). Another sign of secondary damage is the commonly attested separation of shield bosses and other constructive or

Fig. 1.12. Illerup Ådal, shield boss STA with linear damage

decorative parts from the shield boards (ibid., 9) and of the swords from the sheaths (Biborski and Ilkjær 2006a, 14).

Particularly, the phenomena of linear damage were now observed amongst the textile material from Illerup. The similarity is striking e.g. on shield bosses RGZ and STA (Fig. 1.12) as well as on lancehead ADDP. Yet, weapons and textiles were seemingly hit independently, because the cuts in the textiles do not reach down into the metal as can be seen e.g. on STA. Sometimes, e.g. on shield boss RBA, one straight, obviously cut edge of a textile is preserved, although without facing a corresponding edge. Nevertheless, the origin may be identical, i.e. a weapon stroke. This is a clear indication that the textiles were part of the battle and of the subsequent rituals in a similar manner to the weapons. Following the hypothesis that the weapons and other items belonged to foreign warriors, the same may be concluded for the textiles. The textiles therefore most probably represent the clothing of the defeated warriors. They are sacrifices in themselves.

Wrapping

The bulk of the textiles would not have survived if they had not been in close contact with iron. This fact implies that the weapons and other metal items were not merely placed in a heap and then covered with one big cloth or collected in a sack. Jørgen Ilkjær claimed in 2001 (2001a, 17) that parts of shields were kept in place by textiles wrapped around them. Indeed, many items clearly demonstrate that single weapons were wrapped individually. Examples of this phenomenon are sword QMZ, lancehead YWN, axe QPA and knife FMH. Sometimes two or more layers are evident, e.g. on spearhead IUK, on the above-mentioned sword QMZ and lancehead TXB.

On the shield bosses, textiles are often preserved on both the outside as well as on the inside. Theoretically, the fabrics particularly on the inside, i.e. on the concave side of the dome and the adjacent flange, may have had nothing to do with the deposition but could have been fixed to the metal earlier in order to provide some protection for the hand and/or to fulfil a function between the metal flange and wooden board. In certain instances, however, e.g. on IWR, one can follow the remains of a fabric running around the rim of the boss, demonstrating a functional connection between the textiles outside and inside in terms of individual wrapping. Yet, the wrapping of a single shield buckle would possibly not result in textile remains on the inner dome, since the weave would rather cover the hole. Therefore, those bosses must either have been stuffed or stuck together, thereby keeping the textile layer between them in contact with the iron. This can be demonstrated not only from the site maps, e.g. from find cluster 151/119 (Ilkjær 1993a, 109) but also from the items themselves. Textiles were often preserved on the outside in the fold or angle between dome and flange, e.g. on UFN and AAME. This may be explained by one boss having been pressed onto the other. On other bosses, such as XBK and ZAR, the opposite is the case, i.e. the textile does not follow the angle between dome and flange but runs straight from the upper part of the dome down to the rim of the boss. Seemingly, such a shield boss was either not included in such a combination of bosses or it represents its uppermost element.

Although wrapped up individually, more than one weapon could be covered by one and the same fabric within a cluster, e.g. shield bosses UFF and UFN in find cluster 79/104 by a spin-patterned twill. It is likely that several metal objects were laid onto a larger cloth one after the other, each being folded in the package before the next object was added, which would result in a larger bundle of homogeneous fabric. An alternative explanation is that a cloth was divided into suitable sizes for this purpose, using the smaller parts for individual wrappings. Such small units of metal wrapped in textile could thereafter be wrapped up together in a larger piece of cloth of either the same or a different fabric if larger units were desired. Indications of this scenario are first, the above-mentioned series of shield bosses and second, the sequences of two different textile layers on some objects. A third argument for, more or less, voluminous packages is traces of textiles in the sediment which were recorded during excavation (Ilkjær 1993a, 16). According to the site maps, such traces partly filled the gaps between other objects, whether made of iron or not, e.g. in find cluster 111/100.

The best opportunity of identifying a common cover for several already wrapped items was provided in find cluster 57/90 which contained twelve objects with textiles located in an area of only c. 2 m². On four of these objects, combinations of two textiles were preserved. In all four cases, one particular type of weave is present, a z/s diamond twill. Moreover, it seems likely that these four twill fragments derive from the same cloth but this is not certain since the thread counts vary considerably (see above). However, most noteworthy in this context is that, this diamond twill makes up the upper or outer layer (on shield bosses STA and TYF) only twice, while at least on lancehead VFD and probably also on lancehead TWT, the diamond twill was found as the lower or inner layer. Consequently, however probable they may seem, the evidence for large packages is still lacking.

This observation – that microstratigraphies of two different textiles do not necessarily result from larger bundles – is further supported by the textile remains on shield boss RGZ. Here, both a tabby and a diagonal twill were found on the outside as well as on the inside. Seemingly, both fabrics belong to the boss as individual wrappings. Other possible explanations for these microstratigraphies are the following: The outer layer represents the wrapping of a neighbouring metal object from which it was separated e.g. during excavation. Alternatively, a wrapped metal item could have lain on a separate piece of textile which had not been used for wrapping but was sacrificed independently. The corrosive products of the iron were able to preserve both the wrapping and the neighbouring cloth. The latter interpretation refers back to those remnants or imprints in the sediment which might also derive from textiles that had nothing to do with wrapping.

In any case, bundles may have been held together with cords or ropes. Such material was registered at many places in Illerup, as the site maps prove. Although the cords are not part of this research and therefore not examined as such, some aspects are considered here. The raw material of the ropes including the above mentioned cord, TEX, is seemingly of vegetal origin. This may suggest that the absence of textiles made of plant fibres is not due to the environment in the bog but that no such vegetal fabrics were included in the sacrifice. Information referring to another aspect is provided by the site maps. On the one hand, the maps often exhibit pieces of ropes which might indeed be interpreted as parts of such bundles. Find cluster 111/100 provides examples of this phenomenon. Often, the cords lay more or less far away from iron; as they were made of plant fibres, they did not depend on the metal corrosion for preservation. Although rope material lay e.g. on top of the textile-bearing weapons QPA and QPC in find cluster 1/68, there is no proof of any close connection between ropes and textiles – no piece of cordage was found adhering to textile. Nevertheless, packages with fabrics and cords should not be excluded. On the other hand, the excavation of neatly coiled up bundles of rope such as in find cluster 1/68 and particularly in 79/104 (Fig. 1.13) add another perspective. These bundles of rope were clearly not used for keeping other things together. Instead, they were meant as sacrificial objects in themselves. This in turn supports the above mentioned suggestion that textiles may have been offered in their own right as well.

The findings on wrapping and packages may be summarised as follows:

- textiles were frequently used for wrapping items deposited in the bog;
- single weapons were wrapped individually in one or maybe more weaves, forming small packages;
- larger packages with a common outer cover may have existed but cannot be substantiated due to the lack of evidence;
- the use of cordage for binding packages seems logical, but here too, no evidence exists to support this view;
- at least some of the cordage was definitely not used as a means for keeping bundles together but must be regarded as being sacrifices in themselves;
- it is possible or – similar to the cordage – even probable that not all textiles were used for wrapping; fabrics too may have constituted as sacrificial objects.

Intended selection?

From the above descriptions, it is clearly evident that various types of weave can be recovered from any cluster and often in the direct vicinity of one another. The question is whether a selection of fabrics took place, i.e. whether certain weaves and/or textiles with certain functions were used in combination with certain weapons or personal belongings. Since the determination of primary functions was practically impossible, apart from indications of clothing in general, the second part of the question cannot be answered. The first part, however, is investigated here.

The material consists of twelve different kinds of metal objects and six different kinds of weaves. Within the most numerous group of metal items, i.e. the shield bosses, all six types of fabrics were

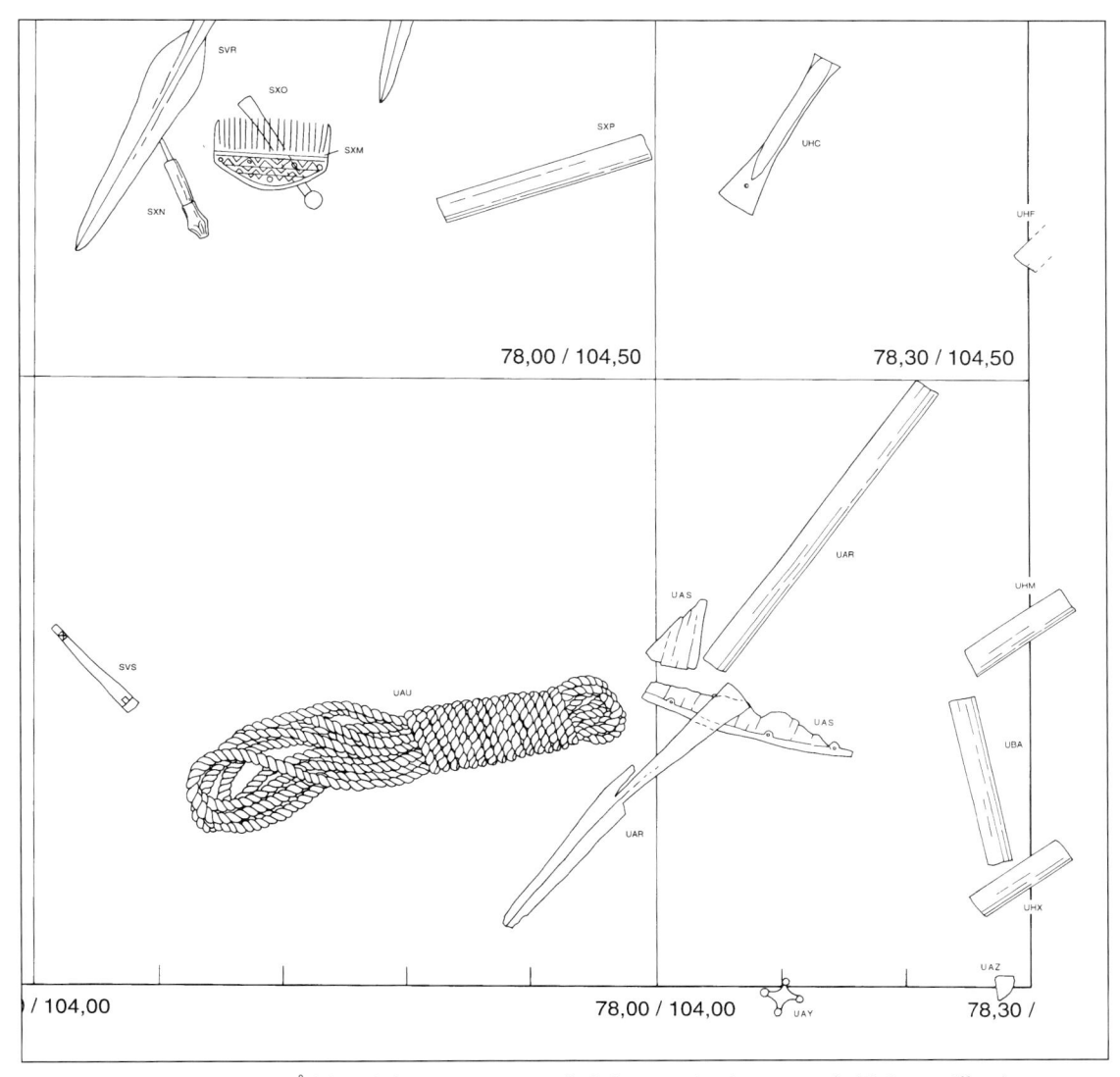

Fig. 1.13. Illerup Ådal, coiled up rope UAU in find cluster 79/104, not to scale (© Jørgen Ilkjær)

encountered. The largest group of textiles, i.e. the diamond twills in z/s, are known from six or seven object categories. The same holds true for the diagonal twills in z/z as well as in z/s. Swords – as the most valuable weapons – were found in combination with diamond twills in z/s as well as with a diagonal twill in z/z. On the other hand, knives – as objects of rather low value – were also observed wrapped in z/s diamond twill and in z/s diagonal twill. Thus, fabrics do not seem to have been deliberately selected according to the objects.

Another aspect of this issue refers to the question of whether particular fabrics were preferred for either inner or outer wrappings. Regrettably, only one type of weave per metal object was preserved in most cases, while microstratigraphies of two different textiles or textile and fur are rare. As inner wrappings, fur (2 ×), tabbies (3 ×) and diamond twills in z/z (2 ×) as well as in z/s (1 ×) were recorded. Tabby (1 ×), diagonal twills in z/z (2 ×) and z/s (1 ×) as well as a diamond twill in z/z (1 ×) and z/s (3 ×) were determined as top layers. Although fur was only found as inner wrapping and diagonal twills only on top, the numbers are too low and the picture is too diverse to provide any definite answer.

Spatial context

The spatial context within each cluster was discussed above. In the following, the bog in its entirety is considered. Within the lake, the various materials were not distributed randomly but were deposited systematically in certain combinations (von Carnap-Bornheim and Ilkjær 1996a, 15). As a rule, each cluster of artefacts contained items of various find categories, i.e. various weapons, tools, raw materials etc. (ibid.; Ilkjær 1993a, 16). Moreover, they generally contained items of different metals and thus of different levels within the hierarchy of the army (von Carnap-Bornheim and Ilkjær 1996a, 15, 483). Another interesting result of previous research concerning the distribution of the weapons was that fragments of a single weapon may appear in different clusters quite far apart from one another (Ilkjær 1993a, 17, Abb. 1). It seems worth verifying whether this might also hold true for the textiles. Regrettably, the majority of weaves is so unspecific that they do not allow for any overall conclusions. Unusual fabrics, which might be used for any comparison, are the spin-patterned examples, possibly those in combination with tubular side edges and the tablet weaves – yet, the latter are not considered here. Spin patterning occurred within three find clusters (-6/60, 79/104 and 111/100) and once without a connection to any cluster. Yet, while more than one fragment of the cloth in question were found within find clusters 79/104 and 111/100, no correspondence among those four places can be stated. The four fabrics clearly differ from one another. The four or five tubular edges all belong to 2/2 z/s diamond twills, distributed within three clusters (56/78, 57/90 and 85/85). Regrettably, these edges themselves could not be determined in every detail, thus preventing a direct comparison. The identical problem occurred in the pattern units of the diamond twills in question which could only be calculated on those two items from find cluster 85/85. Thus, the data provided turned out to be insufficient for tracing this idea.

Notes

1. They are dated to c. 1978, 22.11.1978 and 23.5.1980. Lise Bender Jørgensen kindly gave the manuscripts to the present author.
2. Sometimes the thread count could not be determined.
3. The thread count could not be determined in every case.
4. Klaus Tidow (2000, 108): very coarse ≤ 10, coarse ≤ 16, medium fine ≤ 24, fine ≤ 36, very fine > 36, calculated as threads per cm in warp plus threads per cm in weft.
5. E.g. the shield SAUE was distributed over five find clusters and four isolated spots (von Carnap-Bornheim and Ilkjær 1996a, 73, Abb. 42).
6. The measurements taken by Lise Bender Jørgensen are somewhat higher.
7. On a sixth lancehead, SUP, the signature for textiles is shown in a map in Ilkjær (1993a, 58).
   Pattern units in the warp: ≥ 8, 11, 18, 18, 14, 18, 12; in the weft: ≥ 5, 10, 3, 13, 13, ≥ 13. Weaving mistakes in warp and weft.
9. Pattern units in the warp: ≥ 3, 14, 14, ≥ 5; in the weft: ≥ 12, 13, 13.
10. "Rapport" in warp and weft according to Lise Bender Jørgensen: 26 which is an equivalent to pattern units of 13.
11. Pattern units in the warp on a loose fragment: 9, 7; in the weft: not determinable.
12. Pattern units in the warp on the iron: ≥ 23, 11, 12, 8, 9; in the weft: ≥ 3, 8, ≥ 4. Pattern units in the warp on a loose fragment: ≥ 36; in the weft: ≥ 5, 9, ≥ 10.
13. Pattern units in the warp: ≥ 17, c. 13, ≥ 21; in the weft: c. 11.

3. VIMOSE

3.1. INTRODUCTION

Site and research history

Vimose is a bog situated near Odense on the Danish island of Fyn. When Conrad Engelhardt commenced his excavation there in 1868, the site had already been known for many years. Engelhardt published some of the material in 1869. However, the vast majority of the large number of objects – amounting to c. 5000 today (von Carnap-Bornheim and Ilkjær 2008, 13), remained unknown. More recently, Vimose has again received attention as a parallel for the other weapon deposits (e.g. Ilkjær 1993a). A major result of this renewed interest is Xenia Pauli Jensen's PhD thesis from 2008. Pauli Jensen's main topic was the weapons, particularly those pertaining to the earlier part of the Roman Iron Age. She provided an overview of the research history, presented a refined chronology and introduced new aspects on the origin of the foreign warriors.

All material from Vimose examined in this context are housed at the National Museum of Denmark in Copenhagen.

Chronology

According to Xenia Pauli Jensen (2008, 34–40), the bog contained eight different weapon deposits and some non-military sacrifices. The first weapons were dated to the beginning of the Common Era (Vimose 0), the last deposit belongs to the time around AD 600 (Vimose 6). Although the finds from Vimose encompass a large time span, those with textiles – including the so-called cloth bundle – primarily belong to the Vimose 3 deposit, dated to period C1b.[1] This period corresponds to the decades AD 210/220 to 250/260 (*Sejrens triumf* 2003, inside back cover). Only few items may be older. Six lanceheads (NM 18655, NM 18727, NM 23798, NM 24761, NM 24762 and NM C7306) were part of either Vimose 2a or 2b or Vimose 3 (i.e. period B2–C1/C1b). The only examined weapon clearly dated to Vimose 2b is shield boss NM C1806, but whether or not any textile survived on this particular item cannot be definitely ascertained. Finally, the age of lancehead NM UI160, is rather uncertain (i.e. period B–C).

Origin of non-textile finds

Together with the finds from Illerup Ådal, Jørgen Ilkjær discussed the provenance of the materials found in Vimose, in particular the personal belongings of the warriors. As far as the Vimose 2 deposit is concerned, Ilkjær located the areas of origin either on the island of Fyn and in the south of Jutland, i.e. more in the vicinity of Vimose, or further to the south and southeast on the Continent (1993a, 376). Regarding Vimose 3, he described the material as Scandinavian, as in Illerup Platz A (ibid., 378–380), which implies south and west Norway and west Sweden. Later, Xenia Pauli Jensen subdivided the Vimose 2 deposit into 2a and 2b. According to her (2008, 284–285), the parallels for the weapons and personal belongings of the Vimose 2a deposit are widespread, from Norway and Sweden down to the Baltic countries and Poland where the majority of types can be found within the northern Przeworsk Culture. Regarding the finds of the Vimose 2b deposit, the general picture is quite similar, although the focus on Poland is less clear. The later deposits were not investigated by Pauli Jensen.

Textiles

In Vimose, the conditions for preserving the various prehistoric materials are comparable to Illerup. This implies that textiles are restricted to iron finds. Both mineralisation and conservation enabled the weaves to survive but destroyed or concealed many details. Textiles from Vimose were already mentioned by Conrad Engelhardt (see below). Subsequently however, these materials hardly received any attention until the present. A group of lanceheads and spearheads found in a so-called cloth bundle formed the focus of an article by Jørgen Ilkjær (1975). Yet, Ilkjær's interest was not the textiles but the weapons.

3.2. TECHNICAL ASPECTS OF THE TEXTILES

Of the 58 metal items from Vimose examined: 40 were lanceheads, eleven spearheads, six shield bosses and one a baldric fitting. Not all of them show clear textile remnants. A bundle of three spearheads (NM 24760) is held together by plant fibres, and similar fibres were found on spearhead NM 23935. Possible or undeterminable traces of textiles were observed on nine pieces, amongst them the baldric fitting. In five cases, tablet weaves were found (see Lise Ræder Knudsen, this volume). On one of the remaining 41 weapons, two different textiles survived (NM 24764). Thus, the following description is based on 42 textile remains.

Material

Due to the iron content of the weapons, the organic material was widely mineralised. Since the examination was restricted to the use of optical instruments, many details of the fibres could not be identified. However, in a few cases, e.g. on NM 23798, seemingly non-mineralised, original fibres were found and interpreted as unpigmented wool. This is in accordance with Conrad Engelhardt's description of some items of woven, woollen cloth and a woollen band (1869, 4). Vegetal fibres may have survived as ropes, as in Illerup and, as described below, in Thorsberg and Nydam. Concerning Vimose, Engelhardt wrote (1867, 32):

> "*Paa mange Steder laa større Stykker tynde og tykke Reb, spundne af to og tre Traade, lige ud eller i Klumper*"
>
> ("In many places, larger pieces of thin and thick ropes, spun from two or three threads, lay separately or in heaps.")

Thus, Engelhardt did not mention the material. Yet, he did mention "bast" for a certain cord (ibid.).

Weaving types

Only five tabbies in z/z were recovered (12%). In all other cases (88%), diagonal 2/2 twills were found, all of them again woven with z-spun yarns both in warp and weft.[2] No other types of weave were attested, apart from the tablet weaves. The latter represent the only edges, but regrettably, no example of a tablet weave in combination with a well-determinable ground weave was recovered.

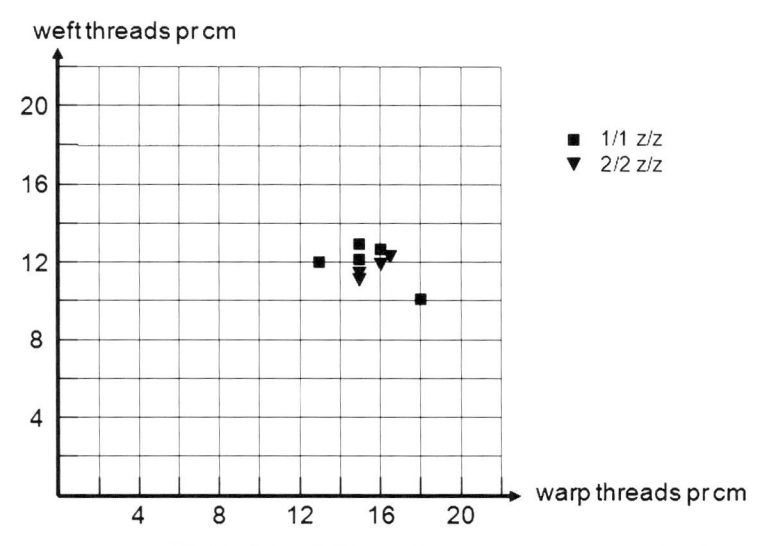

Fig. 1.14. Vimose, thread counts. The "cloth bundle" is considered as one item (15 × 11 tpc)

Consequently, it is impossible to define the warp and weft of any textile. Despite the results found on some z/s twills from Illerup Ådal (see above), but based on material from other sites, the thread system with the highest thread count is considered to be the warp. Not only is the spinning direction of the yarn material identical, the thread diameter too is very similar in all pieces. The typical thickness is 0.5–0.6 mm. Some variation occurs in practically every cloth, with few threads being a little thinner (mostly 0.4 mm), clearly more examples being up to 0.8 mm thick and a few exceptions with a diameter of up to 1.0 mm. Despite these variations, the yarns appear homogeneous and well prepared. The same applies to the weaving which was undertaken with care.

The thread counts are presented in Fig. 1.14 which again emphasises the homogeneity of this material. Four of the five tabbies cluster around c. 15 × 12 tpc. Only one of them (NM 18727) is less balanced, with 18 × 10 tpc and a dominating warp or first system, but still representing a comparable quality. It seems that the coarsest tabby (NM 23798, with 13 × 12 tpc) was napped, indicated by short hairs near the tip of the lancehead and more fibres on the blade.[3] A similar situation was found on lancehead NM 24764 which is the item with two different textiles. Regrettably, it is impossible to ascertain if these fibres derive from the tabby or the twill.

As stated above, 88% of the textiles from Vimose were registered as 2/2 diagonal twills in z/z. Although the technical aspects are in focus in this chapter, it must be mentioned in advance that 37 of the examined weapons of this group – 31 lances and six spears – belonged to the so-called cloth bundle, a closed find already mentioned in the introduction to Vimose.[4] Three of them did not provide any detailed information in this technical context, but the fabrics of the other 34 items will be discussed here, before turning to the rest of the twills. Their thread counts are shown in Fig. 15. It appears that they are – with one exception – very similar, varying between 13 and 17 tpc in the warp combined with 10 to 12.5 tpc in the weft. The thread diameters including the variations are as described above. It seems highly probable that these 33 pieces belong to one and the same cloth which was probably napped. Only on item NM 24745, which was also part of the bundle,

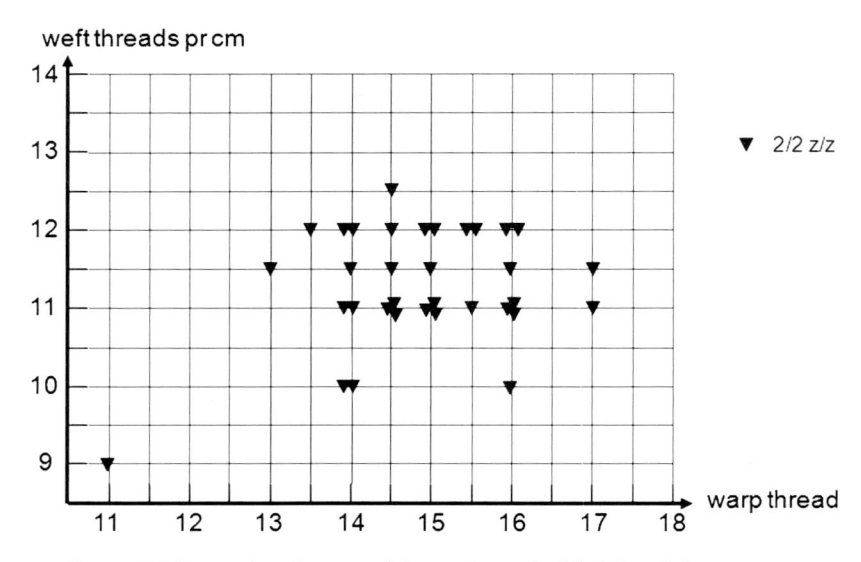

Fig. 1.15. Vimose, thread counts of the textiles in the "cloth bundle"

do the measurements suggest a different textile: The thread count is lower, 11 × 10 tpc, while the threads were mostly 0.7–0.8 mm thick. Yet, the general impression is similar including indications of napping.

Textile quality
As far as may be ascertained, the textiles were made with care in terms of fibre preparation, spinning and weaving. Except for one part of the so-called cloth bundle, all textiles may be called fine, i.e. they consist of at least 24 but less than 36 threads per cm² (see Tidow 2000, 108). Moreover, the indications of napping which were found in the cloth bundle and elsewhere are signs of high-quality products.

3.3. CONTEXT AND FUNCTIONS
Cloth bundle
Engelhard described the contents of the so-called cloth bundle as "*indpakkede samlede i vævet, uldent Tøi*", i.e. "*packed together in woven, woollen cloth*" (1869, 4), regrettably without providing further details. The technical analysis of 37 lances and spears revealed that most probably, only one cloth was used for wrapping all these items. Only in one case (NM 24745), do the measurements yield slightly different results, but here, the textile on this particular lancehead is interpreted as an integral part of this one twill. If it is correct that only one cloth was used, it is obvious that the original textile must have been of considerable size. A cloak or a blanket seems most likely at this point of the discussion. This issue will be taken up again below. It may be added that the idea of a large, torn, or more probably cut cloth is in accordance with the fact that no traces of edges or seams were found.

The description of the cloth bundle suggests that the collection of objects lay in e.g. a bag or one large wrapping. On most weapons, however, textile fragments or at least fibres were observed on both sides, often clearly continuing from one side to the other. There is therefore no doubt that each lance and spear was wrapped separately. Moreover, there are two lanceheads (NM 24744 and NM 24752) on which the weave covers the opening of the socket to some extent. This implies that the wooden shafts were removed or broken off – fragments are still visible in one of the sockets – and this supports the observation of individual wrapping. Yet, it may well be and is easy to imagine that subsequenlty, the entire assemblage was covered again by a piece of the same or another textile.

Returning to the wrapping of each weapon, the comparison between them revealed a striking pattern. The first aspect of this pattern refers to the orientation of the weave in relation to the axes of the weapons. The probable warp runs in right angles to the long axis of the weapons (Fig. 1.16) on the vast majority of lances as well as spears. This is particularly true on the sockets where diagonally positioned threads were observed only twice (NM 24734 and NM 24740). On the heads, the orientation may be oblique to some extent, but often it follows the axes again despite the curved outline of the metal.

The other aspect of the pattern is related to the structure of the twill. Weaving a plain twill produces a pattern of diagonal lines running over the entire cloth. These features are called "twill lines" here. As with the spinning direction, such a twill line may be described as either "Z"- or "S"-orientated. As a rule, i.e. in 31 out of the 32 clearly determinable cases, the fragments on the weapons in the cloth bundle exhibit a twill line in S. Yet, twill lines in Z do exist too, and they do so more often than in merely the one sample above. On the socket of lance NM 24724, spots of differently orientated twill were preserved side by side. If one does not wish to propose a broken twill – in which the twill line changes its direction at some point – this observation supports the idea of several layers of cloth, even though no stratigraphy can be established here. Similar situations were met on NM 24742 and NM 24752. And indeed, in seven other cases, twill lines in Z were found on top of a typical S-layer, e.g. on NM 24721 and NM 24733 (Fig. 1.17). Moreover, the orientation of the threads according to the axes of the weapons is usually the same in these upper layers as it is in those areas with twill lines in S. One conclusion from this phenomenon is that the cloth for wrapping was folded in two – otherwise one would find the same twill lines in both (or more) layers. A further conclusion to be drawn is that the wrapping was carried out with extraordinary care.

Other weapons
The two lanceheads NM 18655/56 are preserved as a unit, with fragments of cloth on the sockets and the blades. On the sockets, at least two layers of the same weave can be distinguished. The textile definitely held the weapons together. Its fragmentary status, however, does not seem to be a result of decay in the bog, but appears to be strips of cloth running around both pieces. This impression is supported by a drawing in Conrad Engelhardt's publication (1864, 4, fig. 1), in which Engelhardt described the cloth as twill ("*firskæftet Vævning*").

Other such units of two or more metal objects are NM 18727 and NM 24760. The latter consists of three spearheads; plant material which appears to be grass or leaves were used for holding them together, referred to as "*Bastbaand*" by Engelhardt (1869, 4). Engelhardt mentioned a similarly made bundle with two lanceheads or spearheads, an arrowhead and a hand brace (ibid.). These items were not included in this investigation, at least not all parts of it; NM 23925, however, may belong to it. The package NM 18727 contains one lancehead and two knives. A tabby was laid rather loosely around these three objects, resulting in folds between the lance and the knives.

Lancehead NM 24762 was clearly wrapped as a single piece in tablet-woven material, i.e. a c.

Fig. 1.16. Vimose, wrapping according to the axes on lancehead NM 24756

Fig. 1.17. Vimose, wrapping laid double on lancehead NM 24721

3 cm wide band. Perhaps it was this piece that Engelhardt had in mind when he wrote of an iron tip wrapped up in a tightly woven band made of wool with a width of "*1 2/12 Tommes Brede*", i.e. c. 3 cm.[5] Yet, he described this weapon as being bent which is not true for NM 24762. Other lances and spears also show textile patches or at least fibres on both sides, thus indicating individual

wrapping. These are nos. NM 23798, NM 24761, NM 24763, NM 24764, NM C7306, NM C9400 and NM UI160. Only one of them (NM 24764) possesses a twill, in a good enough state of preservation to compare it to the cloth bundle. Here again, the twill's orientation corresponds to the axes of the weapon and the twill line may be described as "S". Yet, the twill was only determined on the blade, while on the socket, a tabby was preserved. Since the latter textile does not follow the axes and no stratigraphy can be established, it can only be presumed that the lancehead was at first wrapped in twill and the tabby then used for another wrapping, possibly for keeping a certain number of weapons together. Another lancehead requiring closer scrutiny is NM 24761. A typical twill covers parts of both sides, on one of them parallel to the axes and with an "S"-like twill line. On the reverse side, it is interrupted by a probably originally underlying strip of similar cloth but in "Z", the inner edge of which is folded. Seemingly, it is one and the same cloth which had a narrow fold at the very beginning of the wrapping. This detail is worth mentioning as the innermost edge is neither woven nor finished in any way. It suggests that a cut or torn piece of cloth was used for wrapping which matches the observations on the cloth bundle.

In all, seven shield bosses are included in this investigation. On five of them, textile structures or at least fibres were observed or are probable on the inside, i.e. under the flange and/or on the concave side of the domes. Regrettably, no details could be identified and thus, they cannot be compared to the remnants on the outside of the bosses. Yet, in parallel to Illerup, individual wrapping and then sticking one boss into another may be assumed. Indeed, Conrad Engelhardt excavated several such clustered examples (1869, 4), and up to the present day, two bosses of the small group examined here make up such a unit (NM 22858). There are holes in the dome of the outer one which allow for some inspection. Organic material – possibly structured and of regular thickness – adheres to the inner side of the outer boss. Between this layer and the inner boss, plant material which resembles the wrappings of NM 23935 and NM 24760 is preserved. On the outside of the domes too, the state of preservation is mostly poor. Engelhardt (1869, 4) mentioned a shield boss with woven cloth, edges and fringes which matches NM 24766 with its tablet weave.

Moreover, Engelhardt (ibid.) enumerated a few other textiles which cannot be correlated with the examined material: an iron tip "sewn into" woollen cloth, 30–40 iron fragments of the rim of a shield wrapped in cloth together with the tip of a sword, a shield boss wrapped in cloth together with a fragmented axe and finally some jewellery "*i en lille Lærredsbylt*", i.e. "*in a little bundle of linen tabby*" – the word "lærred", however, should not be taken literally (see chapter 5.3.1.).

Primary functions

As in Illerup, the textiles from Vimose do not yield any direct information about their primary function. Using the same cloth in at least two layers for the individual wrapping of at least 36 weapons – as were found in the cloth bundle (NM 24721–57) – makes clear that this cloth must have been of considerable size. Furthermore, considering its good quality, a cloak or perhaps a blanket seems reasonable. This explanation would be in accordance with the absence of woven or hemmed edges or seams within the cloth bundle. Here again, broad tablet weaves – perhaps in combination with fringes as on shield boss NM 24766 and on spearhead NM 24763 – may be regarded as high quality features of clothing. A tablet-woven band as on lancehead NM 24762 may once have been a belt.

Wrapping and intentional damage

Conrad Engelhardt concluded that the metal objects were deposited as rather small units, each bound together with cords or bands, or wrapped in cloth (1869, 3–4). The wrapping was not only confirmed by the present investigation, but it could be demonstrated that at least in the case of the cloth bundle, it was carried out with extraordinary care. Conversely, the tabby on shield boss NM 24767 exhibits linear cuts like those described on several weapons excavated in Illerup Ådal. They seemingly attest to ritual destruction.

Intended selection?

Lanceheads as well as spearheads are both found in combination with tabby as well as with twill. On shield bosses, only tabbies have been recovered. However, since determinable textiles were observed only twice on this kind of weapon, the lack of twill is not an argument for any firm conclusion. The tablet weaves may also be mentioned again in this context. Tablet-woven material was found on two or possibly three lanceheads, one spearhead and one shield boss. On shield boss NM 24766 and probably on spearhead NM 24763, the combination of tablet weaves with fringes and patches of unidentified weaves may indicate edges of e.g. a cloak. Lancehead NM 24762, on the other hand, appears as if it was totally covered by a tablet weave of c. 3 cm width which may be explained as a band or possible belt rather than the edge of a ground weave. The preservation on NM C9400 and NM Ul160 is not good enough for any interpretation. The occasional use of grass-like plant material points in the same direction, i.e., that there is no particular correlation between a certain type of weapon and a certain textile material. The leaves cover the surface of one single spearhead (NM 23935), it keeps together a group of another three spearheads (NM 24760) and was possibly placed between two shield bosses (NM 22858) before being stuck one into the other.

Spatial context

The information on the position of certain finds in the bog is very poor. Conrad Engelhardt noticed, however, that their distribution was not totally random (1869, 3–4). He mentioned e.g. that small items were often found in the domes of the shield bosses. This observation may also indicate that the bosses were encountered with their concave sides upwards.

Chronological context

The group of textiles that possibly originates from the Vimose 2a deposit and thus represent the Early Roman Age is very small. It encompasses two tabbies in z/z and two diagonal twills in z/z along with two tablet weaves. The thread count of these four weaves ranges from 18 × 10 tpc down to 13 × 12 tpc, i.e. within a small spectrum. The same homogeneity applies to the yarns' thickness which was measured as 0.5 mm at most spots, sometimes a little thicker up to 0.8 mm. However, it is quite possible that these pieces were not deposited in Vimose 2a but in either Vimose 2b or even Vimose 3, both periods belonging to the Late Roman Age.

When the finds of the so-called cloth bundle are considered as one cloth, the group of determinable weaves definitely dating to Vimose 3 is only slightly larger than the one just described. It contains three tabbies in z/z and two diagonal twills in z/z as well as two or perhaps three tablet weaves. Here, the thread counts lie between 16–17 × 12–13 and 15 × 12 with yarn diameters of around 0.5 mm. Thus, the differences between both groups – if they are indeed two chronologically different groups – are insignificant.

Notes

1 Xenia Pauli Jensen, National Museum, Copenhagen, Denmark, personal communication (list of all relevant datings), November 2008.
2 The z-spin of the second system in the twill of NM 24764, however, is uncertain.
3 The traces of napping are very faint on the material from Vimose. They probably would not have been recognised at all if such a phenomenon had not been observed before in more obvious versions on the weapons from Illerup, the examination of which was the first part of the project.
4 The bundle contained 38 tips and one bronze plate, so the plate and one tip are not included in the current investigation.
5 1 T. or tomme corresponds to 1 inch (2.54 cm).

4. THORSBERG

4.1. INTRODUCTION

Site and research history

The Thorsberg bog is situated in the village of Süderbrarup, c. 25 km southeast of Flensburg in northernmost Germany. The main excavations at Thorsberg were carried out in 1860–1861 by Conrad Engelhardt, resulting in over 1,300 finds (von Carnap-Bornheim 2005, 16). Engelhardt's publication of the site (1863) still represents a major source. The catalogues compiled by Klaus Raddatz constitute further basic information on Thorsberg (1987a; 1987b). Moreover, Raddatz published a reconstructed map of Engelhardt's excavation area with its numerous trenches (1987b, 11, Abb. 1). More recently, small test excavations undertaken in the bog in 1997 have to be mentioned, although only wooden artefacts were found (Hartz 2002/2003). They prove, however, that Engelhardt did not recover the material in its entirety. The state of research was summarised by Claus von Carnap-Bornheim in 2004 (pp. 16–18). Preliminary results of current research on various materials such as leather and wood were published in 2008 (Abegg-Wigg and Rau 2008). In the context of the present research, the above-mentioned map was revised digitally and the locations of the finds entered as far as they could be reconstructed.[1] The bulk of the Thorsberg material is housed at Archäologisches Landesmuseum, Schloss Gottorf, in Schleswig. Smaller collections belong to other museums, particularly the National Museum of Denmark in Copenhagen.

Chemically, this bog contains an acidic environment, in contrast to Illerup Ådal, Vimose and Nydam. Therefore, the conditions for the preservation of iron as well as textiles are the opposite to those of the other three sites: while the iron was mostly dissolved, some woollen items were very well preserved.

Chronology and origin of non-textile finds

As on the other sites, several deposits may be distinguished within the Thorsberg bog. While two Bronze Age items may belong to hoards from that period, and ceramic vessels were laid down from the 2nd century BC onwards (Raddatz 1952, 78–82), the deposition of weapons began in period B2 of the Early Roman Iron Age or in the 2nd century AD (Ilkjær 1993a, 374–386; Bemmann and Bemmann 1998 vol. 1, 338, Abb. 144a, and 341; Ilkjær 2003, 60–61; Lund Hansen 2003, 88–89, with fig. 4), with material originating within the region itself or further south, i.e. more or less corresponding to the non-Roman areas of Germany. The major deposition took place in period C1b, i.e. the first half of the 3rd century AD. Again, the likely provenance is the Continent, south and west of the river Elbe. The material includes many finds of Roman origin. Finally, an even later sacrifice is dated to period C2 or the time around AD 300. In this case, the owners of the weapons are thought to originate from the Scandinavian peninsular, around central Norway and central Sweden.

Textiles

Due to the chemical composition of the bog, the textiles from Thorsberg are not attached to weapons but are finds of their own. Most of them are stored in Schleswig. The collection includes two well-known items, a tunic (3683) and a pair of trousers (3684). Additionally, some 15 finds are registered here. Yet, as with other find categories, Schleswig is not the only repository of textiles from Thorsberg. Some are kept in the National Museum of Denmark and single pieces found their way to yet other museums and institutions, e.g. Moesgård Museum and Sorø Akademi, both in Denmark.

The above-mentioned publication by Conrad Engelhardt (1863) is supplemented by his diary for 1860. Later, the material was presented in several publications. Beginning in the 1930s, Karl Schlabow published books as well as smaller papers focused on prehistoric textiles. One of the best preserved cloaks from Thorsberg particularly caught his interest (1951). In 1976, he presented an overview of Iron Age textiles found in northern Germany where he described those items from Thorsberg that are stored in Schleswig. As far as the Copenhagen material is concerned, Margrethe Hald had published it already in 1950 together with the prehistoric textile finds from Denmark. Thirty years later, in 1980, an English version of her book became available. The present investigation is the first publication to deal with the Thorsberg textile assemblage almost in its entirety.[2]

Since the textiles from Thorsberg were not found in direct connection with datable materials such as weapons or wood, the question of which deposits they belong to remains uncertain. Possible datings are periods B2, C1b and C2 (see Erdrich and von Carnap-Bornheim 2004, 99–100). If they were consecrated in connection with the major deposit, the dating is the first half of the 3rd century AD.

4.2. TECHNICAL AND FUNCTIONAL ASPECTS OF THE TEXTILES

4.2.1 Description according to find numbers

Compared to the textiles from the other sites, the state of preservation is generally quite good although the material has suffered damage over time (Farke 1994a). Perhaps the most famous item, a tunic (3683), as well as one pair of trousers (3684) are mounted in such a way that only one side is visible and accessible, while the reverse side as well as the inside are hidden. Since both items had to be maintained that way during the current investigation, many aspects could not be examined. Some large pieces of cloaks and another pair of trousers are sewn onto cloth, thus again keeping the reverse or inner side out of view and reach as long as new conservation treatments are not undertaken. This holds true for the following numbers: 3685, 3686, 3687, 3688, 3689, 3690, 3691, 3692, 3693, 3696 and partly 3684. Other items, often small ones, are sewn onto boards, with the identical result that the reverse side cannot be investigated. This applies to the following fragments: 3696 (together with the modern cloth mentioned above) and 3699–3705. One textile is glued to a glass sheet: 3695. Finally, some pieces are additionally covered with a fine net: 3691, 3692, 3698.

The following section includes the general descriptions of the finds. On many of the textiles, one or more original edges, often tablet-woven borders, may be observed. Their investigation and documentation was carried out by Lise Ræder Knudsen (this volume). Yet, they cannot be treated independently from the ground weaves, especially as they contain information about the weaving process of the items as a whole. In order to avoid discussing the tablet-woven bands continuously throughout the text, the edges are presented in a chapter of their own, followed by some reflections on the looms.

3683 Tunic
(Schlabow 1976, 69–71 and Abb. 135–142)
(Hald 1980, 339)

When Conrad Engelhardt discovered this tunic in 1860, he described it in his diary as follows:

> *"en ulden bluse af følgende dimensioner*
> *Længden 35 T*
> *Bredde 21 T*
> *Kort ærme 21 T*
> *Ved ærmerne og på den ene side forneden særligt vævede sirater.*
> *Stykkerne er sammensyet og kantet med sort tråd. Delt i to stk.*
> *Ved det ene hænger det ene ærme endnu fastsyet og det andet ærme er*
> *Også til stede, i øvrigt er det stærkt pjaltet; det andet stykke har på*
> *Oversiden en rundet kant [...] og er på xxxx[3] revet over, men de to stykker er dog sammenholdt på den ene side ved kanten"*

> ("a woollen blouse of the following dimensions
> length c. 90 cm[4]
> width c. 55 cm
> short sleeves c. 55 cm
> On the sleeves and on one side at the bottom specially woven decorations.
> The pieces are sewn together and edged with black thread. Divided in two pieces.
> One of the sleeves is still fastened to one of the pieces, and the other sleeve is also there; furthermore, it is heavily torn; the other piece has a rounded edge on top [...] and is torn on xxxx, but the two pieces are still held together on one side at the edge.")

In his publication of 1863 (p. 18), Engelhardt's description contained a few amendments:

> *"En Kjortel af vævet, uldent Tøi, 33 ½ T. lang, 20 T. bred; Ærmernes Længde er 20 ½ T. [...] Den er sammensyet af to Stykker Tøi, ligesom ogsaa Ærmerne ere syede til senere. Oppe ved Halsaabningen er Kanten ombøiet, og forneden er der en vævet Bord. [...] Ved Haandleddene derimod er der paasyet særligt vævede uldne Linninger af en fastere Vævning [...] og lysere Farve end Kjortlen, der nu er brunrød. Begge Ærmerne ere af en anden og stærkere Slags Tøi end Kjortlen, idet Tøiet er vævet i rudret Mønster [...] ligesom Foden ved Beenklæderne [...]. Ærmerne og Fodbedækningen vare udsatte for mest Slid, og det er vel Grunden til, at der er valgt stærkere Stoffer dertil. Kjortlen er aldeles fuldstændig; men det ene Ærme var revet løst, og flere store Flænger vise, at den som saa meget Andet i dette Fund øiensynlig er bleven nedlagt i en ubrugbar Tilstand"*

> ("A tunic of woven, woollen cloth, c. 87 cm long, c. 52 cm wide; the length of the sleeves is c. 53 cm [...]. It is sewn together from two pieces of cloth, as also the sleeves were sewn onto it later. At the top, at the neck opening, the edge is folded, and at the bottom, there is a woven border. [...] At the wrists, on the other hand, especially woven, woollen cuffs of a tighter weave [...] and lighter colour than the shirt which is now brownish red, are sewn on. Both sleeves are of another and stronger type of cloth than the shirt, the cloth being woven in a chequered pattern [...] like the foot of the trousers [...]. The sleeves and the foot cover were exposed to the heaviest wear, and this is possibly the reason why stronger fabrics were chosen for them. The tunic is totally complete; but one of the sleeves was torn loose, and several large cuts prove that it, as so many other items in this find, was obviously rendered useless before being laid down.")

Despite Engelhardt's generally acute observations, not all of the described details can be confirmed. Particularly, no difference is visible between the fabric close to the body and that of the sleeves. Both are of the same 2/2 diamond twill in z/s. Within the z-spun system, the warp, the pattern units consist regularly of ten threads; only once within a length of more than 10 cm, was a unit of nine yarns to be found. In the other system, the units usually comprise nine yarns including some irregularities like seven, ten and thirteen. The unpigmented fibre material is unusually fine, curly and homogeneous. It is not easy to understand why Conrad Engelhardt observed a difference between the fabric of the body part and the sleeves. Hypothetically, it could have had something to do with the fabric's surface. No indications of napping or fulling were found. Instead, the surface appears homogeneously rubbed. However, the fibres sticking out from the weave seem to be bent, although this is apparently not due to their natural curliness. Possibly, the tunic was treated in some unknown way after the excavation, resulting in a now more homogeneous surface than it once was.[5] The cloth was produced using a tablet-woven starting border (Fig. 1.18), the structure of which is discussed below.

As mentioned by Engelhardt, the body section consists of two large parts. As can be observed on the side on display, the cloth starts with the tablet-woven border, which is placed at the bottom of the tunic. Thus the warp runs vertically through the piece of clothing. The cloth continues over the shoulders to the inaccessible side. According to photographs,[6] it reaches down for about 35 cm where it ends in a transverse seam. The part below the seam is c. 45–50 cm long and ends in a trimmed edge, secured with blanket stitch. According to hand weaver Anna Nørgaard, Roskilde who examined the tunic in 1998 before it was mounted in the present form, the stitches of the trimming are 4 mm away from each other and reach 4 mm into the cloth (1998, 1).[7] This side is a few centimetres shorter than the one on display where a length of 88.5 cm was measured. The reason might be the transverse seam in connection with the conservation or restoration of the tunic (see below). The measurement of the outer width of the tunic was 56 cm.

The neck opening was cut out and is c. 25.5 cm wide. The edge was folded once and hemmed with blanket stitch. A dark, twined yarn, hardly visible on the outside, was used for sewing. On the displayed side, the cut of the opening is straight while it was made a little rounder on the other side. This is an indication that Karl Schlabow's reconstruction has to be revised to some extent, i.e. that the side on display represents the back of the tunic. This was already stated by other scholars, e.g. by Margrethe Hald (1980, 339). It implies moreover that the location of a conspicuous detail, an edged hole, is not on the right front but on the left back, c. 12.5 cm below the shoulder and c. 8 cm away from the side edge. The function of this hole still seems to be open to question. It was described by Schlabow as a spot where the fibula for closing a cloak could be fixed but this explanation depends on its location in front. Inga Hägg (2000, 28) agreed with Hald and others that the side on display and thus the side with the hole is the back and suggested that it was a buttonhole for fixing a baldric for a sword or quiver. It may be argued, however, that it seems inconvenient to place such a feature in exactly the spot where it was most difficult for the warrior to fix or loosen it by himself. Yet, no better explanation has so far been proposed. Anna Nørgaard (1998, 2) regarded it merely as a possible repair. The hole itself is c. 0.5 cm wide, surrounded by an edging of c. 0.3 cm width. The edging was made in blanket stitch, using a twined yarn in zS and carried out firmly but not very carefully (Fig. 1.19). Its colour is the same as the adjacent cloth.

The preserved seams of the tunic are of a specific type called "Torsberger Naht", i.e. "Thorsberg seam", by Johanna Mestorf. She found this type not only on the tunic but on other items as well (1907, 48). The two edges that meet are each folded backwards (Fig. 1.20). Each side forms a loop or roll. The two adjacent rolls are then fixed to each other by a running stitch, resulting in four layers of fabric kept together. The edges do not lie within the rolls but face outwards. Other items from Thorsberg confirm that the edges were usually left raw. However, here, as an exception to the general rule, they are hemmed.

Fig. 1.18. Thorsberg, edge of the tunic (3683) with starting border and selvedge

Fig. 1.19. Thorsberg, edged hole on the tunic (3683)

The sides of the tunic constitute another striking feature. On the left of the mounted garment, i.e. on its right side, the selvedge of the fabric was used as edging. The selvedge was reinforced by using several z-yarns as the outermost warp (Fig. 1.21). While the sleeve was fastened with a dark, twined thread, a light-coloured twined yarn was used for the adjacent beginning of the downward seam. It gives the impression of a secondary feature and stops after only c. 2 cm. From that point downwards, the side is open. Along the following c. 60 cm, generally very close to the outermost edge, a thin, dark, bluish cord protrudes here and there from the cloth (Fig. 1.21). Often, both ends of a piece of cord appear close to each other, c. 1–2 cm away from each other, the connecting step stitch being visible on the inside. The distance between such pairs of cord ends is irregular and some cord ends are apparently missing. Slightly further away from the outermost edge, a row of stitching holes was observed but there was no corresponding thread. If one does not wish to ascribe these stitching holes to some restoration work from the 19th or early 20th century, it might have served to close the seam. This would tally with the observation that the cloth around the protruding cords is generally intact, which – in contrast to Karl Schlabow's reconstruction – makes it unlikely that the cords were used for tying up the tunic. Moreover, the cords are uncomfortably thin and the ends too short to serve that purpose. Yet, the construction remains obscure. The most probable variant of seam is certainly the "Thorsberg" type which, however, is hard to confirm. In any case, the outermost centimetre of the cloth or a little more appears as if it was once turned inwards (Fig. 1.21) which would place the cord ends inside the tunic. Possible stitching holes can be suspected about 1 cm further away from the edge (Fig. 1.22). Here, the cord ends may have penetrated the cloth. On the other hand, the abrasion of the surface as described above reaches to the very edge. This could not be expected in this context unless the rubbing had occurred only after the excavation. After all, if the cords were not used for tying up, they may rather be the remains of some kind of decoration. The identical cord reappears on the sleeves.

On the sleeves, the warp runs around the arms, and at the openings, the selvedge of the cloth is once again visible. According to Richard Stettiner (1911, 43) and Anna Nørgaard, the other selvedge was used at the upper ends of the sleeves, i.e. the length of the sleeves corresponds to the width of the cloth of c. 55 cm. The seam running down the sleeve is of the "Thorsberg" type. On the inside, the edge is secured with blanket stitch. Parallel to the seam, at a distance of c. 1 cm or a little less, rows of stitching holes, characterised on the outside as shallow depressions, are visible (Fig. 1.23). Around these holes, the

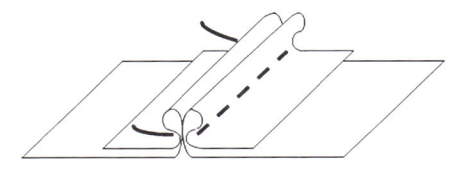

Fig. 1.20. Sketch of the "Thorsberg seam", not to scale

Fig. 1.21. Thorsberg, open seam along the side of the tunic (3683) with cord ends along the edge and stitching holes c. 1 cm inwards; warp horizontal

Fig. 1.22. Thorsberg, open seam along the side of the tunic (3683) with possible stitching holes c. 2 cm away from the edge; warp horizontal

Fig. 1.23. Thorsberg, seam in the left sleeve of the tunic (3683), with stitching holes and probable remnant of bluish cord

surface of the cloth is still woolly. Apparently, the fibres were not rubbed within these protected areas. In one hole, a dark thread is visible. Probably, these fibres belong to a bluish cord as described above. The holes and the dark thread create the impression that the thread (or cord) was sewn across the seam as embroidery. Near the lower end of the sleeve, the seam is left open to a length of c. 11 cm. Here, the cloth is folded further inwards so that the sleeve narrows. At the beginning of the slits, the bluish cord known from the sides of the tunic reappears (Fig. 1.24). Stitching holes as well as some

Fig. 1.24. Thorsberg, beginning of the slits at the lower end of the sleeve (3683)

Fig. 1.25. Thorsberg, faded outside and partly red threads along a cut on the tunic (3683)

cord ends follow the folded edges. This observation supports the notion that the bluish cord served as a decoration along the sides of the body as well. At the lower end of the sleeves, a tablet-woven band of c. 1.4 cm width is sewn onto the edge (see Ræder Knudsen, this volume).

Today, the tunic is of a light reddish hue on the outside while the tablet-woven band along the wrists appears a little more purple. On the inside, the red colour is amazingly vivid and strong. Having the tunic on display in the museum for such a long time must be one reason for the faded colour on the outside. Yet, another reason is that the colour may have faded already in the past. This is indicated by those threads which are cut along the strokes (Fig. 1.25). Their ends turn up to the surface, i.e. the entire diameter was exposed to light for a considerable length of time. However, they do possess a lighter outside while on the inside, they are clearly darker red. When Christian-Herbert Fischer (1997, 108) analysed some samples, he found madder in the body part of the tunic while the tablet weave contains madder as well as some blue dyestuff, "indigo". According to Fischer, this mixture was known as "Egyptian purple", a relatively cheap imitation of genuine purple.

Moreover, because of the conspicuous cuts, the tunic was analysed using forensic methods. According to Anette Kühl's report (2000, 2–5), the linear damages on the "front", i.e. the side with the tablet-woven border, are so similar to each other that they were probably all caused by the same implement, a sharp blade. The same seems to be true for a tongue-shaped tear inflicted on the same side. Regarding the question of when the fabric was damaged, three hypotheses were examined: when a person still wore the tunic; in context with the sacrifice; or during the excavation. Kühl considered the last interpretation as extremely unlikely. The first mentioned hypothesis could not be excluded but was regarded as improbable. Consequently, Kühl favoured the view that the damage was incurred after the battle, with a knife. On the so-called back, she described the transverse damage as well as a long tear running parallel to the right side close to the opening, as characterised by long protruding threads probably resulting from tearing. It remains uncertain, however, whether this happened during the Iron Age or during the 19th century. Small damage rather close to the bottom seems to derive from a stab while the tunic was folded. Again, the date of this incident is unknown. Moreover, Anette Kühl examined the openings along the sides. It was impossible, however, to decide whether they were originally open or closed.

3684 Trousers
(Schlabow 1976, 76–77 and Abb. 162–169)
(Hald 1980, 328–329)
Conrad Engelhardt provided quite a detailed description of the trousers (1883, 18–19):

> "*To Par Beenklæder[8] af uldent, vævet Tøi af en grovere Slags end Kapperne og Kjortlen [...]; Strømperne, der ere syede fast til Beenklæderne, have samme Slags rudrede Mønstervævning som Ærmerne paa Kjortlen [...], kun at Ruderne her ere noget mindre [...]. Paa Vrangsiden af dette rudrede Tøi [...] er Luven hævet ved Kartning [...], hvorved Stoffet vinder i Varme. Det Par Beenklæder, som er bedst bevaret,[9] har en Længde af 45 T., Vidden om Livet 38 ½ T., Fodlængden 11 ¼ T., – Maal, som tyde paa en sværtbygget Eiermand af over Middelhøide. Ved Livlinningen ere flere smalle Stropper fastsyede ved begge Ender; de have vel tjent til at fastholde Livbeltet, som blev stukket derigjennem. En bred og klodset Søm, fremkommen ved en Sammensyning, gaaer langs Midten af Fodsaalen, og paa flere Steder er der Lapper. De fandtes sammenrullede i en Byldt, men vare ufuldstændige, idet den ene Fod og det nærmeste Stykke Tøi manglede. Af det andet Par var der kun større Levninger tilbage.*"

> ("Two pairs of leg coverings of woollen, woven cloth of a coarser type than the cloaks and the tunic [...]; the stockings, which are sewn onto the leg covering, have the same kind of lozenge-patterned weave as the sleeves of the tunic [...], only that the lozenges are somewhat smaller here [...]. On the inner side of this lozenge cloth [...] the nap was lifted by carding [...] by which the fabric gets warmer. The pair of trousers which are best preserved have a length of c. 117 cm, a width of c. 100 cm around the waist and a length of c. 30 cm in the foot, a size that points to a heavily-built owner of more than medium height. Several small straps fastened at both ends are applied around the waist, probably to keep the belt that was put through. A broad and clumsy seam, resulting from stitching together two parts, runs right under foot along the middle of the sole and there are several patches. They were found rolled up in a bundle but were incomplete, i.e. one foot and the adjacent cloth was missing. Only some larger fragments were left of the other pair of trousers.")

Similarly to the tunic, the trousers are mounted today in such a manner that only the front can be examined. In previous years, they were examined and described by various scholars, amongst them Karl Schlabow and Margrethe Hald. Both presented a dress pattern, which however, differ slightly from each other. According to Anna Nørgaard who analysed the trousers before they were mounted this way, Margrethe Hald's diagram is closer to reality than Karl Schlabow's (1998, 1).[10] The following description is based on the author's own examination unless otherwise stated.

A fine, reddish 2/2 diamond twill in z/s with 18–19 × 14 tpc is the ground weave for these trousers with integrated stockings, one of which is missing as described by Engelhardt. The wool is fine, unpigmented and well prepared. The pattern units of the diamonds are very regular, with 14 threads in the warp and nine in the weft. Within the examined sections of more than 10 cm, no exceptions were observed. This pattern of 14/9 clearly differs from the units on the tunic which were found to be 10/9, and the weave of the trousers is even more regular. Thus, the tunic and these trousers were not tailored from the same fabric.

From top to toe, the trousers measure about 125 cm; at the waist, the front is c. 46 cm wide. They consist of one large piece of cloth for each leg up to the waist – with the warp running straight downwards – plus several smaller additions, all of the same fabric. A rather large, trapezoid piece makes up the back, two smaller ones were used for the crotch and the middle of the front. The seams are plain on the outer surface and, as far as may be ascertained, all of the "Thorsberg type" which is confirmed by Schlabow and Nørgaard (ibid.). The upper edge of the narrow strip of cloth in the middle front is frayed but it seems that it was once trimmed, in the same manner as the piece which serves as the edge on the left hip. This latter strip is 4–7 cm wide (seam not included) with the warp running parallel to the waist. It is hemmed along the outer edge with a blanket stitch, using a doubled zS-twined yarn which is darker than the weave but also reddish in colour. The long seam between this addition and the leg piece is again of the "Thorsberg" type but this time turned outwards and the edges hemmed with rough blanket stitches. The counterpart on the right hip is comparable but with a selvedge used as the outer edge (Fig. 1.26); the outermost warp along the selvedge consists of several threads. The strip around the right hip is 7.5 cm wide throughout which results in an asymmetrical middle section in the front of the trousers as there, near the middle, the strip on the left side is only 4 cm wide. In the back, both strips – the hemmed one and the one with the selvedge – meet in the middle. Anna Nørgaard (ibid.) and Richard Stettiner (1911, 44) describe a narrow tablet-woven starting border there which belongs to the part with the selvedge. According to Stettiner, this border made with four tablets resembles that on the tunic, i.e. with a securing doubled thread along the outmost edge.

The strips around the waist are used as a basis for six loops for keeping a belt in place. Two of them are attached in front, two at the sides and another two in the back. Their lower ends seem to have reached down to the horizontal seam which could have served as a strong basis. Their upper ends were folded around the edge of the trousers and fastened on the inside. The loops are made very roughly, varying in width between 2 and 4 cm (as far as those in front and on the sides are concerned) and their edges are not hemmed (Fig. 1.26).

On the back, the lower edge of the trapezoid insertion is, according to Richard Stettiner, again a part of the above described tablet-woven border. The sides of the insertion are set forth in two long seams which run down to the calves and further to the feet. While the right leg is destroyed up to a height of c. 30 cm above the heel, the left leg possesses some remarkable details. About 32 cm above the heel, the seam stops or is left open further down. Therefore one can see that the fabric was folded inwards for about 2 cm. The inner edge is cut and hemmed with a blanket stitch which is

Fig. 1.26. Thorsberg, upper edge on the right hip of trousers 3684, with belt loops, selvedge and "Thorsberg seam" turned outwards and hemmed

Fig. 1.27. Thorsberg, cords along the open seam on the lower leg of trousers 3684; warp horizontal

used at the same time for fastening the edge to the ground weave. On the outside, this seam is almost invisible. At a point c. 6.5 cm down from the beginning of the open seam and c. 2.2 cm away from the fold along the opening, protrudes a thin bluish cord similar to the one already known from the tunic (Fig. 1.27). At this spot, it is 4.5 cm long, with a knot at its end. This cord can be followed on the inside over 1.5 cm before it comes up to the surface again, this time with a length of 5.5 cm and again knotted at its end. About 3 cm and another 3.5 cm further down, stitching holes may be ascribed to such cords. As those before, they are pierced only through one layer of ground weave, not through the doubled fabric along the fold. Another c. 1.5 cm further down, the next cord appears.

Fig. 1.28. Thorsberg, heel with gore and hemmed "Thorsberg seams" on trousers 3684

It is 3.5 cm long but this time knotted directly above the fabric. Its stitching hole lies closer to the folded edge than those before, only c. 1.5 cm away from it, i.e. within the doubled strip along the fold. Yet, it is pierced only through the upper layer. It can be followed within the fold and reappears after c. 1.5 cm, again c. 1.5 cm away from the edge. Its preserved length is about 4.5 cm, again with a knot sitting directly on the fabric. It seems likely that the knots are not original but were placed there after the excavation in order to secure the cords. The weave around the stitching holes for the cords is usually – not always – intact, i.e. the fabric does not appear to have undergone stress by being pulled. This may be an argument against the notion that the cords were used for closing the seam because pulling them regularly must have stressed the fabric. Therefore, a decoration – as on the tunic – seems a more probable interpretation. On the other hand, if the seams were closed by using some kind of wrapping, such a decoration would not be visible.

At ankle height, the cloth of the left leg ends in a "Thorsberg seam" turned inwards and is followed by a strip of cloth around the ankle. Within this 2 cm wide strip, the orientation of the warp is turned by 90°. Then, after another seam of the same kind, the foot of the stocking follows. It consists of one larger piece – in which the warp is again turned by 90° – and a gore of max. 4 cm width. The gore runs for 13 cm from the back of the ankle down under the foot (Fig. 1.28). Its edges are also sewn with "Thorsberg seams" but this time turned outwards with their edges hemmed in blanket stitch. The same applies to the seam from the tip of the gore to the toe where it ends after 17 cm. The area of the ball of the foot is heavily worn. Its position indicates that the surprisingly thick seam sat underneath the foot.

3685 TROUSERS
(Schlabow 1976, 77 and Abb. 170–174)
These trousers are much more fragmentary than 3684 and Conrad Engelhardt found them hardly worth describing (see above, 3684). Nonetheless, they are a highly valuable parallel to trousers 3684 (Fig. 1.29). Like 3684 and several cloaks, the original cloth is sewn onto a brown fabric, which

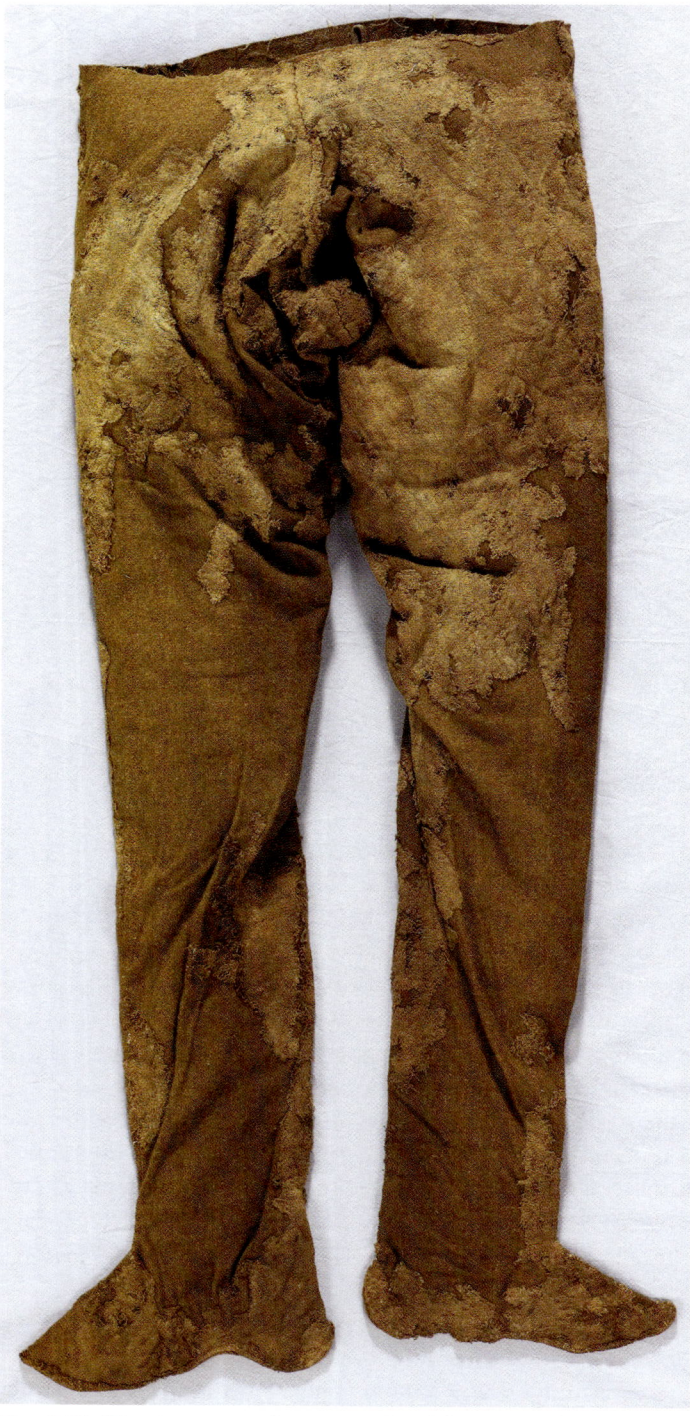

Fig. 1.29. Thorsberg, pair of trousers 3685 (Photo. © Roberto Fortuna, National Museum of Denmark)

– according to Karl Schlabow – was carried out by Johanna Mestorf already around 1907. The prehistoric material is a 2/2 diamond twill in z/s with a thread count of c. 15–17 × 13–14 tpc. Measured near the waist, the breaks creating the diamonds occur after every 10th yarn, in the other system after every 9th yarn. Counted on the right leg, there are 9–10 z-spun yarns and 9 s-spun threads per unit. The diameter of the threads is around 0.5 mm in both systems, no general difference is discernable. In both systems, the twist varies between medium and hard, and in both systems, loops occur because of too much twist. The fibre material was not analysed with high magnification but it is, seemingly, of sheep wool. The unpigmented fibres of homogeneous diameter are not very curly and were well prepared. The colour is a rather light reddish brown today. The surface of the fabric is rubbed off in most places, presumably due to wear. It is woollier along the seams where it is possible to observe parts of the weave that were originally hidden. Due to the mounting, it is difficult to examine the seams in detail, but most of them seem to be "Thorsberg seams". The sewing material includes more than two, probably four yarns, each plied in zS and of the identical colour as the fabric. No woven edges are visible.

Like 3684, trousers 3685 are not open at the bottom but have integrated stockings. The entire

Fig. 1.30. Thorsberg, cut upper edge of trousers 3685

piece of clothing consists primarily of five parts: two for the legs, two for the feet and a quadrangular one set in on the back at the waist. The stockings are mounted in a way that they point straight outwards to the left and right. The long seams on the back go down in a position where they are very comfortable when riding.[11] Further down the legs, these seams sit on the calves where they are left open.

Due to the mounting, no exact figures of the size can be given. Furthermore, the original uppermost edge of the trousers is not preserved. Yet, in many parts, the fabric does reach a straight line which was cut (Figs. 1.29 and 1.30). This cut edge measures c. 90–95 cm around the body. From there down to the line under the middle of the foot, the trousers are c. 120 cm long, while their length from the crotch to the bottom measures c. 80–85 cm. However, since there is no original connection between the two main elements of the trousers and the stockings, it is not known how much is missing, and the original length therefore remains unclear. The cut of the legs is narrow. All in all, it may be surmised that its owner was a tall, slim person. The preserved length and the missing upper edge suggest that the trousers once reached rather far up the body. Therefore, it seems unlikely that loops for a belt as on trousers 3684 should be assumed for the missing part still further up. Another explanation for how to keep the trousers in place is that the uppermost part was rolled down over a simple, hidden belt. Similar trousers with rolled down upper ends are depicted e.g. on the column of Marcus Aurelius in Rome which was completed in AD 193 (see Schlabow 1976, Abb. 61[12]).

As stated above, the seams were left open along the calves, namely on a length of c. 20 cm, starting about 17 cm above the seam beneath the foot. It is not possible to ascertain how it was once fastened. However, it is clear that the stockings were not merely the elongation of the trouser-legs but separate pieces sewn onto the legs: further up, the z-system runs from top to bottom while down at the stockings, it is placed around the leg. The fabric is probably the same, although the size of the diamonds seems more variable, with a change of direction again after every 9th or 10th z-spun thread and usually after every 9th in the other direction, but varying between 7 and 12 in this latter system.

The preserved parts of the stockings are very fragmentary and mounted in a quite arbitrary way. There is no sole but a single seam of the "Thorsberg type", turned outwards, continuing from heel to toe. The sewing thread consists of four z-spun yarns similar to the material in the fabric.

3686 Cloak ("Prachtmantel I")
(Schlabow 1976, 63–65, Abb. 116–119 and Farbt. I)
In his diary for 1860, Conrad Engelhardt wrote the following about this piece (p. 50):

> "*en skønt vævet kappe, grøn af farve med gul og mørkegrøn bort med frynser*"

("a beautifully woven cloak, green in colour with a yellow and dark green border with fringes.")

Shortly after, in his publication of 1863 (p. 18), Engelhardt provided a little more detailed description (together with cloak 3687):

> "*To Kapper, hver af et fiirkantet Stykke vævet, uldent Tøi. [...] Den anden Kappe [= 3686] derimod har bevaret sin grønne Farve i Bunden, medens Borden er guul og mørkegrøn. Vævningen er i begge disse Klædningsstykker megt fiin og jevn, af den saakaldte kiprede Dreils-Vævning*"

("Two cloaks, each of a quadrangular piece of woven, woollen cloth. [...]. The other cloak [= 3686], in contrast, has preserved its green colour in the ground weave while the border is yellow and dark green. The weave in both these pieces of clothes is very fine and even, of the so-called twill-weaving.")

Already in the 19th century, the term "Prachtmantel" was employed for this item signifying a splendid or luxurious cloak. Later, Karl Schlabow proposed a definition for this term. He defined a cloak as a "Prachtmantel" when at least one of its borders was made with more than one hundred tablets combined with the use of more than one colour (1976, 66).

Today, the fragments are still fixed onto a cloth in the same way as when Schlabow examined it, giving the impression of a cloak of 168 × 168 cm. As Schlabow has already demonstrated, one fragment is placed incorrectly, indicating – when the fragments would be rearranged – an original length of at least 236 cm. Another way of rearranging the fragments, resulting in a mantle not larger than it is now, is suggested by Lise Ræder Knudsen (this volume). Yet, the width might have been larger as well since no weft thread running from one side edge to the other is preserved.

The ground weave of this fabric is a 2/2 twill in z/s with 13–14 × 11 tpc. As mentioned above, Engelhardt described the cloak as green with a border in dark green and yellow. The greenish impression may be due to chemical changes that occurred in the bog. The fabric indeed consists of unpigmented wool in different colours, i.e. a lighter and a darker bluish brown in the ground weave. The two blue shades differ slightly in the yarn material, i.e. in diameter. Both of them occur in both thread systems, thus creating a checked pattern. Karl Schlabow reported on indigo but did not say whether it was found in both shades and both thread systems. He described the pattern in detail, so this will not be repeated here. The surface is rubbed off and there is no indication of napping on either side. Although the fragments are fastened to the supporting cloth, the reverse side is partly visible, namely on the wrongly placed piece. On that particular fragment, the oblique twill lines follow the same direction as on the other parts but the orientation of the z- and s-spun threads is the other way around. If someone were to rearrange the fragment correctly, it would necessitate turning it over.

All four edges are worked with tablets (see Ræder Knudsen, this volume). The narrow starting edge is reddish in colour as is one of the side edges. The starting edge and side edge are very much alike, but no connection exists between them. Only a small piece is preserved of the other side edge, a broad tablet band. It consists of two colours, a reddish yarn resembling the narrow tablet weaves and a very dark material. To the naked eye, both correspond to the threads used for the broad, tablet-woven finishing edge. These two edges constitute the only original corner. Their surface is rubbed off to a greater extent than the main fabric.

4. Thorsberg

3687, 24820, 24821 Cloak
(3687: Schlabow 1976, 61–62 and Abb. 109–110)
(24820: Hald 1980, 70)
(24821: Hald 1980, 70 and fig. 52, 191–193)

There are three items with different numbers which originally belonged to only one find. In 1863 (p. 18), Conrad Engelhardt described this piece as follows:

> "*Den fuldstændigere af disse [kapper] har, efter Brudstykkerne at dømme, været en 50 Tr. bred og 40 Tr. lang. Den har forneden en Række af 3 Tommer lange Fryndser; paa de tre andre Sider findes Border. Den er nu mørkebruun, saaledes som uldne Stoffer sædvanlig farves ved længe at henligge i Mosevand; men dens oprindelige Farve lader sig neppe bestemme.*"

> ("The more complete of these cloaks was, judging from the fragments, c. 130 cm wide and c. 105 cm long. At the bottom there is a row of fringes c. 8 cm long, on the other three sides there are borders. It is now dark brown, in the way that woollen fabrics usually become discoloured after lying in the bog for a long time, but its original colour can hardly be determined.")

Parts of the Thorsberg and later Nydam material were brought to Copenhagen in the late 1850s and after. The related inventory lists still exist. In one of them, one can read (Kat. Kopenhagen):

> 24820: "*Brudstykke af en Kappe af uldent, vævet Tøi, med Fryndser ved den ene side*"

> ("fragment of a cloak of woollen, woven cloth, with fringes on one side.")

> 24821: "*Brudstykke af en Kappe af uldent vævet Tøi, med korte Fryndser og ombøiede Traade ved den ene side*"

> ("fragment of a cloak of woollen, woven cloth, with short fringes and threads turned over along one side.")[13]

Similar to many other textiles stored in Schleswig, the fragments of this cloak (3687) were sewn onto some supporting material. The mounting is about 135 × 110 cm in size, i.e. corresponding to the measurements given by Engelhardt. The preserved parts primarily encompass two separate fragments which allow neither the length nor the width of the original size to be estimated. The additional pieces are c. 47 × 17 cm (24820) and c. 41 × 10 cm (24821) in size. Engelhardt mentioned "*13 Tr. l. 5 Tr. bredt*" for 24820 and "*15 Tr. l. 3 ½ Tr. bredt*" for 24821. The second statement corresponds well with the dimensions given above, while in the case of 24820, Engelhardt's information would imply a size of only c. 34 × 13 cm. Both smaller pieces would easily fit into the gaps of the main part.

The cloak primarily consists of a 2/2 twill in z/s with only c. 10 × 8 tpc and relatively thick threads. The well-prepared fibres are dark brown today. The loose fragments 24820 and 24821 allow for the possibility of examining both sides of the fabric, but no signs of napping or fulling were observed. Along the sides, remnants of all four original edges are preserved. The starting edge, which still exists on 3687 and 24821, is characterised by untwisted loops of an even length of c. 10 mm (Fig. 1.31). However, the loops differ in width according to a – generally – clear pattern: One loop encloses four other warp threads, the next loop only two, then again four, again only two and so on; occasionally, it is five or three yarns, in rare cases only one. This method of warping may have been used to obtain very fine stripes of different colours.

Taking the starting edge as the "top" of the mounted cloak, the right side may be described as a simple selvedge. The left side is also characterised by a selvedge but in this case, it is tubular woven. At the bottom, the fabric ends in fringes, often of a length of c. 10 cm (3687, 24820). Each fringe

Fig. 1.31. Thorsberg, starting edge on cloak 3687

Fig. 1.32. Thorsberg, transition from ground weave to fringes along the finishing border on cloak 3687

Fig. 1.33. Thorsberg, cloak 3687 with transition from regular ground weave to weave with missing threads in warp and weft

Fig. 1.34. Thorsberg, cloak 3688 with cuts

consists of two warp ends – usually adjacent ones – which lie parallel for a little more than 2 cm before they are entwined (Fig. 1.32). The tips of these entwined fringes are open, no loops were observed.

Missing threads are a distinct feature of this cloak. The simple selvedge mentioned above makes up the edge of a c. 13 cm wide strip in which threads are lacking, i.e. two adjacent warp ends out of every four are missing. Due to this, every 4th weft has lost the binding (Fig. 1.33). Regrettably, nothing remains of the starting edge in this area, therefore it is impossible to make any conclusions about the warping. A similar strip, almost 40 cm wide, occurs parallel to the bottom. Again, two threads out of four are absent, the weft in this case, resulting in long floating warp ends. Theoretically, the floating threads should remain loose until they reach an edge. However sometimes, they are reintegrated because of weaving mistakes. One such mistake or rather correction during the weaving process, is a wedge which can be seen in Schlabow, Abb. 110a, on the top left. At the bottom of the weave, however, this irregular strip does not reach to the very edge but is followed by a small strip of regular 2/2 twill, only six weft threads wide. In the corner where both strips with missing threads meet, the fabric is in total disorder and the threads arbitrarily stitched to the supporting cloth. The lost material, tiny fragments of which can be seen here and there, may have been either of plant origin or of wool which had been treated chemically in some way so that it deteriorated in the bog. According to Karl Schlabow, the latter is the valid explanation since samples revealed the cortex of wool fibres. In any case, it is highly probable that the now lost material was used for adding another colour as had already been assumed by Johanna Mestorf (1900, 33–34).

3688, 24823a and 24823b Cloak
(Schlabow 1976, 62 and Abb. 111–113)
(Hald 1980, 70 and Fig. 55–56)
The fragments of 3688 are also sewn onto a brown cloth and give the impression of a c. 75 × 108 cm large fabric. The original size remains unknown but it was certainly much larger. Two fragments

belonging to 3688 are stored in Copenhagen, labelled 24823a and b and are respectively c. 40 × 31.5 cm and 43 × 25 cm in size. For this number, i.e. 24823, Conrad Engelhardt listed only one piece of cloth:

> "*Større Stykke af en Kappe af fiint vævet, uldent Tøi, med Bord og korte Fryndser ved den ene Side*"
>
> ("Larger fragment of a cloak of finely woven, woollen cloth, with a border and short fringes on one side.")

The size that Engelhardt mentioned was "*15 Tr. l. 11 Tr. bredt*" which is about 39 × 29 cm, thus roughly corresponding to the size of piece 24823a. Yet, both pieces, marked as "a" and "b", were in Copenhagen when Margrethe Hald examined the material.[14]

The weave consists of a 2/2 twill in z/s with c. 12 × 10 tpc. The threads in both systems are slightly thicker than in many other Thorsberg items, resulting in a dense weave despite the relatively low thread count. Given a certain light, both systems appear to be striped in pairs of only two threads, resulting in a pepita or dogtooth-like pattern. The surface is rubbed, while there are no indications of napping or fulling. An edge, a transverse border, is preserved on the largest fragment of 3688 as well as on 24823a and b. No. 3688 is furthermore characterised by straight cuts spread over the entire piece (Fig. 1.34). For further discussion, see 3689.

3689
(Schlabow 1976, 63 and Abb. 114–115)
Seven fragments are sewn onto a piece of cloth measuring about 94 × 19 cm. It is a 2/2 twill with c. 14 × 11 tpc. The warp spun in z clearly shows fine stripes, consisting of two lighter and two darker threads each. Seemingly, the same applies to the s-spun weft, thus creating pepita or dogtooth-like checks as observed in piece 3688. The surface of the fabric does not seem to be abraded. The warp threads end in a transverse tablet-woven border. On one fragment, this transverse border meets a tablet-woven side edge. Both are rather coarse but still of decorative width although their outer edges are not even preserved. In conclusion, the ground weaves of 3688 and 3689, including the fibre material and the thread diameter, are much alike and could derive from the same fabric. The tablet-woven borders, however, are not identical, see below.

3690, 3705
(Schlabow 1976, 80–81, 83, Abb. 197a–c and Abb. 204a–b)
Sewn onto a cloth of 62 × 45 cm, several fragments of a 2/2 diamond twill labelled as no. 3690 are preserved. The fine fabric of c. 18–19 × 15–16 tpc is woven from z-spun warp and s-spun weft. The pattern units of the diamonds consist of usually ten (17 ×), in two cases of nine warp threads while the weft is more irregular. A set of nine weft threads is most common, but other numbers such as ten, thirteen and also four and five occur as well. The surface appears rubbed. The fine, curly fibres are unpigmented and reveal a reddish tone. The wool of a narrow, tablet-woven transverse border is darker (see Ræder Knudsen, this volume).

Fragment no. 3705 is c. 21 × 13 cm in size. The thread count was stated as 18–19 × 18 tpc, i.e. a little higher in the weft compared to 3690. However, the figures are close enough to possibly represent one weave. Another slight difference is the structure of the surface. Most of it is again rubbed, while fewer areas are woolly, showing some fibre loops. On 3690, the structure is not as woolly and no fibre loops were observed, which however, may be due to the abrasion, i.e. that neither woolly areas nor loops have survived. An important argument for regarding both pieces as one fabric is the irregular pattern units. Again, most common in the warp are sets of ten (19 ×), interrupted by smaller units of six (1 ×) or eight (3 ×) yarns. In the weft, units of nine threads prevail again on this fragment, while other figures are two, five, six, seven, eight, ten and thirteen. A simple selvedge marks the s-spun yarn as weft. A sample of the weft was used for a test on strontium isotopes (see below).

3691 Leg wrap ("Wickelbinde")
(Schlabow 1976, 89, Abb. 226 D and 228a–b)
This fragment of a broad band is about 30.5 cm long and 10.5–12 cm wide. It is one of only three pieces from Thorsberg in which both thread systems consist of yarns spun in an s-direction and amongst these, it is the only 2/2 twill. The thread count is c. 16 × 16 tpc, the non-pigmented and well-prepared fibres give a reddish impression. Both long edges are tablet-woven with only five tablets each (see Ræder Knudsen, this volume), while the two short ones are not original. Adjacent to one of the tablet weaves, the surface is woolly within a narrow strip, while in general, it is irregularly rubbed. Loops of fibres may indicate napping.

3692 Leg wrap ("Wickelbinde")
(Schlabow 1976, 89–90, Abb. 226 C and 229–231)
A fragment of another broad band is preserved as a c. 77 × 13.5 cm large piece of fabric. In contrast to no. 3691, this band was woven as tabby with only 9 × 6 tpc. Although it is woven firmly, it was much less carefully made than most others. The fibres are very variable in thickness,[15] the threads are unusually thick, around 1 mm in diameter, and there are some weaving mistakes, the warp running over more than one weft. Most of the fabric was woven in z/z, but there is broad strip of c. 9 cm width with only s-spun yarns in the weft. Since this part appears slightly darker than the rest, it may have been used as a decoration or patterning. The side edges are a little concave-shaped in this area. At its beginning, one z- and one s-spun thread lie within the same shed and it starts about 50 cm below a very narrow, tablet-woven starting border (see Ræder Knudsen, this volume). Both long sides also consist of tablet weaves.

3693
(Schlabow 1976, 81 and Abb. 198a–d)
This large piece of a 2/2 twill, 86 × 22 cm in size, was made from z-spun yarn in one system combined with s-twisted threads in the other. It is one of the coarser fabrics, with c. 10 × 10 tpc from possibly pigmented wool, with evidence of abrasion. One of the long edges parallel to the z-spun thread system was hemmed, c. 13 cm of which are still preserved. Since the cloth is sewn onto a supporting fabric, it is impossible to study the hem in detail. It seems to be folded twice and then fastened with a simple hemming stitch, using a paired s-spun yarn of c. 0.8 mm thickness. The distance between two stitches is about 1 cm.

3694
(Schlabow 1976, 81 and Abb. 199a–c)
Compared to the majority of textiles found in Thorsberg, no. 3694 is a rare fabric. It is one of only two tabbies in s/s[16] (see 24824c) and one of only two very coarse weaves, with just 4 × 4 tpc (see 1232a). The preserved size is c. 36.5 × 23 cm, without original edges. In contrast to most other items from this site, the structure of the weave is rather loose and the surface of both sides is felted.

Under the microscope, small loops of fibres emanating from the threads become visible. Moreover, tiny locks of wool are observable within the threads, demonstrating a less careful preparation of the raw material compared to the other finds. Furthermore, the generally fine fibres contain a rather high amount of very coarse ones. In conclusion, this piece rather gives the impression of a Bronze Age textile, as already mentioned by Karl Schlabow. It was submitted for strontium isotope analysis (see below).

3695
(Schlabow 1976, 81 and Abb. 200a–b)
The only 2/2 broken twill in z/z[17] has a thread count of c. 8 × 12 tpc. The preserved size is about 39 × 20 cm. From a narrow, tablet-woven starting border (see Ræder Knudsen, this volume), groups of six warp threads protrude. Yet, there are no hints as to missing ends between these groups. The weft has almost totally disintegrated along a length of c. 17 cm from the starting border, making any unambiguous explanation for the groups of warp yarns impossible. The tiny remnants of the weft prove, however, that it is of animal origin, too, but lighter in colour. Some distance from the starting border, more of the weft material still survives, revealing different coloured stripes. However, the weft is poorly preserved. The remaining warp ends again make up groups, often but not always consisting of six threads. Despite the rather large size of the fragment, due to its poor state of preservation, only few changes of weaving direction may be discerned. Only one in the warp and three in the weft can be observed. The distances between the latter constitute 4.5–5 cm in both cases, possibly suggesting a regular pattern, i.e. a diamond twill. Yet, in that case, some more breaks should be detectable, so it seems reasonable to assume a plain twill with weaving mistakes instead. Where the surface is more or less intact, there is one rather woolly side while the other is smoother and rubbed.

3696
(Schlabow 1976, 82 and Abb. 201a–c)
This 2/2 twill of c. 18.5 × 16 cm is another rare item without parallel within the Thorsberg material. It is unique because of its obvious spin patterning. In both thread systems, groups of four z-spun yarns interchange regularly with similar sets of s-spun yarns. Minor irregularities in the pattern occur in both directions. Additionally, it appears as if different colours were used. However, while in system A the z-spun material seems to be of a lighter colour than the s-spun yarns, the impression is the other way round in system B. The higher thread count of 21 tpc may be an indication for A being the warp while 16 tpc were counted in system B, the possible weft. The surface is rubbed.

3697 Probable cloak ("Prachtmantel III")
(Schlabow 1976, 65–66 and Abb. 121–123)
Dyed threads of three different colours – reddish, greenish and blackish blue today[18] – constitute the fragment of c. 8.5 × 18.5 cm, with about 12.5 cm of the length being fringed. The solid part consists of a broad, tablet-woven edge, probably a finishing border with complex blackish blue fringes (see Ræder Knudsen, this volume). Nothing remains of the main fabric, so the border may even have been wider. Still, the warp of the main fabric is represented as the weft of the border. This weft partly consists of s-spun and Z-twined elements, partly of z-spun and S-twined threads (Fig. 1.35), both in the reddish and in the dark parts. This indicates a spin-patterned ground weave. Moreover, the different colours indicate stripes in the direction of the warp. Since a striped warp combined

Fig. 1.35. Thorsberg, 3697, finishing border with variable spinning and twining directions in the border's weft = warp of the ground weave

with a monochrome weft would be very unusual, a chequered design of the whole cloak may be expected. Due to the border's width, or rather the substantial number of tablets needed to create it, and the use of different colours, Karl Schlabow interpreted this item as a parallel to no 3686, i.e. the so-called "Prachtmantel I".

3698, 24822 Cloak?
(Schlabow 1976, Abb. 124a–b)
(Hald 1980, 70 and fig. 53–54)
A great number of tablets combined with different colours were also used for these two pieces which originally belonged together (see also Ræder Knudsen, this volume). The larger one, 3698 located in Schleswig, measures c. 21 × 9 cm, the other one, 24822 located in Copenhagen, c. 10 × 7 cm. In both cases, all four sides are torn, while a break, along which the turning direction of all tablets was changed, is preserved only on 3698. Based on the comparison with the other finds, it might be suggested that this tablet weave once decorated an edge of a cloak. In Conrad Engelhardt's inventory list, no. 24822 appears as a

> "*Lille afrevet Stykke fiint vævet Tøi*"
>
> ("Small torn off piece of finely woven cloth.")

Thus, Engelhardt did not propose any function for the fabric. Nevertheless, he found the pattern worth reproducing in his publication (1865, Pl. 2,5).[19] Both warp and weft are striped. A striped weft in a tablet band would be invisible in an independent weave such as a belt. Instead, it implies a once existing ground weave that was striped or possibly checkered. Moreover, the co-existence of z- and s-spun yarns in the border's weft indicates a spin-patterned fabric, namely in the warp since Ræder Knudsen regards this piece as a finishing border.

3699
(Schlabow 1976, 82 and Abb. 201d–f)

To the naked eye, this 2/2 diamond twill of c. 16.5 × 12.5 cm appears to have been dyed red. On the other hand, given a certain light, the z-spun yarns look darker in colour than the s-spun material. The fabric was woven with 9 tpc in the z-spun system and 11 tpc in the s-spun system. Karl Schlabow determined the s-spun yarns as warp, the z-spun material as weft. Since no original edges determining warp and weft are preserved, Schlabow possibly based his opinion on the breaks in the pattern which are more striking along the z-system. A drawing of two weaving mistakes (Fig. 1.36) was discussed and interpreted by Lena Hammarlund and Martin Ciszuk, both qualified hand weavers with great experience in analysing archaeological textiles. They arrived at an opposite conclusion to Schlabow's. Their result is as follows:[20]

> "The warp is the z-spun yarn. There are two mistakes in the fabric:
> 1: a mistake when knotting the heddles – generating an extra break in warp direction.
> 2: a mistake when lifting the heddles generating the long floats. [...]
>
> The argument for a z-spun warp is that despite the mistake in entering the heddles, there are two sheds [...] where the warp runs two by two. This is a basic system for entering 2/2 twill and 2/2 diamond twill on a warp-weighted loom. When the warp is made with a band as a starting border, the warp will come two by two [...]. This division will form two of the sheds. When the other two sheds [...] are selected the breaks are made.
>
> If the s-spun yarn would be considered as warp, the sheds where the warp threads run two by two cannot be found. We tried this hypothesis by making a drawing [...] where the fault with the floats was corrected by adding two more warp threads which might have been broken, and completing the weave. Still all sheds contain single threads."

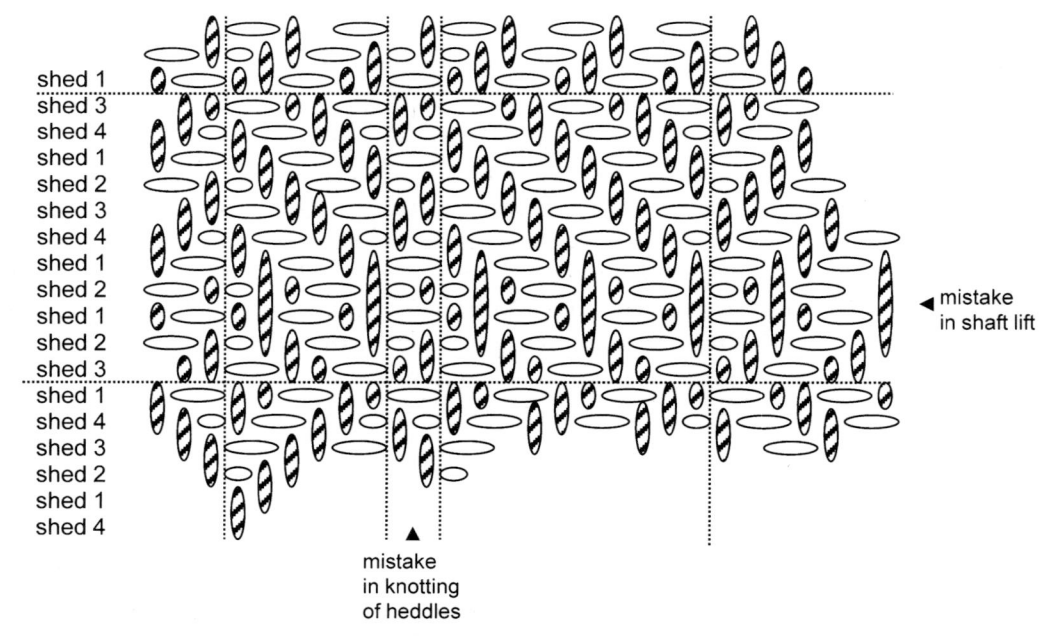

Fig. 1.36. Thorsberg, weaving mistakes on 3699 (Drawing by the author including information by Martin Ciszuk and Lena Hammarlund on sheds and errors)

For further information on how the set up of a loom is reflected in a fabric, see Martin Ciszuk (forthcoming). Here, on 3699, the mistakes and the rather low thread count correspond to some other features denoting lower quality. The wool material includes a rather high proportion of coarser fibres and the yarns are comparatively variable and thick, up to 0.8 mm. The pattern units of the warp usually encompass ten threads, with exceptions like two and six, while in the weft, they vary between ten and 17 with 13 threads being the most common set. Furthermore, the weave is rather loose and there are more weaving mistakes than those already mentioned. Both sides have suffered abrasion to some extent.

3700, 3702, 3703, 3704
(Schlabow 1976, 82–83, Abb. 202a–b, 205, 207a–c and 206a–b)
Four fragments of this fine 2/2 diamond twill are preserved. They are all roughly rectangular in shape, measuring c. 8.5 × 7 cm (3700), c. 55.5 × 8 cm (3702), c. 18 × 6.5 cm (3703) and c. 36 × 6 cm (3604). They are sewn onto a board. The weave is worked in z/s and with c. 18 × 14–15 tpc on average.[21] The very regular pattern units include ten threads in the warp and nine in the weft. Only one exception was found, with eight threads in the warp on 3702. The wool is seemingly non-pigmented and reddish.

One of the short edges of 3700 is a hem including a corner. The hem is 3–4 mm wide, securing the edge with a blanket stitch. The stitches measure c. 3 mm in width. As the hem follows the weft accurately, its slightly curved outer edge must be a secondary feature. The sewing thread resembles the threads of the fabric as far as the fibres are concerned, but is twined in zS. Two such twined yarns were utilised as sewing thread. The hem is turned around a corner at a 90° angle, after which it continues for only 0.8 cm before it is interrupted. Further down that edge, two very short sequences of the hem are preserved, with two stitches and with one stitch, respectively.

The surface of 3700 reveals differently structured parts or stripes, running parallel to the z-spun system (Fig. 1.37). There are two such stripes with a woolly surface and two where it is rubbed and smooth. The boundaries between these stripes are very clear in two cases, but gradual in the third instance. The smooth parts end at the hem, i.e. the surface is woolly below the sewing thread. Within these woolly areas, some fibre loops protrude from the yarns, indicating napping rather than fulling or secondary effects. These parts clearly show coarser fibres than the rubbed surface does.

On 3702, a long and narrow strip of cloth, the surface is again partly woolly, partly smooth resulting in stripes parallel to the warp, although they are less evident here. The stripes reoccur more obviously on 3703, with fibre loops in the woolly areas. Furthermore, 3703 possesses a hem similar to 3700, again following the weft and covering a woolly surface. There is nothing particularly noteworthy about 3704, the final fragment belonging to this twill. From all four fragments, samples of the warp were tested for strontium isotopic ratios (see below).

3701
(Schlabow 1976, 82 and Abb. 203a–b)
This piece is c. 6 × 5.5 cm in size. The fabric is woven in z/s, constituting a 2/2 diamond twill. While the pattern units in the z-direction – the probable warp – regularly contain ten threads each, they vary in the other direction between eight and 13 threads. The impression of lower quality compared to e.g. no. 3700 is confirmed by the thickness of the yarns of a diameter between 0.4 and 0.7 mm in both systems, as well as by the thread count of 14 × 12 tpc. Yet, the raw material is non-pigmented,

with only few coarser fibres. The surface is partly woolly, with fibre loops pointing to napping. No original edge is preserved. The warp was selected for an isotope analysis (see below).

3706
(Schlabow 1976, 83 and Abb. 208a–d)
No. 3706 consists of two fragments, c. 37 × 16.5 cm and 14 × 10 cm in size. The surface of both sides is woolly, concealing the pattern units of this 2/2 diamond twill in z/s. The thread count is high, 19 × 18 tpc. The unpigmented fibres appear a little reddish and in some spots, they form little loops, again interpreted as an indication of napping. Only very few fibres are rather coarse. There is a narrow, tablet-woven starting border which is lighter in colour than the ground weave (see Ræder Knudsen, this volume).

24824a and 24824b
(Hald 1980, 70 and 72)
This 2/2 twill in z/z with 14 × 11 tpc is preserved in two reddish-brown fragments. The wool appears unusual compared to most other pieces found in Thorsberg. It seems non-pigmented, fine, curly and very homogeneous – "possibly lamb's wool", as Margrethe Hald wrote. However, according to fibre measurements by Penelope Walton on 24824b (1988, 152, table 3), the hair

Fig. 1.37. (above left) Thorsberg, 3700 with woolly and smooth stripes

Fig. 1.38. (left) Thorsberg, 24824a with trimmed edge

material in one system should be described as "generalised medium", with a mean diameter of 24.4 micron and a maximum of 46 micron, in the other system as "hairy medium", with 31.9 micron and 62 micron, respectively. Both are very common categories. It should be added, however, that no pigment was found. The textile surface is felted, which is – again according to Hald – "due to fulling". Yet, in those parts where the felted layer is abraded one can see little loops, made up of a tiny bundle of parallel fibres, protruding from the yarns. This may rather indicate napping, although the fact that both sides are felted, may indeed signify fulling. A long side of fragment 24824a as well as a small loose fragment kept together with it are characterised by a tubular selvedge.

On both fragments, there are blue, sometimes blackish yarns made of seemingly non-pigmented and dyed wool, often twined and encompassing different features. Fragment 24824a was edged by using a blanket stitch along one side. The trimming reaches c. 5–6 mm into the weave, but is carried out irregularly. For this edging, two blue/black z-spun yarns were twined into S-plied threads, three of which were finally twined again in an Z-direction (Fig. 1.38). The fabric inside the edging was cut. From the opposite side of the fragment, a cut parallel to the system with the higher thread count splits the fabric for c. 9 cm. The inner end of this cut is secured by some stitches with a dark doubled thread. Along the cut, stitching holes on both sides as well as some remnants of the double thread are observable. However, it is not clear whether the cut was edged along both sides or whether it was a seam across the cut. Finally, a hem secured one edge of fragment 24824b parallel to the system with the lower thread count. The fabric was cut, folded once and then fastened with hem stitches. The twined yarn is dark and made of thicker fibres than the tissue. On the obverse side of the weave, the stitches are much less obvious than on the reverse – in spite of the colour it was possibly not meant as a decorative feature.

Most probably, it is these two fragments that Conrad Engelhardt referred to in his diary (p. 52):

"I samme dybde og et par fod derfra;
Et stykke, uldent, vævet tøj 10½ T langt og 10 T bredt med kant på de to sider. På et stykke er det sammensyet med sort tråd"

("In the same depth and a few feet away from it [i.e. the tunic];
One piece of woollen, woven cloth c. 40 cm long and c. 36 cm wide with borders on the two sides.
One spot, is sewn with black thread.")

"og tæt herved
et 10 2/12 T langt og 7 ¾ T langt lignende stk med en med sort tråd syet kant på den ene af de smalle sider"

("and close to this
a similar piece of c. 37 cm in length and c. 28 cm in length [certainly = width] with a border sewn with black thread on one of the short sides.")

Returning to the list compiled by Engelhardt, he provided the following description:

"2 Stykker uldent, vævet Tøi med Syning med sort Traad"

("2 pieces of woollen, woven cloth with stitches of black thread.")

In this case, Engelhardt did not suggest any function. The size he gave was "10 Tr. brede, 7 ½ og 10 Tr. lange", i.e. about 36 × 27 cm and c. 36 × 36 cm, respectively. These dimensions are larger than what Margrethe Hald described and what can be measured today. Cut edges on both fragments support the conclusion that the preserved remnants represent only parts of the original find.

24824c
(Hald 1980, 72)

Conrad Engelhardt did not mention a third piece of cloth belonging to this find number when he compiled his list of items to be sent to Copenhagen. However, Margrethe Hald annotated Engelhardt's list to the effect that such a piece existed in 1941, 10 × 7 cm in size, labelled "e". It may, however, rather be "24824c" – the letter on the label is not easy to decipher.

Besides 3694, this is the other tabby in s/s amongst the Thorsberg material. However, both pieces do not belong together since this one is clearly less coarse. Nevertheless, the thread count of 9–10 × 7 tpc is low. The preparation of the fibres was carried out without care and the thickness of the threads varies between 0.6 mm and more than 1.0 mm. A narrow tablet-weave edges one of the long sides, and is – according to Lise Ræder Knudsen (this volume) – either a starting border or a side border. Spread over the piece, one can observe some probable stitching holes but no pattern could be determined. Yet, given a certain light, it appears as if two rows of rhombi appear, on the front as well as on the reverse side. Therefore it seems possible that, once, a rhomboid decoration had been sewn onto this tabby.

Without number, here named "o.Nr. -1" and "o.Nr. -2"

These two pieces are kept together and are followed by an old tag remarking "*2 prøver af vævet tøj*", ("*2 samples of woven cloth*"). Although the thread counts are not identical, they seem to derive from one fabric, a 2/2 twill in z/s. On fragment "-1", 12–13 × 9–11 tpc were determined, on fragment "-2" the thread count is 9–10 × 10–11 tpc. In both cases, the fibres vary a great deal in colour and diameter but lie parallel in the thread as the wool was processed. Fragment "-1" possesses a cut edge which roughly follows the s-spun direction, although part of it runs obliquely to the thread systems. Along this edge, at a distance of about 5 mm from each other, the fabric is torn, reaching up to c. 5 mm into the cloth. Some kind of trimming appears to have been ripped off. Traces of a seemingly vegetal thread may belong to this trimming. The surface of the weave under this hypothetical edging is woolly, while in the main parts of the piece, it appears rather abraded.

Without number, here named "o.Nr. -3"

According to a label, this fragment of 10.5 × 7 cm is a "*Prøve af et par benklæder*" (a "*sample of a pair of leg coverings*"). Yet, it neither belongs to the trousers nor to the leg wrappings mentioned above. This fabric is a 2/2 twill in z/s with 13 × 13 tpc, the surface of which is mostly felted. The fine, homogeneous fibres are reddish.

M 607.1, here named "M 607.1 a" and "M 607.1 b"

Two fragments from Thorsberg are in the possession of Moesgård Museum near Århus, Denmark.[22] Fragment "a" is c. 14 × 14 cm in size, fragment "b" 14 × 9 cm. The weave is a 2/2 twill in z/s with c. 13 × 9–10 tpc. Tablet weaves are preserved on both pieces (see Ræder Knudsen, this volume). On fragment "a", the tablet border runs parallel to the s-spun system, while on fragment "b", it follows the z-directed system. There, on fragment "b", the thread count in the z-system becomes a little denser. Today, the edges are c. 3 cm and 2 cm wide but were originally broader than this.

1232a

Fragments 1232a and 1232b are housed at Sorø Akademi on Zealand, Denmark.[23] No. 1232a resembles 3694. Like the latter, this piece is a very coarse tabby with only 4 × 3–4 tpc. Yet, the two items do not belong together since in 1232a, z-spun yarns in one system were combined with s-spun material in the other system. The raw material is sheep wool.[24] A woven border is preserved on a length of c. 9.5 cm. It runs parallel to the s-spun threads, thus possibly representing a starting border. The size of the fragment is about 22 × 15 cm.

1232b

The other Thorsberg textile kept in Sorø is a plain 2/2 twill. The size of the folded piece is c. 6 × 5 cm, the fibres are of sheep wool.[25] Neither the selected yarn material with z in one direction combined with s in the other nor the thread count of c. 13 × 10 tpc is unique within this assemblage. However, since no detailed information can be provided about the quality of the yarns and the surface of the cloth – besides the fact that the weaving pattern is very clear, probably a result of abrasion – no further comparisons may be drawn.

4.2.2 Technical aspects: comparative overview
Material

The vast majority of fibre material found in Thorsberg is of animal origin. Karl Schlabow (1976), Margrethe Hald (1980) and Heidemarie Farke[26] described the various items as made of sheep wool. Most of it is non-pigmented and well prepared. Only traces of a sewing thread on item "o.Nr. -1" are seemingly vegetal. Yet, the ropes – which were not investigated in the present context – have to be considered here. They were described by Conrad Engelhardt as follows (1863, 60), demonstrating that in principle, vegetal fibres could be preserved in the Thorsberg bog:

> "*En Mængde Touge og Snore, flettede eller snoede af Bast, bleve hyppig fundne i større Klumper og undertiden sammenbundne i Knuder*"
>
> ("A number of ropes and cords, plaited or twisted of bast, was often found in larger heaps and sometimes bound together in knots.")

Weaving types

The Thorsberg material presented here consists of 23–25 different fabrics[27] as well as two unconnected tablet weaves. The majority, 17 or 18 of them, are 2/2 twills in z/s. Of these, eight to ten are woven as plain twill while the others are diamond twills. The remaining seven fabrics encompass six different varieties: one plain 2/2 twill in s/s, one plain 2/2 twill with spin patterning, one 2/2 probable diamond twill in z/z, one tabby in z/z+s, one in z/s and finally two in s/s. Both loose tablet weaves indicate the previous existence of a spin-patterned ground weave.

Fig. 1.39 provides an overview of the thread counts observed in the Thorsberg material. The four tabbies range from very coarse to coarse, with 24824c being on the borderline of medium fine quality (see Tidow 2000, 108). The plain twills in z/s constitute a distinct cluster centring around 11–13 × 10–11 tpc. Referring to Klaus Tidow's categories of fineness, they belong to the "medium fine" and the lowest part of the "fine" group. The latter category encompasses most of the diamond twills in z/s, with two exceptions, one being very fine, the other only medium fine. The fine twill in s/s and the very fine spin-patterned piece are comparable to the diamond twills.

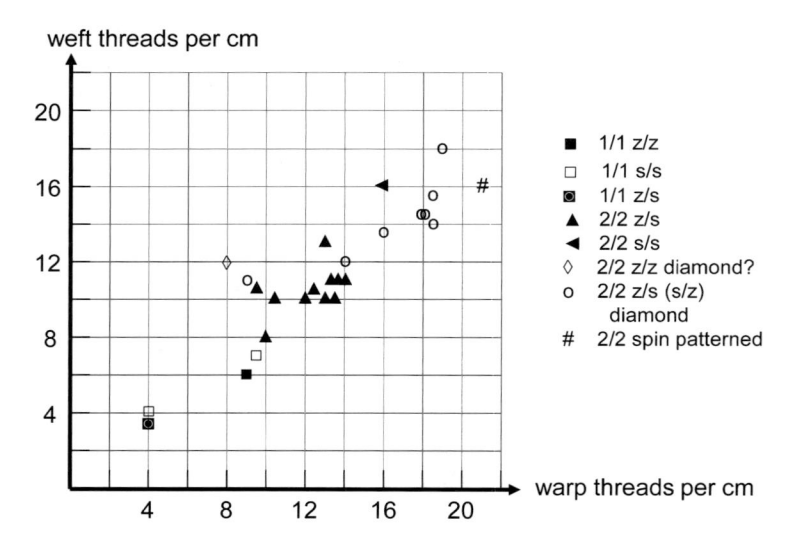

Fig. 1.39. Thorsberg, thread counts. Items "o.Nr. -1" and "o.Nr. -2" are marked individually as are 3688 and 3689

Edges
Compared to most other assemblages – weapon deposits as well as others – an unusual number of original, woven edges is preserved. On most textiles from Thorsberg there is at least one. The majority are combined with tablet weaves which are described in detail by Lise Ræder Knudsen (this volume). Besides their decorative character, there are functional aspects as well. Each edge is briefly described here.

3683: The patterned bands around the wrists of the tunic are sewn onto the ground weave. While their decorative character is obvious, they also reinforced these parts of the tunic which are exposed to heavy wear (Ræder Knudsen, this volume). An integral part of the tunic is the tablet weave along the bottom of its back. Its primary function as a transverse border is proven by the adjacent side borders. The outermost tablets, however, do not represent the outermost edge, since the loops constituting the weft of the tablet weave reach further out (see Figs 1.18 and 1.43). These loops of a slightly different length are turned over a cord which prevents them from being pulled out. The cord runs straight along the tablet weave, but seemingly with little or no tension in it. The side borders were made rather simply without tablets, but the outermost warp is multiplied.

3684: Two original borders were observed on these trousers. One is a narrow, tablet-weave, manufactured with a doubled thread as the outermost edge. It is integrated in a seam on the back. The other is a selvedge used as the upper edge on the right hip. Several warp ends make up the outermost edge.

3686: Four tablet weaves belong to this cloak. The yarn loops within the starting edge, which make up the warp of the ground weave and the weft of the tablet band, do not all possess the same length, they vary between c. 0.6 cm and 1.1 cm. In several instances, they do not even reach the outer edge of the band (Fig. 1.40). Furthermore, the tablets were not turned between the two legs of a loop. Instead, the loops are twined and each lies within one shed of the tablet weave.

Within the narrow side edge, the weft loops of the tablet weave are again of different length, each lying in one shed without a securing outer cord. Compared to the starting edge, the sole difference is that the loops are only very slightly twisted. The other side border as well as the finishing border are much more elaborate than the preserved parts of the other two, but the principle is identical: all these tablet weaves are secondary (see Ræder Knudsen, this volume).

3687: All four original edges are preserved on this cloak. The loops along the starting edge are of different width which was interpreted as a method of creating stripes of different colour. Depending on the loom in use, and thus on the process of warping, one might assume the presence of either two or three different colours. It seems unlikely that – while the cloak was worn – the loops protruded as freely from the weave as they do now. Since they are of equal length – in contrast to e.g. 3686 – they could have functioned as the weft of a primary, tablet-woven starting border. However, a secondary tablet weave might be possible as well. In either case, the warp of this hypothetical tablet weave has disappeared. Its deterioration would be in accordance with the loss of warp and weft threads along one side and the bottom of this fabric.

The side edge along the stripe with missing warp threads is a simple selvedge. The visual effect of a decorative border was probably achieved by the colours of this stripe, not by a tablet weave. Along the other side, the edge was woven in a tubular manner. The bottom end of the cloak is decorated with fringes. After a c. 2 cm wide strip, two threads each are entwined to serve as a fringe (see Fig. 1.32). This strip between ground weave and twined fringes may have been used as a weft for a tablet weave, the warp of which has deteriorated totally. Or – as proposed by Karl Schlabow – it was a regular 2/2 twill with only the warp remaining. In this case, the decorative effect would again be based on the colours only. In any case, this fabric, including its comparatively low thread count, is clearly less elaborate than many others.

3688, 24823a, 24823b: The only original edge of this fabric is a transverse border with a tablet weave described by Margrethe Hald as a finishing border (1980, 71 and 73, figs 55 and 56). The tablet weave has disappeared to a great extent, whole groups of warp threads are missing, thus exposing the weft and resulting in the impression of "fringes". On 24823a and b, the warp of the twill, i.e. the weft of the tablet weave, reaches about 4.5–5 cm beyond the ground weave. The threads are usually grouped into four, sometimes twined very firmly, in other cases without hardly any twist. In certain sections, their tips are seemingly cut, particularly on 24823a, but often they seem frayed. Among them, Margrethe Hald found one preserved loop, i.e. one spot where a "fringe" was neither cut nor frayed but turned back into the tablet weave as another "fringe" and was finally cut at the transition between ground weave and tablet border.[28] Another such loop was now observed on 3688. These loops may mark the former outer edge of the tablet border (Fig. 1.41). Accordingly, Hald interpreted those "fringes" that are kept in place by the tablet weave but cut near the ground weave, as fragments of such loops. On 3688, a different type of "fringe" was observed, besides the warp threads running throughout the tablet weave. Here, in many cases the warp ends were turned already after c. 1.5 cm. They run back towards the ground weave within the same shed of the tablet weave and are then cut.[29] A doubled thread was pulled into the loop at their end, bent and twined, thus extending the "fringe" (Figs 1.41–1.42). The common features of both variations are that each shed or "fringe" contains four threads and that eight "fringes" correspond to c. 20 threads of the ground weave. All these variations and irregularities were originally concealed within the tablet border. See 3689 and Ræder Knudsen (this volume) for further discussion.

Fig. 1.40. Thorsberg, cloak 3686, starting edge. Centre top, two dark loops not reaching the outermost edge of the border

3689: The outer edges of both the side and the transverse border are destroyed. Although their original width therefore remains unknown, the preserved width emphasises their decorative character. As in 3688 and 24823a/b, the weft of the tablet weave exhibits a variable structure with firmly twisted ends besides others with almost no twist, with four threads per "fringe" and with eight fringes per c. 20 threads of the ground weave. On the other hand, the fibres used for these tablet weaves are unusually straight. Moreover, the warp threads of the transverse border lie side by side; no groups apart from at the outermost edge are missing as in 3688 and 24823a/b, to which, 3689 possibly belongs. On the other hand, the weft of the tablet weave exhibits the same structure with firmly twisted ends besides others with almost no twist.

3690, 3705: Wool of contrasting colour was chosen for the narrow, tablet-woven transverse edge on 3690. Each shed of the tablet weave contains a complete weft loop, but no securing cord along the border is documented. The side edge on 3705 is a simple selvedge.

3691: Both side edges of this leg wrap are tablet woven. Neither their small width nor their colour indicates any particular decorative intention. Since the fabric is mounted and covered by a net, the technical details demonstrating e.g., the production process, remain largely hidden.

3692: Three sides of this leg wrap are preserved as original, narrow tablet-woven edges including two corners. Regrettably, they could not be analysed in detail due to the mounting and the covering net. One corner consists of the beginning of a tablet band. After about 1 cm, its weft continues as warp of a side border and then the ground weave. The edge continues for about 12 cm before it turns by 90° and becomes the other side border.

3695: The outermost threads of the tablet-woven starting border are missing, resulting in loops of equal length, 4–5 mm long. Yet, the tablet weave might have once filled that strip. It was composed of darker wool.

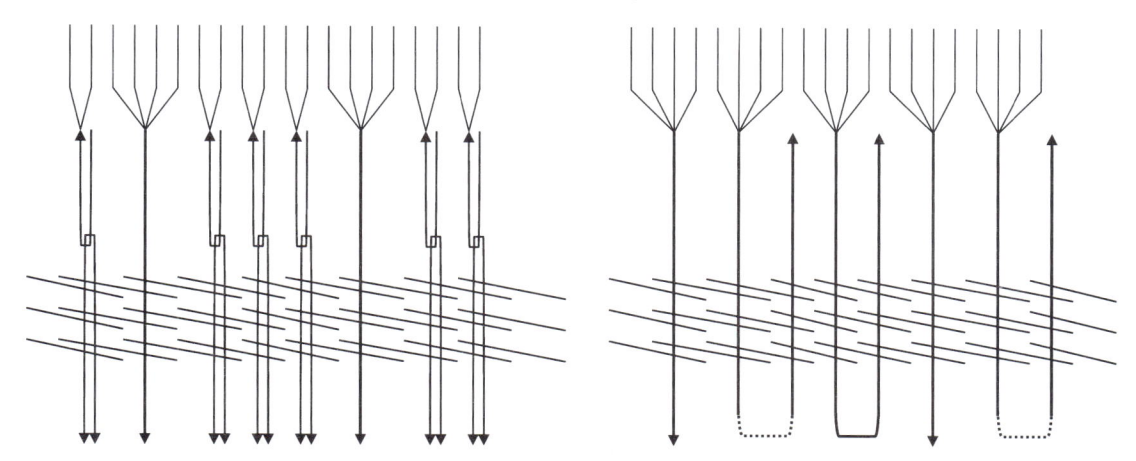

Fig. 1.41. Thorsberg, cloak 3688 and 24823a/b, two variations of border, not to scale. Left, mostly "fringes" with inserted threads and few "fringes" running throughout, as typical for 3688. Right, mostly long loops generally cut open and few "fringes" running throughout, as typical for 24823a/b

Fig. 1.42. Thorsberg, cloak 3688, warp ends turned over with extending threads inserted

3697: Stripes in three different colours constitute the warp of this broad border, probably signifying a finishing edge. The tablet weave is additionally decorated with monochrome, plaited fringes which are inserted into the loops of the tablet weft (see Fig. 1.35).

3698, 24822: Both fragments of this tablet weave are very dark today, but are nevertheless striped. In a strict sense, no original edge is preserved. Yet, the striped, twined weft with variable spinning directions indicates that the pieces represent the prolongation of a spin-patterned ground weave. The stripes in the warp are based on the orientation of the tablets and the colours. Karl Schlabow's drawing (1976, Abb. 124a–b) includes three different colours which seems indeed to be the case.

3706: Within the narrow transverse border of this fabric, each of the loops of the weft, i.e. the warp of the ground weave lies in one shed of the tablet weave. Thus, the tablet band would easily rip off if it was not secured by an outermost thread running through the loops, as in 3683.

24824a: For this item, only a tubular-woven side edge can be mentioned. It was made in tabby, the warp being doubled (see Ciszuk forthcoming).

24824c: A starting or side border woven with tablets constitutes the one original edge of this find.

M 607.1a and b: Two plain tablet weaves are preserved, on piece "a" following the s-spun direction and on fragment "b" parallel to the z-spun thread system. According to Lise Ræder Knudsen (this volume), the first one is a finishing border while the other one was used along one side edge, and they may be seen in connection with 3688/3689.

1232a: According to photographs, the possible starting border on this item does not seem to be tablet woven, but no further information can be given.

Looms
The edges described above are not only important features as such, but they may also reveal information about the weaving device used. Particularly, the tablet-woven starting borders are generally interpreted as proof of the use of the warp-weighted loom.[30] Amongst many others, Margrethe Hald (1980, 165) and Karl Schlabow shared this opinion, the latter ascribing e.g. the large cloak 3686 to this type of loom (1976, 65). However, the current investigation by Lise Ræder Knudsen and the present author shed more light on this issue.

Through the centuries, in a common variant of tablet-woven starting borders, the yarns of the outermost tablet constitute the outermost edge of the whole fabric (see Ræder Knudsen forthcoming). During the process of warping, the yarn ball with the weft of the tablet weave, which is the warp of the planned ground weave, most probably lay on the outer side of the edge, not on the side of the future fabric. From there, long loops of warp thread were pulled through the tablet border, according to the desired length of the ground weave. Consequently, this thread turns directly from one shed to the next of the tablet weave and is barely visible when examining the cloth from above. Of course, variations occur when the warping is carried out with more than one ball of yarn, e.g. in the use of two colours. Among the Thorsberg material, this kind of tablet-woven starting border was used for the tabby, 24824c, and for one of the leg wraps, 3692, also woven in 1/1. Moreover, borders of this type may have belonged to 3687 – a medium fine plain twill in z/s discussed below – and to 3695. The latter is most probably a plain twill in z/z of medium fine quality.

Of a somewhat different appearance are the tablet-woven transverse borders on 3683 (the tunic), 3706 and probably 3684 (one pair of trousers), all three of them comprising fine or even very fine diamond twills. Along the outer edge, the weft of the tablet weave turns around a cord which is not integrated into the tablet weave. Karl Schlabow (1976, 70) regarded them as starting borders. Yet, he considered this method as inappropriate because when the edge was worn down, the tablet weave could unravel. In his description, he assumed that during the process of warping, this cord was stretched and fixed. According to him, the yarn for the ground weave – seemingly the entire ball – was taken through the shed of the tablet weave, turned around the cord and taken back through the tablet band to become the warp of the ground weave. However, this does not need to be the

4. Thorsberg

case. If – during warping – only the tablet band is fixed but the cord left loose, the ball of yarn could remain on the side of the ground weave (Fig. 1.43). Only a short loop is needed to be pulled through the shed of the tablet weave. Both legs of the loop thus lay within one and the same shed. Then the cord was threaded through this loop to keep the loop and the whole border in place. This method speeds up the process of warping, as a test carried out by hand weaver Anna Nørgaard has demonstrated.[31] On the other hand, Lise Ræder Knudsen regards this type of border as a finishing edge added to a tubular warp (this volume).[32] However, in at least two cases, 3683 and 3684, they appear on tailored garments. If the weaves were planned for these purposes, finishing borders – in contrast to typical cloaks – would be dispensable on any type of loom while the warp weighted loom would require a starting border.

Similar to the last mentioned starting border in one respect, but nevertheless very different, is the narrow transverse edge of cloak 3686 ("Prachtmantel I"), a fine plain twill in z/s. Again, the wefts of the tablet-woven border do not go from one shed to another, but lie as a loop within one shed. As a parallel to e.g., tunic 3683, Karl Schlabow (1976, 64) described an additional thread outside the tablet weave, which however, could not be traced. Instead, it is striking that the loops differ in length and particularly, that not all of them reach the outer edge. This indicates that the border is secondary as is confirmed by Lise Ræder Knudsen (this volume). It was thus not an integral part of the warping process and consequently, this transverse edge is not a starting border for a warp-weighted loom. Instead, a two-beam loom with a tubular warp seems to be the most likely solution. This appears from a comparison with the Danish material as presented by Margrethe Hald (1980), from the experience of modern hand weavers[33] and from Ræder Knudsen's latest observations. The other three tablet weaves on this cloak do not contradict this result.

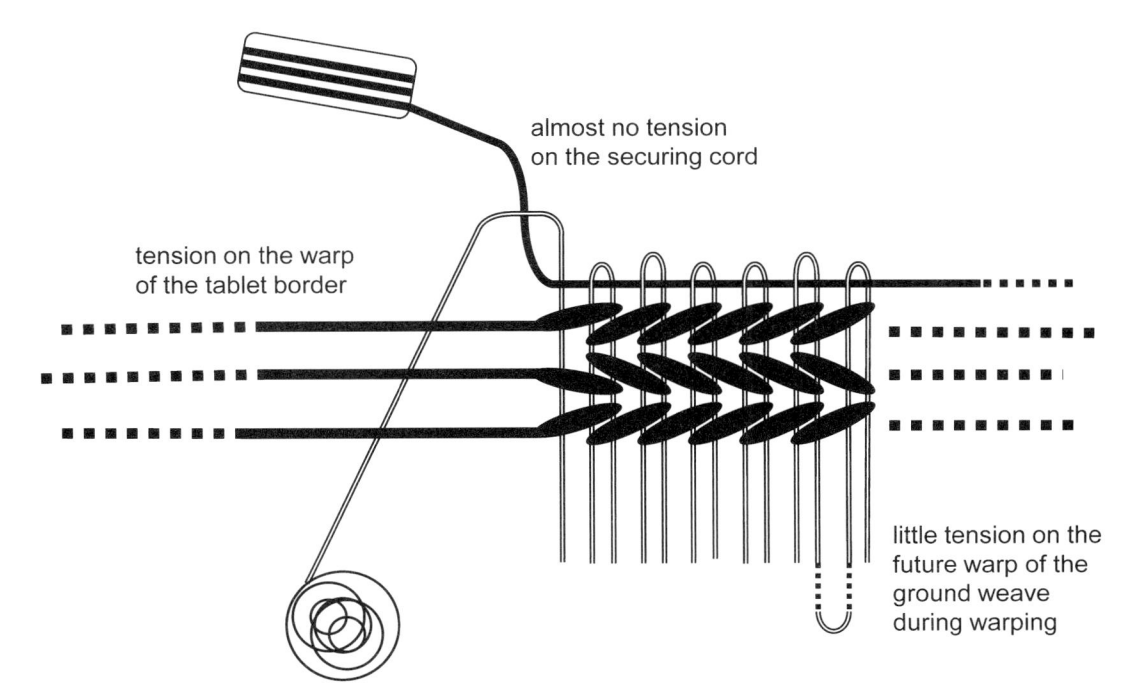

Fig. 1.43. Hypothetical warping method for tablet weaves with outermost securing cord

A tubular warp was also postulated by Margrethe Hald for cloak 3687/24820/24821 (1980, 175, 177). It has a transverse border with loops of practically identical length but of different width. Hald described two possible ways of warping, both resulting in loops of varying width similar to those found on this fabric. However, if the variable length of loops was an argument for a tubular warp in the case of 3686, the equal length of the loops on this piece may suggest an alternative interpretation. Karl Schlabow, on the other hand, reconstructed a tablet-woven starting border (1976, 61–62 and Abb. 109) the warp of which had disappeared. Compared to other fabrics with tablet-woven starting borders, this idea should be in accordance with the loops' length. The pattern of their varying width would then indicate the use of two or three different colours. Since many threads both in warp and weft, including the finishing border, are missing from this fabric, a deteriorated tablet-woven starting border prepared for a warp-weighted loom cannot be ruled out.

In addition to the starting edges just described, other transverse borders may also shed light on the question of looms. In the case of the just discussed cloak 3687/24820/24821, the warp threads end in twined, fraying fringes. No loops being found, the characteristic features of a tubular warping are thus absent here. Instead, a strip of apparently missing threads in the weft direction may once have been covered by a tablet weave. These observations support the notion that this fabric was produced on a warp-weighted loom instead of a tubular one. It may be added though, that the suggested tablet border was not a typical one, since its weft threads coming from the fabric were not turned by 180° and cut along the transitions to the ground weave, but continued as fringes.

Another cloak of medium fine quality, woven as plain, but chequered, twill in z/s, is preserved as nos. 3688, 24823a and 24823b. Within its transverse edge, the warp ends were turned over at different lengths and cut where they reached the ground weave again. Many of the resulting loops were extended by inserted threads. This construction served as the weft of a broad tablet weave. Thus, these features may be interpreted as a finishing border of a cloth woven on a warp-weighted loom. Yet, such a tablet band could have been added to a fabric produced e.g. on a two-beam loom as well, although probably without tubular warping, since the latter is characterised by closed loops both at the beginning and at the end of the cloth. As indicated above, the fabric of 3689 is similar to that of 3688, including the number of "fringes" per unit of length and the varying twist of the hidden threads within the transverse edges. As with 3688, the transverse edge on 3689 might be interpreted as a probable finishing border. Yet, those two edges are not identical. The hair material seems to be different, as is the tablet pattern, and no missing thread groups were observed on the edge of item 3689. Thus, they do not represent fragments of one and the same finishing border. A simple explanation is to consider 3688 and 3689 as one fabric with remnants of the starting edge preserved on one of these pieces, and fragments of the finishing edge on the other. This is possible when a two-beam loom without tubular warp was used for the production of the ground weave and the tablet borders woven onto it later. For a different interpretation, see Lise Ræder Knudsen (this volume).

4.2.3 Context and functions: comparative overview

Conrad Engelhardt's documentation contained notes and drawings of some, but not all, of the textiles. With regard to their function, there was no doubt in the case of the tunic and the two trousers. Nevertheless, there are some features that require a closer examination, particularly as far as the cloaks are concerned.

Cloaks

When Engelhardt discovered the fragments of the polychrome cloth which later received the number 3686, he called it "*kappe*", i.e. cloak, in his diary (p. 50). This is the only term he used for this fabric as well as for 3687 throughout his diary, his publication of 1863, and his list of items to be sent to Copenhagen. Apparently, he had no doubts about this, since large sleeveless cloaks continued to be in use in his time. An example is reproduced in Bemmann and Bemmann (1998 vol. 1, 80, Abb. 45) which depicts the Prince of Arenberg, an Austrian army officer who attempted to find some artefacts of interest in Nydam in the August of 1864. The function must have been so obvious to Engelhardt that he proposed the same for smaller pieces as well (1863, 18):

> "*Flere Stykker vævet, uldent Tøi tildeels med Border og Fryndser forneden er formodentlig Levninger af lignende Kapper, og blandt disse findes den fineste Vævning i Mønster, som vel er bevaret fra en saa fjern Tid; et lille Stykke deraf er fremstillet ved Fig. 5 paa Tavle 2.*"

> ("Several pieces of woven, woollen cloth partly with borders and fringes at the bottom, are presumably fragments of similar cloaks, and amongst these, the finest patterned weaves preserved from such a distant time, are to be found; a small piece of this is depicted in fig. 5 on table 2.")

Engelhardt's last note referred to the tablet-woven piece no. 3698/24822, of which no ground weave is preserved. In Karl Schlabow's publication, function is the main systematic criterion. In his text, he described the following numbers as cloaks: 3686, 3687, 3688/24823, 3689 and 3697. Additionally, no. 3698/24822 which is missing in his text, is depicted as a fragment of a cloak. Margrethe Hald agreed "that the rectangular textiles [...] were primarily used as capes or mantles" but she emphasised that such items of clothing may also belong to women's dress and that other uses than cloaks too were possible, e.g., "covering at night" (1980, 322).

Based on the evidence of several large pieces, not only from Thorsberg – following Engelhardt and then Schlabow – the main criterion for defining a fabric as a cloak are broad, tablet-woven borders. Otherwise a small fragment like 3698/23822 could not be listed as such a piece of clothing. If this is accepted, one should add the number M 607.1 to the list of cloaks. As indicated above, 3688 and 3689 are regarded as one fabric. Within this group of now six textiles,[34] two are no longer connected to any ground weave (3697 and 3698/23822). The other four do have more in common than the broad tablet weaves. The first point is that the spinning direction is invariably z/s which, however, applies to the majority of the Thorsberg finds in any case. More striking is the fact that all four are woven as plain twills. Their thread count is medium fine or at the lower end of the "fine" group, i.e. it is clearly lower than the thread count in the tunic and in the trousers, and the yarn diameter is a little larger than in the diamond twills. None of them possesses indications of napping.

This combination was possibly typical for cloaks. Therefore, it might be worth recalling the other items with these characteristics. These are the numbers 3693, o.Nr. -1/-2, o.Nr. -3 and possibly 1232b and 24824 a/b. At least the first of these, i.e. 3693, is preserved in a remarkable size, 86 × 22 cm, which would correspond well with the idea of a cloak. Only its hem does not seem to fit into this picture, at least at first sight, since the best examples of cloaks are not hemmed. The hem with its actual length of 13 cm, is preserved along one of the longer edges parallel to the probable warp, and may therefore originally have been of at at least 86 cm in length. Considering the most important items of clothing, i.e. cloaks, tunics and trousers, a cloak still seems most likely. Another simple explanation might be a leg wrap, possibly made from a reused cloak. Fragments o.Nr. -1 and -2 are comparatively small. The larger of these, o.Nr. -1, possesses a cut and probably once trimmed edge which is an argument against a cloak, unless the fabric was reused. Together with the even smaller fragment o.Nr. -3, a note is preserved to the effect that this piece belonged to some leg clothing. It does not match, however, with leg wraps 3691 and 3692 or with trousers 3684 and 3685. Nothing concerning its function can be concluded about fragment 1232b. The last twill to be mentioned here is that of 24824 a/b. While the thread count is in accordance with that of the cloaks, it differs from them in being napped. Moreover, several features like seams and coloured sewing make clear that these pieces did not function as cloaks. In conclusion, a plain twill in z/s, of medium fine quality or a little finer and without napping, might be typical for cloaks. Yet, other functions were found as well, although whether the latter are primary or secondary remains unknown.

Tunic and trousers
No obvious parallel of tunic 3683 is preserved amongst the Thorsberg material. Therefore, the technical details may be the sole method of determining possible tunic fragments. A very similar cloth is the reddish diamond twill of 3690/3705. The thread count and diamond pattern are essentially identical. Moreover, the fine, curly fibres are very similar. 3690 is mounted on a cloth 62 × 45 cm in size, but the fragments are much smaller. Thus, the size does not provide any hint as to the function, but the technical similarities are remarkable.

Another cloth of comparable character is represented by the numbers 3700 and 3702–3704. It is again a reddish diamond twill in z/s with the identical high thread count and pattern units. The main difference is the napping. Other characteristics are difficult to interpret in terms of function. There is a hem including a corner, the main part of which runs parallel to the z-system. Woolly sections alternate with abraded areas. The largest piece is 55.5 cm long. In any case, they constitute proof of tailoring. Finally, the other diamond twills are briefly considered here. Even finer than the above-mentioned items is cloth 3706 which appears reddish and was napped. Its starting border is of the same kind as the tunic's, emphasising the similarities. The last two diamond twills, 3699 and 3701, are clearly less fine.

Apart from these fragments, the cloth of both pairs of trousers provides excellent parallels. In the case of 3684, the thread is almost identical while the diamond pattern differs, i.e. the pattern units of 14/9 result in somewhat larger diamonds on the trousers. Regarding 3685, the pattern unit of 10/9 is identical to the tunic's, but the thread count is slightly lower. Thus, smaller fragments of the above-mentioned pieces are possible parallels of the trousers as well. Tunic, trousers and the fragments of diamond twills share many technical details including the absence of broad tablet borders which are considered as one typical feature of cloaks.

However, the two pairs of trousers have more in common than merely the similarities of the weaves. The integrated stockings constitute the most obvious parallel. They may suggest a specific function, as discussed in chapter 7.2. It is beyond the scope of this book to present the dress patterns in any detail, but some observations are noted here. Both consist of two major parts, one for each leg (without stocking) up to the hips or waist, supplemented by a rectangular section on the back and smaller pieces in the crotch and higher up. In both cases, the seams along the calves are left open because the legs are tight fitting. Moreover, this may imply the use of either boots or leg wraps – the latter being more probable for two reasons. Firstly, such wraps are known from this site (3691, 3692) and secondly, because no boots, but rather, sandals were found (most recently: Gräf 2008, 216–218). The main difference between the two pairs is to be found at the upper edges. On one of the pairs, 3684, loops for a belt are sewn onto the cloth. On the other pair, 3685, no traces of loops were recorded. Yet, this does not seem to be due to the cutting off of the original upper end since the trousers still reach higher up. It is more likely that the cloth was rolled down over a belt. In both cases, a rather narrow belt not meant to be visible may be assumed.

The sacrifice

As far as the textiles' function within the sacrifice is concerned, Conrad Engelhardt's statement that some of the textiles – the largest ones – were found rolled up is highly interesting:

"*en ulden bluse [...]. – lå sammenrullet i en klump*" (Diary 1860, 52)

("a woollen blouse [...]. – lay rolled up into a lump.")

"*De [= kapper 3686, 3687] laa hver for sig rullede sammen i en Byldt af temmelig ringe Omfang og vare meget sønderrevne*" (1863, 18)

("They [= cloaks 3686, 3687] lay apart from each other rolled up in a lump of rather small circumference and were very much torn.")

"*De [= beenklæder 3684] fandtes sammenrullede i en Byldt*" (1863, 19)

("They [= trousers 3684] were found rolled up in a lump.")

Engelhardt did not mention that any items were found within these clumps. Of course it must be kept in mind that only little iron was preserved in Thorsberg. Yet, it may well be that these textiles were not used for wrapping other artefacts. Instead they were apparently deposited as sacrifices in themselves. The same may be true for some of the ropes which Engelhardt described as being knotted, though not in the sense of a net (1863, 60). This seems to be the identical phenomenon as in Illerup Ådal.

Parallel to the other sites, damage inflicted on the weapons as well as on the textiles were described and are interpreted as the result of ritual destruction. Although iron finds are widely absent in Thorsberg, the same pattern was found here, e.g. on some shield bosses depicted by Klaus Raddatz (1987b, Tafel 80 and 81). Even more striking are the cuts on the textiles. They are very clear on the tunic (3683) as well as on one of the cloaks (3688). The tunic received strokes on the front as well as on the back. Cuts are also visible on fragments 3689 and 24823a. This is a further argument for these pieces belonging to one cloak because such cuts were not observed on every textile, e.g. neither on the large cloaks 3686 and 3687 nor on the trousers. Although it cannot be excluded that some of the damage on the fragmented pieces are in fact also due to ritual destruction, but have become indistinct over time, it does not seem that all textiles were treated this way. This is again a parallel phenomenon to the metal finds, some of which were left intact.

Apart from arbitrary strokes, another form of damage seems to have played a role. As shown above, the upper edge of trousers 3685 was not preserved. In many spots, the remaining fragments reach up to a virtual waistline where e.g. a starting border or a reinforced edge and perhaps loops for a belt should be placed. Instead, the fabric was cut. Since it might be difficult to keep the trousers in place this way, it seems reasonable to conclude that this is the result of destruction after the battle. Some fragments of cloaks may be interpreted in a similar way, particularly the pieces of tablet-woven borders. Whether the loss of one foot of the trousers 3684 was only due to deterioration over time, cannot be answered.

Spatial context

Since the excavations took place 150 years ago, the documentation cannot be compared to modern standards, although it must be emphasised that Conrad Engelhardt's documentation was excellent for his time. For instance, his diaries are valuable sources. These, as well as other documents, were used for creating a digital map containing the find spots of the various materials.[35] Their location was entered as precisely as possible, but nevertheless remains somewhat inexact. Regarding the textiles, the main source is the diary of 1860. The first fabric found (p. 50) was cloak 3686, the corresponding entry was given above. The cloak lay in the trench named I,1.[36] The following day, Engelhardt (p. 52) wrote about trench K, laid out directly east of I,1 and I,2:

> "*Lige ved kappen [...] og lidt over den lå en ulden bluse*"
>
> ("Just beside the cloak [...] and also a little above it lay a woollen blouse.")

Engelhardt then continued on trench K:

> "*I samme dybde og et par fod derfra*"
>
> ("In the same depth and a few feet further away from it [i.e. the tunic].")

lay the fragment which later received the number 24824a. Moreover,

> "*og tæt herved*"
>
> ("and close to this.")

he found cloth number 24824b. As discussed above, these two seem to represent a piece of garment, but not a cloak. Furthermore, "*Resterne af kappen*", i.e. "*fragments of the cloak*", were recovered at this spot. Thus, a cloak, a tunic and fragments of another piece of clothing were found close to each other and might be interpreted as an ensemble. It should be recalled that the tunic was rolled up. Later that year, when clearing up parts of the site, another fragment turned up which – according to Engelhardt – might belong to this ensemble (p. 138):

> "*Et 9 ¼ T langt og 4 8/12 T bredt stk. uldent tøj, som er afrevet for de længste ender. Hører det til koften S. 52*"
>
> ("A c. 34 cm long and c. 17 cm wide piece of woollen cloth which was torn along the long sides. Belongs to the jacket page 52.")

Seemingly, Engelhardt referred to the tunic. It cannot be ascertained, however, how this fragment could fit into the pattern of the tunic. After all, this assemblage seems to derive from an area of c. 7 × 7 m or probably less in size. Besides the above-mentioned fabrics, one textile can be located at least 10 m north of this find place, but which one this is, is impossible to confirm. Furthermore, three leather sandals could also be located. One of them was found close to the above-mentioned unidentified textile, another one somewhere between the first sandal and the textile ensemble with the tunic, and the third sandal about 20 m further west. Thus none of the sandals can be considered in the immediate context of the textile ensemble.

Isotope analyses

Along with the recent investigations into the Thorsberg material – textile and non-textile – samples of leather and cloth were analysed for their strontium isotope ratios (von Carnap-Bornheim et al. 2007). It proved to be difficult to distinguish definitely between local and non-local items. Yet, eight samples, of which four are textiles (numbers 3701, 3703–3705) are possibly of local origin. Three other specimens, including the weaves 3700 and 3702, may be non-local but possibly originate "from a smaller distance" (ibid., 1544). According to the microscopical analyses presented above, four of these textiles belong to one fabric: 3700 and 3702–3704. Thus, for this cloth, two results point to local provenance, the other two to an origin rather close by. All four samples were taken from the warp.[37] The fabric is a fine, reddish diamond twill in z/s with regular pattern units, well comparable to the tunic (3683) and the trousers (3684). Both other items regarded as locally produced (3701 and 3705) are also diamond twills in z/s, one of a little lower quality, the other even finer and again reddish. These findings are in accordance with the results based on the investigation of non-organic materials, which indicate a provenance primarily south of Thorsberg, possibly rather close by.

Two samples, a piece of leather as well as textile 3694, produced data quite different from those above. The fabric is a unique find, a very coarse tabby in s/s. Both these samples show strontium isotope ratios after mechanical pre-treatment which suggest a possible origin in Norway or northern Scandinavia because of crystalline rocks that prevail there. However, other regions with similar geological structures should not be excluded, as already noted by Julia Gräf (2008, 216). Such regions are e.g. the Black Forest, the Vosges and parts of the Alps as well as the Harz and Bohemia. The method is still under development, the techniques and thus future results continue to be refined (Frei et al. 2009).

Notes
1. This work was undertaken by Ruth Blankenfeldt, Nina Lau and Suzana Matešić, Schloss Gottorf, Schleswig.
2. The possibility always exists that other textile fragments belonging to Thorsberg may lie unrecognized in museum collections. Flensburg museum for instance possesses some metal items, but no textiles (Dorothee Bieske, Museumsberg Flensburg, pers. comm. July 2008). Regrettably, investigating the matter further did not lie within the scope of the present volume.
3. Apparently, the word could not be identified in the manuscript.
4. As already noted, 1 T., a "tomme", is equivalent to an inch (2.54 cm).
5. For instance, the textiles from Bernuthsfeld in Lower Saxony which are discussed later, were brushed and ironed by Johanna Mestorf (Hahne 1919, 50).
6. Unpublished photographs taken by Heidemarie Farke, formerly conservator at Archäologisches Landesmuseum, Schloss Gottorf, Schleswig. They are kept in a file at that museum containing various items of information on the textiles from Thorsberg. It is referred to as the "Thorsberg file" below.
7. Anna Nørgaard kindly made her report available to the present author.
8. 3684 and 3685.
9. = 3684.
10. However, one part – the small piece in the crotch, see below – is missing in Hald's depiction.
11. Andreas Sturm, Aachen, Germany, personal communication, May 2008.
12. Another relief is depicted in Hald 1980, 331, Fig. 394.
13. In another catalogue, referring to a delivery in 1861, another item is listed, no. 19504: "*Et henved 17" langt og 10" bredt Stykke af en Kappe af uldent Tøi, af treskaftet Vævning, forneden kantet med en ci 1 ¾" bred aldre (?) Fryndse. (No. 3687 i den slesv. Olds.samling)*", i.e. "*A c. 44 cm long and 26 cm wide piece of a cloak of woollen cloth, woven as twill, at the bottom edged with a c. 4.5 cm wide ??? of fringes. (No. 3687 in the archaeological collection of Schleswig)*". Copies of the relevant parts of these lists or catalogues were kindly provided by Suzana Matešić, Archäologisches Landesmuseum, Schloss Gottorf, Schleswig.
14. This is indicated by an annotation in Engelhardt's list by Margrethe Hald.
15. "Mischwolle", i.e. wool of mixed diameter, according to Heidemarie Farke. Unpublished note in the Thorsberg file, 8.8.2000.
16. Schlabow: z/s.
17. Described by Schlabow as 2/1 twill with a single change in the weaving direction.
18. In 2000, Christian-Herbert Fischer, Berlin, Germany tested 11 samples of this item. The results are listed in a

letter to Heidemarie Farke who was then conservator at Schloss Gottorf, Schleswig. This letter is kept in the Thorsberg file. While no dyestuff was found in two samples of the warp, all other samples contained "indigo". In seven cases, the contents of this dye were marked as high, resulting in a blue colour. The last two samples – both taken from the weft – had less "indigo", combined with purpurine, a great deal of pseudopurpurine and a little alizarine. According to Fischer, the appearance can be reconstructed as a bluish violet. However, there remains some uncertainty due to the mordant used and to possible selective losses of single dye stuff components (also personal communication, May 2010). Currently, new samples have been taken for analysis by Ina Vanden Berghe, KIK-IRPA, Brussels, Belgium.

19 The drawing in Engelhardt's publication does not show the entire item: two sides appear cut rather than torn and there are too few stripes in the weave. Accordingly, in his inventory list, Engelhardt refers to this drawing as a depiction of the pattern, not of the complete piece.
20 Personal communication, February 2009.
21 3700: 18 × 14 tpc; 3702: 19 × 15–16 tpc; 3703: 16–18 × 13–15 tpc; 3704: 18–19 × 16 tpc.
22 The information provided here is based on the interpretation of photographs. Some were taken by Lise Ræder Knudsen, others were made available to the present author by Suzana Matešić, Ruth Blankenfeldt and Nina Lau, all three at Schloss Gottorf, Schleswig. As noted by Lise Ræder Knudsen (this volume), these fabrics may belong to 3688/3689. However, since they were not examined during the present investigation, they will be regarded here as a separate find.
23 Again, the information is limited to the interpretation of photographs. They were taken by Heidemarie Farke and are in the Thorsberg file.
24 Analysis by Heidemarie Farke, unpublished note in the Thorsberg file, 15.2.2002.
25 Analysis by Heidemarie Farke, unpublished note in the Thorsberg file, 15.2.2002.
26 Unpublished notes in the Thorsberg file, various dates 1998–2000.
27 It is possible that 1232b belongs to one of the other twills in this group. The items 3688 and 3689 are discussed separately but may also represent one fabric.
28 Regrettably, although the particular spot was found, this loop could not be identified further.
29 Because of these loops, Karl Schlabow described this border as a starting border (1976, 62). Yet, the loops do not continue into the ground weave as indicated by Schlabow's drawing, but are cut.
30 An overview of the research history is given in Möller-Wiering (forthcoming a).
31 Personal communication, May 2008.
32 If it was a starting border for a warp weighted loom, the weight down at the end of the warp would – according to Ræder Knudsen – pull the outermost securing thread into the border. It might be argued, however, that the frictional forces within the border could be strong enough to compensate for the traction force. The weight per thread in such a weave would lie around 20 g (Eva Andersson Strand, Centre for Textile Research, Copenhagen, personal communication, February 2010). An experiment might shed light on this question.

A securing thread pulled into the tablet-woven border can be seen on a drawing in an earlier publication by Karl Schlabow (1952/53, Abb. 2). There, in contrast to his description of 1976, the securing thread is not fixed but kept loosely. From this thread, short loops are pulled though the tablet weave and the ball of yarn for the future ground weave is passed through. This method seems clearly more practical than his later version. However, it would be difficult to keep the securing thread straight.
33 Personal communication (May 2008) with Lise Ræder Knudsen, Anna Nørgaard (Roskilde, Denmark), Lena Hammarlund (Göteborg, Sweden) and Martin Ciszuk (Borås, Sweden). The latter three are professional hand weavers with great experience in investigating and reconstructing prehistoric textiles.
34 It is only five fabrics if M 607.1 belongs to 3688/3689, as indicated by Ræder Knudsen (this volume).
35 This work was undertaken by Ruth Blankenfeldt, Nina Lau and Suzana Matešić who made it available to the present author.
36 In the copy used here, the trench with the cloak is named I,1, although the headline of the entry of this day is trench I,2. Both trenches lay adjacent to each other, I,2 just north of I,1.
37 Gabriele Zink, Archäologisches Landesmuseum, Schloss Gottorf, Schleswig, personal communication, July 2009.

5. NYDAM

5.1. INTRODUCTION

Site and research history

Nydam is a bog in southern Jutland, about 8 km northwest of Sønderborg. The site lies only c. 1 km away from the Baltic Sea and quite close to the present Danish-German border. There, the first excavations were carried out by Conrad Engelhardt in 1859 and later in 1862/63, a few years before the German-Danish war, also termed the 2nd Schleswig war. The conflict in 1864 affected his archaeological work in various ways. The excavations could not be completed, the site was partly plundered and subsequently, the finds were divided between Denmark and Germany. Engelhardt's excavations covered 10 % of the deposit at the most (Ilkjær 1990, 20), split up into various pits, the exact location of which was not always reported. Soon after, in 1865, Engelhardt published his main results. More than 100 years later, Güde Bemmann and Jan Bemmann (1998) presented a comprehensive account of the Nydam material excavated in the 19th century, including smaller excavations conducted up to 1980. New large campaigns were initiated in 1984, the results of which are not fully published as yet. An overview of the various excavations and their spatial distribution was provided by Erik Jørgensen and Peter Vang Petersen (2003, 259, fig. 2). Recently, Andreas Rau published some results of his current investigations (2008).

The chemical composition of the bog is comparable to Illerup Ådal and Vimose rather than to Thorsberg. Iron was well preserved as were organic materials such as wood, bone and – to some extent – vegetal cords, while the conditions were unfavourable for wool. Wood is of special interest in Nydam as during the old and new excavations, four boats were discovered, in addition to weapons and personal belongings. The only completely intact ship existing today, often referred to as "the Nydam boat", is housed at Schloss Gottorf, Schleswig. Apart from this boat, many of the older finds belong to this museum while the majority of the material – old and new – is in the National Museum of Denmark in Copenhagen.

Chronology

More than once, weapons and other artefacts were deposited in the Nydam bog or rather lake, the main phases being termed Nydam I–IV. Meanwhile it became apparent, however, that Nydam I could be divided into four parts (Jørgensen and Vang Petersen 2003, 263–266). A excellent point of departure for dating these parts are the wooden finds, particularly the boats. In all, four vessels may be distinguished (Rieck 1998, 267): an oak boat which was ritually destroyed during the sacrifice (A), another more or less intact oak boat which is known today as the "Nydam boat" (B), a third boat made of pine (C), which was destroyed shortly after its excavation, but additional pieces of which were found recently, and finally a few remnants of a fourth vessel (D). Stratigraphically, the parts of boat A were always the lowest (ibid., 281). The trees were felled c. AD 190 and the sacrifice may have taken place in the early 3rd century, i.e. Nydam Ia (Jørgensen and Vang Petersen 2003, 263).[1] The second is the pine boat (C), which could not be dated directly, but only by using the oak of a shield belonging to it. This wood was dated to AD 296, suggesting a sacrifice some time after AD 300, Nydam Ib (ibid.; Rieck 1998, 291). The trees for the complete oak boat (B) were felled between AD 310 and AD 320 which makes a deposition around AD 350 probable (Rieck 1998, 274), Nydam Ic. The sacrifice Nydam Id, parts of which were deposited at the western stern of vessel B, consists of weapons dated to the late 4th or early 5th century AD (Jørgensen and Vang Petersen 2003, 266). The deposits Nydam II–IV belong to the 5th century AD (ibid.).

The bulk of the material in Nydam and almost all the textiles discussed below belong to the assemblages of Nydam I. More detailed information on the datings as well as on the origin of non-textile finds is provided below in connection with the various find categories.

Textiles

Among the many thousand finds from the bog of Nydam, only a few were recorded previously as being connected to textiles. In his publication on these excavations, Conrad Engelhardt did not include a chapter or even a paragraph on woven textiles although such fabrics are mentioned in passing. For example, he found five spearheads as a closed find and described them as being wrapped in woollen cloth (1865, 4). On another spot, 37 metal pieces were discovered

> "*med Levninger af uldent Tøi og tynde Snore rustede fast til Gjenstandene*" (ibid.)

> ("with remnants of woollen cloth and thin cords rusted onto the objects.")

In Güde Bemmann and Jan Bemmann's publication (1998), textiles play an even smaller role. The situation changed to some extent in connection with the new excavations on the site in the 1990s. Since then, many wooden parts of the ships with caulking material on them have come to light. Another group of textiles are tiny amounts of weave adhering to clasps. It is however noteworthy that still hardly any textiles on iron finds were registered. Thus, the Nydam material appears very different from the other weapon deposits. Although comparisons thus remain limited, new perspectives may nevertheless be gained.

Regarding the spatial distribution of the textiles, two spots are of primary interest. The first is pit VI of Conrad Engelhardt's excavations, situated northwest of the boat field, the other is the area of the most recent excavations around the boats. Furthermore, textiles were observed in the closed find Nydam IV, slightly west of the boats (Vang Petersen 1998, 243, Abb. 89; 265).

5.2. TECHNICAL ASPECTS OF THE TEXTILES

The present investigation strongly focuses on the functional aspects of textiles. Therefore, the Nydam textile material cannot be considered and presented as a homogeneous assemblage. Instead, its diversity has to be respected even on the level of the technical analysis. Besides the fibre material, the various functional groups are therefore presented separately. Apart from the random selection of weapons, the bulk of the Nydam material was previously analysed by Ulla Mannering, CTR Copenhagen (2006b), whose results form the basis of the present author's investigation.

Material

In general, as in Illerup and Vimose, animal fibres are not well preserved in Nydam. Nevertheless, as far as may be ascertained without fibre analyses, the great majority of the extant textiles are made of wool. This is most obvious in the tiny, but well-preserved, fragments adhering to clasps. Moreover,

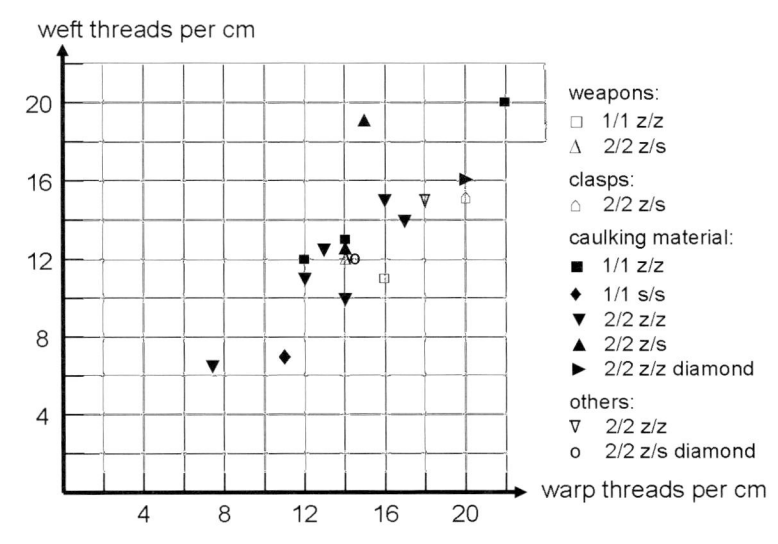

Fig. 1.44. Nydam, thread counts

there are indications of napping and thus of wool on some iron finds. Several cords and ropes – bundles, bindings and a net (Engelhardt 1865, 35; Bemmann and Bemmann 1998 vol. 1, 48) – a group of finds which is not included in this investigation – prove that also vegetal material could survive. According to Flemming Rieck (2003, 309), the ropes are seemingly made of lime bast. Yet, the only weave seemingly made of plant fibres is a coarse twill found amongst the caulking material, i.e. within a group of fabrics which were not directly exposed to the bog environment.

5.2.1 Weapons
Weaving types
Only few weapons possess rather clear textiles remnants. One of them is shield boss 7993, on top of which a tabby in z/z, possibly in two layers, can be seen. On another shield boss, 3411, a 2/2 twill in z/s covers the outside. This twill gives the impression of not having been woven simply diagonally. Yet, no definite break could be observed. Possibly a similar fabric was found on the inner side of its flange (Rieck, unpubl.). Small hairs, observable on both the inside and the outside, may most probably be interpreted as napping. A comparable twill was observed on the socket of spearhead 3264. In this case, the twill lay on top of a tablet weave.[2] Whether or not the twill and the tablet weave belong to the same fabric, remains unknown. Another diagonal twill – this time in z/z – was found on lancehead 7937. A spin-patterned diagonal twill is connected to shield boss 6136. While the threads of one system are z-spun, those of the other system include s- as well as z-spun ones, alternating in narrow stripes. A photograph of spearhead 5372 (Bemmann and Bemmann 1998 vol. 1, 42, Abb. 17) depicts a 2/2 twill which appears irregular. Since no break can be determined, the effect might be caused by spin patterning. The thread counts found on the weapons – as well as on the other Nydam finds – are given in Fig. 1.44.[3]

Besides the above-mentioned items, a random selection of weapons was checked. From the recent excavations, 72 lanceheads and spearheads were examined. On the following 51 pieces, some traces of textiles could be observed:

39, 6007, 6320, 6632, 6667, 7027, 7101, 7262, 7280, 7287, 7616, 7617, 7624, 7628, 7684, 7693, 7694, 7692, 7696, 7701, 7706, 7707 (or 7709), 7712, 7734, 7778, 7815, 7824, 7850, 7867, 7878, 7969, 7982, 7983, 7990, 7992, 8001, 8009, 8012, 8016, 8024, 8062, 8075, 10750, 10758, 10759, 10760, 10761, 10763, 10764, 10766, 10768.

In some of these cases it was possible to identify the spinning direction of single threads. S-yarn was found on 6007, 7616, 7706, 7992 and 10760. Furthermore, on the latter as well as on 7706, a thread spun in z was noticed. Other z-spun fragments were observed on 7101, 7878, 8012 and 10766.

On the remaining 26 items, the traces of textiles are extremely faint and hard to determine if one did not know the better preserved variants described above:

6174, 6415, 6887, 7102, 7152, 7153, 7263, 7626, 7735, 7756, 7784, 7785, 7833, 7849, 7862, 7930, 7991, 8011, 8019, 8021, 8074, 10675, 10679, 10752, 10754, 10767.

All weapons mentioned thus far are stored in Copenhagen and were recovered – with the exception of 5372 – during the recent excavations. As far as the material from the 19th century stored in Schleswig is concerned, 21 weapons were checked (see list in Appendix 11.5). Possible 2/2 twills may be mentioned with regard to two shield bosses, F.S. 4764 and one without F.S. number (new catalogue no. 1941). On most other pieces, faint traces of textiles were observed, although again, their details are undeterminable. Amongst the selection examined, the preservation of fibres is uncertain only on two arrowheads (5402, 5403) and one lancehead (5405).

Textile quality
The few measurable thread counts belong to the category "fine", according to Klaus Tidow's classification (2000, 108). Some indications of diamonds and/or spin patterning, which are generally signs of high quality, were found, although unambiguous proof of the former is missing. Moreover, the traces of napping may be interpreted as a feature characterising good quality.

5.2.2 Clasps
The Nydam material includes more than 200 clasps.[4] With the exception of a small group belonging to Nydam IV and thus to the Migration Period, all others were examined during this investigation. As a rule, several pieces or fragments found together belong to one item number. A pair of clasps usually consists of a hook and an eye, each decorated with a button on top of a pin. The state of preservation of the textiles is often quite good. However, since the diameter of most of the clasps is less than 1 cm and often even only 0.5 cm, since their pins often pierce the textiles and since the tissues are either squeezed in and hidden between the button and hook or eye, or they have loosened and opened up, it is usually impossible to determine any technical details. No fibre analyses were performed, but the visual impression is that of well-prepared wool.

Weaving types and textile quality
One tabby (14704) was identified with z-spun threads in one system while the spinning direction of the other system remained obscure. In two cases, a 2/2 twill in z/s could be discerned (6992, 7968). These are regarded as plain twills, although – due to the fragments' small size – it cannot be excluded that they were diamond twills instead. The same applies to a similar tissue with 20 × 15 tpc. This latter item (7289) is a loose one, stored together with the clasps, but the connection between clasps and 7289 is unclear. It is the only fabric in this context where the thread count could be determined. It is fine – almost very fine – in terms of Klaus Tidow's categories (2000, 108). The combination

of z- and s-spun yarns, however, was observed on several items and may – in all cautiousness – be considered characteristic for this group. There is one attestation of a possible spin-patterned twill, indicating high quality (7093; Fig. 1.45). Amongst the fragments of six find numbers (25 %), pieces which appear to have been dyed red were observed (6878, 6879, 7093, 7274, 7639 and 7289). Wherever the thread diameters could be measured, the results lie within the spectrum known from the other sites.

5.2.3 Caulking material

Preservation conditions for this group of textiles were quite different compared to the general situation in the bog. While the fabrics on the weapons and those adhering to the clasps were in direct contact with the chemically active substances in the ground, the caulking textiles were protected by some water-repellent matter and by being pressed between wooden planks. The heavily pressed combination of textile and repellent kept the boat watertight. In a strict sense, the term "caulking material" is not correct when referring to the tightening of clinker built vessels, of which the Nydam boats are examples. Instead, "caulking" describes the method of tightening carvel built vessels.[5] However, due to the lack of a general, handy term reflecting the specific maritime context, the term "caulking material" was chosen here.[6] All the finds presented here came to light during the 20th-century excavations and belong to either the complete oak vessel (B) or the pine vessel (C).[7]

Weaving types

All the caulking material from Nydam is woven. The group consists of 25 find numbers and 27 textiles or imprints of textiles, although two are uncertain. The binding as well as the spinning direction in both systems and the thread count could be determined for only eleven of them (see Fig. 1.44). In all other cases, some data are missing. Nevertheless, there is valuable information. The most common type of fabric is a 2/2 twill in z/z which was determined six times and which is furthermore the probable weave for another four pieces. One of them (5911) appears to be made of vegetal material. A 2/2 twill in z/s occurred twice (Fig. 1.46). Usually, the fragments are large enough to distinguish a plain twill from a broken or – more probably – diamond twill, assuming a "normal" size of the diamonds. Yet, such a fabric was found only twice, a diamond twill in z/z (11545) and another of uncertain spinning direction (5512). At least two, possibly four textiles are tabbies, three of them woven in z/z, one in s/s. No spin patterning was observed.

Taking into account binding, spinning directions and thread count, the technical variations within this group of textiles are so numerous that it is almost impossible to determine any fabrics which hypothetically may be represented by more than one fragment. Possible exceptions within the group of plain twills might be 5785 and 10510 as well as 5902 and 5925.

Textile quality

The thread counts are quite variable, ranging from 7–8 × 6–7 tpc to 22 × 20 tpc or from coarse to very fine according to Klaus Tidow's categories (2000, 108). This whole range – coarse, medium fine, fine and very fine – is represented amongst the tabbies and probable tabbies, i.e. with one fabric in each group. On the other hand, the twills seem to be slightly more similar. With the exception of the coarse vegetal piece, they are medium fine or fine, with one of the diamond twills (11545) on the upper limit of the fine group. Based on the comparison with Illerup, in the latter case, the system with the higher thread count is regarded as possible weft.

Fig. 1.45. Nydam, hook of a pair of clasps (7093)

Fig. 1.46. Nydam, caulking material on plank 5780 (lower right)

Depending on a textile's function, a low thread count does not necessarily signify low quality. The open weave of a veil-like fabric, e.g., is characterised by rather few threads per cm² in combination with thin and carefully spun yarns. Here in Nydam, it is difficult and often impossible to evaluate the quality of the spinning since the material is not preserved very well and sometimes has totally disappeared, leaving only imprints behind. Yet, the density of the cloths, i.e. the thread count in relation to the thickness of the yarn material, indicates rather simple weaves as far as the fabrics of low thread count are concerned. In this context, it may be useful to include those three textiles for which the thread count was calculated although the binding could not be determined, and to distinguish between planks – which are considered as original components of the vessels – and repairs. All three additional fabrics belong to planks. The average thread count of textiles adhering to planks is 15.5 × 14 tpc, that of the three repairs is only 11 × 10. It may be added that the repairs consist of the common twill in z/z. Napping or dyeing were not observed but may not be excluded, particularly on the finer pieces.

5.2.4 Others
A few textiles found in Nydam cannot be ascribed to any of the above-mentioned groups. On a wooden head (2860), were found several woven fragments which originally belonged to one fabric, as can be evidenced from their homogeneity. It is a fine 2/2 twill in z/z with 18 × 14–16 tpc (see Fig. 1.38). Yet, it is not a completely plain twill since in one spot, there is a break in one direction. This particular fragment is approx. 3.1 cm × 2.6 cm. Its size should therefore be sufficient to detect a possible broken or diamond twill if its pattern lay roughly within the well-known dimensions. Other fragments are even up to 9.7 cm × 5.8 cm in size but do not show any breaks. Therefore, the one break should be interpreted as a weaving mistake. The largest fragment possesses a narrow, tablet-woven edge (see Ræder Knudsen, this volume). The fibre material is well prepared, mainly non-pigmented hair, i.e. wool as far as can be ascertained without a more detailed analysis.

A piece of a 2/2 twill, broken or diamond, is preserved without a connection to any other item. It is spin patterned. One system consists of only z-spun yarn with 12 tpc. In the other system, there are threads of s- as well as of z-direction but the thread count could not be determined. Neither was it possible to identify a particular pattern, which of course is due to the small size of the fragment. Thus, it is quite possible that the first system of which only z-spun yarns are preserved was originally patterned as well. The thread count of 12 tpc in one system indicates a medium fine or fine quality which is supported by the spin patterning.

At least 30 loose fragments are labelled as "præp. 3404", the largest of which measures 3.8 cm × 2.7 cm.[8] This diamond twill was woven in z/s with c. 14–15 × 12 tpc. Regrettably, the size of the diamonds could not be determined. Some fragments have a slightly bluish appearance.

The tiny textile fragment which adhered to the pin of fibula 13794 when excavated, is not preserved.[9]

5.3. CONTEXT AND FUNCTIONS
5.3.1 Weapons
Weapons in pit VI
Among the pits which Conrad Engelhardt opened already in 1859–1860, is pit VI. Engelhardt referred to two closed finds within this pit. In his notes quoted by Bemmann and Bemmann (1998 vol. 1, 119), he described the smaller one as follows:

> "5372/76. 5 Jernspyd [...] fandtes i en Lærredsindpakning. Tydelige Levninger af Lærred og tynde Snore findes endnu paa dem alle. I Skafthulungerne er der Levninger af Træskaftet; men de laae afbrudte uden Skafter i Indpakningen."

> ("5 iron points [...] were found packed in canvas. Obvious fragments of canvas and thin cords can still be found on all of them. In the holes of the sockets are fragments of wooden shafts; but in the package they lay broken off, without shafts.")

This implies that remnants of textiles and cords were observed on all five weapons of this group which seemingly once again suggests individual wrapping. This does not necessarily contradict Engelhardt's observation of one piece of cloth where his description is taken literally. It might well be that the weapons were wrapped in a way that at least one layer of textile lay between every two spearheads. However, one must be careful with Engelhardt's use of the term "Lærred" which usually indicates a simple tabby made of linen or – in modern times – of other vegetal material. The drawing and photograph of one of these spearheads clearly show a 2/2 diamond twill on the socket (Bemmann and Bemmann 1998 vol. 1, 42, Abb. 17 [cat. no. 1126]; = 1998 vol. 2, Taf. 124). And indeed, in the publication (1865, 4), Engelhardt gave a slightly different description:

> "*Fem Jernspydspidser med afbrudte Skafter vare indpakkede i et Stykke uldent Tøi; de have alle været ubrugelige ved Nedlægningen*"

> ("Five iron spearheads with the shafts broken off were wrapped in a piece of woollen cloth; they had all been rendered useless when deposited.")[10]

Thus, in the publication, Engelhardt referred to a woollen cloth, which accords better with the weaving type, i.e. the diamond twill, and with the finds in general. Three of these weapons were investigated in the present study. On no. 5374, textile is preserved in large areas on both sides. In the case of 5375, a patch on the socket and a few traces here and there may be ascertained. On the socket, the threads run obliquely to the long axis of the weapon. Fabric is observable on one side of the blade of 5376 as well as on its socket where it goes around to the other side. This may also be the case on no. 5372, a photograph of which is reproduced in Bemmann and Bemmann (1998 vol. 1, 42, Abb. 17). Here, the threads run parallel to the long axis. In conclusion, the above-mentioned individual wrapping is confirmed in at least two or three of these spearheads. Moreover, a fragment of a thin cord was indeed found on the socket of no. 5376.

The second closed find within pit VI was larger than the one just described (Engelhardt 1865, 4):

> "*Paa en lille Plet, ikke een Fod i Kvadrat, laae med Levninger af uldent Tøi og tynde Snore rustede fast til Gjenstandene: 4 Skjoldbuler stukne indeni hverandre, 19 Brudstykker af Spydspidser af forsklellige Former, 8 Jernpilspidser, 2 smaae Bronzeringe, Spidsen af en damaskeret Jernklinge, et Mundblik til en Sværdskede, et massivt Bronzebeslag til en Sværdknap og en Jernpig til en Spore.*"

> ("On a small spot, of less than one square foot, lay these items with fragments of woollen cloth and thin cords rusted onto them: 4 shield bosses stuck to each other, 19 pieces of spearheads of various shapes, 8 iron arrowheads, 2 small bronze rings, the point of a damasked iron blade, one mount of a scabbard mouth, one massive bronze mounting for a sword's pommel and one point of a spur.")

Several items of this group were examined in this study. No textile is preserved on the bronze artefacts. However, all seven spearheads examined here (5381, 5382, 5384, 5386, 5389, 5390 and 5391) possess traces of textiles visible on both sides. This holds true also for lancehead 5394. Better preserved textiles were found on one side of the sword blade (5409) as well as on one of the arrowheads (5401). Thus, the situation is comparable to the smaller closed find of pit VI.

This pit encompasses the only spatial context in which textiles on weapons were described to some extent at that time. It might well be that for some unknown reason, the conditions for the preservation of textiles were better in pit VI than in other places. Nevertheless, woven fabrics were observed in other places as well:

> "*Spydspidser fandtes oftere samlede i Bunker, som det synes, oprindelig nedlagte indsvøbte i Tøi*" (Engelhardt 1865, 29)

> ("spearheads were often found in bundles which seemingly were originally deposited wrapped in cloth.")

Other weapons
The few fabrics preserved on other weapons do not allow for any far-reaching interpretations. Yet, they match the picture of wrapped weapons observed in the Illerup Ådal and Vimose material. For instance, here again shield bosses 3411 and 7993 which were found in undisturbed areas during the recent excavations, lay upside down (Rieck, unpubl.), preserving some textile below them. Traces under the flange and on the inner side of boss 3411 are not preserved well enough to ascertain whether or not they belong to one and the same fabric. However, Flemming Rieck (unpubl.) depicts a fragment originating from the lower side of the flange, which may well belong to the twill from the outside as described above. Moreover, the indications of napping are to be found on its inside as well as its outside, supporting the idea of only one textile and of individual wrapping. The material on the inner flange – i.e. further up in the stratigraphy – is described by Flemming Rieck (unpubl.) as "*et stort kompakt korrosionslag med tekstilspor*", i.e. traces of textiles in a compact corrosion layer. On top of this lay several spearheads. It is impossible to say whether these spearheads were part of the same wrapping or whether there was another fabric.

Individual wrapping must be proposed for a number of shield bosses, spears and lances where traces of textiles were observed on both sides. Among poorly preserved examples are at least five shield bosses from the old excavations: 4751, 4764 and new catalogue numbers 1938, 1954 and 1976. One of the better preserved items is 3264, a piece of a spearhead where textile was found clinging to the socket. In this case, there are two layers, a tablet weave directly on the iron and a twill above this which both may or may not belong to one fabric. On spearhead no. 39, textile could be observed on the blade as well as on the socket. Although hardly any details are discernible, it may be noted that there is more than one layer and that the uppermost layer lies obliquely to the long axis. On spearheads 7815 and 8075, the orientation of the tissue is also oblique in relation to the long axis.

The situation is different on shield boss 7993 where textile could only be observed on the outside. It lay within the huge cluster of finds immediately southwest of the pine boat. This area also contained a great number of shield boards. Karin Göbel and Andreas Rau from Schleswig succeeded in reconstructing complete shields including their bosses and handles.[11] The boss labelled 7993 constitutes a part of one of them, seemingly not torn off the wood but offered as a shield in its entirety. Therefore, it is not surprising that no textile was detected on the inner side, particularly on the inner flange, of this boss. Textile is preserved only on its outside. Yet, this weave was not intact but damaged by a weapon stroke, providing a parallel to the intentionally damaged weapons and textiles described from the other deposits.

Primary functions
Today, the textile remnants are too few, too small and too diverse to allow for any interpretations. The only hint appears in Conrad Engelhardt's observation of the closed finds. His descriptions suggest that cloth of considerable size was used for wrapping. In all cautiousness, this may refute the notion of items of clothing such as tunics or trousers and rather indicate cloaks or blankets.

The sacrifice
Summing up the results obtained here, it appears that the weapon material from Nydam reveals the same primary features connected to rituals as already known from the other sites. The intentional damage of the weapons themselves was observed on several instances (Engelhardt 1865, e.g. pl. XI) as were

linear cuts on the textile covering shield boss 7993. Indications of individual wrapping are preserved on the weapons of both closed finds from pit VI as well as on some other items. Moreover, those closed finds may represent larger packages including e.g. several shield bosses pressed into each other.

Chronological context
Güde Bemmann and Jan Bemmann stated that the possibilities of ascribing the weapons to certain closed finds within the Nydam I phase are limited, but that particularly the lances and spears as such may be dated quite accurately (1998 vol. 1, 297). Yet, it lies beyond the scope of this volume to date the single weapons and thus the adhering textiles. Therefore, only one hint is provided. According to Bemmann and Bemmann, who proposed only two phases within Nydam I, the finds in pit VI belong to the second deposition which is thought to correspond to the 2nd half of the 4th century AD (ibid., 302–303). Compared to the subdivision based on the dendrochronological datings presented above, this could refer to either Nydam Ic or Id.

Origin of weapons
Due to the distribution of the various types of weapons, Bemmann and Bemmann excluded all regions south of the river Elbe and east of the Mecklenburg region in the northeast of Germany as possible places of origin for the entire material found in Nydam (1998 vol. 1, 311). Based on the knowledge gained in the 1990s, they proposed only two deposits within Nydam I (ibid., 299). For the older one ("By-Gruppe"), Denmark including the islands as well as Schleswig-Holstein were described as probable areas of provenance for the weapons. For the later one ("Mollestad-Gruppe"), the authors suggested the Jutland peninsula including Schleswig-Holstein.

According to Andreas Rau (2008, 153), most weapons of the Nydam Id deposit originate from the Continent, from Germanic groups in the west and along the River Elbe. Additionally, based on research on fibulae, Rau defined the regions of origin as Schleswig-Holstein and West-Mecklenburg.

5.3.2 Clasps
Primary functions
In male costumes, clasps are primarily found on long-sleeved tunics, placed at the cuffs or sometimes at the waist, although they are also known from trousers from the knees downwards as well as from other pieces of clothing (Nockert 1991, 108–111; Hines 1993, 76). Following a classification proposed by John Hines in 1993, the Nydam clasps may be described as consisting of plate and button and are therefore to be grouped into Hines' class B (p. 12). As far as grave finds are concerned, clasps of this group were "regularly used by men, and in regular use in other places than at the wrists", although examples worn on the wrists are also known (ibid., 78). In any case, they must be regarded as parts of clothing[12] as was – with reference to the Nydam material – also claimed e.g. by Erik Jørgensen and Peter Vang Petersen who, moreover, ascribed the clasps and thus the textiles to the defeated warriors (2003, 271). The vast majority of the clasps found in Nydam must be seen in context with the pine boat,[13] i.e. with the Nydam Ib deposit of the first half of the 4th century, and the following discussion refers to this group. Most often, textile was preserved around the pin beneath the button, i.e. between button and hook or eye. It is these fabrics which the clasps were pierced through, representing the hems or the cuffs. Accordingly, two or more layers of fabric could be observed there on several instances.

Spatial context and sacrifice

In many instances, textiles covered the top of the decorative buttons. Textiles below the hook or eye are rare, but do exist as well. Neither the remnants on top of the buttons nor those beneath the hook or eye owe their preservation to the clasps' function. Instead, their survival may be interpreted in connection with the sacrifice. They demonstrate that when the clasps were cast into the bog, they were in close contact with textiles. Apparently, they were not cut off the clothes and sacrificed separately. Theoretically, this might have been a possibility, seen as a parallel to the shield bosses and many lanceheads and spearheads which were deposited without the wood. However, generally, jewellery and costume accessories remained undamaged (Bemmann and Bemmann 1998 vol. 1, 318) which also holds true here, i.e. the clasps remained on the clothes. This is in accordance with the observation made during the excavation that sometimes, the clasps lay in little rows (Rieck, unpubl.).

Since the clasps with preserved textiles still adhered to the clothing when they were deposited, it seems reasonable to assume that this also holds true for those clasps in this sacrifice which are no longer combined with textile. Further perspectives may be gained by taking this group also into account. There are about 50 find numbers representing clasps, about one half with the textiles discussed above and the other half without organic remains. Further information about them may be drawn from the site maps. In order to create an overview as well as to enable detailed interpretation of spatial contexts, all finds of the modern excavations were registered in a computer programme.[14] The corresponding area around the vessels can then be divided into sections. When e.g. a grid of 21 sections – each measuring c. 28–35 m² – is laid upon the area, it appears that shafts of lances or spears can be found in every section. The distribution of hooks and eyes, however, is quite different.[15] Out of a total of 44 find numbers relevant here, 21 find numbers (47.7 %) belong to the section that covers most of the eastern half of the pine boat (C) as well as the sediment southwest of this vessel (section 15). Here, 19 find numbers or 43.2 % of the total, were encountered within an area of only c. 6 m² along the southwestern edge of the boat. Another 11 find numbers (25 %) came to light in the adjacent section surrounding the eastern stern (section 18), but mostly southeast of the ship, at least 5 m away from the above mentioned cluster. Only six find numbers (13.6 %) were registered in other sections, further away from this boat, while no location is given for the last six numbers (13.6 %). Conrad Engelhardt who had excavated the major parts of the pine vessel, had already then realised that the artefacts within the boat

> "*oprindelig ere nedlagte samlede i Bunker og i en vis Orden*" (1865, 4)
>
> ("were originally deposited gathered in heaps and in a certain order.")

This observation was later confirmed by Bemmann and Bemmann (1998 vol. 1, 318). In the case of the clasps, this signifies that the tunics and possibly trousers were gathered together and laid down in an identical manner to the various kinds of iron artefacts. In other words: the clothes were not used for wrapping metal pieces here and there but represented votive offerings in themselves. Furthermore, this correspondence between the clothes and the other artefacts supports the premise that the clothing in the bog once belonged to the same people to whom the weapons, combs and other items did. Thus this material is supposed to originate from abroad.

Despite the fact that all clasps belonging to John Hines' class B may be "treated as a unit" in various respects (1993, 78), many subdivisions are distinguishable which, however, are mostly irrelevant in this context. Concentrating on the Nydam material, the clasps may be divided into several different types, seven of which are of interest here. Each of these types was encountered in more than one spot and therefore labelled with more than one find number. On the other hand, several find numbers contain more than one type of clasp. Thus there is a mixture which is at least partly due to the fact that during excavation, running water dislocated some of the clasps (Rieck, unpubl.). Assuming that as a rule, each piece of clothing possessed a uniform set of clasps (see examples in Nockert 1991, 108–111), this mixture requires closer scrutiny. It is not known how many clasps belonged to one tunic or pair of trousers. Generally, there should be at least two pairs – one for each sleeve or ankle, respectively – consisting all in all of two hooks and two eyes together with four buttons. Yet, often more than one pair were used immediately adjacent to each other (ibid.).

A very small group consists of a roughly triangular type ("type 5")[16]. Four buttons and two hooks of this type are preserved, although no eyes have been recovered. They represent a minimum of two pairs which could hypothetically belong to a single tunic. These few pieces are distributed among three find numbers, 4433, 4434 and 2211. The first two, 4433 and 4434, came from section 18, perhaps only 20 cm away from each other.[17] The find-place of 2211 is unknown.

Another very small group of clasps is that of a longish, rectangular type ("type 6"). Remnants of at least three such pairs were found, theoretically representing one or two tunics, but labelled with four different find numbers. All of them come from section 15, three of them (7091, 7289, 7640) from within an area of about 40 cm × 20 cm, the last one (6991) lying almost half a meter away from the others.

The buttons of a cruciform shape are the largest ones, measuring approx. 1 cm ("type 8"). All in all, ten hooks, seven eyes and 17 buttons of this type were found, all in section 18,[18] constituting at least ten pairs of clasps. They might have been used for one to five (or even more) tunics. Among these pieces, five hooks, four eyes and nine buttons have all received one and the same find number (2270) and it may be assumed that they belonged to the same piece of clothing. At a distance of c. 70–90 cm lay another group of four hooks, two eyes and five buttons (2386, 2387, 2509, 2510). They may represent either a second piece of dress or, alternatively, the other sleeve or leg of the first one. Only one hook, one eye and two buttons (2304, 2396, 3183; possibly also 3184) were found 1–2 m away from these two clusters and not in combination with other clasps. Presumably, the cruciform clasps may be assigned to not more than three items of clothing.

Thus, in all these cases, the above-mentioned notion of clothing with uniform sets of clasps is supported by the find distribution in Nydam. Undoubtedly, the situation becomes more complicated when examining the larger groups. The biggest one is that of a round, flat type with a circular pattern ("type 9"). The material contains at least thirty pairs of clasps. Even if one assumes a row of pairs on each sleeve or leg, it seems likely that this huge amount derives from several items of clothing. No attempt is made here to assign the clasps in detail. However, there is no reason to assume that the situation differs from the smaller groups.

This result may now be combined with the information derived from the textiles themselves.

- For the small group of "type 5" clasps which might represent just one tunic, one possible combination of z-spun yarn in one direction with s-oriented threads in the other was observed (4433).
- "Type 6" clasps may derive from one or two tunics but it is uncertain whether a piece of 2/2 twill in z/s (7289), which was stored together with these clasps, in fact belongs to them.
- For "type 8" clasps, the third small group mentioned above, no specific information on the textiles could be gained.
- The largest group with at least 30 pairs, "type 9" clasps, provided one 2/2 twill in z/s along with one s-spun yarn, which may belong to the same tunic (both 7968).

- In another large group, "type 10/11" clasps, spin patterning was found, once as a possible twill (2/2 ? z+s/s) while in another case, the binding remained unclear. Since both pieces belong to the same find number (7093), they may well originate from the same tunic. Furthermore, z- as well as s-spun yarns were observed on 7343, which lay only a few centimetres away from 7093 and may therefore again represent the spin-patterned fabric.
- A 2/2 twill in z/s was determined (6992) within "type 1/2" clasps. The combination z/s was found in another three instances, although the binding could not be stated (again 6992, 7091, 7092). 6992 and 7092 lay close to each other, 7091 – with further z- and s-directed threads – less than 1 m away from them. It seems that these finds belong to one fabric woven as z/s twill, although a second piece of possibly the same type of weave is not unlikely.
- "Type 4" clasps only yielded a z-spun thread.

On the whole, these results correspond very well with those gained solely from the site maps. Finally, it must be recalled and emphasised that often, textiles were not only found between button and hook or eye but also on top of the former. A satisfactory explanation for this phenomenon is that the pieces of clothing were rolled up for the sacrifice.

Nydam IV
One specific type of clasp belongs to the late Nydam IV sacrifice, immediately outside the boat field, dated to the second half of the 5th century AD. These few pieces were not included in this investigation. Yet, traces of woven textiles were observed on top of these clasps and Peter Vang Petersen therefore regarded them as part of elite clothing and as part of the sacrifice (1998, 261). This is in accordance with the observations discussed above.

Chronological context and origin of clasps
Besides the above-mentioned specific clasps of Nydam IV, all other pieces belong to the Nydam Ib period,[19] i.e. to the consecration of the pine vessel some time after AD 300. John Hines described the provenance of clasps of class B as a geographical belt reaching from the island of Öland in the east via Scania, to the islands of Zealand and Fyn, and further west to the neighbouring area of Jutland (1993, 87).

5.3.3 Caulking material
Structural context
Conrad Engelhardt observed woven caulking material during his excavations. For the oak ship (B) he stated (1865, 7):

> "*Mellem Plankerne, hvor de dække hinanden, er der tættet med uldent Tøj og en beget og klæbrig Masse*"
>
> ("Between the planks where they cover each other, [the boat] is sealed with woollen cloth and a pitch-like and sticky matter.")

Concerning the pine vessel (C), he wrote (1865, 12):

> "*Paa Undersiden er der Levninger af et tættende Stof af uldent, vævet Tøi og en klæbrig, beget Masse af samme udseende som den, der er brugt til Beviklingerne paa Pilskafter*"
>
> ("Underneath, there are patches of a sealing substance of woollen, woven cloth and a sticky, pitch-like matter which appears similar to that used for winding around arrow shafts.")

In the case of the pine vessel (C), Engelhardt had its repairs in mind, whereas regarding the oak ship (B), he referred to the original planks. The pine boat – as far as it was excavated in the 19th century – was destroyed soon after its discovery, but some textile caulking material was preserved on recently found fragments of its planks (Rieck 1998, 285). The textiles presented above belong to the oak vessel (B) and the pine boat (C).[20] Some of them were pressed onto fragments of planks while others adhere to rounded wooden strips which were used for repairs.[21] When discussing the weaving types, it was mentioned that twill patches 5785 and 10510 may derive from one cloth as possibly do the coarser twill fragments 5902 and 5925. It may now be added that the first two pieces were found on the original planks while the latter two belong to the repairs. Thus the correlation based on textile characteristics is in accordance with the structural context.

Functional context
The discussion of the technical aspects demonstrated that a variety of fabrics was used, which holds true for the textiles between the original planks as well as for those used as repairs. Apparently, no special type of fabric was produced for caulking but only reused material was employed for this purpose. When focusing on the planks with original caulking, it appears that diamond twills as well as twills in z/s are rare, although no functional reason for this seems to be apparent. Possible explanations are discussed below. As far as the repairs are concerned, the situation is almost identical. The thread count could only be determined for three pieces, but it is clearly lower than the average in the textile material from the original planks. Furthermore, another difference between planks and repairs has to be stated: While on the planks the threads of the cloth are usually orientated parallel to the edges of the wood, often, they run more obliquely on the repair strips. Perhaps one was more careful when building the boat than when repairing it subsequently.

Chronological context and origin of the Nydam boat
The oak of vessel B not only provided information about the age of the boat but also about its possible provenance. Its wood was dated to AD 310–320 (Rieck 1998, 274). The region of origin may be described as Schleswig-Holstein, Denmark and Scania (Rieck 2003, 307). No information on the origin of the pine boat (C) and its repairs is provided.

5.3.4 Others
During recent excavations, faint impressions of seemingly fine textiles were observed in the ground on four spots (3223, 5240, 6940, 8792; Rieck, unpubl.). They could not be saved and no technical details are reported. However, their existence is yet another proof of the extensive use of textiles in the ceremony.

The textiles recovered with the wooden head (2860) were not embedded in any sticky substance as the caulking material was. It is easy to imagine that the figure was wrapped in this fine fabric, particularly since no other item seems to have been in contact with this piece when it was discovered. The head is one of three such finds which were in use on the Nydam boat, i.e. vessel B (Rieck 2003, 307). The other loose textile finds (3264, præp. 3404) do not offer any information apart from the technical aspects. The latter, however, place them clearly amongst the other material.

Probably independent from the ritual in a strict sense was a fine textile that lay within a box (3701) but which could not be saved (Rieck, unpubl.). It may have constituted part of the personal belongings of the owner of the box and lay in the container already before the battle.

No technical information can be provided about a tiny fragment of textile once adhering to the pin of fibula 13794, found during the latest excavations. Of course, it might be the remnants of some clothing, possibly a cloak. Earlier, similar fibulae were excavated in the 19th century, seven of them near the bow of the oak boat, one within it (Bemmann and Bemmann 1998, vol. 1, 113). None of them form a pair, thus suggesting that they belonged to male clothing (ibid.). As a parallel to the clasps, it is tempting to propose their deposition in the vessel's bow during one and the same deposition but this may be problematic. Seemingly, the fibulae were used for a considerable length of time and are therefore dated rather to the end of the 4th century AD (ibid.). However, as stated above, the oak boat probably had been sacrificed already c. AD 340–350 (Rieck 1998, 274). Thus, the fibulae in Nydam may originate from a later stratum than the ships do (Rieck, unpubl.). Yet, their distribution or rather concentration emphasises the systematic deposition of certain finds in certain places. If the fibulae were attached to clothing this would be a direct parallel to the tunics. Regrettably, one tiny fragment of textile on merely one fibula cannot prove this. As far as the provenance of these finds are concerned, it may be added that this particular type of fibula may have been produced in northern Germany but that it is also well known from western Scandinavia (Bemmann and Bemmann 1998 vol. 1, 113). Andreas Rau (2008, 153) considers their origin to be in the area of Schleswig-Holstein and West-Mecklenburg.

5.4. COMPARISONS WITHIN THE NYDAM MATERIAL

After presenting and interpreting the textiles separately according to their functional background, these groups are now compared to each other. These comparisons are limited because of the low number of items within each group. Nevertheless, certain attributes may be highlighted.

5.4.1 Technical aspects of the textiles
Weaving types
Although it was impossible to determine all technical details for most of the finds, it is obvious that the majority of textiles were woven as 2/2 twills while only few tabbies are preserved. Comparing the largest group, the caulking material, with the rest, it appears that three varieties (1/1 z/z, 2/2 z/z and 2/2 z/s) occur in the caulking material as well as in the other contexts (see Fig.1.44). Diamond twills are very rare, with merely one example in z/z preserved with a plank and another loose fragment in z/s.

Yet, besides these similarities, there are differences. Plain twill in z/z is dominant in the caulking material. Outside this group, however, this variation was found only once, i.e. among the group called "others" but neither with weapons nor with clasps. Moreover, the spinning directions require closer scrutiny. In addition to the six z/z twills, the caulking material encompasses ten items with z-spun threads in at least one system, while no s-orientated material was determined within these ten patches. Yarns spun in s, on the other hand, were found only three times, twice as z/s twills and once as a probable tabby in s/s. Of the four weapons on which the spinning direction could be determined, two items possess s-spun material, the two others solely threads in z, i.e. the distribution is balanced. Within the group called "others", there are only two relevant examples, one with s-spun yarns, one without. On the clasps, however, the situation is different. Here, among fourteen relevant weaves, s-orientated material, mostly representing weaves in z/s, was observed in twelve instances, supplemented by two or three finds of spin patterning (all numbered as 7093) and one item of uncertain yarn combination. The last two fragments have z-spun material in one system while the other system could not be determined. In other words: within this group of fourteen find numbers, at the most two fabrics or perhaps none were woven in z/z. Possible reasons for this discrepancy between the caulking material and clasps are discussed below.

Textile quality
Spin patterning was found once in combination with a shield boss (6136) and once with clasps (7093). Indications of napping were observed once on the few weapons, on shield boss 3411. Neither on caulking material, nor with clasps, was any napping found, but this may be due to the different preservation conditions and the very small sizes respectively. Possible dyeing may be noted in several fragments on the clasps and on loose pieces (præp. 3404). Most of the fabrics used for caulking may be termed fine as are all of the other groups. Thus, except for the coarse twill made of plant material and used as caulking (5911), all observations indicate textiles of good to high quality.

5.4.2 Context and functions
Primary functions
The textile material found in connection with weapons does not provide direct information on its former use. Based only on comparisons, it was proposed above that the fabrics may represent clothing and if so, that they may rather belong to cloaks than to any tailored and sewn items. Weaving types, thread counts and – in one case – possible dyeing place the two well documented finds of the group called "others" in the immediate vicinity of weapons and clasps, but as with the weapons, there is no independent proof of the original function. The situation is much better, however, in the case of the clasps. Nothing speaks against an interpretation as clothing. Whether they originate from tunics or rather from trousers remains open to question.

Within the last group, the caulking material, its primary functions are again left to the realm of supposition. Theoretically, the textile quality in terms of thread count, weaving type, napping and dyeing is of little importance for caulking; only seams and other features of irregular thickness may possibly have been avoided. This is reflected in the high variability of thread counts as demonstrated in Figure 1.44. Nevertheless, the difference between cloth associated with original planks with 15.5 × 14 tpc on average and weaves connected with repairs with 11 × 10 tpc on average may be significant. Thus, on comparing the former number with the average tpc of the non-caulking material found in Nydam which is 16.5 × 13 tpc, the similarity is striking. It appears as if high quality textiles such as good clothing were preferred caulking materials when building the boat. A possible explanation may be that the boat builders aspired to a symmetry between the high value of the vessel on the whole and all its components. Such an ambition is – beyond functional reasons – reflected e.g. in beautiful carvings on the pine boat (e.g. Rieck 2003, 302, fig. 10).

The sacrifice
Well-preserved textiles are rare on the weapons. Yet, together with those faint traces observed on dozens of lanceheads and spearheads as well as on a few shield bosses, often on both sides, individual wrapping may well be postulated. The fabric found together with one of the wooden heads belonging to the oak vessel (B) too may be interpreted as wrapping. Ritual damaging seems to have occurred some time before the wrapping, as is suggested by some cuts on a shield boss.

In contrast to the weapons, the clothing represented by clasps and the tiny textile remnants preserved on them was seemingly not intended for wrapping. Instead, these pieces were apparently left intact and rolled up before their deposition. The reason may be the exceptional value of these items implied by the silver clasps.

Textiles used for wrapping as well as bundles of clothes should be regarded as deliberate and integral parts of the sacrifices. Only the caulking material was definitely not intended as an offering as such. Although the original functional background may be comparable – many fabrics are of good quality and may have belonged to high-quality clothing – these textiles were invisible and of no relevance to the sacrifice. It was the boat in its entirety as a valuable item that was of interest. Yet, since the vessels were rather warships than traders, even these caulking fabrics may well be regarded as textiles for war.

Origin of non-textile finds
Summing up the relevant information mentioned above, it follows that:

- the weapons at least of the Nydam Id period are thought to originate from northwest Germany;
- the clasps seem to originate from a geographical belt including Öland, Scania, Zealand, Fyn and the adjacent areas of Jutland;
- the oak boat was built in the region of Danmark, Schleswig-Holstein or possibly Scania;
- certain fibulae indicate northern Germany, particularly Schleswig-Holstein and western Mecklenburg, possibly western Scandinavia.

Comparing these data and provided that the non-textile finds do represent the home country of the warriors, they seem to have originated from the Schleswig-Holstein area or the neighbouring southernmost part of Jutland.

Chronological context
Recalling the information given above for the various find categories, the results are as follows: The oldest textiles may be those on the planks of the pine vessel (C). Since it is part of the sacrifice dated to Nydam Ib or some time after AD 300, the ship itself including its original caulking is probably slightly older. The clasps belong to the same sacrifice. The fabrics used as caulking material on the original planks of the oak boat which was built c. AD 320 are almost of the same age. They were sunk in the lake around AD 350 – Nydam Ic – together with the wooden head and its probable wrapping (2860). Of the same age or somewhat younger – Nydam Ic or Id – are the weapons found in pit VI, one of which was included in this examination (5372). Thus, all these finds may be regarded as material belonging to a period of c. 100 years. Chronologically, they may therefore be interpreted as a homogeneous group. Whether the other five weapons and the one assemblage of loose textiles (præp. 3404) belong to the same era, cannot be ascertained here.

Clasps vs. caulking material
Finally, the textiles found with the clasps are once again compared to those of the caulking material. The former are seemingly characterised by s-spun yarn, either as weaves in z/s or possibly in s/s or as spin-patterned fabrics. Amongst the weaves found with the vessels, on the other hand, s-spun yarn material is rare, with z-threads clearly prevailing. No chronological difference exists. Nor can any chorological contradictions be ascertained either. Provided that the difference in spin direction is not accidental, an explanation should be sought within the primary functions. Yet, the generally fine quality of the caulking material applied during the boat building (in contrast to later repairs) matches the notion of clothing as do the clasps. Thus there may be other inherent differentiations.

Firstly, tunics and trousers represented by valuable clasps should be considered as clothing which could not be afforded by everyone. Secondly, not being used for wrapping, they were deposited separately. And thirdly, they are likely to contain s-spun yarns. A similar observation was made amongst the Thorsberg material: tunic, trousers and several cloaks were woven in z/s, the cloaks primarily as plain twills, tunic and trousers as diamond twills. These items which are preserved as large pieces were laid down as consecrated pieces in their own right. Regrettably, nothing is known about textiles used for wrapping in Thorsberg. However, textiles woven in z/s instead of z/z and particularly woven as diamond twill were possibly connected to a certain high social stratum. Their scarcity amongst the caulking material may signify that the boat builders had only little access to such material. Another possibility is that they were not keen on re-using sewn clothing because of the seams and hems.

Notes

1. According to Ilkjær (2003, 46, fig. 2) however, the earliest deposit in Nydam occurred in period C2 which according to the list in *Sejrens Triumf* (inner back cover), began only around AD 250/260.
2. This tablet weave was not investigated by Lise Ræder Knudsen.
3. Iron pieces 1993 with their tablet weave (Ræder Knudsen, this volume) are not included here.
4. Currently, this material is being systematically studied by Andreas Rau, Schloss Gottorf, Schleswig, Germany.
5. The relevant difference between clinker building and carvel building in this context is that in the former, the planks overlap for several centimetres and the caulking material is laid between them while the vessel is built. In carvel tradition, the planks are set one against the other, with much less area of contact. The caulking material is pressed in later and then sealed with a strip of wood.
6. See discussion in Möller-Wiering 2001, 151–153.
7. Flemming Rieck, Vikingeskibsmuseet, Roskilde, Denmark, personal communication, January 2008.
8. Find number 3404 is the socket of a spear or lance. The textiles "præp. 3404", however, do not seem to originate from such a socket.
9. Andreas Rau, personal communication, April 2008.
10. Today, only four catalogue numbers can be assigned to this closed find: 1086, 1108, 1116 and 1126 (Bemmann and Bemmann 1998 vol. 1, 39).
11. Personal communication Karin Göbel, Schloss Gottorf, Schleswig, Germany, April 2008.
12. The few half-moon shaped items found separately northeast of the boats and seemingly belonging to a leather bag prove an exception. Andreas Rau, personal communication, March 2008.
13. Andreas Rau, personal communication, February 2008.
14. This task was mainly performed by Karin Göbel, Schloss Gottorf, Schleswig, Germany.
15. In the following description, the clasps of a leather bag found in the very north (section 3), as well as those of a bag belonging to the later closed find of Nydam IV (section 12), are disregarded. The discussion is based on the present author's own examinations, on lists provided by Andreas Rau and on the above mentioned maps produced by Karin Göbel. No clasps are known from the first excavations – seemingly due to the working procedures of the time. Andreas Rau, personal communication, February 2008.
16. Classification according to Andreas Rau, see footnote above.
17. On the corresponding site map, the items 4433 and 4434 are classified as belt fittings. Yet, in both cases, there is textile between hook and button.
18. The location of one find number (2214) in uncertain.
19. Andreas Rau, personal communication, February 2008.
20. Flemming Rieck, personal communication, January 2008.
21. Flemming Rieck, personal communication, October 2007 and March 2008.

6. GREMERSDORF-TECHELWITZ

The site of Gremersdorf-Techelwitz is situated further south than the large deposits of e.g. Illerup or Thorsberg, in the very east of Schleswig-Holstein, about 2.5 km away from the Baltic coast. The assemblage is very small, containing half a dozen metal finds, i.e. a shield boss, two lanceheads, two sockets and an arrowhead. The material which is stored at Schloss Gottorf, Schleswig, has been known since around 1900 but without the site being investigated. Its character as a weapon deposit is therefore likely but not verified (Bemmann and Bemmann 1998 vol. 1, 336). The probable dating is period C1.

On the shield boss (11392d), traces of textiles are preserved within a large area of the dome (Fig. 1.47), outside as well as inside, and on the outside of the flange. Regrettably, their preservation is not of sufficient quality to determine further details, and it is impossible to ascertain if the same fabric covered both sides. In comparison to the results from the sites discussed above, it seems highly likely that the shield boss was wrapped. Moreover, the patches on the inner side of the dome seem to indicate that either the wrapping was pressed against the metal by another boss or some textile was stuffed into the concave form. Provided that no other shield boss existed within this deposit, the latter explanation may be more reasonable.

As far as the other weapons are concerned, the situation is quite similar: traces of textiles can be found but their structure remains obscure. Some fibre material was observed on both sides of the arrowhead (11800c), the two lanceheads (11392c and 10763) and one of the sockets (10763h), once again suggesting individual wrapping. The same probably applies to the second socket (again 10763). Whether or not the entire assemblage was then made into a bigger package remains unknown.

Fig. 1.47. Gremersdorf-Techelwitz, shield boss 11392d

7. COMPARISONS

7.1. COMPARISON OF THE SITES

7.1.1 Technical aspects

Material

In the present investigation, no fibre analyses using high magnification were undertaken. Most of the textiles from Thorsberg have previously been examined by other scholars, particularly Karl Schlabow (1976) and Margrethe Hald (1980). They determined the fibres as sheep wool. Based on low magnification and the present author's experience, it may be claimed that, as far as the state of preservation allows for an evaluation, sheep wool was also used for the other textiles. This applies to the few textiles from Thorsberg, which were hitherto less well known to the public, as well as to the weaves from the other sites, apart for one seemingly vegetal exception. No indications of other animal hair, e.g. goat, were found, except perhaps for the warp in the tablet-woven section of 3689 from Thorsberg. As far as the other sites are concerned, the fibre determination is limited by mineralisation, loss, and certain conservation procedures. The wool quality varies, but is most often good, i.e. the fibres had been sorted out carefully and then spun with the same care. The vegetal exception was found in Nydam (5911), as caulking material. As such, it was better protected against external influences from the environment than most of the other fabrics. This does not necessarily mean, however, that plant fibres would generally speaking have been destroyed, since ropes made of vegetal materials demonstrate their ability to survive.

Weaving types and textile quality

In order to facilitate the comparison of the various weaves, the average thread counts were calculated according to type, site and – in case of Nydam – to function. The results for the tabby group are presented in Figure 1.48. Tabbies were found at all four sites, though as a minority amongst a larger amount of twills. Yet, if the "cloth bundle" found at Vimose is considered as one textile, the distribution is about half and half at this site.

Two groups are distinguishable in terms of the average thread counts: a fine one and a clearly coarser one. The group of fine tabbies encompasses material from Illerup, Vimose and Nydam – only Thorsberg did not yield any examples. They were used for wrapping weapons and as caulking material between original planks. All of them are woven in z/z.

The coarser group consists of four entries, representing only five fabrics. The finest of them, of medium fine quality according to Klaus Tidow's classification (2000, 108), is a piece of caulking material from the original planks of the Nydam boat and it is one of the rare tabbies in s/s. Among the other four items – all excavated in Thorsberg – there are two more examples in s/s. In this particular case, the average as marked in Fig. 1.48 and Table 1.2, is misleading since one of them possesses a thread count of 9.5 × 7 tpc which is medium fine and comparable to the fabric from Nydam, while the other was woven with only 4 × 4 tpc which is very coarse. The only tabby in z/s too is very coarse. Functionally, just one coarse tabby from Thorsberg can be determined: the leg wrap 3692, woven in z/z with an integral part of z/s.

Plain twills occur on all four sites and in four variations: z/z, z/s, s/s and spin patterned. As indicated in Figures 1.49 and 1.50, their average thread counts generally belong to the "fine" category, thus constituting a much more homogeneous group than the tabbies. One exception, a z/z twill of medium fine quality, comes from a repair on the Nydam ship. The other plain twills in z/z include original caulking material and possible wrapping from Nydam as well as weapon wrappings from Illerup and Vimose. On the latter site, the diagonal twill in z/z is the only twill variant preserved. In contrast, Thorsberg does not contribute to this group, as with the fine tabbies. On the other hand, a comparable fabric in s/s originates from Thorsberg. It is a unique find in relation to the material as a whole.

Diagonal twills in z/s were excavated in Illerup, Nydam and Thorsberg, with the latter providing the lowest average thread count. The entry for clasps from Nydam only represents one item, the size of which is so small that it might well derive from a diamond twill. Its high thread count of 20 × 15 tpc, which is clearly higher than the other numbers within this group, would accord well with this assumption (see below). The thread counts of spin-patterned twills recovered in Illerup and Thorsberg are of either almost very fine or very fine quality. Here, Thorsberg defines the upper end of the whole spectrum of diagonal twills.

As with most of the plain twills, the diamond twills belong to the "fine" category and often even to the higher section of this (Fig. 1.51). The group includes items from Illerup, Thorsberg (only z/s) and Nydam (only z/z). The averages lie quite close to each other, in the case of the variants in z/s from Thorsberg and Illerup, they are even identical. The two lowest thread counts in Fig. 1.51 belong to broken twills in which the breaks may probably be regarded as weaving mistakes. If they were considered as plain twills, their thread counts are in accordance with the other diagonal twills in z/z and z/s, respectively.

Countable pattern units were observed in Illerup and Thorsberg. In the Thorsberg material, the units were counted on seven find numbers. In five instances, the most common sets encompassed 10 threads in the warp and 9 in the weft. Once, 14/9 was found and once 10/13, irregularities disregarded. The pattern units within the textiles found in Illerup turned out to be highly variable (see Table 1.1). Yet, units of 10 threads in the probable warp were most common, and also 18 occurred rather often. In the probable weft, units of 9 were most popular, followed by 13. Thus, the most typical sizes of pattern units are identical in Thorsberg and in Illerup. On a slightly more general level, it may be stated for both sites that usually even numbers were chosen for the warp, and odd numbers for the weft. This suggests common traditions. Yet, while 10/9 was an apparently well-known and popular size of pattern unit, the deviations on single fabrics as well as within the entire corpus of material are too numerous to regard it as a clear standard.

In Table 1.2, the average thread counts are listed according to weaving type and site, and in the case of Nydam split according to functions. It might be unwise to go further into too much detail when interpreting this list. One reason is that the number of attestations per category is often small. Another reason is the different preservation conditions which may have influenced the structure of the textiles to some extent. Only few remarks are therefore made here. Disregarding the broken twills which are probably the result of weaving mistakes, most weaving types were found at more than one site, emphasising the general similarities which were already visible in Figures 1.48–1.51. Thorsberg is the site with the widest range of weaves. Moreover, it is the site with the lowest overall thread count. At first sight, this seems to be due to the very low thread counts of the tabbies which indeed play a major role in this respect. Yet, even when only the twills are taken into account, the

Table 1.2. All sites, average thread counts of all weaving types. Number of items given in parentheses

	Illerup	Vimose	Thorsberg	Nydam: weapons	Nydam: original planks	Nydam: repairs	Nydam: clasps + others
all	16 × 14 (88)	15.5 × 12 (9)	13 × 11.5 (26)	15 × 11.5 (2)	15.5 × 14 (10)	11 × 10 (3)	17.5 × 14 (3)
1/1 z/z	15.5 × 11 (12)	15.5 × 12 (5)	9 × 6 (1)	16 × 11 (1)	16 × 15 (3)		
1/1 s/s			7 × 5.5 (2)		11 × 7 (1)		
1/1 z/s			4 × 3.5 (1)				
2/2 z/z	17 × 14 (17)	15.5 × 12 (4)			15.5 × 13 (3)	11 × 10 (3)	18 × 15 (1)
2/2 s/s			16 × 16 (1)				
2/2 z/s	12.5 × 12.5 (9)		12.5 × 10.5 (11)	14 × 12 (1)	14.5 × 16 (2)		20 × 15 (1)
2/2 z/z broken (prob. mistake)			8 × 12 (1)				
2/2 z/s broken (prob. mistake)							14.5 × 12 (1)
2/2 z/z diam.	15 × 17.5 (8)				20 × 16 (1)		
2/2 z/s diam.	16.5 × 14 (35)		16.5 × 14 (8)				
2/2 spin patt.	17.5 × 15 (7)		21 × 16 (1)				

situation continues to be the same: Thorsberg 14 × 12.5, Vimose 15.5 × 12, Nydam 15 × 13 and Illerup 16 × 14.5. However, as mentioned above, such results should not be overrated.

Indications of napping were found on fabrics from all four sites and on all types of weaves, except for tabby in z/s, of which only one item was discovered.[1] It must be reiterated that it does not only occur on common plain twills but also on diamond twills and on the finest spin-patterned fabrics. This phenomenon was observed on textiles from Illerup and Thorsberg, i.e. from two sites with very different conditions in terms of preservation.

Edges
Since the material from Thorsberg contained a large amount of well-preserved tablet borders, this type of edge was already discussed above. The borders revealed information about different methods of warping and, obviously, of weaving. Some must be regarded as primary borders in the sense that they were an integral part of the weaving process. Others were woven onto the edges later, after weaving the cloth. Apart from Thorsberg, tablet weaves were found on several weapons from Illerup and Nydam. They are discussed in detail by Lise Ræder Knudsen (this volume).

Tubular edges were recorded on textiles from Thorsberg and Illerup Ådal. At Illerup, all tubular edges were encountered along diamond twills in z/s. At Thorsberg, they occur in combination with plain twills in z/s. Yet, tubular edges possess less information on textile production than the tablet-woven borders. In Early Iron Age material from Denmark, tubular edges were preserved on fabrics woven on warp-weighted looms as well as on looms with tubular warping, on tabbies and on 2/2 twills (Ciszuk forthcoming).

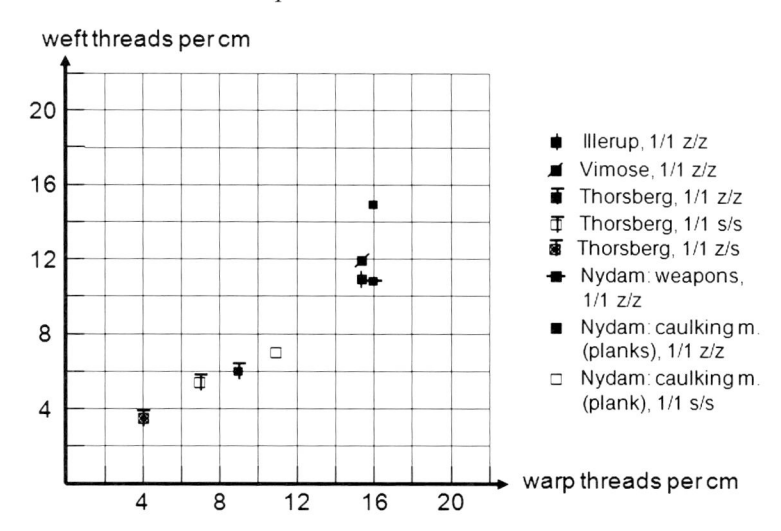

Fig. 1.48. All sites, average thread counts of tabbies

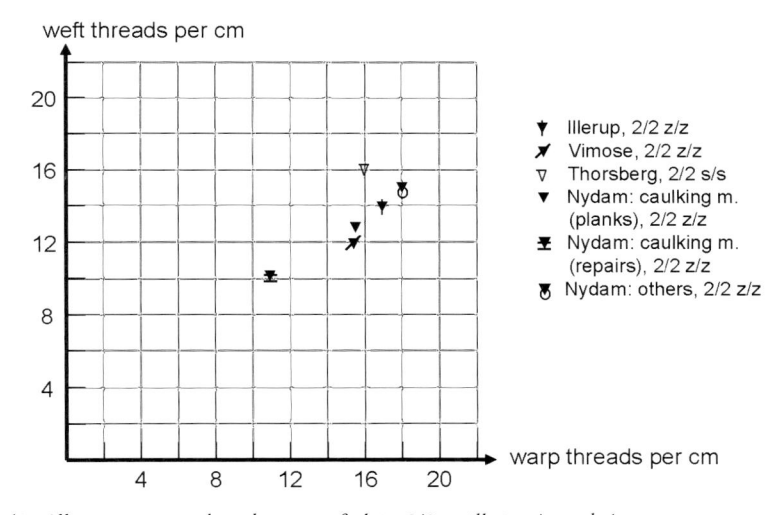

Fig. 1.49. All sites, average thread counts of plain 2/2 twills in z/z and s/s

7.1.2 Context and functions
Primary functions
For a comparison of the primary functions, Thorsberg may be taken as a point of departure since items of unambiguous function such as a tunic, trousers and cloaks were excavated there. In addition, the similarities among the sites in terms of weaves and quality including napping should be recalled. This signifies that on a general level, the vast majority of textiles from all sites may ultimately have derived from clothing.

Besides the weaving type and quality, the tunic as well as the trousers found in Thorsberg are characterised by many seams, tablet-woven borders of only very limited width and without fringes, red

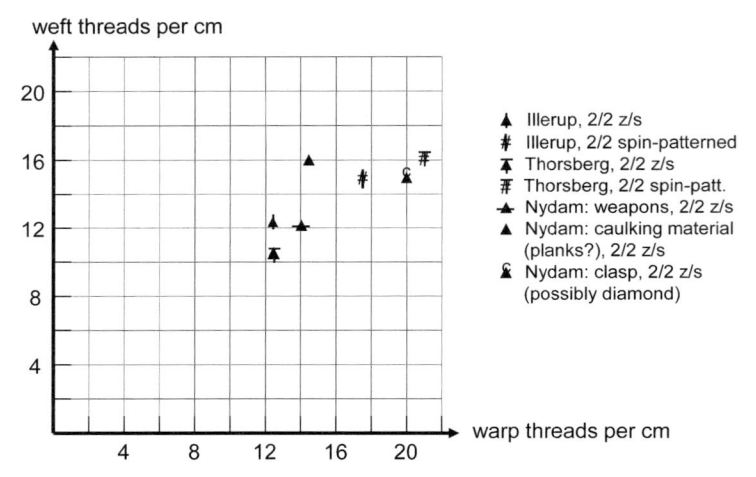

Fig. 1.50. All sites, average thread counts of plain 2/2 twills in z/s and spin patterned

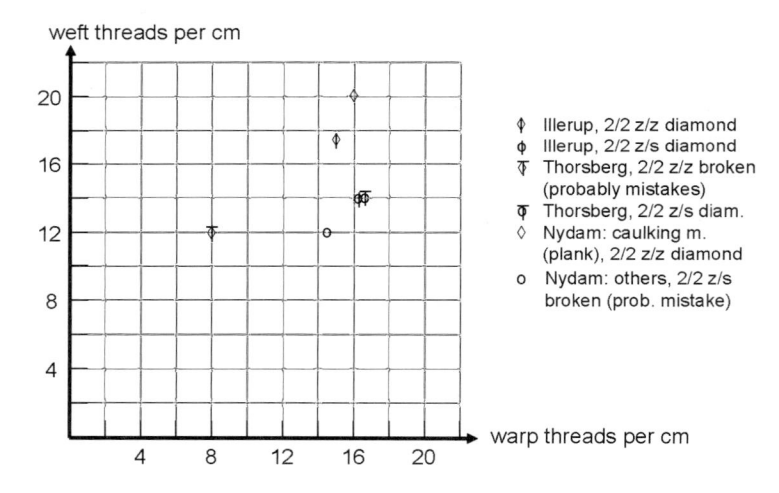

Fig. 1.51. All sites, average thread counts of broken and diamond twills in z/z and z/s

dye, and decorative additions. Based on these criteria, possible parallels within the Thorsberg material were discussed above. Clasps as decorative additions were found in Nydam. They are combined with high-quality fabrics and – at least sometimes – red dye, and there is almost no doubt that they derive from tunics and/or trousers. Inconspicuous belt buckles from Illerup – as an addition to trousers – match very well with the upper edges of both pairs of trousers from Thorsberg and confirm the iconographic evidence of the trousers having being worn under the tunics.

The absence of seams and other features typical of tailoring constitutes one general aspect of the materials from Illerup Ådal, Nydam and Vimose. On the other hand, broader tablet weaves and sometimes fringes similar to those from the cloaks from Thorsberg were observed on the material from these sites. Indications of large-sized cloths come from Vimose, Nydam and obviously Thorsberg.

Unsurprisingly, the large, flat cloaks provided an ideal source of wrapping material and it may well be that such pieces of clothing were preferred for this purpose.

Finally, other primary functions that may be of importance need to be discussed briefly. As indicated in the sections on the sacrifices, the textiles may be ascribed to the defeated warriors. Regrettably, very little is known about the equipment of a Germanic army besides their weapons and personal belongings. A few possible needs may have been blankets, tents and materials for transport such as sacks, bags and tarpaulins on the ships. As far as blankets are concerned, the cloaks may well have served as such. For covering the other needs – as far as they were relevant at all – leather may have been a suitable option. Instead of leather, robust cloth could have been used. It is not impossible to imagine bags made of e.g. plain twill with 12 × 10 tpc, particularly small ones for personal belongings. Otherwise, one might expect less fine, but tightly woven fabrics, using less well-prepared fibres.

From all four large sites, only seven items are recorded with less than 10 tpc both in warp and weft. The only twill within this group, MYP from Illerup Ådal, seems to have loosened over time as a secondary effect. YSW from Illerup is a tabby in z/z. No observations can be made about the fibres; but the weave is quite dense. The only example from Nydam, 5911, must be disregarded in this context since it belongs to the caulking materials. Four relevant tabbies come from Thorsberg. One of them, 3692 (z/z with a strip of z/s), is commonly regarded as a leg wrap. The fibres of 3694 (s/s) resemble Bronze Age material and the structure of the weave is loose. The investigation of 1232a (z/s) was restricted to the examination of photographs, thus nothing is known of the fibres, but the weave might be called rather tight. The same is true in the case of 24824c (s/s), combined with a carelessly accomplished fibre preparation. Thus only three finds match the hypothetical criteria for e.g. a sack. However, leg wrap 3692, the quality of which would fit into this group, demonstrates that even such simple fabrics could be used for clothing.

The sacrifice

Information on the use of textiles during the sacrifice subsequent to the battle was gained from all sites. On a general level, one can primarily distinguish between fabrics used for wrapping and pieces of clothing that apparently played a different role during the rituals.

More or less completely intact items of clothing are a characteristic feature of the Thorsberg material: a tunic, two pairs of trousers, two leg wraps and several cloaks. Some of them were excavated rolled up and nothing seems to have been found within these rolled up bundles. Their significance during the rituals is thus comparable to that of the weapons. It is not impossible that these pieces themselves were originally wrapped. The identical procedure was most probably followed in Nydam, which is represented by the fibres and fabrics found on top and underneath the clasps which derive from tunics and/or trousers. It is not surprising that comparable material is missing in Illerup Ådal and Vimose, since the conditions for preserving wool were poor there and no clasps were found within these complexes since they are older than that of Nydam. The sacrifice of entire items of clothing and possibly even complete sets of clothing accords well with the non-textile finds, among which complete sets of the warriors' equipment can be distinguished. In this context, it may be recalled that rope too was sacrificed, that entire bundles of rope were discovered in Illerup Ådal and probably in Thorsberg.

On the other hand, more cloaks were apparently recovered in Thorsberg than tunics, trousers, leg wraps and shoes. Moreover, the size of their preserved remnants is highly variable. Based on these observations, it may be assumed that cloaks fulfilled two functions within the rituals. While at least one piece was laid down as such, others may have been used for wrapping. The large, rectangular cloths were ideal for the latter purpose, both for binding large bundles and for being cut into smaller pieces for separate, individual wrappings. Assuming that rather broad and thus decorative tablet weaves are a characteristic feature of cloaks, the use of such mantles for wrapping may also be stated for Illerup Ådal and Vimose. When, additionally, the considerable size of a cloth is also interpreted as an indication of a cloak, Nydam and again Vimose may be included.

The wrapping of weapons is the most common feature of the entire material. It was observed in Illerup Ådal, Vimose, Nydam and Gremersdorf-Techelwitz. Sometimes, a few weapons, particularly points, were bound together either with e.g. grassy material or with textile. In many cases, though, it was possible to demonstrate that each weapon – no matter whether shield boss, lancehead, axe or anything else – was wrapped individually. In the case of Vimose, the weapons of the so-called cloth bundle were wrapped with extreme accuracy while in Illerup, the orientation of the threads does not correspond to the orientation of the long axes of e.g. swords or lanceheads, but is highly variable.

Microstrata in the sense of metal with two or more superposed layers of fabrics were found in Illerup Ådal, Vimose and Nydam. Often, the layers are of the same fabric, and sometimes it is apparent that the cloth was laid double before wrapping. In other cases, different weaves were found on one weapon. It seems possible, therefore, that several, individually wrapped items were then packed together into larger bundles. One example from Illerup, however, demonstrates that the combination of different fabrics does not always corroborate this hypothesis. Yet, fragments of ropes which are known from all large sites, seem to support the idea of larger bundles. Finally, it should be noted that no correlation between certain metal items and certain weaves was found.

The ritual damage of the weapons which was found on the materials from all large sites,[2] has been discussed ever since Conrad Engelhardt (1865, 25). Recently, Marcin Biborski and Jørgen Ilkjær (2006a, 343) summarised this topic, postulating that the ritual was meant as "killing the weapon". The well-known cuts in the Thorsberg tunic, however, were disregarded in their discussion. Focusing on this site, Inga Hägg (2000, 28) identified the officers and their dress as the principal target of the act of ritual damaging. The present examination of all the textiles demonstrates that such damage is also a common feature on weaves, observable again on the textile material from all four sites. Thus the idea behind the ritual – the reason for the damage – was not restricted to weapons. On the other hand, personal belongings such as jewellery or combs were hardly affected. Possibly, the theory of "killing the weapon" may be extended to "killing the enemy".

This may well have taken place during some kind of rage as is described in ancient texts (see Chapter 1). Whether it occurred shortly after the battle and in the neighbourhood of the battlefield or at some spatial and/or chronological distance, cannot be confirmed. However, it is unequivocal that a certain time span must have passed between the damaging and the deposition in the bog. The deposition was well prepared which becomes evident e.g. in the fact that the materials were not cast in randomly. Moreover, some time was needed for preparation if the sacrifice was intended as a ceremony e.g. including the entire community. Finally, and most importantly, the textiles prove this. Unquestionably, the meticulous wrapping of up to thousands of weapons needed time. Whether this was done by the warriors themselves or possibly by their women, is left to speculation.

The conclusions above demonstrate that many aspects of the textile materials as well as of the rituals and depositions were met on two or more sites. These results are listed in Table 1.3. In combination with Table 1.2, they confirm two main conclusions:

7. Comparisons

Table 1.3. All sites, features characterising the sacrifice

	Illerup Ådal	Vimose	Thorsberg	Nydam
Textiles of high quality	x	x	x	x
Textiles of low quality			x	x
Decorative tablet borders	x	x	x	
Large size of cloths		x	x	x
Whole pieces of textiles rolled up			x	x
Wrapped weapons	x	x		x
Two or more weapons in bundles		x		x
Individual wrapping	x	x		x
Possible wrapping of larger units	x	x		?
Ritual damages on textiles	x	x	x	x
Ritual damages on weapons	x	x	x	x
Fragments of ropes, possibly indicating larger units	x	x	x	x
Complete bundles of ropes	x		x	x

Firstly, there are no general differences between the sites in terms of weaving techniques and qualities. Thorsberg contained a somewhat larger variety of weaves and thread counts while plain twills in z/z are missing. However, the similarities outweigh the differences. Only the tablet-woven borders with a securing outermost thread may be worthy of note as a possible peculiarity of the Thorsberg material.

Secondly, the various items of information on what had happened after the battles, reoccur from site to site. They demonstrate that in connection with battle and war, certain practices were known and cultivated at least from Illerup in the north down to Thorsberg in the south.

Chronological context

The vast majority of textiles may be ascribed to the period C1b with a time span over the decades from c. AD 200 to 260. Only some Nydam material may be younger, dating to the early 4th century. Therefore, the similarities between the sites correspond to their chronological uniformity. One may speculate, however, whether the slightly higher overall thread count found in the Nydam material – when disregarding the repairs in the boat – may be due to some development or perhaps rather increased experience in weaving, although there are no indications of a change in weaving equipment.

7.2. COMPARISONS WITH OTHER MATERIAL

A thorough comparison of the various aspects discussed above would constitute a project of its own. Yet, it is necessary to set the materials characterising the weapon deposits into a wider framework. This frame is extended to the south – to Germany and even to the Mediterranean – rather than to the north. The reason for this is the question of whether the textile materials might be of Roman origin. Weapons, particularly swords, and other items crafted in the Roman Empire were recovered from all large deposits.[3] Moreover, as described above, the warriors whose belongings ended up in the bogs of Thorsberg and Vimose are thought to have come rather from the south than from the north. Therefore, it is no surprise that a Roman provenance was also claimed for some of the textile finds, as is presented below.

Technical aspects

Wool as the typical material in the weapon deposits is too commonly encountered all over Europe and even the eastern Mediterranean to be a suitable means of comparison or differentiation.

At Illerup Ådal, two combinations of spinning direction are very common: z/z and z/s, supplemented by a few spin-patterned pieces, while s/s is missing. The only combination observed at Vimose is z/z. In Thorsberg, z/s clearly prevails, while z/z was found only twice as was s/s. Spin patterning occurred three times. Finally, in Nydam, there is more z/z than z/s, with spin patterning and possibly s/s each found once. All in all, z/z and z/s are numerous while s/s and spin patterning are very rare. Apart from the weapon deposits, the prevailing spinning direction in Europe of the time is z/z, with z/s occurring mostly in some twills. This applies to Scandinavia and the Barbaricum as well as to the northwestern Roman provinces, France and Italy (Schlabow 1976; Hald 1980; Bender Jørgensen 1986a and 1992; Desrosiers and Lorquin 1998; Wild 2002). The s/s combination is common in Spain and in the eastern Mediterranean (e.g. Bender Jørgensen 1992, 30, 107; Wild 2002, 30; Shamir 2006).

Considering the weaves, various scholars have demonstrated that tabby and its extended versions, i.e. half basket and basket weave, were more common in the Mediterranean area than further north. Particularly half basket weave is regarded as Roman influenced (Wild 2002, 20) but this type is completely absent in the materials from the weapon deposits. In central and northern Europe including Great Britain, twill is more often found than tabby (Bender Jørgensen 1986a, 1992; Wild 2002, 15), which is also true for the weapon deposits. In these areas, the weaves are generally rather well balanced, while in the Mediterranean, the textiles are often characterised by an unbalanced thread count resulting in a weft-dominated surface.

Some further technical aspects are reconsidered in context with the tunics, trousers and cloaks, e.g. the question of tablet-woven edges which is also discussed by Lise Ræder Knudsen (this volume).

Tunics

On a general level, including iconographical sources, a large number of tunics can be compared with the Thorsberg find. Therefore, the following define the criteria on which the comparisons may be based:

- material, i.e. wool,
- weave, i.e. diamond twill,
- tablet-woven starting border,
- selvedge reinforced using a bundle of threads,
- "Thorsberg seams",
- direction of warp and weft in the dress, i.e. the warp running perpendicularly,
- dyed red,
- decorated seams and hems,
- otherwise unpatterned,
- almost straight, horizontal neck opening,
- attached sleeves,
- hole on the left shoulder.

Sizes and proportions will not be considered in detail. As indicated above, some textile material from Nydam may be regarded as originating from tunics – or trousers – as suggested by clasps and fabrics comparable to the Thorsberg example. Similar weaves were also found in Illerup as well as among the fragments excavated in Thorsberg, but other features supporting the interpretation as tunics are mostly lacking in this context.

It may be reasonable to begin the wider comparisons with other north German bog finds. Among the tunics that were presented by Karl Schlabow in 1976, two are ^{14}C dated. The chronologically closest is the one from Obenaltendorf in Lower Saxony, dated AD 260–380 (van der Plicht et al. 2004, 483). Parallels to Thorsberg are the use of wool, the perpendicular warp and the simple, straight neck opening (Möller-Wiering 2007, 249–250, 255–260). All other features of this sleeveless shirt, however, differ from the Thorsberg tunic, including a few indications that it was made from a cloak of Roman – possibly Italian – origin. Amongst the latter is a type of selvedge resembling Thorsberg in terms of bundles of yarn used as reinforcement, but here, this feature is doubled, i.e. the two outermost warp ends are enlarged this way. Another sleeveless shirt, found in Marx-Etzel, Lower Saxony, is dated to AD 45–125 (van der Plicht et al. 2004, 483). Following Hans Hahne (1919, 11–23) and Karl Schlabow's (1976, 72 and Abb. 146–148) descriptions, the similarities comprise the material, the perpendicular warp, the unpatterned cloth and the straight neck opening. The "Thorsberg seams" constitute another common feature, according to Johanna Mestorf (1907, 48), who found them in various pieces of clothing, not only in examples from Germany but also from Denmark. It may be added here that, according to Graham Sumner (2002, 4; 2003, 5–6), rectangular, sleeveless tunics were a typical item of dress in the Roman Empire before sleeved variants became popular, at the latest in the 3rd century AD.[4]

Highly remarkable is a third comparable example, the tunic from Reepsholt, Lower Saxony. This item was repeatedly described, particularly by Hanns Potratz (1942), Irmingard Fuhrmann (1941–42) and Karl Schlabow (1976, 73–76).[5] No ^{14}C dating was undertaken but an origin in the Roman Iron Age seems reasonable.[6] The material is wool, of different colours – though possibly undyed, woven in plain twill. Its long sleeves are not attached but are an integral part of the cross-shaped weave. Narrow, tablet-woven starting borders are present along one side of the body (and certainly originally around the opening of one sleeve), resulting in a warp running across the finished dress. According to a drawing reproduced by Fuhrmann (ibid., 352, Abb. 10), in contrast to the Thorsberg tunic, no securing thread accompanying the tablet border was used here. Instead, the loops of the main weave's warp turn from one shed to the next in the tablet band, while in every second shed, the threads cross each other.[7] The finishing edges were hemmed and cut. The selvedges were reinforced with a bundle of thread. Both sides of the tunic were sewn right down to the bottom with the so-called "Thorsberg seam". Red bands of only 2 mm width woven with tablets were added along the straight opening for the neck and the arms.

Margrethe Hald (1980, 338) and Frances Pritchard (2006, 46–49) describe cross-shaped, but tabby-woven tunics from Egypt where they represented the most common or even only sleeved variant. Typically, they were ornamented with clavi and orbiculi. Clavi are stripes woven into the fabric and running perpendicularly across the shoulders. Orbiculi are coloured patches on the shoulders and near the bottom of the tunic, again woven into the cloth. They became popular around AD 300 (Croom 2002, 34). Besides these ornaments, decorated edges were also attested.

From Palmyra in Syria, Annemarie Stauffer (2000, 29, 34–35) mentioned cruciform tunics in tabby as well as decorations like in Egypt. Her survey of seams observed at this site does not include the "Thorsberg seam". Wool as well as linen was used. The textiles from Palmyra date to the 1st and 2nd century AD (Schmidt-Colinet 2000, 2). Within the materials from Dura Europos in eastern

Syria which was deserted in AD 273, the wool tunics were again cross-shaped, but the ornaments on the mostly white clothes were restricted to clavi and decorated edges. Selvedges along the horizontal neck aperture could be reinforced with three cords (Pfister and Bellinger 1945, 13–15, 17–19).

This does not signify, however, that only cruciform tunics existed in the eastern Mediterranean area. Older variations from Egypt presented by Margrethe Hald are rectangular in shape with a perpendicular warp and colourfully trimmed edges but with a vertical neck opening and without sleeves. The weave is linen tabby. Examples are dated to 1250 BC and to Roman times (1946, 53–54, 61–66). Later, this tradition seems to have survived besides the cruciform tunic as is suggested by an item from Halabiyah in Syria, a city which was destroyed in AD 610 (Nockert 1991, 118–119). It is a child's linen tunic with a rounded neck opening and gussets in the sides, but principally shaped as a rectangle with perpendicular warp and short, inserted sleeves.

Tunics with attached sleeves and colourfully trimmed edges and seams are attested from inner Asia. The burials of Pazyryk in the Altai Mountains in Siberia, Russia, dated to the 5th century BC are well known. Sergei Rudenko (1970, 83–84) presented a tunic from a man's grave, woven from plant fibre in tabby, with a horizontal opening for the head. Its body consists of four pieces, two constituting the front, the other two the back. Gussets inserted from the bottom widen the lower part. Various red braids and cords follow the seams and hems. Fragments of a very similar tunic were found along with the first one. Another example from the Pazyryk culture, dated to before c. 200 BC, is a yellow silk tunic discovered in a grave on the Ukok plateau (Polosmak 1998, 127, 140–142). It is the burial of a woman but the shape of the tunic is described as being identical for both sexes. In this case, the main part was sewn together from two pieces of cloth, again with gussets at the bottom,[8] and the edges and seams are decorated with red braids and cords which, according to N. V. Polosmak, may have had a protective symbolic meaning. Southwest of Pazyryk, Shanpula in the Tarim Basin yielded a large amount of textiles which are chronologically closer to Thorsberg, dated between the 3rd century BC and the 4th century AD (Bunker 2001, 15). One type of woollen tunic (Wang and Xiao 2001, 66–67) is made from one piece of cloth folded on the shoulders as in Thorsberg but with gussets inserted from the bottom and with a collar added to the horizontal neck opening. One item described in detail is made of "cream-colored" tabby and possesses red bands and braids stitched to the seams, hems and down the middle of the front. The other type is made without gussets, sometimes with slits in the sides. A light yellow example of this group is decorated with bands in yellow and blue.

As another comparison of a rectangular tunic with inserted sleeves, the long garment of a woman buried c. AD 180 in Les Martres-de-Veyre, France deserves mention (Hald 1980, 338–339; Desrosiers and Lorquin 1998, 62; van Driel-Murray 1999, 11). Yet, the warp in this half basket weave runs horizontally in a similar way to the cross-shaped dresses. From a Roman cemetery at Lankhills in England, two probably linen tabby fragments and one piece of fine woollen twill were interpreted by Elisabeth Crowfoot as probable tunics (1979, 329–330).

Among the examples younger than the Thorsberg finds, the tunic from a male grave excavated at Högom in Sweden is the first to be included here. The burial was dated "to c. 500 or slightly earlier" (Nockert 1991, 8, 13–20, 32–33). The weave is a diagonal 2/2 twill in z/z, with a thread count of generally 19–24 × 17–20 tpc, and the warp running perpendicularly as in Thorsberg. Selvedges are characterised by bundles of yarn. Yet, according to Margareta Nockert's reconstruction, the dress pattern is quite different because those pieces making up the sleeves also contribute to the body part of the tunic, resulting in seams on the breast and on the back. Another consequence of this pattern is apparently a different shape of the neck opening which, regrettably, is not preserved. If it were a simple horizontal aperture, it would be too narrow. Therefore, Nockert suggested a construction based on two layers of cloth. Another possibility might be a vertical slit, either in the middle or a little to the left, but Nockert rejected this idea as no means of fastening was found. Along the bottom line as well as around the sleeve openings, tablet-woven bands of up to 6 cm width are added. The bands are not only multicoloured but display figurative motifs. Furthermore, large clasps were used both at the slits in the sides and on the cuffs.

A roundish neck opening with a collar and an asymmetrical, vertical slit was used in the tunic from Bernuthsfeld in Lower Saxony (Hahne 1919, 51–52; Schlabow 1976, 72–73; Farke 1998). The long sleeves are attached to a rectangular body. The latter, however, does not have a ground weave but consists of more than 40 woollen patches of various weaving types and qualities, but all woven in z/s. A chequered patch decorates the breast. The selvedge of at least one piece possesses one bundle of warp threads as reinforcement (Farke 1998, 102, Abb. 4). The ^{14}C dating for the Bernuthsfeld assemblage is 1290 ± 45, i.e. the 7th century AD (van der Sanden 1996, 192). Based on microstratigraphical analyses, two tunics were identified in male graves from Liebenau, Lower Saxony (Möller-Wiering 2005, 60, 69). Both were made of wool and designed in z/s. For the first one, a coarse, plain twill was used, for the other one a medium fine diamond twill. The datings are the 2nd half of the 6th century AD and the end of the 6th or first half of the 7th century AD, respectively.

Finally, the red colour of the Thorsberg tunic is briefly discussed here. Reddish textiles were also found around some clasps in Nydam and as loose fragments in Illerup Ådal. Inga Hägg (2000, 28) reported on Roman written evidence indicating that foreigners in the Roman army could be awarded a decoration in the form of a red tunic, a "tunica rossa". She therefore considered the Thorsberg item as a possible example of such a gift. According to Graham Sumner who had examined various sources from Roman times, literature as well as iconography, the "overwhelming impression" is that soldiers usually wore white tunics up to the end of the 3rd century AD when red became more common (2003, 39–40). Sumner considered red as the typical colour within the military milieu because it corresponded to Mars, the god of war. As a possible example, he reported on the dress of, as it was believed, St. Gereon who was a soldier and was buried in the beginning of the 4th century AD in Cologne, Germany (ibid., 34). When the sarcophagus was opened in the 12th century, the corpse was dressed in a white under tunic and a red over tunic. Based on archaeological and iconographical sources from Egypt – particularly mummy portraits – Frances Pritchard (2006, 49) ascribed colourful tunics to women and white ones to the men. These people were, however, civilians.

The results achieved thus far are collated in Table 1.4. In some cases, only one particular find is described, so the information is very specific. Other entries, such as "Palmyra", refer to more than one piece and only an overall picture based on the above-mentioned sources can be given. An "x" denotes the existence of a particular feature, a hyphen, the statement of a different variation. In many cases, however, information is lacking. The use of wool is so common that only closer examination, possibly including isotope analyses, might provide further information. Among the finds from northern Germany and Högom in Sweden, twill clearly prevails, albeit in different variations. As for the absence of twill in the Mediterranean area, it must be kept in mind that particularly for Egypt, only few sources were taken into account. For the majority of more or less intact tunics, decorations

Table 1.4. Characteristic features of tunics compared to Thorsberg. Entries in the same order as in the text

	wool	2/2 twill	tablet-woven starting border	selvedge with 1 yarn bundle	Thorsberg seams	warp perpendicular	dyed red	decorated seams/hems	otherwise unpatterned	horizontal neck opening	inserted sleeves	dating
Thorsberg	x	z/s diam	securing thread	x	x	x	x	x	x	x	x	2nd cent. AD–c. AD 300
Nydam	x	z/s					x	x				early 4th cent. AD
Obenaltendorf	x	-	-	-	-	(x)	-	-	-	x	-	3rd–4th cent. AD
Marx-Etzel	x	z/s plain	-	-	x	x	-	-	x	x	-	1st–2nd cent. AD
Reepsholt	x	z/z+s plain	no securing thread	-	x	-	-	x	-	x	-	Roman Iron Age
Egypt	x, -	-					x, -	x	-		-	AD 300 ff
Palmyra	x, -	-				-	-	x	-			1st/2nd cent. AD
Dura Europos	x	-	-	-		-	-	x	-	x	-	before AD 273
Egypt	-	-	-			x		x	x	-	-	1250 BC, Roman
Halabiyah	-					x				-	x	before AD 610
Pazyryk	-	-					x	x	x		x	5th cent. BC
Ukok	-	-					-	x		-	x	before c. 200 BC
Shanpula	x	-					-	x	x	(x)	x	3rd cent. BC–4th cent. AD
Les Martres-de-Veyre	x	-				-	-	-	-	x	x	AD 180
Lankhills	-	-										Roman Iron Age
Lankhills	x	x										Roman Iron Age
Högom	x	z/z plain				x	-	x	x	-	(x)	c. AD 500
Bernuthsfeld	x	(x)	-	x	-	-	-	-	-		x	c. AD 660
Liebenau	x	z/s plain										2nd half 6th cent. AD
Liebenau	x	z/s diam										c. AD 600–650
Köln							x, -					early 4th cent. AD

along seams and/or hems are a common feature. The type of decoration differs – e.g. tablet-woven bands, clasps or braids – but the idea is apparently very similar while patterns on the plain cloth like clavi and orbiculi have quite a different visual effect. Tunics with inserted sleeves originate from inner Asia, from a younger stratum in Syria (Halabiyah) and from Gaul. Moreover, attached sleeves are typical of caftans, i.e. jackets or coats open at the front. This type of dress, however, is not considered here any further and it may suffice to mention the essays by Elfriede Knauer (1985, 607–662) and Geo Widengren (1956, 237) who described caftans as a typical garment of peoples in the Middle East and inner Asia, i.e. of those used to riding.[9] The other features of the Thorsberg tunic can be found here and there, without any obvious pattern. Only the trimmed hole of the

Thorsberg tunic seems to be unique which may indicate that this is not a functional feature. This last issue is addressed again in the section about settlements.

Trousers

Trousers are well documented for many non-Mediterranean peoples. Celts as well as Germanic men wore trousers and so did the peoples of the Asian steppes as well as those of Iran and neighbouring regions (e.g. Widengren 1956). During the Roman Iron Age, i.e. the 3rd century AD, they also became part of the clothing of Roman soldiers (Sumner 2003, 5). When seeking comparisons for the Thorsberg trousers, it is again the specific features that are in focus and that constitute the defining criteria, i.e. the basic product – the weave, the integrated stockings and the slim shape, but other variations also have to be taken into account. As far as the textiles from the other weapon deposits are concerned, the relevant results were recalled in connection with the tunics (see above).

According to Inga Hägg (2000, 29), the cloth of the Thorsberg trousers – if not the whole item – should be of Roman origin because of the extremely fine diamond twill, with parallels found in Syria. Regarding the weave as such, the current investigation has added other parallels, particularly from Illerup Ådal which are very close to the Thorsberg material. On the other hand, diamond twills are very rare in Palmyra (Stauffer 2000, 23) as well as in Dura Europos (Pfister and Bellinger 1945, 22), the most important sites for comparison in Syria. In Palmyra, trousers are made of wool and possibly cashmere, they are much finer, with 23×54 to 26×106 tpc (Stauffer and Schmidt-Colinet 2000, 135), and they possess a quite different visual effect because of the dominating weft. The latter is also true for the only example from Dura Europos which is also made of wool but with a thread count of 14×36 tpc, i.e. closer to the Thorsberg pieces but still dominated by the weft. Similar tissues were further encountered e.g. among the textile materials from the late Roman fort at Abū Shaʿār in Egypt (Bender Jørgensen 2006, 169–170) where their percentage is a little higher than in Syria. Their thread count is not given but they are described as somewhat coarser than the items from Palmyra and with an almost invisible warp. Also very fine, but more balanced, and therefore, more similar to the Thorsberg trousers is the garment of a princess dated to the 5th to 8th century AD from Cologne, Germany, constituting of a very fine diamond twill in z/s with 32×24 tpc (Bender Jørgensen 1985, 85–86). These figures may indicate different traditions in weaving diamond twill in the eastern Mediterranean and in central Europe in a wider sense.

Seeking contemporary, regionally close items of which function and weave is known, the most promising group of textiles are again those found in the bogs. Yet, only two items consist of diamond (or perhaps goose-eye) twill, both in z/s. One was found in the bog of Damendorf, only c. 25 km south of Thorsberg. According to its ^{14}C dating – AD 135–335 (van der Plicht et al. 2004, 483) – it is slightly older or perhaps of the same age as some of the weapon deposits. Detailed information was provided by Johanna Mestorf (1900, 10–13), Richard Stettiner (1919, 30–34), Karl Schlabow (1976, 77–78) and Heidemarie Farke (1994b). The thread count of $12–14 \times 11–12$ tpc[10] is clearly coarser compared to the Thorsberg trousers. Yet, it still belongs to the "fine" category, and the diamond weave, the possible napping and the red dye prove the good quality of the product as a whole. Narrow, tablet-woven edges occur as starting and finishing borders and as side edges of the weave. The existence of four tablet-woven edges may be the reason why John Peter Wild (Wild and Bender Jørgensen 1988, 84) considered the trousers as made from a cloak. The starting border was made without a securing outermost thread, i.e. they differ from the Thorsberg trousers and tunic. The seams, on the other hand, are a common feature, being of the "Thorsberg" type. Generally, they are turned inwards but outwards on the front, on the belly. In this area, Schlabow reconstructed a semicircular insertion, nothing of which was found. Indeed, Farke could demonstrate that this addition did not exist. Thus, the dress pattern is quite similar to trousers 3685: the two main parts constitute the legs, reach up to the hips and meet in front on the belly. An almost quadrangular piece was inserted in the back, in this case supplemented by two triangular pieces below. As the upper end, a strip of cloth was added using the starting border as the outermost edge. On this strip, Johanna Mestorf observed traces of former buttons or laces (1900, 12). Down at the bottom, the legs end in flaps which were interpreted by Mestorf (ibid.) and Hjalmar Falk (1919, 118) as straps in the sense of stirrup pants. These flaps are irregularly cut and torn. This contrast to the other features of the trousers may suggest that this shape, although old, is not the original one. Yet, Mestorf wrote that the flaps seem to have been sewn together under the feet. The trousers had been deposited at the feet of a bog body, wrapped around two leg wraps, shoes and a leather strap whilst a cloak (see Table 1.5) covered the body.

The other site is the above-mentioned bog near Marx-Etzel in Lower Saxony (Hahne 1919, 11–23; Schlabow 1976, 79–80); the related ^{14}C dating is AD 45–125 (van der Plicht et al. 2004, 483). In this case, the legs are much shorter, about knee-high, so these are breeches rather than trousers. The weave is of medium fine quality, i.e. coarser than the finds from Thorsberg. One later example – although not from a bog – is from a male grave at the above-mentioned site of Liebenau (Möller-Wiering 2005, 10–12). This diamond twill of medium fine quality was dated to the second half of the 6th century.

Furthermore, three items of different weave may be added. The first was found at Dätgen in Schleswig-Holstein and is ^{14}C dated to AD 345–535 (van der Plicht 2004, 483). It is woven in plain twill with a medium fine thread count (Mestorf 1907, 19; Schlabow 1976, 78). Basically, the dress pattern of these breeches seems to be identical to the trousers from Damendorf, with two pieces of cloth for the legs and the hips, joined on the belly, and with a rectangular addition in the back. The triangular insertions are larger here, reaching up to the upper edge of the trousers. This edge is hemmed and runs around the hips, i.e. it does not reach as far up as the other trousers do.

The next example is from the above-mentioned site of Obenaltendorf in Lower Saxony. It possesses a fine thread count, but this fabric in half basket weave seems to be a reused Roman tunic (Möller-Wiering 2007, 258). The last item is a pair of trousers from a burial at Högom, Sweden, excavated together with the already discussed tunic and dated to c. AD 500. Although this site is much further away from the weapon deposits than the examples from Schleswig-Holstein and Lower Saxony, it is still quite closely related. Like the tunic from Högom, the trousers are decorated with wide tablet-woven bands and clasps (Nockert 1991, 23–24, 34). Moreover, as in Thorsberg, the ground weave corresponds to the fabric of the tunic; here it is a diagonal 2/2 twill in z/z with c. 20 × 20 tpc.

Evidence of trousers with stockings is rare, although generally, the iconographic evidence for trousers is plentiful. Regrettably, however, the men depicted usually wear shoes or boots which make it impossible to ascertain if the trousers may have stockings. Yet, two well-known examples deserve mention. The older one is a relief from Persepolis in Iran, depicting a Scythian delegation presenting, amongst other things, tight-fitting trousers of this type hanging over the arms (e.g. Haussig 1992, 19, Abb. 8). Regrettably, the upper end of the garment remains obscure. The relief is dated to around 500 BC. The other example is a painting which was discovered in a grave in the Roman city of Durostorum, now Silistra in Bulgaria. The dating is the second half of the 4th century AD (Schneider 1983, 39; see also e.g. Hägg 2000, 29). A slave carries his master's trousers on his arms together with a pair of shoes. Again, the trousers are of the tight-fitting type. Most interesting is the upper end where a narrow belt running through a loop is clearly evident. Thus both in the details of the trousers as well as chronologically, this is a close parallel to Thorsberg. It may be added that on another painting in the same grave, another servant carries a broad belt on his arms, confirming the combination of a functional narrow belt used for the trousers under the tunic with the conspicuous military belt worn visibly over the tunic.

According to Hjalmar Falk (1919, 118–120) who used the Nordic sagas as his database and added information about Scandinavia of later times, trousers with attached feet were well known and called "leistabrókr". They were made of either: textile ("Fries"), leather or fur. Falk reports on a white example mentioned in *Gunnlaugs saga* and on a particularly slim one described in *Eyrbyggja saga*. Moreover, woven pieces of this kind were said to be common in the region of Bergen in Norway in the 18th century, while similar ones made of leather ("skinnbrókr") were used by Icelandic seamen up to Falk's times. And finally, linen trousers usually worn underneath other clothes could be strapped under the foot.

Returning to archaeological textiles, it may be useful to consider inner Asia again. A pair of very wide trousers with attached socks was found at Daiqintala sumu, northeast China (Gremli 2007a, 29–30). Legs and socks were made from similarly coloured silk, yet "different kinds of twill-patterned tabby". The burial is dated to around AD 940 (ibid., 26). In a tomb in A'cheng, still further northeast in China, the male deceased – probably a king – wore trousers of a light silken tabby, without stockings but strapped under the feet (Gremli 2007b, 59). They date to the Jin dynasty (AD 1112–1234). Going further back in time, another find is of interest here, a single leg of trousers with stockings from Noin Ula in Mongolia. The site is dated to the beginning of the Common Era (Rudenko 1969, 10) or a little older, i.e. the 1st century BC (Haussig 1992, 213). A foot made of felt is sewn onto the extremely wide leg made of silk (ibid., 74, Abb. 117). The carefully trimmed upper end proves that this is not a fragment but a complete item which was fastened to a belt. According to Hans Wilhelm Haussig (ibid.), grave figures demonstrate that single leggings as those from Noin Ula were worn by Chinese soldiers on horseback. Other examples – although possibly without stockings – were described by Geo Widengren (1956, 241–246) as leggings which are known at least from the 1st century BC onwards, with items e.g. from Nimrud in Turkey, Palmyra in Syria and later from Antinoë in Egypt. Quite recently, some Egyptian examples without feet – seemingly parts of an "oriental" riding dress (Bénazeth and Fluck 2004, 190) – were discussed by Marie Schoefer (2004, 110–112) and Petra Linscheid. Linscheid (2004, 153–154, 157) described pieces with a woollen warp combined with a cashmere weft, covering "voluminous linen trousers", dated to the 5th–7th century AD. Returning to trousers as such and leaving aside the usually very wide, differently constructed and often silken trousers from the Tarim Basin, Mongolia and northeast China, the number of examples is low, as is generally their relevance to any details concerned here. An exception is an item from Halabiyah in Syria (Nockert 1991, 118–119). Although made of linen, designed for a child and most probably later than the Thorsberg trousers – dated to before AD 610 – it displays some similarities to those pieces, i.e. a rectangular piece inserted on the back, the seams of the legs running down on the back and having loops for a belt.

Besides the stockings, the slim shape is another common feature of both pairs of trousers found in Thorsberg. A narrow, dress pattern is also characteristic of the above-mentioned examples from Damendorf, Dätgen and Marx-Etzel. In the case of Högom, at least the area around the ankles had a slim shape. Furthermore, this type of dress pattern is depicted in both Persepolis and Silistra.

Particularly slim trousers are typical for some statuettes representing priests in a Zoroastrian temple situated on the river Amu Darya (Oxus) in Tajikistan, dated to the late 6th century BC (Pichikyan 1997, 313–321). On many other depictions, the trousers are clearly wider, or it is impossible to ascertain – often due to incomplete preservation – whether a tight-fitting garment or bare legs are meant. As far as the Scythians are concerned, with their abundance of very precise representations, the evidence of clothes for the legs is usually that of rather wide pieces. Taking wide leggings into account, tight-fitting trousers may have been worn beneath such leggings. Geo Widengren mentioned the Parthian statue of the so-called prince of Shami, Iran, as an example of such a combination (1956, 244). Moreover, he claimed that in the Scythian world, the slim variants were made of leather while the wider pieces were sewn from cloth (ibid., 229). Yet, such a differentiation, if correct, does not need to be true for the regions under investigation here.

In general, trousers were apparently preferred by horsemen and perhaps even invented by them as claimed e.g. by Margareta Nockert (1991, 116)[11] and Graham Sumner (2002, 37). According to Sumner, Celts as well as Germanic people took over the idea of wearing trousers from the Scythians. In any case, the men of both these peoples are generally depicted in trousers which are usually a little wider than the Thorsberg examples. They introduced them to the Roman army, where during the 3rd century AD, trousers became part of the uniform (Sumner 2003, 5). A. T. Croom suggested that particularly trousers or rather hoses "with integral feet", as she terms it, were generally introduced during the 3rd or 4th century AD together with the long-sleeved tunic (2002, 55). Pointing to Silistra as a parallel, Inga Hägg (2000, 29) argued that in the case of the Thorsberg trousers, the thick seams of the stockings indicate their use as a riding outfit because the seams would be uncomfortable and even dangerous during a long march, but guarantee a good fit when riding. Wearing a replica of trousers 3684, Andreas Sturm, Aachen, Germany, noticed that the seam under the foot slid aside, away from the sole, not being awkward in any way.[12] In this context, the grave of the woman in Les Martres-de-Veyre can be considered again (Desrosiers and Lorquin 1998, 63; van Driel-Murray 1999, 11, 14). It contained stockings which were far too large for the deceased and which – according to an embroidery – probably belonged to a man. These stockings of napped plain twill had a thick seam under each foot. On a replica of these worn by Angharad Beyer, Aachen, the seam remained beneath the foot but did not cause any problems.[13] Similar stockings were used over a long time by Christine Wenzel, Halstenbek, Germany.[14] According to her experience, the flat and quickly felting seam remained under the foot, albeit not in the middle, but a little away from the outer rim. She easily became used to it. Johanna Zimmerman presented two insoles from 16th-century Groningen in the Netherlands, each consisting of two fragments of woven bands sewn together lengthwise, thus with a seam under the middle of the foot (2007, 220, Afb. 4.99). Referring to *Njáls saga*, Hjalmar Falk (1919, 119) concluded that trousers with stockings were impractical when riding.[15] It remains unknown, however, whether these particular trousers were made with seams under the feet.

According to the various examples presented here, attached feet do not seem to be a typical or even necessary feature of trousers worn by riders; while on the other hand, seams under the feet do not necessarily cause problems when walking. Yet, among Celts and Germans, trousers were a primary item of male dress, no matter whether the owner was a horseman or not. In such an environment, when trousers are absolutely common but riding is restricted to a certain group of people, it might be tempting for a man to manifest his status by wearing special riding trousers, e.g. characterised by the dress pattern. The deceased buried in the grave in Silistra may be taken as an example. He should be considered as a member of the upper class, although not of the high aristocracy (Schneider 1983,

39). Some paintings in the grave refer to hunting. Nobles of the time used to ride when hunting (ibid., 51), and this gentleman possessed such trousers with feet. Among the archaeological examples presented above, the combination of riding and high status is demonstrated by valuable materials, silk in Daiqintala sumu, A'cheng and Noin Ula, and cashmere in Antinoë.

The high quality of the weaves used for the Thorsberg trousers has repeatedly been emphasised. This is in close accordance not only with the quality of many other artefacts found in Thorsberg, including the equestrian equipment (Lau 2008, 49), but also with this range of high status owners as are reflected in the various parallels including the Scythian delegation to the court of Persepolis. Moreover, the deposition of the Thorsberg trousers as items in their own right – not used for wrapping – may imply their special value. It seems reasonable to ascribe these valuable items to a leading minority, the officers. This was also suggested by Inga Hägg (2000, 29) who interpreted the pieces as Roman military trousers, the shape of which resulted from a mixture of various traditions.

Cloaks

The third major item of the male dress was the cloak. Again, the depictions are countless and even the archaeological evidence is too numerous to consider all. Within the boundaries of the Roman Empire, various types of capes and cloaks were in use (see Kolb 1973 for a comprehensive description). Amongst these were woollen semicircular ones with or without hoods. Such curved cloaks (chlamys or paludamentum) were preferred by the Roman officers (e.g. Harlow 2004, 59–60; Wild and Bender Jørgensen 1988, 85). More recent archaeological examples with hoods – excavated at Lahun in Egypt and dated to around AD 600 – were presented by Hero Granger-Taylor (2007) who demonstrated how these pieces were woven to shape. Other items from Egypt were described by Frances Pritchard (2006, 117–120). The round shape was in use already in pre-Roman times, not only in Etruria (Stauffer 2002, 196–203) where they could be combined with broad tablet weaves (Ræder Knudsen 2002, 220–228) but also in northern Europe from where the Bronze Age item from Trindhøj deserves special mention (Hald 1980, 318, fig. 378). Roman soldiers, on the other hand, wore rectangular cloaks (sagum) already from the 3rd century BC (e.g. Sumner 2003, 10–11; Wild and Bender Jørgensen 1988, 85). This shape was also reported as typical for the Celts and Germanic peoples. Corresponding iconographical and written evidence is quoted by Johanna Mestorf (1900, 30) and Lise Bender Jørgensen (Wild and Bender Jørgensen 1988, 72–73).

The Thorsberg finds match this picture. Besides the shape, their other typical feature is decorative, tablet-woven edges of considerable width. Furthermore, the ground weaves are all very similar: all five fabrics are plain twills in z/s with thread counts of between 10 × 8 and 14 × 11 tpc, i.e. clearly less than in the tunic and the trousers. Apparently, this slightly coarser and thicker quality met functional as well as aesthetic and social requirements. In the case of Vimose, the overall size of the fragments belonging to the so-called cloth bundle also suggested a cloak. The weave is again a plain twill, though in z/z, with 15 × 11 tpc which corresponds well with Thorsberg. It may be surmised that amongst the textiles from Illerup Ådal, this type of garment too played a role as wrapping material. Here, finer weaves also seem to have been used as cloaks, particularly 2/2 diamond twills in z/s since they are so common in Illerup.

The north German bogs yielded a considerable number of more or less complete Iron Age cloaks as described by Karl Schlabow (1976). Lise Bender Jørgensen and John Peter Wild took up a discussion on the provenance of these fabrics (Wild and Bender Jørgensen 1988). Referring to the distribution of weaves in z/s, to their repeated combination with Roman imports like glass and terra sigillata in Scandinavian graves, and particularly to depictions of Dacian prisoners who seem to

Table 1.5. Weaves and thread counts of cloaks. Data based on Karl Schlabow (1976), if not otherwise mentioned; ^{14}C datings after van der Plicht et al. (2004, 483–485); data for Högom, Vrangstrup and Blindheim, see text

	type of weave	thread count	tablet weaves	dating	remarks
Obenaltendorf	1/1 half basket	7 × 18 (Möller-Wiering 2007, 248–249)	-	AD 260–380	with body; no starting border, no finishing border
Kibitz-Moor (Hayen and Tidow 1982)	1/1	5 × 5	-	c. 50 BC	bundle; rips starting border; many repairs
Bernuthsfeld	2/2 z/s chevron	7 × 5 (Hahne 1919, 62)	-	AD 680–775	around body (Hahne 1919, Tafel XXXVI); starting cord
Rendswühren	2/2 z/z	7 × 6.5	-	AD 135–255 AD 305–315	plaited starting border; stripes; repairs (Mestorf 1900, 18)
Neddenaverbergen	2/2 z/zz chevron	8 × 6 pairs	-	-	bundle; starting cord
Dätgen	2/2 z/z	7.5 × 6	max 3 tablets	AD 345–535	bundle?; many repairs
Bökener Moor	2/2 z/z diamond	(not given)	max 6 tablets	-	
Damendorf	2/2 z/z diamond	8.5 × 10	poss. > 8 tablets	AD 135–335	covering body; several repairs
Hunteburg A	2/2 z/s	12.5 × 7	max 16 tablets	AD 245–415	around body
Hunteburg B	2/2 z/z	11 × 9	max 27 tablets		around body
Vaalermoor	2/2 z/z diamond	(not given)	max 42 tablets	-	
Vehnemoor	2/2 z/s diamond	12.5 × 9.5	max > 100 tablets	-	"Prachtmantel II"; wrapped around a Roman bronze vessel
Högom	2/2 z/z	13–16 × 10–12	max ≥ 85 tablets	c. AD 500	rich grave; connection to ground weave not confirmed
Vrangstrup	2/2 z/s diamond	16–18 × 13–16.5	max ≥ 73 tablets	AD 250/260–310/320	rich grave
Blindheim type 1	2/2 spin-patterned	14 × 12	52 tablets	4th century AD	rich woman's grave
Blindheim type 3	2/2 spin-patterned	20 × 18	36 tablets		

wear cloaks with broad tablet weaves, Bender Jørgensen argued for a provincial Roman origin of the entire set of textiles from Thorsberg (pp. 71–74). Wild, on the other hand, discussed a number of features typical of Roman textiles – "Mediterranean-Roman" as well as "Gallo-Roman" – which are missing in Thorsberg and instead compared the Thorsberg set to bog finds (pp. 75–84). Moreover, he emphasised the absence of "elaborated", tablet-woven borders within the Roman Empire and regarded the spread of z/s woven fabrics as a phenomenon independent of Roman influence. Therefore, in his opinion, all the Thorsberg cloaks should rather be of Germanic origin.

Three examples from Scandinavia may be added. The first is from Vrangstrup in Denmark, situated only about 35 km north of Illerup Ådal and dated to period C2 or AD 250/260–310/320 (Ræder Knudsen 1998, 79).[16] The main fabric is a 2/2 diamond twill in z/s with 16–18 × 13–16.5 tpc (Hald 1980, 93), thus this fine weave is comparable to the fabrics from Illerup Ådal rather than to the cloaks from Thorsberg. On this piece, Lise Ræder Knudsen could demonstrate that the broad tablet border was woven onto the cloth after completing the ground weave (1998, 81–82). Based on the scholarly discussion of the origin of the fabrics and the tablet-woven borders, Ræder Knudsen suggested that ground weaves may have been produced in Roman workshops with the edges added later by Germanic weavers. The second example is of a woman's burial from Blindheim, Norway, dated to the 4th century AD (Raknes Pedersen 1988, 116). It contained two fabrics with broad tablet borders, thus possibly cloaks. Both are spin-patterned diagonal twills, one with 14 × 12 tpc, the other with 20 × 18 tpc (ibid., 117–124), i.e. of fine and very fine quality, respectively. According to Inger Raknes Pedersen, the broad borders were sewn onto the main cloth on both items. At least in one case, however, the yarns are identical in the cloth, the tablet weave, and the seam. This indicates that the entire textile was manufactured in the same place.[17] As a third site in Scandinavia, Högom has to be reconsidered. A 2/2 twill was recovered from various spots in the grave and interpreted as a cloak because of these locations (Nockert 1991, 27–31, 35). Moreover, a wide tablet band with tassels seemed to belong to this cloak, although no connection between band and twill could be observed.

The secondary combination of cloth and borders is also considered in the section on edges in Thorsberg, and is discussed in detail by Lise Ræder Knudsen in this volume. As far as the north German pieces are concerned, a thorough re-investigation would be very useful. Since Karl Schlabow's time, several ^{14}C datings which help interpret the fabrics have become available. Moreover, additional finds have come to light – not only from bogs – and particularly, knowledge of Roman textiles has increased considerably. For example, the re-examination of the Obenaltendorf finds revealed that the cloak and the entire assemblage are of Roman origin (Möller-Wiering 2007, 260). A piece with selvedges similar to Obenaltendorf was found in the bog of Kibitz Moor in Lower Saxony (Hayen and Tidow 1982), but according to Hajo Hayen and Klaus Tidow, no function could be determined. However, because of its size of 185 × 124 cm, it is tempting to construe it as a cloak. It was dated to c. 50 BC by dendrochronology.

In the following, John Peter Wild's group of cloaks (1988, 82–84) is briefly considered.[18] Weaves and thread counts according to Karl Schlabow (1976, 51–69, 85) are given in Table 1.5, together with data on the cloaks discussed above. The pieces from Rendswühren in Schleswig-Holstein and Neddenaverbergen in Lower Saxony are conspicuous because of their technical details which are described as similar to the Obenaltendorf finds with their Roman origin as noted above. At least technically, the same might be true in the case of the later find from Bernuthsfeld with its starting cord. A common feature of the other finds from Germany – besides the general use of 2/2 twill – is the frequently quite low thread count of coarse to medium fine quality. It can also be concluded that apparently, such coarser weaves were combined with less costly tablet weaves. At the upper end of the scale, as far as German sites are concerned, appears the so-called "Prachtmantel II" from Vehnemoor in Lower Saxony, which in terms of thread count and tablet weaves meets the qualities found in Thorsberg. Yet, the Vehnemoor cloak was woven as diamond twill which is not attested in this function in Thorsberg but – in even finer quality – in Vrangstrup, Denmark, and probably in Illerup Ådal. Regrettably, the thread count of two other diamond twills – from Bökener Moor and Vaalermoor – was not included by Schlabow. The find context of all those examples is very different from the weapon deposits. Some of the bog finds were saved together with other artefacts or with human remains but high-quality assemblages are missing except for Vehnemoor. Here, the combination of a valuable Roman bronze vessel with a "Prachtmantel" resembles the combinations in the weapon deposits. High quality items were also found in the three Scandinavian graves, e.g., glass, gold and a sword in Högom (Nockert 1991, 6, fig. 1), gold in Vrangstrup (Hald 1980, 93) and a bronze sieve in Blindheim (Magnus 1988, 111).

In this context, one result gained from the analysis of non-textile materials is noteworthy. Evaluating the finds from Illerup Ådal, Claus von Carnap-Bornheim and Jørgen Ilkjær emphasised that artefacts of Roman origin or character, particularly the swords, needed badges of Germanic style to characterise the high rank of the owner (1996a, 16–17; 245; 248). In other words, regarding status in contrast to practical aspects, the origin was less important than the appearance. In view of this background, it seems reasonable to interpret the wide, tablet-woven borders as not Roman, but rather Germanic, fabrics. This means that the weavers in the Barbaricum possessed the material as well as the knowledge to produce polychrome fabrics of high quality. As they were able to weave these fine borders, there is no reason to assume that they were incapable of manufacturing diagonal twills of medium fine quality or fine diamond twills. Indeed, recent isotope analyses confirm this conclusion. Moreover, the use of looms with tubular warping, the products of which are well known from the north and indications of which were observed amongst the Thorsberg finds, points in the same direction. Of course, this does not exclude the use of Roman textile material, either dyed yarns or complete weaves. Future analyses of dyes and particularly isotopic traces may shed more light on this question.

Caulking material

All the caulking material found in Nydam is reused, consisting primarily of fine woven fabrics. According to the categories proposed by the present author (2004), these items may be described as secondary and entirely processed textile material. Comparative contemporary finds within northern Europe are very rare. The only rather close parallel is the boat found in Halsnøy, western Norway, dated to the Late Roman Iron Age or Early Migration Period. In this case, two woollen twills were recorded, a diamond twill in z/s with 13 × 18 tpc and a plain, but spin-patterned variant with 15 × 16 tpc (Magnus 1980, 22–25). Both are high-quality products related to the upper class of that time, as Bente Magnus stated (ibid.). In this respect, they correspond well to the fine patches between the original planks of the Nydam boat. The difference is the use of s-spun material which is scarce in the caulking material from Nydam. Regrettably, no information is given of the location where the ship found at Halsnøy was built.

Chronologically close material excavated further south is based on different traditions in ship building as well as – possibly – in textile manufacturing rendering them a little difficult to use as comparisons. Yet also here, woven textiles were sometimes used for caulking (Bockius 2000, 448–450), amongst them dyed fabrics such as in the Gallo-Roman vessels from Chalon-sur-Saône (Monthel et al. 1998, 36).

In the north European tradition, ships of later periods can be taken into account. Here again, woven fabrics were occasionally encountered (Möller-Wiering 2004, 117, Tab. 2). However, more often, the majority of caulking consisted of primary, little processed materials, particularly of sheep wool that was loosely spun into rolls. Woven pieces were seemingly preferred for repairs. This signifies that the tradition of using weaves as caulking material continued, but was reduced from being a general application to mainly repairs, relying primarily on simpler material during boat building.

It may be surmised that, this change of preferred type of caulking material is a parallel to the development in boat building in general. A review of north European boat building traditions in any detail is beyond the scope of this study, but it is possible to state that some of its roots may be related to textile work. A very good example is the Pre-Roman Iron Age boat from Hjortspring – excavated on the island of Als, only c. 10 km northeast of Nydam. The vessel was a sacrifice, too, and contained numerous weapons. Its major structural components were kept together by "sewing" (Randsborg 1995, 21). Sewing is also known from the much older vessel of Ferriby in eastern England which was dated to the Middle Bronze Age (ibid., 24). Even the boats excavated in Nydam itself (A, B and C) possessed indications of such a tradition since the ribs were tied to other structural elements (Rieck 1998, 269–270, 276). This contributes to the high elasticity of such vessels. In this context of sewing a boat, it may have been logical to use well-prepared textiles for such an important purpose as caulking. Moreover, all components utilised in building such a valuable boat would perhaps be of the finest quality, even if they were not visible, or their function, for instance, caulking did not require textiles of the highest quality. For, a vessel of that importance would be considered as requiring only the highest quality building materials. However, nails were meanwhile used on most components. Thus, the connection between textile work and boat building disappeared, reducing the value of the caulking to its practical aspects. The woollen rolls could be prepared by the boat builders themselves while the repairs were possibly carried out during the voyages where some textiles were always at hand.

Consecrated textiles
Sacrifices were neither restricted to textiles – as the weapon deposits prove – nor to the context of battles, nor to the Roman Iron Age. A Bronze Age example of consecrated textile material consists of some red-dyed cords found in Bad Frankenhausen, Saxony-Anhalt, Germany (Farke 1991, 128–129, 132, 140). Out of the ample literature dealing with sacrifices in prehistoric times – though not with textiles – only the thesis by Wolf-Rüdiger Teegen (1999) is introduced here because it focused on the Roman Iron Age. Furthermore, Teegen cited some written sources which are either older or younger than that period and which are of interest here because they refer to clothes (pp. 349–350). Pieces of clothing were e.g. sacrificed in Greek temples. Gregory of Tours who lived in the 6th century AD, described rituals from France where clothes, wool and food were cast into a lake. Reference to written evidence of the Roman Iron Age on the consecration of textiles subsequent to battle is mentioned in the introduction to this volume.

A recurring question is how to determine a particular find as a sacrifice, how to distinguish an offering from a hoard and from simply lost items. Teegen's postulate that a sacrifice must consist of something valuable (1999, 241) seems valid, but is difficult to take as a guideline since anything might have been of great value for a certain person on a certain occasion. In connection with textiles, the following thoughts may be useful. Valuable textiles are not likely to be put into a hoard to be hidden in the earth, in a bog or in water since the environment would harm the fabrics. Moreover, a bog may generally be a rather unsuitable place for a hoard because of the seemingly uniform, but rapidly changing and treacherous surface. Otherwise, the immediate find context can shed more light on this problem. For instance, a large, carefully folded bundle may be less likely to have got lost than e.g. a small bag with some everyday utensils. The discarding of textiles may have been more likely in settlements than when people were travelling. Some probable sacrifices are now described, with the exception of the bog bodies in general as well as the Iron Age material found in Denmark presented in detail by Ulla Mannering and Margarita Gleba (forthcoming).

Among the already discussed materials, four bog finds from Lower Saxony, Germany may be considered as probable sacrifices. The oldest is a cloth bundle, the possible cloak, from Kibitz-Moor. It was laid down on some birch twigs beside a boardwalk, in the same stratum as the planks (Hayen and Tidow 1982). The weave is a tabby with only 5 × 5 tpc and with many repairs. Despite its seemingly low quality, the bundle bedded on twigs may suggest a sacrifice. The cloak from Neddenaverbergen was also folded into a bundle, without accompanying finds (Schlabow 1976, 20). The thread count is medium fine, repairs are absent, thus it seems to have been quite new when it ended up in the bog. Folded into a bundle was also the well-made Reepsholt tunic (ibid., 21). Its inside was turned outwards (Fuhrmann 1941–42, 340, 359–360). Some small cuts on the proposed front, in the area of the heart, were interpreted by Irmingard Fuhrmann as resulting from a stabbing weapon, possibly a lance. The Vehnemoor cloak with its splendid tablet-woven border was wrapped around a bronze vessel, a parallel to which was found in the Czech Republic (Schlabow 1976, 24).

A bog find from the Netherlands, from Deurne, consisted of several valuables of a Roman soldier, including some textiles, particularly a 2/2 chevron twill in z/z (Leene 1973, 81, 83). The function of the latter is unclear. Yet, it is noteworthy that despite the low thread count of c. 4 × 10 tpc,[19] the appearance is closer to the east Mediterranean diamond twills than to those of the weapon deposits, simply due to the dominating weft. Moreover, J. E. Leene reports on a roundish woven edge. It is tempting to recall here the curved chlamys woven to shape. According to a re-evaluation by Carol van Driel-Murray (2000), the assemblage can be dated to the 1st half of the 4th century AD and may represent an offering by a former soldier leaving the army. Another chronologically closely related example is a piece of a woollen fabric found in a raised bog near Strückhausen in Lower Saxony (von Buttel-Reepen 1930, 64; Halpaap 1991). It can be dated to the last quarter of the 4th century or around AD 400. The fabric constitutes of a half-basket weave and according to a photograph, it is very fine.[20] It was used for fastening 28 almost identical bronze fibulae with decorations made of tin.[21] The fibulae were new, so Rainer Halpaap regarded them as a hoard rather than a sacrifice (ibid., 65). Yet, the deposition in a bog may be inconsistent with this hoard interpretation. If the thread count of the weave is indeed very fine, the quality of the weave reflects that of the jewellery – a possible parallel to Vehnemoor. In general, these examples correspond well with Wolf-Rüdiger Teegen's claim for valuable items as well as with the results from the weapon deposits.

Textiles in graves
A highly interesting material to compare with, yet difficult to interpret, is the textiles found in graves. They may possibly be seen as consecrated textiles as well. The fact that graves with preserved textiles are rare in relation to the total number of known burials, and that these graves belong to the richer examples since they contain metal, leads to the hypothesis that the weaves from graves may resemble the fabrics from the weapon deposits in type and/or quality. When including the possible regions of origin of the weapons, the textile material becomes too vast, despite the above-mentioned restriction to only burials containing metal items. To make optimal use of such a comparison, it would be necessary not only to analyse the technical aspects of grave textiles but also to determine their primary functions as well. This, however, has rarely been done and is a task beyond the scope of the present study. Therefore, only few items from single graves were included in the comparisons above, such as Högom, Blindheim, Vrangstrup, Liebenau and Lankhills. Here, a few more sites are briefly considered.

The grave fields of Sievern and Flögeln-Voßbarg are both situated in Lower Saxony, close to the coast, and are dated to the 4th/5th century AD (Tidow 2001). In Sievern, only 2/2 twills were found, five fabrics woven in z/z, three in z/s. One of the latter is a diamond twill. All the thread

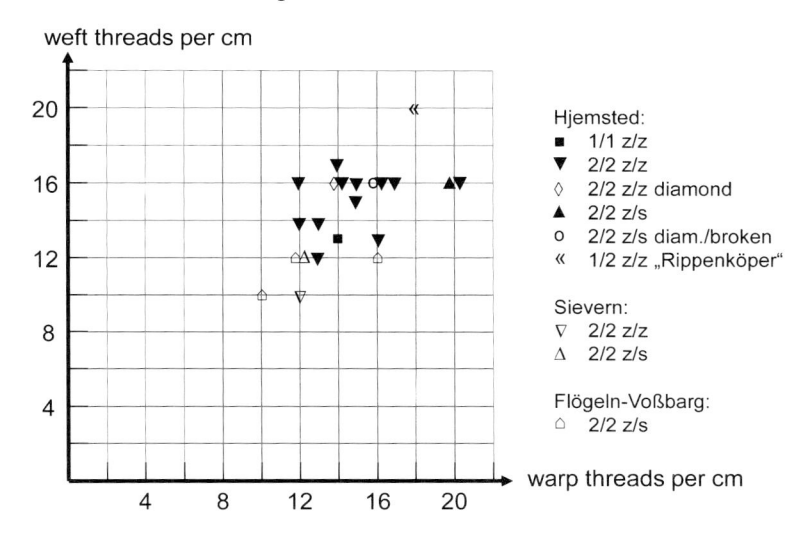

Fig. 1.52. Hjemsted, Sievern and Flögeln-Voßbarg, thread counts

counts belong to the medium fine group (Fig. 1.52).[22] At Flögeln-Voßbarg, two burials yielded weaves, plain 2/2 twills in z/s. One grave contained three fragments of medium fine quality, found on a miniature tool and below two fibulae placed on the shoulders, i.e. this was a woman's grave. The twill in the other burial comes from a strap-end and possesses 16 × 12 tpc, i.e. it belongs to the category "fine".

Of similar age is the grave field of Hjemsted in Denmark (Bender Jørgensen 1986b, 99–100), situated near the west coast of Jutland, c. 100 km northwest of Thorsberg and 70 km west-northwest of Nydam. The majority of textiles in the 13 relevant burials are plain twills in z/z (Fig. 1.52) which resemble the corresponding twills from Illerup Ådal in their thread count. Thus these Danish grave finds of textiles are clearly finer than the examples from Lower Saxony. On the other hand, the Hjemsted textiles differ from Illerup and Thorsberg in the scarcity of diamond twills and s-spun yarns. The only two diamond/broken twills as well as the single plain twill in z/s derive from one and the same grave.

None of the sites or graves presented thus far is characterised by particularly rich assemblages. As a contrast to the grave fields but a parallel to the rich graves of Högom, Vrangstrup and Blindheim, two burials with unusually ample furniture from Neudorf-Bornstein, situated only c. 25 km south of Thorsberg, are included here. They are regarded as "Fürstengräber" and are dated to period C2, i.e. the 2nd half of the 3rd century AD (Abegg-Wigg 2008, 279). The textiles from these graves have not yet been analysed and published in detail but some data are available. Heidemarie Farke examined one part of the fabrics found under a bronze vessel in grave 7 (2004). It encompasses seven layers, some of which could be determined rather well. They consist of plain 2/2 twill in z/s, once with 14 × 10 tpc, once with only 7 × 6 tpc. The latter may be due to a secondary effect or it might be an error since Farke considered the fabrics as very fine and very valuable (ibid., 42). This evaluation seems to be based on three aspects: the well prepared wool, the polychrome weft and one layer with an unidentified weft. No dye analyses have thus far been performed but Farke could distinguish three colours: a reddish tone presumably due to madder, (today) brown threads, and bluish yarns of presumably vegetal fibres. Layers of tablet weaves were also observed. In her conclusion, Heidemarie Farke did not exclude the use of silk although silk did not appear in her analysis. She may refer to the unidentified weft threads in one microstratum in which context she considered another type of raw material. Yet, brownish and reddish picks in the same layer suggest that it is at least not a different piece of textile. With all cautiousness, the multi-layered wrapping, the quality of the weave, its colours and the tablet weave match the characteristics of cloaks as described above. From the second burial relevant here, grave 4, Angelika Abegg-Wigg (2008, 287) reported on gold tinsel, observed by conservator Gabriele Zink.

At this juncture, it is impossible to ascertain the degree to which differences between the sites are based on function (practically and contextual), gender, wealth/status, provenance/weaving tradition, perhaps chronology or even other reasons. At least, the distribution of the various features does not appear accidental. In this context, the finds from Liebenau in Lower Saxony dating from around AD 400 to the 8th–9th centuries may be reconsidered. The analyses revealed that tabby and diagonal twill in z/z were more common in female graves than in male burials while fabrics in z/s and diamond twill were attested more often in male graves (Möller-Wiering 2005, 65–72). Moreover, these groups, i.e. textiles in z/s and/or in diamond twill occurred in more well-equipped graves. Seemingly, diamond twills were not used for cloaks in Liebenau. Over time, the weaves generally became a little finer, shifting from medium fine to fine quality, but the spectrum of textiles remained stable. These results shed light on a connection between type and quality of weave, function and status. A similar structure seems to be reflected in the finds from the other grave fields as well as in the weapon deposits but this cannot be determined without further research. In any case, the results emphasise again the prestige value of items such as the tunic and trousers from Thorsberg.

Textiles in settlements

Another group of textiles which sheds light on the quality of the fabrics in the weapon deposits are the weaves found in contemporary Iron Age settlements. Only two sites are considered here. The first is a dwelling mound called Tofting, situated about 60 km south-west of Thorsberg, on the west coast of Schleswig-Holstein. The material was published by Karl Schlabow in 1955 and recently re-analysed by the present author (2009). According to the new results, it consists of five twills of different character and quality: one coarse diagonal twill in s/s, two plain twills in z/s, one of which is coarse while the other may be called fine, as well as two diamond or goose-eye variants in z/s of medium fine quality. They are dated to the 3rd century AD (Schlabow 1955, 94).

Hundreds of fabrics were preserved in the dwelling mound of Feddersen Wierde, on the coast of Lower Saxony. The mound was inhabited from c. 50 BC to c. AD 400 (Ullemeyer and Tidow 1981, 77) but the majority of the textiles belong to the 1st and 2nd centuries AD. Among the 605 woven pieces, there are 337 tabbies, of which 257 were woven in z/z (ibid., 84–94). Thirty-five pieces contained yarns twined in zS in both thread systems. The group of 2/2 twills consists of 252 items, with increasing numbers in the younger strata. Of these 219 constitute plain twills, among which 206 are in z/z. The rest encompasses 25 chevron twills and only eight diamond or goose-eye twills. Among a small group of unusual fabrics, there are three 2/1 twills, one of them (FW 222) with a starting border typical for a warp-weighted loom. The catalogue presented by Rudolf Ullemeyer and Klaus Tidow (ibid., 127–152) reveals the generally rather low thread counts within the entire assemblage. According to Tidow's categories (2000, 108), only one single very fine weave and 16 fine fabrics were found. Amongst these 17 pieces, there are ten plain twills, three chevron twills, three tabbies and only one diamond twill. Chevron as well as diamond twills also occur in other qualities, even as very course weaves, thus there is no clear correlation between weaving type and thread count. A considerable number of starting borders was observed, although more often in reps than as tablet weaves, as well as some tubular edges. However, no "Thorsberg seams" were described (Ullemeyer and Tidow 1981, 110).

Indications of original functions are lacking (ibid., 84). Yet, one item is presented here, FW 575a, a 2/2 twill of medium fine thread count with twined yarns in both systems (ibid., 115, 144). There are three eyes, i.e. oval, edged holes on the fragment which measures c. 15 × 9 cm. The size of the openings is about 1.0 × 0.5 cm and the trimming is c. 0.8 cm wide, thus resembling the hole at the back of the Thorsberg tunic. The trimming is more elaborate on the Feddersen Wierde piece – even using different colours – but the basic technique is the same as in Thorsberg, a blanket stitch. Two of the eyes were placed immediately beside each other while the third one is about 10 cm away. If one does not want to explain the use of twined yarns as a reflection of pre-Roman traditions further south in Germany, one might assume a special function for such weaves, demanding a strong but still rather fine quality. This may prove an argument against clothing. The presence of at least three eyes would also argue against an interpretation as clothing, although no other function can be proposed.[23] Returning to Thorsberg, this parallel is therefore only a technical one, leaving the reason for the hole in the tunic to further speculation.

Two wool tabbies from Feddersen Wierde were examined regarding their fibre material, with warp and weft measured separately (Bender Jørgensen and Walton 1986, 183, table 3). One of them (FW 204) was categorised as "hairy medium", the other one (FW 451) as "hairy". The first one had a mean diameter of 27.9 microns in the warp and of 21.4 microns in the weft, with maximum figures of 118 microns in both systems. The corresponding figures for the second fabric are 42.4 microns and 44.4 microns as mean diameters and 83 microns and 91 microns as maxima. Apart from the categorisation, these figures – particularly the maxima – demonstrate that this material was less carefully prepared than the wool of item 24824b from Thorsberg with a maximum of 46 microns in the warp and of 62 microns in the weft (ibid.).

Notes

1. Provided that the very few irregularly broken twills were not planned as such but are in fact plain twills with weaving mistakes.
2. No certain damage of this kind is observable on the weapons from Gremersdorf-Techelwitz, although this may be due to their poor state of preservation as noted by Bemmann and Bemmann (1998 vol. 1, 336).
3. For the sake of simplicity, only one recent publication is quoted per site. Illerup Ådal: Ilkjær 2003, 50. Vimose: Pauli Jensen 2008, 304–308. Thorsberg: Matešić 2008. Nydam: Sim 1998.
4. Margrethe Hald (1980, 338): c. AD 200.
5. The following description is based on Irmingard Fuhrmann.
6. A palynological dating resulted in a very wide time span, 600 BC–AD 200 (Potratz 1942, 11; Fuhrmann 1941–42, 340). Based on the technical elements of the textile, Irmingard Fuhrmann (ibid., 364) reduced this period to the two first centuries AD.
7. This may indicate the use of two balls of differently coloured yarns in the warp, although the warp is reported as monochrome. Using two colours, they could either alternate or a pattern of the system 2/1/1/2/1/1 etc. could be created. The idea of two colours in the warp may accord with the fact that in the weft, stripes consisting of one and two alternating yarns were woven.
8. The neck opening is described as "a broad horizontal one". In another publication, however, a photograph of this tunic displays a clearly rounded aperture (Polosmak and Molodin 2000, 75, fig. 26).

9   For a recent overview, see Ulla Mannering (2006a, 194–199).
10 Measured by Farke. Schlabow: 11 × 12.5 tpc which would be categorised as medium fine.
11 Nockert refers to Geo Widengren, *Ryttarfolken från öster* (Stockholm, 1960), pp. 7–8, a text which was not included in the present investigation.
12 Personal communication, May 2008.
13 Personal communication, May 2008. However, the type of seam is not mentioned in the case of the original as well as the replica.
14 Personal communication, August 2008.
15 "*Flosi var í leistabrókum, því at hann ætlaði at ganga*" ("*Flosi wore trousers with attached feet because he wanted to walk*") (chapter 134).
16 Margrethe Hald (1980, 93): 4th century AD.
17 Another noteworthy aspect is the napping of the very fine twill. Moreover, a 2/2 diamond twill from the same grave had a finish of the same kind (Raknes Pedersen 1988, 120–122, 125). The phenomenon of concealing the pattern by napping the cloth was also attested in all large weapon deposits.
18 The cloak from Odry in Poland is excluded. Of this piece of garment, only the weave (2/2 z/s) is noted and the wide tablet borders along one side and the bottom.
19 Leene 1973, 81, 3.7 × 10 tpc, ibid., 83, 3.88 × 5.66 tpc. The latter number, however, does not seem to correspond with the photographs on Tafel 29.
20 Halpaap described it as tabby which apparently was a misunderstanding of von Buttel-Reepen's statements. The photographs confirm the half basket weave.
21 Not silver, as was originally thought by von Buttel-Reepen.
22 Classified as such by Tidow. The exact thread count is only provided in few cases.
23 An essentially similar eye is known from a medieval Norwegian sail (Möller-Wiering 2002, 128–131). Yet, that eye is larger and the trimming is reinforced. Whether sails might have existed at Feddersen Wierde, is a question that is not touched upon here.

8. SUMMARY AND CONCLUSION

The four large weapon deposits of Illerup Ådal, Vimose, Nydam and Thorsberg were created as sacrifices subsequent to battles. All of them are situated near the Baltic coast of the Danish peninsula of Jutland including the northernmost area of Germany, and the island of Fyn. The maximum distance, i.e. between Illerup Ådal and Thorsberg, is only c. 150 km. The very small deposit of Gremersdorf-Techelwitz which is included here, was also established close to the Baltic Sea, another c. 80 km further southeast.

Compared to the thousands of metal finds in the large deposits, the number of preserved textiles is small. Yet, the textile materials particularly from Illerup Ådal and Thorsberg should be considered as outstanding assemblages.

The technical and microstratigraphical analyses were performed by using reflected light microscopes. Based on the resulting data, and including information from other – published as well as unpublished – sources, the material was interpreted in terms of primary functions and its role within the sacrifice. This was undertaken separately for each site. The subsequent comparison of the sites constitutes another main section of this work. Again, technical characteristics, primary functions, and aspects of the sacrifices were taken into account. Finally, some material from other sites and other categories of sites and sources such as settlements, graves and written evidence was considered briefly.

ILLERUP ÅDAL

Of the four deposits at the northernmost site, Illerup Ådal, the one termed "Platz A" is important here, dating to c. AD 200 or early in period C1b. By far the most textiles were preserved by the help of iron oxides from weapons such as shield bosses, spearheads, or axes. Technically, the c. 100 well-documented textiles are characterised by an average thread count of 16 × 14 tpc. The generally fine quality is not only reflected in the thread count, but also in the wool preparation and spinning, as far as this could be evaluated despite the often high degree of mineralisation. Only on tabbies, does the thread diameter often vary slightly. The fibre material appears to be of sheep wool. Ropes of vegetal material prove the possible survival of plant materials, but no such weaves were found. All tabbies (12%) are woven in z/z. All other weaves are variations of 2/2 twill: plain or diamond, z/z, z/s or spin-patterned. Most common are diamond twills in z/s. The size of the diamonds is highly variable, i.e. their pattern units vary. This holds true both for diamonds in z/z and in z/s. Nevertheless, it can be confirmed that in the warp, pattern units with even numbers of threads were preferred – most often 10 – while in the weft, odd numbers prevailed, with 9 and 13 as the most common. Indications of napping were observed on at least 17 items.

The small size of the textile pieces found in Illerup hampers the determination of primary functions. Considering napping as a typical feature of clothing, about one sixth of the material should be regarded as clothes. Moreover, it may be argued that textiles of similar fineness, though not napped, can also be considered as clothing. Broad tablet weaves are another characteristic of high quality textiles and possibly of cloaks in particular. The absence of seams and hems may be interpreted as a preference for non-tailored items, i.e. again cloaks. With respect to the sacrifice, these textiles were used for wrapping weapons. Prior to the sacrifice, at least some of the fabrics were damaged deliberately by cuts or strokes. Similar damage is well known from the weapons themselves. This emphasises the similar status of textiles and metal items and thus that the textiles belonged to the defeated.

As a rule, the weapons were wrapped individually. Microstrata of different weaves on one metal find may signify that such individually wrapped items were gathered into larger bundles, with the help of another textile and possibly some rope. Yet, this does not necessarily have to be the case as spatial analyses have demonstrated. Furthermore, the rope fragments could derive from entire bundles of rope offered as sacrifices in their own right. Examples of the latter do exist and may be interpreted as a parallel to completely intact items of clothing, possibly not used for wrapping but deposited as an offering, although such fabrics have not been found in this weapon deposit.

VIMOSE

The second site presented here is the bog of Vimose on the Danish island of Fyn. In current research, eight deposits can be distinguished, already from around the beginning of the Common Era. Possibly all well-documented textiles – 41 items in all – belong to period C1b or the first half of the 3rd century AD. They were all found covering iron weapons. Of these, 34 items constitute the so-called "cloth bundle" together with some weapons on which the textile remains are less evident. Apparently, the various contents of this bundle were all wrapped in one and the same cloth, a fine 2/2 twill in z/z. Taking theses pieces together as one item, the textile material from Vimose is reduced to four twills of the just mentioned type plus five tabbies in z/z, also of fine quality.

The wrapping of the spearheads and lanceheads of the "cloth bundle" was carried out meticulously, emphasising the great significance of this aspect in preparation for the sacrifice. The cloth, which seems to have been napped on one side, was taken double and each weapon orientated to the textile's grain. No seams or other indications of tailoring were observed. Therefore, this apparently rather large piece of cloth is regarded as a probable cloak. The few other weapons were also wrapped. Straight cuts suggest strokes as in the Illerup material.

THORSBERG

Thorsberg is the southernmost of the large weapon deposits and is situated in Germany. Like the others, it contained several depositions. Regrettably, the textiles found at Thorsberg are more difficult to date than the other weapon assemblages. The most probable dating, however, is period C1b or the first half of the 3rd century AD. Due to the chemical composition of the bog, wool was very well preserved and some surprisingly intact items of clothing survived. Technically, the textiles from Thorsberg are slightly more diverse than those from the other three large sites. Yet, among the 36 find numbers, fabrics woven in z/s constitute the great majority and amongst these, plain twills – often cloaks – are more common than diamond twills. The pattern units of the diamond twills follow the identical guidelines as in Illerup Ådal. Although the average thread count is slightly lower than on the other sites, the quality of most pieces is good or very good, including well-prepared fibres, napping and some red-dyed fabrics.

Along with the fabrics, an unusual amount of original edges are preserved. Side edges are simple, reinforced with a warp bundle, tubular woven or combined with tablet weaves. Transverse edges also appear in several variations. Some tablet-woven borders can be related to the warp-weighted loom, either as starting or as finishing borders. Others rather indicate a loom with a tubular warp, while, at least in one case, a two-beam loom without a tubular warp cannot be ruled out. The primary functions of a number of items is evident – a tunic, two pairs of trousers and one cloak. Based on the size of the remains and certain technical details, several other fabrics are also regarded as cloaks. Two other pieces are commonly considered as leg wraps, an interpretation which was not questioned here but which might be worth further investigation. Particularly the tunic and the trousers have previously been examined by various scholars. Nevertheless, some aspects may be added here.

It should be recalled that the trimmed hole on the tunic is not located on the right breast but on the left side of the back. The side on display and reproduced in so many publications is the back of the garment. The tunic was dyed red and at the time of its deposition, it had already suffered from light, which can be demonstrated along certain cuts. If the tunic was worn for some time as the fading indicates, the short, blue, thin cords along the open sides of the garment are hard to explain as a means of fastening. Instead, the cords are interpreted here as a decoration. It might be that the seams were cut open in connection with the sacrifice, damaging the ornamentation at the same time. At least the cuts in the fabric appear to be parallels to the phenomenon of intentional damaging found in Illerup and Vimose.

Short, thin, blue cords of the identical type are also preserved along the calves of one pair of trousers (3684). Here, one might expect some means for fastening the now open seam regularly because of the slim dress pattern. Yet, other slim-patterned trousers apparently do not possess such openings. Principally, the situation is the same as on the tunic, with the cords sticking out from a widely undisturbed weave. No additional stitching holes were recorded. This may be interpreted as a decoration as on the tunic but with a different method of fastening. The similarities between tunic and trousers, including, e.g., a very rare variation of a transverse edge, support the hypothesis that both items belonged to the same costume. However, both pieces do not derive from the same cloth, as the clearly different pattern units of their diamond twills prove.

A well-known feature of these trousers is the integrated stockings, or rather the one preserved attached foot. The other foot is lost. Whether this occurred in the bog or possibly during the preparations for the sacrifice or even earlier, remains unknown. The other trousers (3685) are in generally worse condition but with both attached feet preserved. Its upper edge is cut but not hemmed and fastenings for a belt are absent. Possibly, a short length amounting to some centimetres of the upper rim were cut away before the trousers were consecrated.

Typical features of the cloaks encountered at Thorsberg are the use of diagonal twill in z/s, a somewhat lower thread count compared to tunic and trousers, and broad tablet weaves. The tablet-woven borders may be interpreted as a status symbol, comparable to certain ornaments on swords. Several of them were not woven simultaneously with the ground weave but attached subsequently.

Of the smaller remains, some could be interpreted as cloaks, based on the above-mentioned characteristics. A few others resemble the material of the tunic and trousers and are partly dyed and decorated. Others are too indistinct to determine a particular function but their similarity in terms of quality with the above-mentioned pieces suggests their use as clothing.

In the sacrifice, at least some of these pieces were rolled up and offered as individual items and not used for wrapping as in Vimose and Illerup. Wrapping might be surmised but could not be verified since no combination of metal and textile is preserved. However, in accordance with the observations from the other two sites, deliberate damage on the textiles is attested here too. Most conspicuous are the cuts in the tunic, supplemented by two long tears and probably cut seams. Similar strokes were found on one cloak. On one pair of trousers, the upper end was severed, possibly as a part of the same phenomenon. Whether the missing foot on the other trousers is also due to intentional damage, cannot be confirmed.

NYDAM

The bog of Nydam is situated slightly north of the present-day Danish-German border and it is the latest site considered here. As is typical for the large weapon deposits, sacrifices were performed on several occasions. Here, different types of textiles may be ascribed to different depositions. One group of weaves are those attached to clasps. They were consecrated together with the pine boat (C) some time after AD 300. Possibly around the same time, AD 310–320, the oak vessel (B) was built, thus dating the reused fabrics of the original caulking material as slightly older to this. The textiles found on weapons primarily belong to the 2nd half of the 4th century AD.

Since the weapons are the most obvious parallel to the other sites, i.e. to Illerup Ådal and Vimose, they are discussed first. More than 100 items were examined and found to have traces of textiles on their surface. Their condition of preservation, however, is usually so poor that only six items revealed any significant information. The few determinable features link them to the observations particularly from Illerup Ådal. The same applies to the clasps, of which more than 200 were examined. Again, information is very scarce but still indicates high-quality textiles as may be expected in connection with such valuable decorations. Besides the remaining textiles as such, their preservation partly on top of the clasps and the distribution of the clasps on the site are of interest. The investigation revealed that the clasps were left on the tunics and/or trousers and that these items were rolled up and deposited intact as in Thorsberg.

Finally, the caulking materials may be divided into two groups. Although both groups consist of reused fabrics, the textiles utilised in the building of the boat are of better quality than those employed during later repairs. The former are comparable in quality to the Illerup textiles. A common feature of both groups, however, is the scarcity of weaves in z/s.

Besides the material from the clasps which denote tunics and/or trousers, it is difficult to determine any primary functions. The absence of seams and hems among the caulking material may be due to a preference for untailored textiles. During the sacrifice, the caulking material remained invisible and did not play any particular ceremonial role. The situation is different with the tunics and/or trousers represented by the clasps. They were seemingly regarded as valuables and offered as items in their own right. Other textiles were used for wrapping weapons as is attested at Illerup Ådal and Vimose.

SPECIFIC ASPECTS IN COMPARISON

Although the range of weaves is not identical on the four large sites, the general impression is that of many similarities. These include material, general absence of textiles in s/s, thread count and balance of thread count. Within the variety of weaves, the visual appearance of the fabrics is highly similar. A diamond twill from Illerup resembles a diamond twill from Thorsberg – while both are clearly distinguishable e.g. from such twills in the eastern Mediterranean area. The unusual range of edges and thus of looms found in Thorsberg cannot be confirmed from the other sites, but at least tubular side edges and tablet weaves are not restricted to this deposit.

Searching for comparative textiles, a very wide geographical frame was chosen, which included Europe, Egypt, the Near and Middle East, and Inner Asia. The aim was not to introduce the textile materials from these regions in their entirety, but to trace certain characteristics of the fabrics from the deposits. Using the garments found at Thorsberg as a model, features such as raw material, weave, cut and decorations were compared to chronologically and regionally more or less close parallels.

Starting with the tunics, it emerged that individual characteristics such as inserted sleeves, horizontal neck opening, perpendicular warp, and clasps could be traced here and there, in e.g., Inner Asia, Egypt, France, Denmark, and Sweden. However, as must be expected within such a large area, other features of the tunics in question differ completely from the Thorsberg item. Even the seemingly nearest parallels such as Roman Iron Age bog finds of north Germany, display features which do not suggest a close relationship. The least common factor within this group is the use of wool and often twill.

Wool was also used as raw material for some trousers and breeches found in the bogs. Moreover, they resemble each other in their dress pattern and slim legs, but lack integrated stockings. When this phenomenon is emphasised, the closest parallels come primarily from Asia and from somewhat modern Scandinavian sources. On the question of whether the Thorsberg trousers constitute part of a riding dress, no functional reasons could be found to support this notion, but high status might be an explanation.

As far as cloaks are concerned, it is easier to draw comparisons from closer areas and periods. The cloaks excavated in Thorsberg are highly similar, plain twills of medium fine or fine quality. An analogous find may exist at Vimose. The abundance of finer diamond twills in Illerup Ådal implies that such weaves may also have served as cloaks. The design is rectangular, often decorated with wide, tablet-woven borders. The shape is identical to that worn by the soldiers in the Roman Empire, but the broad borders are apparently absent there. The absence of borders was an argument in a discussion of the origin of these garments between Lise Bender Jørgensen and John Peter Wild. This discussion is now resumed; see also Lise Ræder Knudsen (this volume). As the borders are so typical of the cloaks found in north Germany and Scandinavia, and since visual signs of status should be of Germanic origin within a Germanic army as particularly the decorations of originally Roman swords demonstrate, the borders are considered as domestic products here.

The use of woven, apparently reused textiles as caulking material was not restricted to the north. Contemporary parallels were found in France. Later, woven fabrics were often used for repairs, while during the boat building, less processed materials such as rolls of wool were preferred. As a hypothesis, a connection is suggested between the tradition of "sewing" boats and using woven fabrics, while later on with the development of boat building, this basic correlation increasingly disappeared.

TEXTILES FROM OTHER SOURCES

Two major aspects observed in the weapon deposits – the deposition of complete garments and textiles used for wrapping – are also to be found in non-military contexts. The consecration of textiles as such was practised at least from the Bronze Age onwards and some Iron Age bog finds may be classified as consecrated textiles. The other function, the wrapping, is possibly best represented by the bog find from Vehnemoor with a bronze vessel wrapped in a marvellous cloak. Moreover, it is well known from burials.

Textiles from graves are another important group comparable to the weapon deposits. However, this material is too numerous to be taken into account in this discussion and furthermore, the functional identification of these materials is often lacking. Nevertheless, a few sites were presented in order to ascertain whether a burial may be of comparable significance as a military campaign, possibly reflected in textiles of similar qualities. Methodically, the basis is very weak not only because of the lack of functional determination but also of omitting gender and other factors and because of the low number of graves that can be considered here. Three rather contemporary grave fields were chosen. None of them contained particularly rich burials but the existence of metal enabling the preservation of textiles implies that the deceased were probably not poor. While the few fabrics from Lower Saxony correspond well with the Thorsberg finds in general, the textiles from Denmark resemble the Vimose material. Exceptional burials, however, may provide finer weaves – as were also found amongst the textiles from the weapon deposits – and they may contain unusual materials such as gold tinsel. Such rarities are not known from the weapon deposits.

In contrast to the graves, all social and economic strata may possibly be reflected in settlements. Two contemporary dwelling mounds, Feddersen Wierde and Tofting, were considered here. Tofting provided only five fabrics, all of them twills, ranging from coarse to fine. At Feddersen Wierde, more than 600 weaves were found, over 50% of which were tabbies. The great majority of twills are plain specimens. Fine fabrics are rare while coarse ones are abundant. These figures support the notion that in the settlements, a larger range of textiles was in use, including many simple weaves, while in graves, the better qualities prevail.[1] Moreover, they support once again the result obtained from the weapon deposits that the fabrics found there primarily represent the upper end of the available textile qualities.

ORIGIN

The technical characteristics as well as the qualities are rather similar in the textile materials from the weapon deposits, no matter where their former owners are thought to have originated from, i.e. north Germany or various regions of Scandinavia. Many features differ clearly from the typical finds from e.g. the eastern Mediterranean. On the other hand, on a general level, it may be said that they are also known from the northwestern Roman provinces. In any case, the various details of the best preserved pieces, i.e. the dress items from Thorsberg, do not point to the Roman Empire in particular, since Roman features such as half-basket weave, corded edges or reinforcements with two or more warp bundles are missing. Of course, this does not exclude the exchange of know-how or of material to some extent.

The broad, elaborate tablet borders are a conspicuous element. Their absence within the Roman Empire was an argument in a discussion of the origin of cloaks between Lise Bender Jørgensen and John Peter Wild. This discussion is now reprised (see also Lise Ræder Knudsen, this volume). The borders are considered to be Germanic products, since they are not only typical of the material found in the weapon deposits, but they are also typical of all the cloaks recovered in northern Germany and Scandinavia. Furthermore, as particularly demonstrated by the decorations on what originally were Roman swords, the visual status symbols would have been of Germanic origin within a Germanic army.

On this background, it seems reasonable to assume that the textiles of the weapon deposits were domestic products of the Barbaricum and Scandinavia, based on a common tradition and taste. This is confirmed by some isotope analyses.

When searching for comparisons to the various dress items, a chronologically and regionally wide frame was chosen, which included Europe, Asia and Egypt. It emerged that, parallels could be found for many details in Inner Asia and the Middle East, i.e. in regions where riding played an important role in the lives of people. These details seem to confirm the opinion of earlier scholars that tunic and trousers, the typical dress of Celtic as well as Germanic peoples, have their roots in Asia.

TEXTILES FOR WAR

Considering the complete materials of the weapon deposits, the finds seem to reflect the structure of a Germanic army with principes, comites and pedites (von Carnap-Bornheim and Ilkjær 1996a, 483–484), with rather few, but expensively made equestrian items which have to be seen in the context of the military elite. As previously claimed by other scholars, the well-preserved dress items from Thorsberg may be ascribed to this elite as well, thus possibly to the principes. In the present work, this conclusion is partly based on the fact that these pieces were offered as completely intact items, as valuables, while other textiles were used for wrapping. The general distribution of textiles in the bogs, particularly in Illerup Ådal, indicates their extensive use for wrapping. Certainly, such a large amount would not all derive alone from the equipment of the principes. Instead, garments used by the lower ranks must be included in the preserved textile assemblage. The question of whether the garments of the warriors were partly or wholly provided by the chieftains as were probably the weapons (ibid., 484–485) is left to discussion. In any case, the demand for good and even high quality cloth was obviously large. If the Roman Empire were the best and perhaps only source for such products, one might expect the best qualities in the deposits exhibiting the closest connections to the Roman provinces, i.e. in Thorsberg and Vimose. However, the current observations do not support this assumption. Instead, within the range of generally high quality textiles, the products at the bottom of the range in terms of quality were identified in Thorsberg. The generally finest cloths, on the other hand, come from Illerup Ådal with its catchment area further north. From this perspective too, a Roman origin of the textiles does not seem probable.

WAR AND WORSHIP

Besides the primary functions of the textiles in the weapon deposits, their role as part of ritual action is striking. It is beyond the scope of this work to discuss the religious, cultural and social context in which the depositions took place. Yet, there seems no doubt that war was an occasion which involved all members of society in some way – not least the gods. Assuming worship as an integral part of daily life, it is easy to imagine the exceptional significance of a victorious battle which possibly could not have been achieved without the help of the gods. In such a situation, war and worship were inextricably linked.

Only a few elements of the ceremonial procedures after the battle are tangible. As integral parts of the weapon deposits, the fabrics presented here were, unquestionably, consecrated textiles. They had been worn by the defeated foreign warriors during the battle and were considered worthy as sacrificial offerings to the gods. Thus, the first traceable step of the ritual is that the vanquished warriors were, at least partly, undressed. Then – at almost the same time or subsequently – several garments were intentionally damaged, possibly in rage, thereby killing the enemy once again. At some point, individual textiles perceived to have a value comparable to certain metal items would have been selected. Others – probably the majority – were used for covering and wrapping other offerings for the subsequent sacrifice. The wrapping could be meticulous, as the "cloth bundle" from Vimose demonstrates. Wrapping hundreds, or rather thousands, of items took time. It is the penultimate archaeologically traceable step. The final act was the deposition in the lake. Yet, another element seems most likely: the wish to keep the memory alive. The lake as a place of worship remained sacred. Many years later, after another victorious battle, the people returned, to repeat their ceremonies.

Note
1 The lower qualities occur frequently in the settlements but are rare in the burials. They probably existed in the poorer graves without metal, but there is no way of proving this. Surviving textiles are generally restricted to graves containing metal and thus to richer burials. Provided that the affluence of the deceased is not only reflected in inorganic valuables such as jewellery or glass, but also in fine clothes, high quality fabrics are overrepresented in burials compared to settlements.

9. ZUSAMMENFASSUNG UND ERGEBNISSE

Die vier großen Kriegsbeuteopferplätze Illerup Ådal, Vimose, Nydam und Thorsberg wurden in der Folge kriegerischer Auseinandersetzungen angelegt. Sie liegen alle in der Nähe der Ostseeküste auf Jütland einschließlich des nördlichen Schleswig-Holsteins bzw. auf Fünen. Die maximale Entfernung zwischen ihnen, d.h. zwischen Illerup Ådal und Thorsberg, beträgt nicht mehr als etwa 150 km. Hinzu kommt die sehr kleine Deponierung von Gremersdorf-Techelwitz rund 80 km weiter südöstlich, ebenfalls in Ostseenähe.

Verglichen mit den Tausenden von Metallfunden aus den großen Opfermooren erscheint die Zahl der erhaltenen Textilien gering. Dennoch sind die Gewebefunde vor allem aus Illerup Ådal und Thorsberg ohne Frage als herausragende Kollektionen zu betrachten.

Für die technischen und mikrostratigraphischen Analysen standen Auflichtmikroskope zur Verfügung. Die Kombination aus den so gewonnenen Daten mit Informationen sowohl aus veröffentlichten als auch aus unpublizierten Quellen bildet die Basis, um das Textilmaterial vor allem im Hinblick auf seine ursprünglichen Funktionen sowie auf seine Rolle bei den Opferhandlungen hin zu untersuchen. Dieser Schritt wird für jeden Fundplatz separat durchgeführt. Der anschließende Vergleich der Plätze miteinander repräsentiert einen weiteren Schwerpunkt dieser Arbeit. Wiederum stehen technische Merkmale, Primärfunktionen sowie Hinweise auf Abläufe nach der Schlacht im Mittelpunkt. Zu einem zeitlich und räumlich weiter reichenden Vergleich werden schließlich Informationen und Materialien von anderen Fundplätzen und aus anderen Quellengattungen herangezogen, etwa aus Siedlungen, Gräbern und schriftlichen Nachrichten.

ILLERUP ÅDAL

Unter den vier Niederlegungen in Illerup Ådal, dem nördlichsten Fundplatz, spielt "Platz A" die entscheidende Rolle, datiert auf etwa 200 n. Chr. bzw. in einen frühen Abschnitt der Periode C1b. Die weitaus meisten Textilien blieben mithilfe der Eisenoxide verschiedener Waffen erhalten, auf der Oberfläche z.B. von Schildbuckeln, Speerspitzen oder Äxten. Technisch gesehen zeichnen sich die etwa 100 gut dokumentierten Gewebe durch eine Einstellung von 16 × 14 Fäden/cm im Mittel aus. Die allgemein gute Qualität zeigt sich jedoch nicht nur in der Fadendichte, sondern ebenso in der Aufbereitung der Fasern und der Gleichmäßigkeit des Spinnguts, so weit sich dies trotz der Mineralisierung und konservatorischer Maßnahmen erkennen lässt. Nur bei den Leinwandbindungen sind nennenswerte Variationen der Fadenstärken festzustellen. Als Rohmaterial scheint ausschließlich Schafwolle vorzukommen. Seile aus Pflanzenfasern verdeutlichen, dass auch vegetabiles Material erhalten bleiben konnte, doch liegen keine entsprechenden Gewebe vor. Alle Leinwandbindungen (12 %) sind z/z-gewebt. Bei allen anderen Stoffen handelt es sich um Varianten des 2/2-Köpers: Gleichgrat- oder Diamantköper, in z/z- oder z/s oder aber mit Spinnmusterung. Diamantköper in z/s stellen die größte Gruppe. Die Größe der einzelnen Diamantkaros erweist sich als sehr unterschiedlich, d.h. ihre Mustereinheiten variieren. Dies gilt sowohl für Stoffe in z/z als auch in z/s. Dennoch kann festgehalten werden, dass für die Kette jeweils Mustereinheiten mit einer geraden Fadenzahl bevorzugt wurden – am häufigsten 10 Fäden –, während im Schuss ungerade Zahlen vorherrschen, insbesondere 9 und 13. Hinweise auf Rauung liegen von mindestens 17 Stücken vor.

Die geringe Größe der meisten Textilfunde aus Illerup erschwert die Bestimmung ihrer ursprünglichen Funktion. Geraute Oberflächen können mit großer Wahrscheinlichkeit als Kriterium für Kleidung gelten, so dass etwa ein Sechstel des Materials dieser Kategorie zuzurechnen ist. Daran anschließend erscheint es sinnvoll, Textilien vergleichbarer Qualität ebenfalls als Bekleidung anzusprechen, auch wenn Hinweise auf Rauung fehlen. Breite Brettchengewebe sind ein weiteres Charakteristikum hochwertiger Textilien, und zwar speziell der ärmellosen Mäntel. Der Mangel an Nähten und Säumen spricht für die Bevorzugung nicht geschneiderter Stücke, also wiederum von Mänteln. Im Rahmen der Kulthandlungen dienten diese Stoffe dazu, Waffen und persönliche Gegenstände darin einzuwickeln. Zuvor wurden zumindest einige vorsätzlich durch Schnitte und Hiebe beschädigt, wie es auch von den Waffen selbst her bekannt ist. Diese Beobachtung unterstreicht den übereinstimmenden Status von Textilien und Metallgegenständen und zeigt damit gleichzeitig an, dass die Kleidungsstücke – wie die Waffen – den unterlegenen Kriegern zuzurechnen sind.

In der Regel wurde jede Waffe einzeln in Stoff eingeschlagen. Mikrostraten unterschiedlicher Gewebe auf einem Metallfund deuten darauf hin, dass diese individuell eingewickelten Stücke zu größeren Einheiten zusammengefasst wurden, und zwar mithilfe eines anderen Textils und vielleicht auch Seilen. Die Analyse der Fundkarten ergibt allerdings, dass diese Interpretation nicht notwendigerweise korrekt sein muss. Unter anderem können die häufig beobachteten Seilfragmente von kompletten Bündeln stammen, die als eigenständige Opfergaben in das Moor gelangten. Entsprechende Beispiele liegen vor und können als Parallelen zu möglicherweise vollständig niedergelegten Kleidungsstücken betrachtet werden, die gegebenenfalls nicht als Einschlagtücher verwendet, sondern als Gabe an sich geopfert wurden. Funde dieser Art sind in Illerup allerdings nicht überliefert.

VIMOSE

Der zweite Fundplatz ist Vimose auf Fünen. Untersuchungen der jüngsten Zeit lassen acht Deponierungen erkennen, deren älteste in die Zeit um Christi Geburt fällt. Vermutlich gehören alle 41 gut dokumentierten Textilien der Periode C1b an, d.h. der ersten Hälfte des 3. Jahrhunderts n.Chr. Sie bedecken wie in Illerup die Oberflächen eiserner Waffen. 34 Stücke wurden als so genanntes "Stoffbündel" gefunden, zusammen mit einigen weiteren Waffen, die kaum noch Textilspuren aufweisen. Offensichtlich wurden die Bestandteile dieses Bündels einzeln eingewickelt unter Verwendung ein und desselben Gewebes, eines feinen 2/2-Köpers in z/z. Betrachtet man daher alle diese Stücke als einen einzigen Gewebefund, reduziert sich das textile Material aus Vimose auf vier Köper des genannten Typs sowie fünf Leinwandbindungen in z/z, ebenfalls in feiner Qualität.

Das Einschlagen der Speer- und Lanzenspitzen aus dem "Stoffbündel" erfolgte mit äußerster Sorgfalt, die die große Bedeutung dieses Vorgangs im Rahmen der Opferhandlungen unterstreicht. Das wahrscheinlich einseitig geraute Tuch wurde doppelt gelegt und jede Waffe exakt dem Fadenverlauf folgend darauf ausgelegt. Hinweise auf Nähte oder andere Schneiderarbeiten fehlen. Demnach dürfte es sich um ein recht großes Stoffstück gehandelt haben, das daher als wahrscheinlicher Mantel angesprochen wird. Die wenigen anderen Waffen waren ebenfalls eingewickelt. Gerade Schnitte vermitteln den Eindruck von Hieben, wie aus Illerup Ådal bekannt.

THORSBERG

Thorsberg, der südlichste der großen Waffenfundplätze, liegt im nördlichen Schleswig-Holstein. Ebenso wie die anderen, enthielt auch dieses Moor mehrere Deponierungen. Die Textilien sind in diesem Fall allerdings schwieriger zu datieren als die Waffen. Die wahrscheinlichste Einordnung ist Periode C1b oder die erste Hälfte des 3. Jahrhunderts n.Chr. Aufgrund der chemischen Zusammensetzung des Moores blieb Wolle hier sehr gut erhalten, und einige erstaunlich vollständige Kleidungsstücke überdauerten die Zeit. Technisch gesehen sind die Thorsberger Textilien etwas vielfältiger als das Material der drei anderen großen Opferplätze. Unter den 36 Fundnummern bilden jedoch z/s-gewebte Stoffe die große Mehrheit, und unter diesen überwiegen die Gleichgratköper – oft Mäntel – gegenüber den Diamantköpern. Die Mustereinheiten der Diamantköper folgen den aus Illerup bekannten Richtlinien. Obwohl die durchschnittliche Einstellung etwas unter den von den übrigen Plätzen bekannten Marken liegt, ist die Qualität der meisten Stücke gut oder sehr gut, inclusive gut aufbereiteter Fasern, z.T. Rauung und künstlicher Rotfärbung.

Im Zusammenhang mit den Stoffen blieb eine ungewöhnlich große Zahl an Webkanten erhalten. Seitenkanten kommen einfach oder verstärkt mit einem Bündel aus Kettfäden vor, als Schlauchkanten oder mit Brettchenweberei. Transversale Kanten treten ebenfalls in verschiedenen Varianten auf. Einige brettchengewebte Kanten lassen sich mit dem Gewichtswebstuhl in Verbindung bringen, als Anfangs- oder Abschlusskante. Andere weisen auf einen Rundwebstuhl hin. In wenigstens einem Fall kann ein Webgerät mit zwei Bäumen, aber ohne rund geführte Kette nicht ausgeschlossen werden.

Bei einigen Stücken ist die Originalfunktion offensichtlich – eine Tunika, zwei lange Hosen und ein Mantel. Aufgrund der Fragmentgröße und bestimmter, technischer Details können einige andere Gewebe gleichfalls als Mäntel angesprochen werden. Zwei weitere Funde gelten allgemein als Wickelbinden für die Unterschenkel. Diese Interpretation wird hier nicht infrage gestellt, doch könnte sie weiterer Untersuchungen würdig sein. Insbesondere die Tunika und die Hosen wurden im Laufe der Zeit bereits von verschiedenen Experten analysiert. Dennoch können einige neue Aspekte vorgestellt werden.

Zunächst ist daran zu erinnern, dass das eingefasste Loch in der Tunika nicht auf der rechten Brust zu lokalisieren ist, sondern auf dem linken Schulterblatt. Die Seite, die dem Besucher in der Ausstellung präsentiert und in zahlreichen Publikationen abgebildet wird, ist die Rückseite des Kleidungsstücks. Die Tunika besitzt einen künstlichen Rotton, der bereits zur Zeit der Niederlegung teilweise ausgeblichen war, wie sich entlang einiger Schnitte zeigen lässt. Wenn dieses Hemd also einige Zeit lang getragen wurde, wie es der Verlust an Farbe andeutet, sind die kurzen, blauen, dünnen Schnüre entlang der offenen Seitennähte kaum als Befestigungen zu interpretieren. Statt dessen werden sie hier als Dekoration angesprochen. Möglicherweise wurden die Nähte im Zusammenhang mit den Opferhandlungen aufgeschnitten und die Verzierungen dabei gleichzeitig beschädigt. Zumindest die Schnitte im Gewebe lassen sich als Parallele zu den aus Illerup und Vimose bekannten, vorsätzlichen Zerstörungen deuten.

Kurze, dünne, blaue Schnüre desselben Typs blieben auch entlang der Waden der einen Hose (3684) erhalten. Hier wäre eine Vorrichtung zum wiederholten Schließen der offenen Nähte zu erwarten, da die Hosenbeine sehr schmal geschnitten sind. Andere schmal gehaltene Hosen scheinen entsprechende Elemente jedoch nicht zu besitzen. Grundsätzlich entspricht das Bild dem der Tunika, mit kurzen Schnurenden, die aus einem nicht nennenswert strapazierten Gewebe herausragen. Zusätzliche Stichlöcher wurden nicht beobachtet. Es mag sich also wie bei der Tunika um eine Verzierung handeln, jedoch verbunden mit einer anderen Methode, um die offene Naht zu schließen. Die Ähnlichkeiten zwischen Tunika und Hose, inclusive einer ungewöhnlichen Variante einer transversalen Webkante, stützen die These, dass beide Teile ursprünglich eine Einheit bildeten. Allerdings stammen die beiden Stücke nicht vom selben Gewebe, wie sich aus den unterschiedlichen Mustereinheiten der Diamantköper klar ergibt.

Ein berühmtes Merkmal dieser Hose sind die integrierten Füßlinge. Nur einer blieb erhalten, der andere ging verloren. Ob dies auf die Zeit im Moor zurückgeht oder vielleicht auf die Vorbereitungen zu den Opferungen oder sogar noch älteren Datums ist, bleibt unklar. Die andere Hose (3685) ist insgesamt deutlich schlechter erhalten, doch sind beide Füßlinge vorhanden. Ihre obere Kante ist geschnitten, aber nicht gesäumt, und Schlaufen für einen Gürtel fehlen. Möglicherweise wurden einige Zentimeter am oberen Rand weggeschnitten, bevor die Hose in das Moor gelangte.

Typische Merkmale der Mäntel aus Thorsberg sind die Gleichgratköper in z/s, eine etwas geringere Fadendichte pro cm im Vergleich zur Tunika und den Hosen sowie breite, brettchengewebte Kanten. Letztere können vermutlich als Statussymbol gedeutet werden, vergleichbar einigen Verzierungen auf Schwertern. Mehrere Brettchenkanten wurden nicht zeitgleich mit den Grundgeweben hergestellt, sondern anschließend ergänzt.

Unter den kleineren Gewebesten können aufgrund der eben genannten Merkmale einige als Mäntel klassifiziert werden. Andere ähneln den Stoffen der Tunika und der Hosen, sie sind zum Teil gefärbt und verziert. Manche besitzen keine Merkmale, die auf ihre frühere Funktion schließen lassen, aber grundsätzliche, qualitative Übereinstimmungen mit den genannten Stücken legen auch hier eine Nutzung als Kleidung nahe.

Im Hinblick auf die Opferungen wurden zumindest einige Textilien zusammengerollt und als individuelle Opfergaben dargebracht. Sie wurden nicht als Einschlagtücher verwendet, wie es für Illerup und Vimose typisch ist. Das Einwickeln von Gegenständen darf auch für Thorsberg vermutet werden, doch ist es nicht nachgewiesen, da die Kombination von Textil und Metall fehlt. Als Parallele zu den beiden anderen Fundplätzen ist jedoch auch hier die vorsätzliche Beschädigung der Textilien belegt. Besonders auffällig sind die Schnitte in der Tunika, ergänzt durch zwei lange Risse und vermutlich aufgeschnittene Nähte. Vergleichbare Hiebe wurden auf einem Mantel festgestellt. An einer Hose ist das obere Ende beschädigt, möglicherweise als entsprechendes Phänomen. Ob der fehlende Füßling an der anderen Hose gleichfalls auf mutwillige Zerstörung zurückzuführen ist, lässt sich nicht nachweisen.

NYDAM

Das Moor von Nydam, der letzte hier zu nennende Fundplatz, liegt etwas nördlich der heutigen deutsch-dänischen Grenze. Wie in den großen Waffenopfermooren üblich, wurden auch hier Opfergaben bei verschiedenen Gelegenheiten dargebracht. In diesem Fall können verschiedene Kategorien von Textilien unterschiedlichen Deponierungen zugewiesen werden. Eine dieser Gruppen ist an silberne Agraffen gebunden. Sie kamen einige Zeit nach 300 n.Chr. zusammen mit dem Kiefernboot (C) in das Moor. Wohl um dieselbe Zeit, 310–320 n.Chr., wurde das Eichenschiff (B) gebaut, so dass die zwischen den originalen Planken gefundenen, als Kalfat wiederverwerteten Stoffstücke etwas älter sein dürften. Die einigen Waffen anhaftenden Textilien gehören vor allem der zweiten Hälfte des 4. Jahrhunderts an.

9. Zusammenfassung und Ergebnisse

Da die Waffen die offensichtlichste Parallele zu den anderen Fundplätzen darstellen, d.h. zu Illerup Ådal und Vimose, beginnt die Darstellung mit dieser Gruppe. Die Untersuchung von mehr als 100 Stücken erbrachte zumindest geringfügige Faserreste auf den Oberflächen. Der Erhaltungszustand ist allgemein jedoch so dürftig, dass nur in sechs Fällen signifikante Aussagen getroffen werden können. Die wenigen bestimmbaren Merkmale können unmittelbar mit den Ergebnissen vor allem aus Illerup Ådal verglichen werden. Entsprechendes gilt für die Agraffen, von denen mehr als 200 untersucht wurden. Wiederum ist der Informationsgehalt sehr begrenzt, doch liegen hochwertige Textilien vor, wie es im Zusammenhang mit derartig wertvollen Verzierungen erwartet werden darf. Neben den Textilien selbst ist ihre Lokalisation teilweise oben auf den Agraffen von Interesse sowie auch ihre Verteilung auf der Fundstelle. Die Untersuchung ergab, dass die Agraffen auf den Kleidungsstücken — Tuniken und/oder Hosen – belassen wurden und dass diese Teile wie in Thorsberg aufgerollt und als Ganzes niedergelegt wurden.

Als letztes ist das Kalfatmaterial zu erwähnen, das in zwei Kategorien gegliedert werden kann. Obwohl beide Gruppen ausschließlich wiederverwendete Gewebe beinhalten, sind für die Fragmente, die bereits beim Bootsbau Verwendung fanden, bessere Qualitäten zu konstatieren als für jene, die bei späteren Reparaturen eingesetzt wurden. Erstere sind qualitativ vergleichbar mit dem Material aus Illerup. Ein gemeinsames Merkmal beider Gruppen ist jedoch die Seltenheit z/s-gewebter Stoffe.

Abgesehen von dem den Agraffen anhaftenden Material, das auf Tuniken und/oder Hosen hinweist, ist es schwierig, primäre Funktionen zu bestimmen. Das Fehlen von Nähten und Säumen innerhalb des Kalfatmaterials mag mit der bevorzugten Verwendung nicht geschneiderten Materials zu erklären sein. Während der Kulthandlungen blieb das Kalfat unsichtbar und spielte daher keine Rolle im zeremoniellen Ablauf. Anders ist die Situation bei den durch die Agraffen repräsentierten Tuniken und/oder Hosen. Sie galten augenscheinlich als Wertgegenstände und wurden als eigenständige Opfergaben dargebracht. Andere Textilien nutzte man als Einschlagtücher für Waffen, wie es aus Illerup Ådal und Vimose überliefert ist.

SPEZIELLE ASPEKTE IM VERGLEICH

Obwohl das Spektrum der Bindungen auf den vier großen Fundplätzen nicht identisch ist, prägen die Übereinstimmungen den Gesamteindruck. Dazu gehören das Ausgangsmaterial, der allgemeine Mangel an Textilien in s/s, die Fadendichte und ihre Ausgewogenheit in Kette und Schuss. Innerhalb der Bandbreite an Bindungen ist der visuelle Eindruck, den die Gewebe vermitteln, ausgesprochen ähnlich. Ein Diamantköper aus Illerup gleicht einem Diamantköper aus Thorsberg – während sich beide von entsprechenden Stoffen aus dem östlichen Mittelmeerraum deutlich unterscheiden. Die ungewöhnliche Variationsbreite an Webkanten und damit verbunden auch an Webgeräten, wie sie in Thorsberg beobachtet wurde, ist auf den übrigen Fundplätzen nicht zu verifizieren. Doch zumindest Schlauchkanten und brettchengewebte Kanten sind nicht auf Thorsberg beschränkt.

Für die Suche nach vergleichbaren Textilien wurde der geographische Rahmen sehr weit gesteckt: Europa, Ägypten, der Nahe und Mittlere Osten sowie Innerasien. Ziel ist es nicht, das von dort bekannte Textilmaterial in seiner Gänze vorzustellen, sondern bestimmten Charakteristika der Funde aus den Waffenopfermooren nachzugehen. Ausgehend von den Thorsberger Kleidungsstücken werden Merkmale wie Rohmaterial, Bindung, Schnitt und Verzierungen mit chronologisch und geographisch unterschiedlich nahen Parallelen verglichen.

Angefangen mit den Tuniken zeigt sich, dass individuelle Charakteristika wie eingesetzte Ärmel, eine horizontale Halsöffnung, eine senkrechte Kette sowie Agraffen bzw. aufgenähte Verzierungen hier und dort auftreten, etwa in Innerasien, Ägypten, Frankreich, Dänemark und Schweden. Andererseits, wie in einem solch großen Gebiet nicht anders zu erwarten, unterscheiden sich andere Merkmale der betreffenden Tuniken vollständig von dem Thorsberger Beispiel. Selbst die anscheinend nächsten Parallelen, die römerzeitlichen Moorfunde Norddeutschlands, weisen Eigenheiten auf, die keine enge Verwandtschaft nahe legen. Die Gemeinsamkeiten innerhalb dieser Gruppe beschränken sich auf die Verwendung von Wolle und häufig Köper.

Aus Wolle sind auch die in anderen Mooren entdeckten, langen und kurzen Hosen hergestellt. Darüber hinaus ähneln Schnittmuster und die schmale Form der Beine den Thorsberger Exemplaren, doch besitzen sie keine Füßlinge. Wenn dieses Merkmal im Vordergrund steht, kommen die besten Parallelen aus Asien sowie aus deutlich jüngeren skandinavischen Quellen. Für die These, dass die Thorsberger Hosen als Reithosen anzusprechen seien, konnten keine funktional begründeten Belege beigebracht werden, doch mag der Status des Trägers in diesem Zusammenhang eine Rolle spielen.

Bezüglich der Mäntel ist es leichter, Vergleiche aus näher gelegenen Regionen und Perioden heranzuziehen. Die Beispiele aus Thorsberg ähneln einander deutlich, es sind Gleichgratköper mittelfeiner oder feiner Qualität. Eine Entsprechung scheint aus Vimose vorzuliegen. Die Fülle feinerer Diamantköper in Illerup Ådal legt nahe, dass solche Gewebe ebenfalls als Mäntel gedient haben dürften. Der Umriss ist rechteckig, oft verziert mit breiten Brettchenkanten. Die Form ist identisch mit den Mänteln der Soldaten im Römischen Reich, jedoch fehlen dort augenscheinlich die breiten Brettchengewebe.

Die Verwendung gewebter, offenbar wiederverwerteter Textilien als Kalfat war nicht auf den Norden beschränkt. Zeitgenössische Parallelen sind aus Frankreich bekannt. Später wurden Gewebe häufig bei Reparaturen eingesetzt, während man beim Bootsbau weniger stark aufbereitetes Material bevorzugte, etwa lose gerollte Stränge aus Wolle. Rein hypothetisch ist zu überlegen, ob ursprünglich eine Verbindung existierte zwischen der Tradition, ein Boot zu "nähen", und der Verwendung gewebter Stoffe – eine Verbindung, die im Zuge der Weiterentwicklung des Bootsbaus langsam verloren ging.

TEXTILIEN AUS ANDEREN QUELLEN

Zwei wesentliche Aspekte, die auf den Waffenfundplätzen beobachtet wurden – nämlich einerseits die Deponierung vollständiger Kleidungsstücke und andererseits die Verwendung von Textilien zum Einhüllen anderer Gegenstände – sind auch aus nicht militärischen Zusammenhängen überliefert. Die Weihung von Textilien wurde wenigstens seit der Bronzezeit praktiziert, und einige eisenzeitliche Moorfunde können als Opfergaben angesprochen werden. Die zweite Funktion, als Einschlagtuch, ist vielleicht am besten durch den Fund von Vehnemoor repräsentiert, der eine in einen besonders hochwertigen Mantel gewickelte Bronzeschale enthielt. Darüber hinaus ist dieses Phänomen aus Gräbern bekannt.

Textilien aus Bestattungen stellen eine weitere wichtige Vergleichsgruppe zu den Kriegsbeuteopfern dar. Allerdings ist dieses Material zu umfangreich, um im vorliegenden Rahmen ausführlich behandelt werden zu können. Außerdem mangelt es häufig an einer funktionalen Bestimmung der Gewebereste. Dennoch werden hier einige wenige Fundplätze vorgestellt, um abzuschätzen, ob einer Bestattung eine ähnliche Bedeutung beigemessen wurde wie einem Feldzug, was sich möglicherweise in der

9. Zusammenfassung und Ergebnisse

Verwendung ähnlicher Textilqualitäten widerspiegelt. Methodisch gesehen ist die Basis dafür sehr schwach, nicht nur, weil funktionale Bestimmungen fehlen, sondern auch, weil das Geschlecht und andere Faktoren außer Acht gelassen und insgesamt nur wenige Gräber mit einbezogen werden. Drei etwa zeitgenössische Gräberfelder wurden ausgewählt. Keines enthielt außerordentlich reiche Bestattungen, obwohl die Existenz von Metallbeigaben, die die Erhaltung der Textilien ermöglichte, nahe legt, dass die Verstorbenen vermutlich nicht arm waren. Während die wenigen Gewebe aus Niedersachsen gut mit den Thorsberger Funden im Allgemeinen übereinstimmen, ähneln die Funde aus Dänemark dem Material aus Vimose. Außergewöhnliche Bestattungen, "Fürstengräber", können dagegen auch feinere Gewebe enthalten sowie ungewöhnliche Materialien wie Goldfäden. Derartige Raritäten liegen von den Waffenfundplätzen nicht vor.

Im Gegensatz zu den Gräbern spiegeln Fundkomplexe aus Siedlungen möglicherweise alle sozialen und ökonomischen Schichten wider. Zwei zeitgenössische Wurten, Feddersen Wierde und Tofting, wurden herangezogen. Tofting erbrachte nur fünf Stoffe, alles Köper, qualitativ von grob bis fein reichend. Auf der Feddersen Wierde wurden mehr als 600 Gewebe geborgen, darunter mehr als 50 % Leinwandbindungen. Die große Mehrheit der Köper war als Gleichgrat gewebt. Feine Stoffe sind selten, während grobe in großer Zahl vorkommen. Diese Daten stützen die Überlegung, dass in den Siedlungen eine größere Bandbreite an Textilien Verwendung fand, einschließlich zahlreicher einfacher Gewebe, während auf den Gräberfeldern die besseren Qualitäten vorherrschen. Es darf vermutet werden, dass ärmer ausgestattete Gräber ohne Metallbeigaben auch Textilien geringerer Qualität enthielten, doch mangelt es an Nachweismöglichkeiten. Die sich in Siedlungen und Gräbern abzeichnenden Verhältnisse unterstreichen darüber hinaus das auf den Waffenfundplätzen gewonnene Ergebnis, dass die dort angetroffenen Stoffe vor allem den oberen Bereich der verfügbaren Textilqualitäten repräsentieren.

HERKUNFT

Die technischen Merkmale wie auch die Qualitäten der Textilien ähneln sich auf allen vier Fundplätzen, unabhängig davon, welche Gegenden als wahrscheinliche Heimat der ehemaligen Eigentümer bestimmt wurden, also Norddeutschland oder verschiedene Regionen Skandinaviens. Viele Charakteristika unterscheiden sich deutlich von typischen Funden z.B. aus dem östlichen Mittelmeerraum. Auf der anderen Seite ist auf einem sehr allgemeinen Niveau festzuhalten, dass entsprechendes Material auch aus den römischen Provinzen bekannt ist. Zweifellos ist aber zu konstatieren, dass die Details der am besten erhaltenen Funde, d.h. der Kleidungsstücke aus Thorsberg, nicht speziell in Richtung des Römischen Imperiums deuten, da typisch römische Merkmale fehlen, etwa erweiterte Leinwandbindung, gezwirnte Kanten oder Randverstärkungen mit zwei oder mehr Kettbündeln. Dies schließt einen gewissen Austausch von technischem Wissen oder auch Materialien natürlich nicht aus.

Ein augenfälliges Element sind die breiten, aufwändigen Brettchenkanten. Ihr Fehlen im Römischen Reich war ein Argument in einer Diskussion zur Herkunft der Mäntel, die Lise Bender Jørgensen und John Peter Wild führten. Diese Diskussion wird nun wieder aufgenommen (siehe auch Lise Ræder Knudsen in diesem Band). Aus vornehmlich zwei Gründen werden die breiten Brettchenkanten als einheimisch germanische Produkte angesehen. Zum einen sind sie typisch für die in Norddeutschland und Skandinavien auch unabhängig von Kriegsbeuteopfern gefundenen Mäntel. Zum anderen zeigen germanische Verzierungen an römischen Schwertern, dass die Träger ihren Status durch sichtbare Zeichen germanischen Typus bekundeten. Die zur Herstellung der Mäntel und Brettchenkanten benötigte Ausrüstung war durchaus bekannt, und es gibt keinen Grund, einen Mangel an entsprechenden Kenntnissen anzunehmen.

Vor diesem Hintergrund ist davon auszugehen, dass es sich bei den Textilien aus den Waffenopfermooren um einheimische Produkte des Barbaricums und Skandinaviens handelt, mit einer gemeinsamen Tradition und ähnlichem Geschmack. Einige Isotopenanalysen bestätigen dieses Ergebnis.

Für die Suche nach Vergleichsmaterial wurde ein chronologisch und geographisch weiter Rahmen gewählt, der Europa, Asien und Ägypten einschließt. Es zeigt sich, dass Parallelen zu vielen Details aus Innerasien und dem Mittleren Osten überliefert sind, d.h. aus Gegenden, in denen die Reiterei eine bedeutende Rolle im Leben der Menschen spielte. Diese Übereinstimmungen scheinen die Ansicht früherer Autoren zu bestätigen, dass Tunika und lange Hose, also die typischen Kleidungsstücke sowohl keltischer als auch germanischer Männer, ihren Ursprung in Asien haben.

TEXTILIEN FÜR DEN KRIEG

In ihrer Gesamtheit scheinen die Funde aus den Kriegsbeuteopfern die Struktur eines germanischen Heeres mit principes, comites und pedites widerzuspiegeln (von Carnap-Bornheim and Ilkjær 1996a, 483–484), mit nur wenigen, aber exquisiten Reiterausrüstungen, die im Zusammenhang mit der militärischen Elite zu sehen sind. Wie schon von anderen Autoren bemerkt, dürften die gut erhaltenen Kleidungsstücke aus Thorsberg ebenfalls dieser Elite zuzurechnen sein, also vermutlich den principes. In der vorliegenden Arbeit gründet sich dieser Schluss teilweise darauf, dass vollständige Stücke als eigenständige Einheiten geopfert wurden, d.h. als Wertgegenstände, während andere Textilien zum Einwickeln verwendet wurden. Die flächenhafte Verbreitung von Geweben in den Mooren, insbesondere in Illerup Ådal, zeigt ihre massenhafte Nutzung als Einschlagtücher. Sicher können derartige Mengen nicht allein aus den persönlichen Ausrüstungen der principes stammen. Die überlieferten Textilien müssen auch Kleidungsstücke der unteren Ränge enthalten. Ob die Ausstattung der Krieger mit Kleidung ganz oder teilweise den Heerführern oblag, wie es bezüglich der Waffen gewesen sein mag (ibid., 484–485), ist nicht zu entscheiden. Ohne Frage jedoch war der Bedarf an guten und sogar hochwertigen Textilien groß. Wäre das Römische Reich die beste und vielleicht einzige Quelle für Produkte dieser Art, wären die besten Qualitäten wohl in jenen Deponierungen zu erwarten, die insgesamt die engsten Beziehungen zu den römischen Provinzen aufweisen, d.h. in Thorsberg und Vimose. Die nun vorliegenden Ergebnisse stützen diese Annahme jedoch nicht. Im Gegenteil, innerhalb des Spektrums allgemein hochwertiger Qualitäten nimmt Thorsberg den Platz am unteren Ende der Skala ein. Die allgemein feinsten Gewebe kommen dagegen aus Illerup Ådal mit seinem Einzugsgebiet weiter im Norden. Auch aus dieser Perspektive heraus erscheint eine römische Herkunft der Textilien unwahrscheinlich.

KRIEG UND KULT

Neben den primären Funktionen einiger Textilien aus den Waffenopfermooren ist ihre Rolle im Rahmen ritueller Handlungen augenfällig. Es liegt jenseits der Möglichkeiten dieser Arbeit, den religiösen, kulturellen und sozialen Kontext zu diskutieren, in dem die Deponierungen stattfanden. Dennoch kann kaum ein Zweifel bestehen, dass Krieg ein Ereignis war, das alle Mitglieder der

Gesellschaft betraf – auch die Götter. Wenn man Religion und Kult als integralen Bestandteil des täglichen Lebens annimmt, ist es leicht, sich die außerordentliche Bedeutung einer gewonnenen Schlacht vorzustellen, die ohne göttliche Unterstützung vielleicht unmöglich erschien. In dieser Situation waren Krieg und Kult eng miteinander verknüpft.

Nur wenige Elemente der zeremoniellen Handlungen nach einer Schlacht sind archäologisch fassbar. Als integrale Bestandteile der Waffendeponierungen können die hier vorgestellten Gewebe sicherlich als geweihte Textilien betrachtet werden. Sie wurden während der Auseinandersetzungen von den fremden Kriegern getragen und waren es wert, den Gottheiten geopfert zu werden. Der erste zu erschließende Schritt ist daher die zumindest teilweise Entkleidung der Opfer. Dann – entweder fast gleichzeitig oder später – wurden einige Kleidungsstücke rituell beschädigt, vielleicht in Rage wurde der Feind noch einmal getötet. Zu gegebener Zeit wurden bestimmte Textilien ausgewählt als Wertgegenstände entsprechend den metallenen Beutestücken. Andere – wahrscheinlich die Mehrzahl – wurden benutzt, um weitere Opfergaben zu umhüllen und einzuwickeln und damit einen geeigneten Rahmen für die nachfolgenden Opferhandlungen zu schaffen. Das Einschlagen konnte mit außerordentlicher Akkuratesse erfolgen, wie das "Stoffbündel" aus Vimose beweist. Hunderte oder sogar Tausende Gegenstände einzuwickeln, erforderte Zeit. Es ist der vorletzte Schritt, der mit archäologischen Mitteln nachgewiesen werden kann. Der letzte Akt war die Deponierung im See. Allerdings erscheint ein weiteres Element sehr wahrscheinlich: der Wunsch, die Erinnerung an das Geschehene am Leben zu erhalten. Der See als Ort des Kultes blieb heilig. Viele Jahre später, nach einer weiteren erfolgreichen Schlacht, kehrten die Menschen zurück und wiederholten ihre Zeremonien.

10. BIBLIOGRAPHY

Abegg-Wigg, A. 2008. Zu den Grabinventaren aus den "Fürstengräbern" von Neudorf-Bornstein, in A. Abegg-Wigg and A. Rau (eds), *Aktuelle Forschungen zu Kriegsbeuteopfern und Fürstengräbern im Barbaricum. Internationales Kolloquium, Schleswig 15.–18. Juni 2006, Schriften des Archäologischen Landesmuseums*, Ergänzungsreihe 4, Neumünster, 279–297.

Abegg-Wigg, A. and A. Rau (eds) 2008. *Aktuelle Forschungen zu Kriegsbeuteopfern und Fürstengräbern im Barbaricum. Internationales Kolloquium, Schleswig 15.–18. Juni 2006*, Schriften des Archäologischen Landesmuseums, Ergänzungsreihe 4, Neumünster.

Bemmann, G. and J. Bemmann 1998. *Der Opferplatz von Nydam, Bd 1: Text, Bd 2: Katalog und Tafeln*, Neumünster.

Bénazeth, D. and C. Fluck 2004. Fussbekleidung der Reitertracht aus Antinoopolis im Überblick, in C. Fluck and G. Vogelsang-Eastwood (eds), *Riding costume in Egypt, Origin and appearance*, Leiden, 189–205.

Bender Jørgensen, L. 1978–1980. (Illerup Ådal-textiler). (Three unpublished reports).

Bender Jørgensen, L. 1985 (1987). A Coptic Tapestry and other Textile Remains from the Royal Frankish Graves of Cologne Cathedral, *Acta Archaeologica* 56, 85–100.

Bender Jørgensen, L. 1986a. Forhistoriske textiler i Skandinavien. Prehistoric Scandinavian Textiles, *Nordiske Fortidsminder*, Serie B, 9, København.

Bender Jørgensen, L. 1986b. Textilresterne fra Hjemsted, in P. Ethelberg, *Hjemsted – en gravplads fra 4. og 5. årh. e.Kr.*, Skrifter fra Museumsrådet for Sønderjyllands Amt 2, 92–100.

Bender Jørgensen, L. 1992. *North European Textiles until AD 1000*, Aarhus.

Bender Jørgensen, L. 2006. The Late Roman Fort at Abū Shaʿār, Egypt: Textiles in their Archaeological Context, Textiles in situ, *Riggisberger Berichte* 13, 161–173.

Bender Jørgensen, L. and P. Walton 1986. Dyes and Fleece Types in Prehistoric Textiles from Scandinavia and Germany, *Journal of Danish Archaeology* 5, 177–188.

Biborski, M. and J. Ilkjær 2006a. Illerup Ådal, 11, Die Schwerter: Textband, *Jutland Archaeological Society Publications* XXV:11.

Biborski, M. and J. Ilkjær 2006b. Illerup Ådal, 12, Die Schwerter: Katalog, Tafeln und Fundlisten, *Jutland Archaeological Society Publications* XXV:12.

Bockius, R. 2000 (2003). Antike Prahme. Monumentale Zeugnisse keltisch-römischer Binnenschiffahrt aus der Zeit vom 2. Jh. v. Chr. bis ins 3. Jh. n. Chr., *Jahrbuch des Römisch-Germanischen Zentralmuseums Mainz* 47, 439–493.

Bunker, E. C. 2001. The Cemetery at Shanpula, Xinjiang. Simple Burials, Complex Textiles, in D. Keller and R. Schorta (eds), *Fabulous Creatures from the Desert Sands*, Riggisberger Berichte 10, Riggisberg, 15–45.

von Buttel-Reepen, H. 1930. Ein bemerkenswerter Moorfund von 28 silberverzierten Bronze-Fibeln, *Zur Vorgeschichte Nordwest-Deutschlands, Funde von Runen mit bildlichen Darstellungen und Funde aus älteren vorgeschichtlichen Kulturen*, Oldenburg, 58–65.

von Carnap-Bornheim, C. 2004. Römische Militaria aus dem Thorsberger Moor. Fundzusammensetzung, Kontext, Interpretation, in M. Erdrich and C. von Carnap-Bornheim, *Corpus der römischen Funde im europäischen Barbaricum, Deutschland, Bd. 5, Freie und Hansestadt Hamburg und Land Schleswig-Holstein*, Bonn, 15–24.

von Carnap-Bornheim, C. and J. Ilkjær 1996a. Illerup Ådal, 5, Die Prachtausrüstungen: Textband, *Jutland Archaeological Society Publications* XXV:5.

von Carnap-Bornheim, C. and J. Ilkjær 1996b. Illerup Ådal, 6, Die Prachtausrüstungen: Katalog, Fundlisten und Literatur, *Jutland Archaeological Society Publications* XXV:6.

von Carnap-Bornheim, C. and J. Ilkjær 1996c. Illerup Ådal, 7, Die Prachtausrüstungen: Tafelband, *Jutland Archaeological Society Publications* XXV:7.

von Carnap-Bornheim, C. and J. Ilkjær 1996d. Illerup Ådal, 8, Die Prachtausrüstungen: Fundliste, *Jutland Archaeological Society Publications* XXV:8.

von Carnap-Bornheim, C. and J. Ilkjær 2008. "Jernalderen i Nordeuropa" und "Zwischen Thorsberg und Bornstein" – Archäologische Forschung im internationalen Netzwerk, in A. Abegg-Wigg and A. Rau (eds), *Aktuelle Forschungen zu Kriegsbeuteopfern und Fürstengräbern im Barbaricum, Internationales Kolloquium, Schleswig 15.–18. Juni 2006*, Schriften des Archäologischen Landesmuseums, Ergänzungsreihe 4, Neumünster, 9–17.

von Carnap-Bornheim, C., M.-L. Nosch, G. Grupe, A.-M. Mekota and M. M. Schweissing 2007. Stable strontium isotopic ratios from archaeological organic remains from the Thorsberg peat bog, *Rapid Communications in Mass Spectrometry* 21, 1541–1545.

Ciszuk, M. forthcoming. Early Iron Age weaving technology, in U. Mannering and M. Gleba, *Designed for Life and Death*.

Croom, A. T. 2002. *Roman clothing and fashion*, Stroud.

Crowfoot, E. 1979. Textile remains, in G. Clarke, *The Roman Cemetery of Lankhills*, Oxford, 329–331.

Desrosiers, S. and A. Lorquin 1998. Gallo-Roman Period Archaeological Textiles found in France, in L. Bender Jørgensen and C. Rinaldo (eds), *Textiles in European Archaeology, Report from the 6th NESAT Symposium, 7–11th May 1996 in Borås*, Gotarc Series A, 1, Göteborg, 53–72.

van Driel-Murray, C. 1999. A Set of Roman Clothing from Les Martres-de-Veyre, France, *Archaeological Textiles Newsletter* 28, 11–15.

van Driel-Murray, C. 2000. A late Roman assemblage from Deurne (Netherlands), *Bonner Jahrbücher* 200, 293–308.

Engelhardt, C. 1860. *Diary of the excavation in Thorsberg* (Copy of unpublished manuscript in the Archive of the National Museum of Denmark in Copenhagen).

Engelhardt, C. 1863. *Thorsbjerg Mosefund*, Kjöbenhavn (reprint 1969).

Engelhardt, C. 1865. *Nydam Mosefund*, Kjöbenhavn (reprint 1970).

Engelhardt, C. 1869. *Vimose Fundet*, Kjöbenhavn (reprint 1970).

Engelhardt, C. n.d. *Frederik den Syvendes Privatsamling. Thorsbjerg Mosefund* (Copy of unpublished list in the Archive of the National Museum of Denmark in Copenhagen).

Erdrich, M. and C. von Carnap-Bornheim 2004. *Corpus der römischen Funde im europäischen Barbaricum, Deutschland, Bd. 5*, Freie und Hansestadt Hamburg und Land Schleswig-Holstein, Bonn.

Falk, H. 1919. Altwestnordische Kleiderkunde. Mit besonderer Berücksichtigung der Terminologie, *Videnskapsselskapets Skrifter* II, Hist.-Filos. Klasse, 3, Kristiania 1919.

Farke, H. 1991. Schnüre, Geflechte und Leder aus Höhlen bei Bad Frankenhausen, *Alt-Thüringen* 26, 123–140.

Farke, H. 1994a. Beobachtungen an Textilien nach der Präsentation in einer Ausstellung, *Arbeitsblätter für Restauratoren*, (1), 192–195.

Farke, H. 1994b. Ein zweitausendjähriges Bekleidungsstück – Beobachtungen nach der Präsentation einer Ausstellung, in G. Jaacks and K. Tidow (eds), *Archäologische Textilfunde – Archaeological Textiles, Textilsymposium Neumünster, 4.–7.5.1993* (NESAT V), Neumünster, 69–81.

Farke, H. 1998. Der Männerkittel aus Bernuthsfeld – Beobachtungen während einer Restaurierung, in L. Bender Jørgensen and C. Rinaldo (eds), *Textiles in European Archaeology, Report from the 6th NESAT Symposium, 7–11th May 1996 in Borås*, Gotarc Series A, 1, Göteborg, 99–106.

Farke, H. 2004. Textile Spuren in einem kaiserzeitlichen Grab aus Norddeutschland, in J. Maik (ed), Priceless Invention of Humanity – Textiles, Report from the 8th North European Symposium for Archaeological Textiles, 8–10 May 2002 in Łódź/Poland, *Acta Archaeologica Lodziensia* 50/1, Łódź, 39–43.

Fischer, C.-H. 1997. Historische organische Farbstoffe, *Spektrum der Wissenschaft* 10, 104–108.

Frei, K. M., R. Frei, U. Mannering, M. Gleba, M. L. Nosch and H. Lyngstrøm 2009. Provenance of ancient textiles – A pilot study evaluating the strontium isotope system in wool, *Archaeometry* 51, (2), 252–276.

Fuhrmann, I. 1941–42. Zum Moorgewand von Reepsholt, *Prähistorische Zeitschrift* 32–33, 339–365.

Gräf, J. 2008. Die Lederfunde aus dem Thorsberger Moor, in A. Abegg-Wigg and A. Rau (eds), *Aktuelle Forschungen zu Kriegsbeuteopfern und Fürstengräbern im Barbaricum, Internationales Kolloquium, Schleswig 15.–18. Juni 2006*, Schriften des Archäologischen Landesmuseums, Ergänzungsreihe 4, Neumünster, 215–229.

Grane, T. 2003. Romerske kilder til Germaniens geografi og etnografi, in L. Jørgensen, B. Storgaard and L. Gebauer Thomsen (eds), *Sejrens triumf*, (Exhibition in Copenhagen, accompanying publication), (København), 126–147.

Granger-Taylor, H. 2007. 'Weaving Clothes to Shape in the Ancient World' 25 Years on: Corrections and Further Details with Particular Reference to the

Cloaks from Lahun, *Archaeological Textiles Newsletter* 45, 26–35.

Gremli, L. S. 2007a. The status of research on Liao-dynasty textiles, in R. Schorta (ed), *Dragons of silk, flowers of gold, A group of Liao-dynasty textiles at the Abegg-Stiftung*, (Riggisberg), 17–52.

Gremli, L. S. 2007b. A group of Liao-dynasty textiles and metal objects at the Abegg-Stiftung, in R. Schorta (ed), *Dragons of silk, flowers of gold, A group of Liao-dynasty textiles at the Abegg-Stiftung*, (Riggisberg), 53–68.

Hägg, I. 1974. Kvinnodräkten i Birka. Livplaggens rekonstruktion på grundval av det arkeologiska materialet, *Aun* 2, Uppsala.

Hägg, I. 1989. Historische Textilforschung auf neuen Wegen, *Archäologisches Korrespondenzblatt* 19, 431–439.

Hägg, I. 2000. Geopferte Gewänder, in M. Gebühr, *Nydam und Thorsberg, Opferplätze der Eisenzeit*, (Exhibition in Schleswig, accompanying publication), Schleswig, 28–29.

Hahne, H. 1919. *Moorleichenfunde aus Niedersachsen. – Vorzeitfunde aus Niedersachsen herausgegeben vom Provinzialmuseum zu Hannover*, B (VI), Hildesheim.

Hald, M. 1946. Ancient Textile Techniques in Egypt and Scandinavia, *Acta Archaeologica* XVII, 49–98.

Hald, M. 1980. Ancient Danish Textiles from Bogs and Burials, *Publications of the National Museum, Archaeological-Historical Series* XXI, Copenhagen 1980. Originally published in Danish as *Olddanske Tekstiler*. Nordiske Fortidsminder. Det Kgl. Nordiske Oldskriftselskab, Femte Bind, København.

Halpaap, R. 1991. Der Fibelfund von Strückhausen, Kr. Wesermarsch, *Bodenfunde aus der Wesermarsch, Archäologische Mitteilungen aus Nordwestdeutschland*, Beiheft 5, Oldenburg, 57–66.

Harlow, M. 2004. Clothes maketh the man: power dressing and elite masculinity in the later Roman world, in L. Brubaker and J. M. H. Smith (eds), *Gender in the early Medieval world, East and west, 300–900*, Cambridge, 44–69.

Hartz, S. 2002/2003. Baggersondagen im Thorsberger Moor, LA 53, Elfter Jahresbericht des Archäologischen Landesamtes Schleswig-Holstein, *Offa* 59/60, 302–305.

Haussig, H. W. 1992. *Archäologie und Kunst entlang der Seidenstraße*, Darmstadt.

Hayen, H. and K. Tidow 1982. Ein Wollgewebe vom Bohlenweg VI (Pr), *Archäologische Mitteilungen aus Nordwestdeutschland* 5, 29–31.

Hines, J. 1993. *Clasps, Hektespenner, Agraffen. Anglo-Scandinavian clasps of classes A–C of the 3rd to 6th centuries A.D. Typology, diffusion and function*, Stockholm.

Ilkjær, J. 1975. Et bundt våben fra Vimose, *Kuml*, 117–162.

Ilkjær, J. 1990a. Illerup Ådal, 1, Die Lanzen und Speere: Textband, *Jutland Archaeological Society Publications* XXV:1.

Ilkjær, J. 1990b. Illerup Ådal, 2, Die Lanzen und Speere: Tafelband, *Jutland Archaeological Society Publications* XXV:2.

Ilkjær, J. 1993a. Illerup Ådal, 3, Die Gürtel, Bestandteile und Zubehör: Textband, *Jutland Archaeological Society Publications* XXV:3.

Ilkjær, J. 1993b. Illerup Ådal, 4, Die Gürtel, Bestandteile und Zubehör: Tafelband, *Jutland Archaeological Society Publications* XXV:4.

Ilkjær, J. 2001a. Illerup Ådal, 9, Die Schilde: Textband, *Jutland Archaeological Society Publications* XXV:9.

Ilkjær, J. 2001b. Illerup Ådal, 10, Die Schilde: Katalog, Tafeln und Fundlisten, *Jutland Archaeological Society Publications* XXV:10.

Ilkjær, J. 2003. Danske krigsbytteofringer, in L. Jørgensen, B. Storgaard and L. Gebauer Thomsen (eds), *Sejrens triumf*, (Exhibition in Copenhagen, accompanying publication), (København), 44–64.

Ilkjær, J. 2006. Die Funde aus Illerup Ådal – Der Stand der Forschung im Jahr 2006, in A. Abegg-Wigg and A. Rau (eds), *Aktuelle Forschungen zu Kriegsbeuteopfern und Fürstengräbern im Barbaricum, Internationales Kolloquium, Schleswig 15.–18. Juni 2006*, Schriften des Archäologischen Landesmuseums, Ergänzungsreihe 4, Neumünster, 19–24.

Jørgensen, E. and P. Vang Petersen 2003. Nydam mose – nye fund og iagttagelser, in L. Jørgensen, B. Storgaard and L. Gebauer Thomsen (eds), *Sejrens triumf*, (Exhibition in Copenhagen, accompanying publication, København), 258–284.

Jørgensen, L., B. Storgaard and L. Gebauer Thomsen (eds) 2003. *Sejrens triumf. Norden i skyggen af det romerske Imperium* (Exhibition in Copenhagen, accompanying publication, København).

Kat. Kopenhagen n.d. (Katalog der Funde 24820–25199 aus der Flensburger Sammlung, die von Conrad Engelhardt nach Kopenhagen geliefert wurden).

Knauer, E. 1985. Ex oriente vestimenta. Trachtgeschichtliche Beobachtungen zu Ärmelmantel und Ärmeljacke, *Aufstieg und Niedergang der Römischen Welt* II, 12.3, 578–741.

Kolb, F. 1973. Römische Mäntel, *Mitteilungen des Deutschen Archäologischen Instituts, Römische Abteilung* 80, 69–167.

Kühl, A. 2000. *Untersuchungsbericht* (Unpublished report), Kiel.

Lau, N. 2008. Zügelkettenzaumzeuge der jüngeren und späten Römischen Kaiserzeit – Neue Untersuchungen zu Typen, Verbreitung, Herkunft und Datierung, in A. Abegg-Wigg and A. Rau (eds), *Aktuelle Forschungen zu Kriegsbeuteopfern und Fürstengräbern im Barbaricum, Internationales Kolloquium, Schleswig 15.–18. Juni 2006*, Schriften des Archäologischen Landesmuseums, Ergänzungsreihe 4, Neumünster, 25–55.

Leene, J. E. 1973. Analyse der textilen Reste, in H. Klumbach (ed), *Spätrömische Gardehelme, Münchner Beiträge zur Vor- und Frühgeschichte* 15, 80–83.

Linscheid, P. 2004. Gaiters from Antinoopolis in the Museum für byzantinische Kunst Berlin, in C. Fluck and G. Vogelsang-Eastwood (eds), *Riding costume in Egypt, Origin and appearance*, Leiden, 153–161.

Lund Hansen, U. 2003. Våbenofferfundene gennem 150 år – forskning og tolkninger, in L. Jørgensen, B. Storgaard and L. Gebauer Thomsen (eds), *Sejrens triumf,* (Exhibition in Copenhagen, accompanying publication, København), 84–89.

Magnus, B. 1980. Halsnøybåtens tekstiler, *Arkeo*, 22–25.

Magnus, B. 1988. Blimshaugen – a fourth century mausoleum, in L. Bender Jørgensen, B. Magnus and E. Munksgaard (eds), *Archaeological Textiles, Report from the 2nd NESAT symposium, 1.–4.V.1984*, Copenhagen, 109–115.

Mannering, U. 2006a. Billeder af dragt. En analyse af påklædte figurer fra yngre jernalder i Skandinavien. Ph.d.-afhandling, Københavns universitet.

Mannering, U. 2006b. *Nydam textiles* (Unpublished list).

Mannering, U. and M. Gleba forthcoming. *Designed for Life and Death.*

Matešić, S. 2008. Militaria im Thorsberger Moorfund – Zeugnisse römisch-germanischer Kontakte, in A. Abegg-Wigg and A. Rau (eds), *Aktuelle Forschungen zu Kriegsbeuteopfern und Fürstengräbern im Barbaricum, Internationales Kolloquium, Schleswig 15.–18. Juni 2006*, Schriften des Archäologischen Landesmuseums, Ergänzungsreihe 4, Neumünster, 85–104.

Mestorf, J. 1900. Moorleichen, *Zweiundvierzigster Bericht des Schleswig-Holsteinischen Museums vaterländischer Alterthümer bei der Universität Kiel*, Kiel, 10–34.

Mestorf, J. 1907. Moorleichen, *Vierundvierzigster Bericht des Schleswig-Holsteinischen Museums vaterländischer Altertümer bei der Universität Kiel*, Kiel, 14–55.

Möller-Wiering, S. 2001. Karschau, Haderslev und Lynæs – Kalfat aus mittelalterlichen Schiffen als Ausdruck einer nordeuropäischen Schiffbautradition, *Archäologie in Schleswig – Arkæologi i Slesvig* 9, 151–163.

Möller-Wiering, S. 2002. Segeltuch und Emballage. Textilien im mittelalterlichen Warentransport auf Nord- und Ostsee, *Internationale Archäologie* 70, Rahden/Westf.

Möller-Wiering, S. 2004. Schiffbau und Textil: Ansätze zu einer systematischen Untersuchung von Kalfat, in J. Maik (ed), *Priceless Invention of Humanity – Textiles, Report from the 8th North European Symposium for Archaeological Textiles, 8–10 May 2002 in Łódź/Poland*, Acta Archaeologica Lodziensia 50/1, Łódź, 113–119.

Möller-Wiering, S. 2005. Symbolträger Textil. Textilarchäologische Untersuchungen zum sächsischen Gräberfeld von Liebenau, Kreis Nienburg (Weser), *Studien zur Sachsenforschung* 5.8, Oldenburg.

Möller-Wiering, S. 2007. Italienische Mode im Stader Moor? – Archäologie zwischen Befund und Rekonstruktion, in F. M. Andraschko, B. Kraus and B. Meller (eds), *Festschrift Renate Rolle, Antiquitates* 39, Hamburg, 247–263.

Möller-Wiering, S. 2008. Die Textilien aus Illerup Ådal – erste Ergebnisse, in A. Abegg-Wigg and A. Rau (eds), *Aktuelle Forschungen zu Kriegsbeuteopfern und Fürstengräbern im Barbaricum, Internationales Kolloquium, Schleswig 15.–18. Juni 2006*, Schriften des Archäologischen Landesmuseums, Ergänzungsreihe 4, Neumünster, 209–214.

Möller-Wiering, S. 2009. Ein Seitenblick auf die Textilien aus der Wurt Tofting, *Archaeological Textiles Newsletter* 48, 16–19.

Möller-Wiering, S. 2010. Evidence of War and Worship: Textiles in Roman Iron Age Weapon Deposits, in E. Andersson Strand, M. Gleba, U. Mannering, C. Munkholt and M. Ringgaard (eds), North European Symposium for Archaeological Textiles X, *Ancient Textiles Series* 5, Oxford, 167–173.

Möller-Wiering, S. forthcoming a. Textiles of Bronze Age and Pre-Roman Iron Age in Germany, in M. Gleba and U. Mannering (eds), *Textiles in Context*.

Möller-Wiering, S. forthcoming b. Warrior Costumes in Iron Age Weapon Deposits, in M.-L. Nosch (ed.), Roman Military Textiles, *Historia*, Supplement volume.

Monthel, G., M. Schoefer, O. Valansot, D. de Reyer and W. Nowik 1998. Les tissus gallo-romains de

Chalon-sur-Saône: étude pluridisciplinaire, *Bulletin du CIETA* 75, 21–36.

Nockert, M. 1991. The Högom Find and other Migration Period Textiles and Costumes in Scandinavia, *Högom II, Archaeology and Environment* 9, Umeå.

Nørgaard, A. 1998. *Thorsbjerg, en mandsdragt fra jernalderen* (Unpublished report).

Pauli Jensen, X. [2008]. *Våben fra Vimose. Bearbejdning og tolkning af et gammelkendt fund.* – Ph.d.-afhandling, Københavns universitet, Det humanistiske fakultet, (Unpublished) [Bd. I: Text, Bd. II: Katalog, København].

Petersen, P. 1995. *Nydam Offermose* (Dansk Historisk Håndbogsforlag).

Pfister, R. and L. Bellinger 1945. The Textiles, in M. I. Rostovtzeff, A. R. Bellinger, F. E. Brown, N. P. Toll and C. B. Welles (eds), *The Excavations at Dura Europos, Final Report* IV, *Part* II, New Haven.

Pichikyan, I. R. 1997. Rebirth of the Oxus Treasure: Second Part of the Oxus Treasure from the Miho Museum Collection, *Ancient Civilizations from Scythia to Siberia* IV, 306–383.

van der Plicht, J., W. A. B. van der Sanden, A. T. Aerts and H. J. Streurman 2004. Dating bog bodies by means of 14C-AMS, *Journal of Archaeological Science* 31, 471–491.

Polosmak, N. V. 1998. The Burial of a Noble Pazyryk Woman, *Ancient Civilizations from Scythia to Siberia* V, 125–163.

Polosmak, N. V. and V. I. Molodin 2000. Grave Sites of the Pazyryk Culture on the Ukok Plateau, *Archaeology, Ethnology and Anthropology of Eurasia* 4, 66–87.

Potratz, H. 1942. Das Moorgewand von Reepsholt, Kreis Wittmund, Ostfriesland, *Veröffentlichungen der Urgeschichtlichen Sammlungen des Landesmuseums zu Hannover* 7, Hildesheim.

Pritchard, F. 2006. *Dress in Egypt in the First Millenium AD. Clothing from Egypt in the collection of The Whitworth Art Gallery, The University of Manchester*, Manchester.

Raddatz, K. 1952. Bronzezeitliche Funde aus dem Thorsberger Moor, *Jahrbuch des Angler Heimatvereins* 16, 78–93.

Raddatz, K. 1987a. Der Thorsberger Moorfund. Gürtelteile und Körperschmuck. Katalog, *Offa* 44, 117–152.

Raddatz, K. 1987b. *Der Thorsberger Moorfund. Katalog. Teile von Waffen und Pferdegeschirr, sonstige Fundstücke aus Metall und Glas, Ton- und Holzgefäße, Steingeräte*, Offa-Bücher 65, Neumünster.

Ræder Knudsen, L. 1998. An Iron Age cloak with tablet-woven borders: a new interpretation of the method of production, in L. Bender Jørgensen and C. Rinaldo (eds), *Textiles in European Archaeology, Report from the 6th NESAT Symposium, 7–11th May 1996 in Borås*, Gotarc Series A, 1, Göteborg, 79–84.

Ræder Knudsen, L. 2002. La tessitura a tavolette nella tomba 89, in P. von Eles (ed), Guerriero e sacerdote, Autorità e comunità nell'età del ferro a Verucchio, La Tomba del Trono, *Quaderni di Archeologia dell' Emilia Romagna* 6, Firenze, 4.10, 220–234.

Ræder Knudsen, L. forthcoming. Tablet-woven bands from bogs and burials of the Early Iron Age, in U. Mannering and M. Gleba (eds), *Designed for Life and Death*.

Raknes Pedersen, I. 1988. Analysis of the textiles from Blindheim, Giske, in L. Bender Jørgensen, B. Magnus and E. Munksgaard (eds), *Archaeological Textiles, Report from the 2nd NESAT symposium, 1.–4.V.1984*, Copenhagen, 116–125.

Randsborg, K. 1995. *Hjortspring, Warfare and Sacrifice in Early Europe*, Aarhus.

Rau, A. 2008. Zwischen Südjütland und Nordgallien – Ausrüstungen elitärer Krieger der frühen Völkerwanderungszeit aus dem Nydam mose, in A. Abegg-Wigg and A. Rau (eds), *Aktuelle Forschungen zu Kriegsbeuteopfern und Fürstengräbern im Barbaricum, Internationales Kolloquium, Schleswig 15.–18. Juni 2006*, Schriften des Archäologischen Landesmuseums, Ergänzungsreihe 4, Neumünster, 151–174.

Rieck, F. 1998. Die Schiffsfunde aus dem Nydammoor. Alte Funde und neue Untersuchungen, in G. Bemmann and J. Bemmann, *Der Opferplatz von Nydam, Bd* 1: *Text*, Neumünster, 267–292.

Rieck, F. 2003. Skibene fra Nydam mose, in L. Jørgensen, B. Storgaard and L. Gebauer Thomsen (eds), *Sejrens triumf*, (Exhibition in Copenhagen, accompanying publication, København), 296–309.

Rieck, F. n.d. *Nydam mose* (Unpublished report).

Rudenko, S. I. 1969. Die Kultur der Hsiung-nu und die Hügelgräber von Noin Ula, *Antiquitas* 7, Bonn.

Rudenko, S. I. 1970. *Frozen Tombs of Siberia. The Pazyryk Burials of Iron Age Horsemen*, London.

van der Sanden, W. 1996. *Mumien aus dem Moor. Die vor- und frühgeschichtlichen Moorleichen aus Nordwesteuropa*, Amsterdam.

Schlabow, K. 1951. Der Thorsberger Prachtmantel, der Schlüssel zum altgermanischen Webstuhl, in K. Kersten (ed), *Festschrift für Gustav Schwantes zum 65. Geburtstag*, Neumünster, 176–201.

Schlabow, K. 1952/53. Der Prachtmantel Nr. II aus dem Vehnemoor in Oldenburg, *Oldenburger Jahrbuch* 52/53, 160–201.

Schlabow, K. 1955. Textilfunde und Hausopfer von Tofting, in A. Bantelmann, *Tofting, eine vorgeschichtliche Warft an der Eidermündung, Vor- und frühgeschichtliche Untersuchungen aus dem Schleswig-Holsteinischen Landesmuseum für Vor- und Frühgeschichte in Schleswig und dem Institut für Ur- und Frühgeschichte der Universität Kiel*, N.F. 12, Offa-Bücher, 94–97.

Schlabow, K. 1976. *Textilfunde der Eisenzeit in Norddeutschland*, Neumünster.

Schmidt-Colinet, A. 2000. Einleitung, in A. Schmidt-Colinet, A. Stauffer and K. Al-As'Ad, *Die Textilien aus Palmyra*, Mainz, 1–7.

Schneider, L. 1983. Die *Domäne als Weltbild. Wirkungsstrukturen der spätantiken Bildersprache*, Wiesbaden.

Schoefer, M. 2004. Présentation d'un ensemble trouvé à Antinoé, rapporté par Albert Gayet en 1897–98, in C. Fluck and G. Vogelsang-Eastwood (eds), *Riding costume in Egypt, Origin and appearance*, Leiden, 109–115.

Schumacher, K. 1935. Germanendarstellungen. Teil I: Darstellungen aus dem Altertum, *Kataloge des Römisch-Germanischen Zentralmuseums zu Mainz* 1, Neu bearbeitet von H. Klumbach, Mainz.

Shamir, O. 2006. Textiles and their find spots: Finds from along the spice route joining Petra and Gaza, Textiles in situ, *Riggisberger Berichte* 13, 185–194.

Sim, D. 1998. The reproduction of a late Roman pattern-welded sword, in G. Bemmann and J. Bemmann, *Der Opferplatz von Nydam*, 1: *Text*, Neumünster, 381–387.

Stauffer, A. 2000. Material und Technik, in A. Schmidt-Colinet, A. Stauffer and K. Al-As'Ad, *Die Textilien aus Palmyra*, Mainz, 8–40.

Stauffer, A. 2002. Tessuti, in P. von Eles (ed), Guerriero e sacerdote, Autorità e comunità nell'età del ferro a Verucchio, La Tomba del Trono, *Quaderni di Archeologia dell' Emilia Romagna* 6, Firenze, 4.9, 192–215.

Stauffer, A. and A. Schmidt-Colinet 2000. Katalog, in A. Schmidt-Colinet, A. Stauffer and K. Al-As'Ad, *Die Textilien aus Palmyra*, Mainz, 99–190.

Stettiner, R. 1911. Brettchenwebereien in den Moorfunden von Damendorf, Daetgen und Torsberg, *Mitteilungen des Anthropologischen Vereins in Schleswig-Holstein* 19, 26–56.

Sumner, G. 2002. *Roman military clothing (1). 100 BC–AD 200*, Oxford.

Sumner, G. 2003. *Roman military clothing (2). AD 200–400*, Oxford.

Teegen, W.-R. 1999. Studien zu dem kaiserzeitlichen Quellopferfund von Bad Pyrmont, *Ergänzungsbände zum Reallexikon der Germanischen Altertumskunde* 20.

Tidow, K. 2000. Von Prachtmänteln, Friesischen Tuchen und anderen Wollgeweben, in E. Kramer (ed), *Könige der Nordsee, 250–850 n. Chr. Geb.*, Leeuwarden, 105–110.

Tidow, K. 2001. Gewebefunde aus Gräbern der Gräberfelder Sievern, Fst. Nr. 58B, und Flögeln-Voßbarg, Ldkr. Cuxhaven, *Probleme der Küstenforschung* 27, 241–246.

Ullemeyer, R. and K. Tidow 1981. Textil- und Lederfunde der Grabung Feddersen Wierde, in W. Haarnagel (ed), Einzeluntersuchungen zur Feddersen Wierde, *Feddersen Wierde* 3, Wiesbaden, 77–152.

Vang Petersen, P. 1998. Der Nydam-III- und Nydam-IV-Fund. Ausgrabungen völkerwanderungszeitlicher Waffenopfer durch das Nationalmuseum Kopenhagen in den Jahren 1984, 1989 bis 1992. Ein Vorbericht, in G. Bemmann and J. Bemmann, *Der Opferplatz von Nydam, Bd* 1: *Text*, Neumünster, 241–266.

Walton, P. 1988. Dyes and Wools in Iron Age Textiles from Norway and Denmark, *Journal of Danish Archaeology* 7, 144–158.

Wang B. and Xiao X. 2001. A General Introduction to the Ancient Tombs at Shanpula, Xinjiang, China, in D. Keller and R. Schorta (eds), Fabulous Creatures from the Desert Sands, *Riggisberger Berichte* 10, Riggisberg, 47–78.

Widengren, Geo 1956. Some Remarks on Riding Costume and Articles of Dress among Iranian Peoples in Antiquity, *Arctica, Studia Ethnographica Upsaliensia* XI, 228–276.

Wild, J. P. 2002. The textile industries of Roman Britain, *Britannia* XXXII, 1–42.

Wild, J. P. and L. Bender Jørgensen 1988. Clothes from the Roman Empire. Barbarians and Romans, in L. Bender Jørgensen, B. Magnus and E. Munksgaard (eds), *Archaeological Textiles, Report from the 2nd NESAT symposium, 1.–4. V.1984*, Copenhagen, 65–98.

Zimmerman, J. A. 2007. *Textiel in context. Een analyse van archeologische textielvondsten uit 16e-eeuws Groningen*, Groningen.

11. APPENDIX

11.1. Illerup Ådal: list of textiles

Textiles with indications of napping in italics; LBJ = Lise Bender Jørgensen

find clusters and items	1/1 z/z	2/2 z/z	2/2 z/z diamond	2/2 z/s	2/2 z/s diamond	2/2 spin-patterned	remarks	related find
-6/60								
LCW				10 × 10–11				shield boss
LHH				x				lancehead
LLO			18 × 18					shield boss
MBL						20–22 × 16		shield boss
MDC		x					red	loose fragment
MII					14 × 14			spearhead
1/68								
QLC				16–17 × 13–14				belt buckle
QMZ		17–18 × 16–17						sword
QPA					18–19 × 13			axe
QPC							napped twill, imprint tablet-weave	lancehead
25/66								
QAT				x			diamond twill?	arrow shaft
QZA		x					red	shield boss
QZE					16–17 × 14			shield boss
RBA					15–16 × 16			shield boss
RBB			13–14 × 13–14				fur with seam	shield boss
RBO					14–15 × 13–14			lancehead
RCC					20–21 × 17–18			sword
RCX	14–15 × 10							top of shield boss
RGZ	15–19 × 10–11	16 × 13						shield boss
41/73								
VRL		16 × 13						shield boss
VSG					16 × 11			lancehead
VVB							textile not determinable; strand of rather coarse hair between iron and textiles	spearhead
VZT	14 × 7							shield boss
WME		16–17 × 15						shield boss
WYO		x						rivet / rivet plate
WYR							Z-twined fringes?	shield boss
WYX					23–24 × 12			shield boss
WZO			20 × 18					shield boss
XAZ		20 × 20–21						shield boss
XBK		18–20 × 13–15						shield boss
XBV				10 × 8				shield boss
XBW							2/2 diamond?	shield boss
XBZ	18–19 × 15							lancehead
XFN			11–12 × 14		13 × 13			shield boss
XNW					*x*		napped	shield boss

11.1. Illerup Ådal: list of textiles continued

find clusters and items	1/1 z/z	2/2 z/z	2/2 z/z diamond	2/2 z/s	2/2 z/s diamond	2/2 spin-patterned	remarks	related find
46/119								
ZHL							tabby?	hand brace of shield
ZKI		17 × 12						axe
56/78								
HAK							twill?	lancehead
HAS / HAT					13–14 × 13–14		tubular selvedge	shield boss
HBD				17 × 12			analysis by LBJ	shield rim
HBE				17 × 14			analysis by LBJ	shield rim HBD
57/90								
SQE		13 × 11–12						shield boss
STA			19 × 22–23		15–16 × 10		z/s: tubular selvedge; both red	shield boss
TWT		11–12 × 10–11			13 × 11			lancehead
TWU							twill, z-spin in one system	lancehead
TXB					15–18 × 14–16			lancehead
TXC					14 × 9		tubular selvedge	lancehead
TYF	18–20 × 11–16				11 × 12			shield boss
TYH					11 × 12			shield boss
TYR					x		red	loose fragment
VFB				x			diamond?	shield boss
VFD		11 × 9–10			14 × 12–13		hair; z/s red; tablet weave?	lancehead
VFI				x			diamond twill? red	shield boss
70/114								
YYA					15 × 12			socket of spearhead
79/104								
UFF						16 × 13–14		shield boss
UFN						16–17 × 12		shield boss
ULW	15–18 × 14–15						fur	shield boss
UNK					13–14 × 12–14		tablet weave	shield boss
85/85								
IUK			18 × 11					spearhead
IWC					20–21 × 13–15			shield boss
IWE					20 × 18			shield boss
IWR					16 × 13		tubular selvedge	shield boss
					22–23 × 18–20		red	
IXE		19–20 × 15–16						shield boss
IXK				10 × 12			analysis by LBJ; tablet weave	shield boss
IXL							red tablet weave	shield boss
IXU					20 × 20		analysis by LBJ	sword[1]
IXY	12 × 11			15 × 18 11–12 × 14–15			z/s: red?, higher tpc on loose fragment, lower tpc on boss	shield boss
IXZ	10 × 7–8							wire
IYE					12 × 16		analysis by LBJ	shield boss
IYF		17–18 × 14–15			21 × 18		red tablet weave	shield boss
IYH					20 × 17–18			loose fragment
IYK					16 × 12		tubular selvedge (analysis by LBJ)	shield boss IWR
KAT			13 × 14–17					shield boss
KAZ					18–19 × 12			shield boss

11. Appendix

11.1. Illerup Ådal: list of textiles continued

find clusters and items	1/1 z/z	2/2 z/z	2/2 z/z diamond	2/2 z/s	2/2 z/s diamond	2/2 spin-patterned	remarks	related find
87/89								
MML				18–19 × 14				lancehead
MNL				20 × 16			red?	shield boss MNH
88/109								
YME		17 × 12–13						spearhead
YPL (VPL?)		17 × 16–17						spearhead
YSW	8–9 × 7							shield boss
YWN					13–14 × 13–14			lancehead
89/74								
FMH					12–13 × 11–12			knife
92/97								
MYP				7 × 9			red	knife MYO (?) or lance head MYQ (?)
95/110								
ZAR			19 × 14					shield boss
111/100								
AAIH				x			red	spearhead AAIB
AAII						18–19 × 16–17		spearhead
AAKA						20 × 17		lancehead
AALZ		21 × 12						lancehead
AAMC		18 × 15						axe
AAMD		19–20 × 15						top of shield boss
AAME	14–17 × 8–9							shield boss
AAMX						x		shield boss
AAOI						17–18 × 15–17		shield boss
123/114								
ADDP	20 × 13–14							lancehead
ADDQ	18 × 12–13							lancehead
127/114								
AAYN				x				shield boss
129/105								
ADBZ					16 × 15–16			lancehead
151/119								
AAVU							twill?	lancehead
AAVW					14 × 15–16			lancehead
unknown								
u.Nr.				x				loose fragment
TEX							vegetal s-spun yarn	wooden shaft
ZBP						14 × 14–15		spearhead
ZML							hair > originally napped? no textile left	fragment of shield boss

1. IXU is not mentioned in the description of this concentration by Biborski and Ilkjær (2006, 79–80). It might be part of an ensemble with a different number.

11.2. Vimose: list of textiles

Indications of napping in italics. Items of the 'cloth bundle' marked with an asterisk, thereof several with indications of napping

item	1/1 z/z	2/2 z/z	remarks	related find
18655/56		*15 x 11–12*		lancehead
18727	18 x 10			lancehead
21647			organic material, possibly textile	baldric
22850	15 x 13			shield boss
22858			possibly textile	shield boss
22878			textile, no details determinable	shield boss
23798	*13 x 12*			lancehead
23935			plant fibres, probably no textile	spearhead
24721*		14–15 x 11		lancehead
24722*		16 x 10–12		lancehead
24723*		16 x 11		spearhead
24724*		15 x 11		lancehead
24725*		14 x 11		lancehead
24726*			fibres	lancehead
24727*		14 x 11		lancehead
24728*		16 x 10		lancehead
24729*		14 x 10		lancehead
24730*		13 x 11–12	measurements inexact due to small size	spearhead
24731*		15 x 12		spearhead
24732*		15 x 11		lancehead
24733*		14–15 x 11–12		lancehead
24734*		17 x 11–12		lancehead
24735*		13–14 x 12		lancehead
24736*		not det.	z-spin in one direction uncertain	lancehead
24737*		15 x 12		lancehead
24738*		14–15 x 11		lancehead
24739*		15 x 11–12		spearhead
24740*		14 x 12		lancehead
24741*		15–17 x 12		lancehead
24742*		14 x 11–12		lancehead
24743*		15–17 x 11–13		lancehead
24744*		16 x 11		lancehead
24745*		11 x 9		lancehead
24746*		17 x 11		lancehead
24747*		14 x 10		lancehead
24748*		14–15 x 12		lancehead
24749*		15 x 11		lancehead
24750*		15–16 x 11		spearhead
24751*		13–15 x 12		lancehead
24752*		15–16 x 12		lancehead
24753*		14–15 x 12–13		spearhead
24754*			few fibres	lancehead
24755		15–17 x 11–12		lancehead
24756		15–16 x 11–13		lancehead
24757		13–16 x 11		lancehead
24760			plant fibres, probably no textile	three spearheads
24761		*16 x 12*		lancehead

11. Appendix

11.2. Vimose: list of textiles continued

item	1/1 z/z	2/2 z/z	remarks	related find
24761		*16 x 12*		lancehead
24762			tablet weave	lancehead
24763			tablet weave and fringes	spearhead
24764 -1	16 x 12–13 *napping?*		measurements inexact due to small size	lancehead
24764 -2		16–17 x 12–13 *napping?*	z-spin of second system uncertain; measurements inexact because of small size	
24766			tablet weave and fringes; undeterminable weave	shield boss
24767	15 x 12			shield boss
C 1806			possibly textile	shield boss
C 7306			undeterminable textile	lancehead
C 9400			undeterminable textile, possibly tablet weave	lancehead
UI 160			tablet weave	lancehead

11.3. Thorsberg: list of textiles
Textiles with indications of napping in italics

item	1/1 z/z (+s)	1/1 s/s	1/1 z/s	2/2 s/s	2/2 z/z broken	2/2 z/s	2/2 z/s diamond	2/2 spin-patterned	function	associated find numbers	woven edges	remarks
finds in Schleswig												
3683							18 × 14–15		tunic		3	pattern units 10/9, slightly irregular
3684							18–19 × 14		trousers		1	pattern units 14/9, regular
3685							15–17 × 13–14		trousers			pattern units 10/9, warp irregular
3686						13–14 × 11			cloak ("Prachtmantel I")		4	stripes in warp and weft
3687						9–11 × 8			cloak	24820, 24821	4	stripes in warp and weft
3688						12 × 10			cloak	24823 a/b, probably 3689; ? M 607.1-1/-2	1	stripes in warp and weft
3689						13–15 × 10–12			cloak	probably 3688, 24823 a/b; ? M 607.1-1/-2	2	stripes in warp and weft
3690							18–19 × 15–16			3705	1	pattern units 10/9, irregular (partic. weft)
3691				16 × 15–17					leg wrap ("Binde")		2	broad dark strip in z/s
3692	9 × 6								leg wrap ("Binde")		3	hem
3693						10–11 × 10						
3694		4 × 4										
3695					8 × 12						1	stripes in weft; probably plain with mistakes
3696								21 × 16				spin pattern: groups of 4 yarns in s and z
3697								x	cloak ("Prachtmantel III")		1	stripes; no ground weave
3698								x	cloak	24822		no ground weave; stripes in warp and weft
3699							9 × 11					pattern units 10/13, irregular (partic. weft); colours?
3700							18 × 14–15			3702–3704		pattern units 10/9; seam

11. Appendix

11.3. Thorsberg: list of textiles continued

item	1/1 z/z (+s)	1/1 s/s	1/1 z/s	2/2 s/s	2/2 z/z broken	2/2 z/s	2/2 z/s diamond	2/2 spin-patterned	function	associated find numbers	woven edges	remarks
finds in Schleswig												
3701							13–15 × 12					pattern units 10/9, weft irregular
3702										3700, 3703–3704		hem?
3703										3700, 3702, 3704		hem
3704										3700, 3702–3703		
3705										3690	1	
3706							19 × 18				1	pattern units not determinable
finds in Copenhagen												
24820										3687, 24821	1	
24821										3687, 24820	1	
24822										3698		
24823 a/b						13–14 × 10–12				3688, 3689; ? M 607.1 -1/-2	1	
24824 a/b		9–10 × 7									a) 1	a), b) seam; differently coloured sewing threads
24824c						12–13 × 10–11, 9–10 × 10–11					1	
o.Nr. -1												1 trimmed edge
o.Nr. -2												
o.Nr. -3						13 × 13						
finds in Moesgård												
M 607.1 -1/-2						13–14 × 10			cloak	? 3688, 3689, 24823 a/b	2	
finds in Sorø												
1232a			4 × 3–4									
1232b						13 × 10					1	

11.4. Nydam: list of textiles
Textiles with indications of napping in italics

items	1/1 z/z	1/1 s/s	2/2 z/z	2/2 z/z diamond or broken	2/2 z/s	2/2 z/s diamond or broken	2/2 spin-patterned	not completely determinable	remarks	related find
weapons										
3264								a) 2/2 z?/s? 15 × 11?	b) tablet weave	spearhead
3411					14 × 12				napping; broken twill?	shield boss; kon. 16607–08
5372							?			spearhead
6136							12 × ?		z?/z+s, broken?, diamond?	shield boss
7937			x							lancehead
7993	16 × 11								2 layers?	shield boss
clasps										
2270								undeterminable	1x below button; probably 1x on top of button	
4433								z?/s?	2x below button; probably belonging to 4434	
4434								undeterminable	1x below button; 1x loose s-yarn; probably belonging to 4433	
6878								undeterminable	5x below button; 3x reddish; bronze pin without textile	
6879								a) 1x z, b) undeterminable	7x below button; 1x below hook; 3x reddish	
6992					a) x			b) ? z/s, c) undeterminable	a) below button, probably 2 or more layers; undet. textile on top; b) below button; undet. textile on top; c) 1x below and on top of button; 4x below button; 1x 2 or more layers	
7091								a) ? z/s, b) z; s; undet.	a) on top of button b) on top of / below button; 1x 2 or more layers	
7092								a) ? z/s, b) undeterminable	a) below button; b) 2x below button; 1x on top of button	
7093								a) 2/2 ? z+s/s b) ? z+s/s c) z; s; undet.	a) below button; unpigm. wool b) below button; red? c) below button	
7223								undeterminable	below button, with wood on top (shield [according to label])	
7274								undeterminable	6x below button; red?	
7289					a) 20 × 15			b) undeterminable	a) loose fragments; red? b) below and on top of button	
7343								a) z; s b) undeterminable	a) below button; b) 6x below button; some s-yarns	
7392								undeterminable	2x below button	
7639								undeterminable	below button; 1x z-yarn; red?	
7640								undeterminable	1x below and on top of button; 1x below button	
7681								undeterminable	2x below button + below hook	

11. Appendix

11.1. Nydam: list of textiles continued

items	1/1 z/z	1/1 s/s	2/2 z/z	2/2 z/z diamond or broken	2/2 z/s	2/2 z/s diamond or broken	2/2 spin-patterned	not completely determinable	remarks
clasps									
7795								undeterminable	5x below button; 1x z-yarn
7855								undeterminable	a) below button; b) on top of button
7968					a) x			b) ? s/?; c) undeterminable	a) below button, 2 or more layers; b) s-spun yarn in one system below button; undet. textile on top of button and below eye; c) on top of and/or below button
10503								undeterminable	below button; 1x z-yarn
14704								1/1 z/?	on top of button
14815								undeterminable	a) beneath button; b) on top of button
o.Nr.								undeterminable	below button
caulking material									
5318								a) 2/2 ?; b) 2/2	a), b) plank
5512								2/2 ?/? diam 17–18 × 14	plank
5653a								prob 2/2 ?/?	tablet weave?
5780					14 × 12–13				plank
5785			16 × 15						plank
5858			12 × 11						plank
5902			7–8 × 6–7					x	repair
5911			13 × 12–13						repair; seemingly plant fibre
5925								2/2 ?/z	repair
5940					15 × 19				repair
6269									?
10012								2/2 ?/z	plank
10015								2/2 ?/z	repair
10283								2/2 ?/z	repair
10510			17 × 14						plank
10967								2/2 ?/z	repair
11307		b) ? 11 × 7	a) 14 × 10						a) on front b) on reverse
11356	a) 14 × 13							b) 2/2 ?	a) on front b) on reverse
11378								twill?	plank
11410								textile?	plank
11462								textile?	plank

11.4. Nydam: list of textiles continued

items	1/1 z/z	1/1 s/s	2/2 z/z	2/2 z/z diamond or broken	2/2 z/s	2/2 z/s diamond or broken	2/2 spin-patterned	not completely determinable	remarks	find numbers
caulking materials										
11520b	? 12 × 12									plank
11537a	22 × 20									plank
11545				20 × 16					diamond	plank
P67 Rx 3053 177									2/2 z?/s? 2,5 × 2	?
others										
2860			18 × 14–16						several fragments; one reverse, tablet weave	wooden head
3223									not preserved (Rieck)	impression in ground
præp. 3404						14–15 × 12			blue?; broken (prob. mistake)	loose fragments
3701									not preserved (Rieck)	inside a box
5240									not preserved (Rieck)	impression in ground
6940									not preserved (Rieck)	impression in ground
8792									not preserved (Rieck)	impression in ground
13794									not preserved (Rau)	fibula

11. Appendix

11.5. Nydam: list of examined weapons stored at Archäologisches Landesmuseum Schloss Gottorf, Schleswig

F.S.-no.	old catalogue no.	new catalogue no.	find
4751	1863	1940	shield boss
4764	1857	1941	shield boss
5374	1072	1116	spearhead
5375	1126	1086	spearhead
5376	1070	1108	spearhead
5381	1252	1292	spearhead
5382	1276	1277	spearhead
5384	1272	1276	spearhead
5386	1239	1264	spearhead
5389	1232	1263	spearhead
5390	1273	1274	spearhead
5391	1275	1275	spearhead
5394	909	929	lancehead
5401	1480	1480	arrowhead
5402	1479	1479	arrowhead
5403	1448	1487	lancehead
5405	1452	1498	lancehead
5409	441	431	sword
./.	1858	1938	shield boss
./.	1883	1954	shield boss
./.	1893	1976	shield boss

PART 2

12. TABLET-WOVEN TEXTILES FROM 3RD TO 4TH-CENTURY AD WEAPON DEPOSITS IN DENMARK AND NORTHERN GERMANY

Lise Ræder Knudsen

12.1. INTRODUCTION

Tablet weaving is a textile technique used to make bands, edges and borders. The technique requires only few tools. In Danish prehistory, we see examples of tablet-woven borders produced by weaving techniques from very simple to the most elaborate and intricate techniques (for more on the technique, see Collingwood 1982).

Tablet weavings have been found together with other textiles in various contexts. Many Iron Age tablet weaves were recovered from bogs and graves. The latest research on the subject will be published in connection with Ulla Mannering and Margarita Gleba's investigation on Danish bog finds (Ræder Knudsen forthcoming a; Mannering and Gleba forthcoming). Weapon deposits encompass the second largest group of sites with preserved tablet weaves. However, as these finds from weapon deposits are most certainly the equipment of defeated foreign armies, the textiles do not necessarily have their origin in Denmark (Jensen 2003, 373, 548–549). The examination of this group, as presented here, may shed more light not only on technical questions, but particularly on the potential provenance of the material.

The four weapon deposits considered here have very different preservation conditions. While entire garments are preserved from Thorsberg, only textile pseudomorphs were recovered from Illerup, Nydam and Vimose. These corrosion imprints are thus tiny fragments, found only where metal was present. In comparative terms, statistics derived from finds recovered in various different preservation conditions are more unreliable than those from identical preservation conditions.

12.2. DESCRIPTION OF THE FINDS *(Table 2.1)*

Illerup

From Illerup, fragments of six different tablet-woven borders were recovered. None of these tablet-woven borders have both edges preserved, and therefore, it is only possible to see the minimum width. This varies from 0.3 cm to 3.0 cm. The amount of tablets utilized to make the borders varies from at least 7 tablets to at least 60 tablets. The borders can be divided into two groups: One coarser group of approximately 10 tablets per cm, and one group of finer quality of about 20 tablets per cm (see Table 2.1). One border is too disintegrated for further study (FHM 1880 IXK, cat. no. 01). It is only possible to see that it is tablet woven.

Number of tablets per cm in tablet-woven textiles from Illerup – Nydam – Thorsberg – Vimose

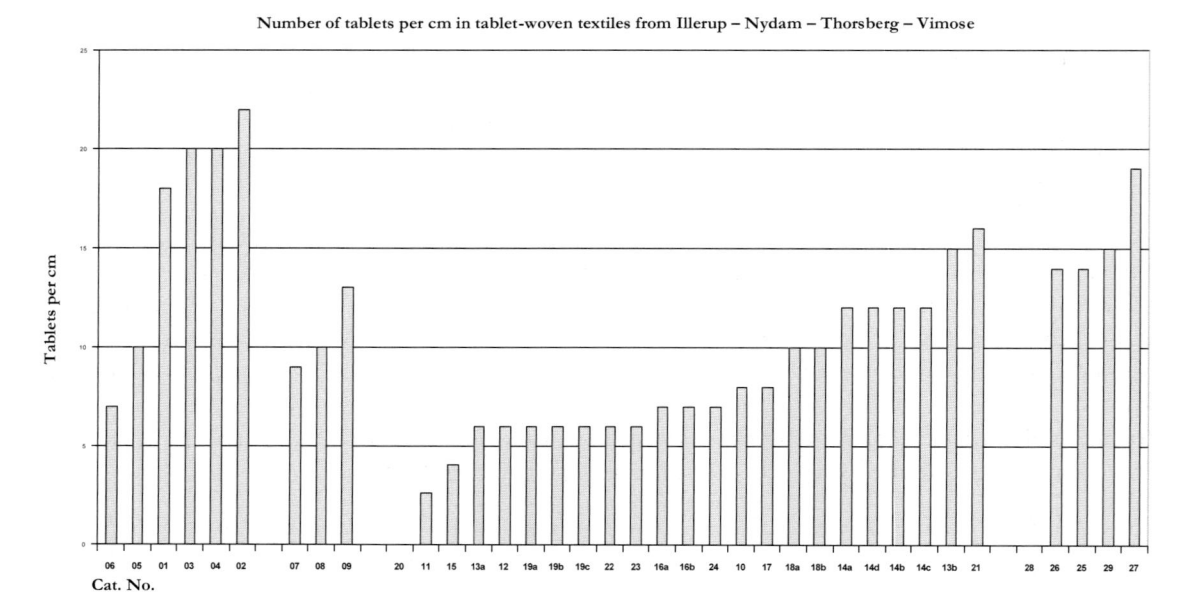

Table 2.1. Number of tablets per cm used to make the borders from Illerup, Nydam, Thorsberg and Vimose. In Illerup it might be possible to see two groups of tablet borders, one of a coarser quality and one of a finer quality. The finds from the other weapon deposits have a more equal distribution of various qualities of fineness.

Cat. no. 01 (FHM 1880 IXK) is the remains of a tablet-woven border preserved in the corrosion of a shield boss. At least 11 alternately opposed tablets were used and the tablet count is 18 tablets per cm. The preserved width is approx. 0.6 cm. It is not possible to see the weft (Fig. 2.1).

Cat. no. 02 (FHM 1880 IXL) is a shield boss on which a tablet border of at least 31 tablets threaded in opposed pairs is preserved. Details are very difficult to see, but as the weft is composed of double threads, this is most certainly a border integrated in a fabric (Fig. 2.2).

Cat. no. 03 (FHM 1880 IYF) comprises two shield bosses with a tablet border of at least 60 tablets preserved as small fragments in the corrosion. The weft is one thread, which most certainly indicates that this is an independent band (For a discussion of integrated versus independent bands see Ræder Knudsen forthcoming a). Furthermore, the weft consists of s-spun double threads as does the warp of the border, which also indicates an independent band. Neither the edge, nor the full width of the central, pattern-woven part of the border is preserved. Thus it is only possible to see that one edge was made utilizing at least 8 tablets threaded in opposed pairs, and this was followed by a pattern woven part of at least 52 tablets. The pattern weaving seems to be a warp-faced, plain-weave double cloth (Collingwood plate 119, p. 217), but it is not possible to discern a pattern even though a reddish colour is preserved in some places. As extant borders of this kind are symmetrical, a cautious estimation is that this border originally might have had two edges of ordinary tablet weaving of at least 8 tablets each, and at the centre, a pattern woven part of at least 52 tablets, in all at least 68 tablets. As twill fabric is also found on the shield bosses, the border might have been sewn on a cloak or it could be a band used to tie the shield to the load (Fig. 2.3).

On cat. no. 04 (FHM 1880 QPC), a simple tablet border of at least 20 tablets is preserved in the waxed and heated surface of a lancehead. The edges or weft of the tablet border is impossible to see. The border can be followed as it is wrapped around the lance. As there are no other fabrics preserved on the lancehead and as the wrapping most likely would leave another deposition of the border if it was part of a fabric, this is presumably an independent band used, for instance, for tying up a soldier's load (Fig. 2.4).

Cat. no. 05 (FHM 1880 UNK) is yet another shield boss on which a tablet-woven border is preserved. Also larger fragments of a twill fabric may be discerned. The border is at least 2.5 cm wide and was woven using at least 26 tablets. It has a kind of pattern where 3 tablets are threaded in one direction, 3 in the other and so on. It is as simple as weaving a border of tablets threaded in opposed pairs, but it gives a more striped look, whereas the threading in opposed pairs appear more knitted. The weft is hardly visible, but in some places, it seems to be made of two threads. A tiny fragment of a fringed edge is preserved, and there is scant evidence of an additional weft. This could be an integrated border edging a cloak with fringes (Figs 2.5 and 2.6).

Cat. no. 06 (FHM 1880 VFD) is a lancehead on which a twill fabric is preserved. On one of the edges of the twill, a tablet border of two tablets threaded in opposed pairs is seen. The border is only 0.3 cm wide. The warp is single spun yarn and the threads of one tablet is s-spun, the other z-spun. The border is integrated in a twill fabric, and the s- and z-spun single threads of the fabric are the wefts of the border. It is a starting- or side border (Fig. 2.7).

Out of the 6 tablet woven borders from Illerup, two are independent bands, whereas three are borders integrated in fabrics, and one is too disintegrated to form any conclusions.

Nydam

From Nydam, only three small fragments of tablet borders are preserved. Most of the excavation took place very early and it is likely, that tiny fragments of textile on metal were accidently destroyed while cleaning. The width of the borders is between 0.2 cm and 2.2 cm and made using between two tablets and at least 13 tablets.

Cat. no. 07 (NM 1993 SL 217 × 6136) comprises two fragments of iron with a border preserved in the corrosion. One fragment seems to be a nail on which the tablet border was hung and on the other, the border lies around the middle. It is made using 12 tablets threaded in opposed pairs. The warp consists of z-spun single threads and the weft of presumably two or more z-spun single threads. The use of more threads as weft and the use of different yarn in warp and weft might indicate that this band was a border integrated in a fabric. However, as the edges of the border seem to be preserved and since the border seems to be going around a nail, it is recorded as an independent band (Fig. 2.8).

Cat. no. 08 (NM 2860) is a little, well-preserved twill textile stored beneath window glass. At one side, the fabric has an integrated tablet border of two tablets threaded in opposed pairs which must be a starting or side border. It is made using two tablets and the weft of the border continues as threads of the fabric (Fig. 2.9).

Cat. no. 09 (NM 5653 a) is an imprint on wood of a border of at least 2.2 cm and 13 tablets. The tablets seem to be threaded from the same side, but the textile is very difficult to see as the wood

Fig. 2.1. Cat. no. 01, Illerup. Imprint of tablet-woven border of at least 11 tablets preserved on fragments of a shield boss (Photo: ©Lise Ræder Knudsen).

Fig. 2.2. Cat. no. 02, Illerup. Imprint of tablet-woven border of at least 31 tablets preserved on fragments of a shield boss (Photo: ©Lise Ræder Knudsen).

Fig. 2.3. Cat. no. 03, Illerup. Imprint of tablet-woven border of at least 60 tablets preserved on fragments of two shield bosses (Photo: ©Lise Ræder Knudsen).

Fig. 2.4. Cat. no. 04, Illerup. A tablet-woven border of at least 20 tablets preserved on a lancehead (Photo: ©Lise Ræder Knudsen).

Fig. 2.5. Cat. no. 05, Illerup. A tablet-woven border of at least 26 tablets and twill fabric preserved on the surface of a shieldboss (Photo: ©Lise Ræder Knudsen).

Fig. 2.6. Cat. no. 05, Illerup. The border is woven in a pattern where 3 tablets are threaded in one direction, 3 in the other and so on (Photo: ©Lise Ræder Knudsen).

Fig. 2.7. Cat. no. 06, Illerup. A lancehead on which a twill fabric is preserved. The fabric is edged with a tablet weaving of two tablets. (Photo: ©Lise Ræder Knudsen).

Fig. 2.8. Cat. no. 07, Nydam. A tablet-woven border of 12 tablets preserved in the corrosion of a nail (Photo: ©Lise Ræder Knudsen).

Fig. 2.9. Cat. no. 08, Nydam. A twill fabric edged with an integrated border of two tablets (Photo: ©Lise Ræder Knudsen).

Fig. 2.10. Cat. no. 09, Nydam. An imprint on wood of a tablet-woven border of at least 13 tablets (Photo: ©Lise Ræder Knudsen).

Fig. 2.11. Cat. no. 10, Thorsberg. A thick border of at least 56 tablets of different threading (Photo: ©Lise Ræder Knudsen).

Fig. 2.12. Cat. no. 11, Thorsberg. A coarse twill fabric edged by a border of at least 12 tablets. (Photo: ©Lise Ræder Knudsen).

is treated with wax. It is not possible to see if this was an independent band or an integrated band (Fig. 2.10).

Thorsberg

The chemical composition of the Thorsberg bog was excellent for the preservation of organic materials and the textiles from this excavation may well contain the largest amount of textile objects and some of the most well-preserved, intact garments of the Iron Age. Moreover, the tunic and trousers are displayed in almost every book written about the Iron Age in Denmark since they were excavated in the mid-19th century.

From Thorsberg, 20 different tablet-woven borders are recorded. Some of them are borders of the same textile, but as they have different functions and often are made using different amounts of tablets, each different border was recorded with an individual number. Furthermore, if the textile was in a poorer condition and the borders belonging to the same textile were impossible to discern, they would be registered as different borders anyway.

The number of tablets used for making the borders of the Thorsberg finds differs from 3 to 178. The width differs between 0.5 cm and 16 cm. The fineness of the tablet-woven borders can be assessed in number of tablets per cm. However, unlike in Illerup where it is possible to distinguish between a finer and coarser group of tablet weaving, in Thorsberg, the difference in variation does not allow such a straightforward division into two clearly identifiable groups (see Table 2.1).

Cat. no. 10 (NM 24822 and F.S.3698) comprises two fragments of a well-preserved and rather coarse tablet border of at least 56 tablets. One is in the Danish National Museum in Copenhagen and the other at Schloss Gottorf. They have a pattern of tablets threaded in different ways, and in one place, the same mistake occurs on both, thus seeming to prove that these fragments were originally part of the same textile. The border is rounded in shape, which seems odd and thus might be intentional. The border is rather coarse and the tablet count is 8 per cm. The weft is composed of 2–3 z- or s-spun single threads. As the weft is both s- and z-spun, this was most likely a border integrated in a fabric, and as the border is very thick, it was most likely a finishing border (Fig. 2.11).

Cat. no. 11 (NM 24823 a and b) consists of two fragments of a coarse, twill fabric edged by a tablet-woven border. The pattern is simple, three tablets twisted the same way are followed by three tablets twisted the opposite way and so on. Three threads from the fabric unites to one twisted weft thread of the border, but the threads are not turned back in the tablet weave, they continue a little beyond the border to form the short fringes. The border appears to lack some of the warp threads of the tablet weave in the middle. This could be intentional, or due to the disintegration of some of the warp threads. The twill fabric is z/s, and the threads used for the weft of the tablet weave are z-spun. The tablet weave of both fragments are most likely a finishing border. The border was woven using at least 12 tablets and the width is approx. 4.6 cm. This border could belong to the same textile as F.S.3688 (Cat. no. 15) (Fig. 2.12).

Cat. no. 12 (NM 24824c) is a woollen tabby edged by a tablet border of four tablets. The border is 0.7 cm and the threads from the fabric form the wefts of the border. It is a starting- or side border (Fig. 2.13).

Cat. no. 13a (F.S. 3683) is the lower tablet-woven edge of the famous entirely preserved shirt from Thorsberg. It is made using 4 alternately opposed tablets. It is normally seen as the starting border of the fabric and is made using four tablets. It is possible to see the starting point of the border at the right side of the shirt, at the left side the remaining threads seems to be fastened off by sewing. The border is made in a different manner, than most of the other borders. It has a locking thread outmost pulled through a looped thread which goes in and out of the same shed. Usually the weft thread goes into one shed and continues into the next thereby forming a loop at the edge. If this way of making the border was used without the locking thread, the loops of the weft could be pulled out of the border. Using a locking thread prevents this. Furthermore, a locking thread has an advantage if used as a starting border as it makes warping easier (Anna Nørgård, pers. comm. from her personal experience when making very long warps for the upright loom for sails). The warp threads of the border are single s-spun threads and the tablets change their twisting direction over an uneven distance, the longest being 25 cm and the shortest 0.6 cm. The width of the band is 0.7 cm (Fig. 2.14).

Cat. no. 13b (F.S. 3683) comprises the fully preserved tablet borders sewn onto the sleeves of the Thorsberg shirt. They measure 1.4 cm across, and each has a length of approx. 18 cm. The outer edge is made using 7 tablets threaded in opposed pairs, the two outmost tablets of which are woven in a special way, resulting in a very strong sleeve edge (see Fig. 2.15), the inner edge is made using 6 tablets threaded in opposed pairs. In the middle, 9 tablets create a pattern based on double weave, but as the colours are faded to an equal light brown it is not possible to see the pattern. In all, the border was made using 22 tablets. It is sewn onto the sleeve and seems to have two functions: It reinforces the edge of the sleeves and also decorates the sleeves of the shirt. As only the outer edge has the reinforcement, the border is most likely purpose made. Both warp and weft consists of very fine double S-2z threads. The borders are densely woven using 15 tablets per cm (Fig. 2.16).

Previous research on the borders of the sleeves:

Stettiner (1911, 49–51) writes that, the edges of the border are made by 6 and 7 tablets and that all the tablets have 4 threads each. "Ein mir noch unbekannter Kunstgriff" (a method still unknown to me) is the basis for the pattern section which is made by 12 tablets. The entire border consists of 25 tablets in all.

Schlabow 1976 (93–94) understands the pattern of the sleeves as being woven with four hole-tablets where one of the holes is left empty and the tablets have the empty hole placed in a way, where it is in hole no. 1 in the first tablet, hole 2 in the second, 3 in the third, 4 in the fourth, and first hole in the 5th tablet and so on. All the tablets are twisted forward, and they will leave an empty grove in a diagonal line. He writes that the border was woven using 21 tablets, six tablets for each edge and 9 tablets for the pattern.

Hansen (1990) notes the special way the outermost tablets are woven and suggests that the pattern is woven in 2/1 double twill (pp. 47 and 54), and that it originally had two colours. He analysed the find using photographs and did not examine the original find. He writes that the border was woven using 25 tablets, seven and six tablets for the edges and 12 tablets for the pattern.

Cat. no. 14a (F.S. 3686) (Prachtmantel I). The finishing border of the large cloak from Thorsberg. The border is 12.3 cm and was woven using approx. 136 tablets. In one place the warp threads of the border is not preserved, but the gap suggests that there originally were approx. 12 tablets (see Fig. 2.17). All tablets are threaded in opposed pairs. The warp of the border is made of three different colours: possibly white, light blue and darker blue. The border is an edging of a fabric, and two

Fig. 2.13. Cat. no. 12, Thorsberg. Tabby edges made by four tablets. Note the loop at the left, which was the weft of the border before it was torn (Photo: ©Lise Ræder Knudsen).

Fig. 2.14. Cat. no. 13a, Thorsberg. The tablet-woven edge of the Thorberg tunic with edging cord (Photo: ©Lise Ræder Knudsen).

Fig. 2.15. In this cross-section, four o's represent the four threads in each tablet, and the line represents the weft of the tablet border. A: The selvedge of a normal tablet-woven border, where two threads of each tablet belong to the upper layer of threads and two threads belong to the lower layer of threads. B: The outmost selvedge of the border of the sleeves from Thorsberg. The edge is made in a different way, which seems to be as in this drawing, but as the threads lie very close together, it is difficult to see. The weft is put in the normal way until it reaches the two last tablets. Here only one thread is in the upper layer and three in the lower layer. C: When the weft is inserted again, the two outmost tablets are avoided and thus a tiny round woven edge of only two tablets is made (Photo: ©Lise Ræder Knudsen).

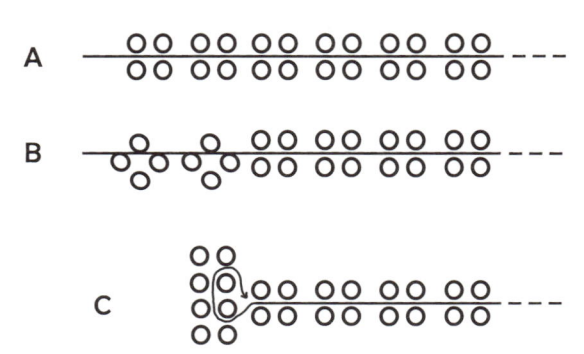

Fig. 2.16. Cat. no. 13b, Thorsberg. Tablet-woven border with pattern sewn onto the sleeves of the tunic (Photo: ©Lise Ræder Knudsen).

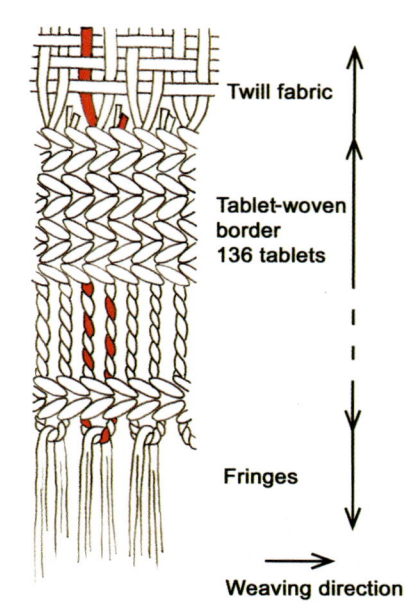

Fig. 2.17. Cat. no. 14a, Thorsberg. Drawing of the finishing border of the large cloak (Drawing: ©Lise Ræder Knudsen).

Fig. 2.18. Cat. no. 14a, Thorsberg. Tablet-woven finishing border of the large cloak. (Photo: ©Roberto Fortuna).

Fig. 2.19. Cat. no. 14b, Thorsberg. Tablet-woven border opposite the finishing border of the large cloak. This is normally seen as the starting border (Photo: ©Lise Ræder Knudsen).

threads from the fabric are used as the weft of the border. The weft passes from the fabric as two single z-spun threads, unites to one s-twined weft thread of the border, in the outer edge it is linked to another thread, which most likely has formed fringes, goes back in the next shed and is cut in the nexus between the border and the fabric. The border was woven from the left side to the right side (Fig. 2.18).

Cat. no. 14b (F.S. 3686) The starting border of the large cloak from Thorsberg. At the opposite side of the finishing border, a small edge is seen, where the eyelets of the fabric and tablet weave appear, but not much is preserved. The place which is best preserved show warp threads of 9 tablets. However, there is no outer edge; the loops merely pass out of the tablet weave, as part of the border has disappeared. Two threads of the fabric unite to one weft of the border and the weft threads are both in the same shed. The loops of the fabric are firmly twisted, both where the warp threads of the fabric are missing and where the warp threads are present, which proves that the twist was made during the manufacture of the cloak. The loops are not of the same length. The difference in length of neighbouring loops is up to ½ cm. All these little details are important pieces in the big puzzle when trying to figure out how the cloak was originally made (Fig. 2.19).

Cat. no. 14c (F.S. 3686) The right side border of the large cloak from Thorsberg. A small tablet-woven border of at least 5 tablets can be seen at the right side of the cloak. The edge of the border is very uneven and the outer edge is not preserved. Little loops of varying length are seen going out of the border. The loops are hardly twisted in comparison to the loops of the starting border, and there is a clear difference between the twisted loops of the starting border and the untwisted loops of the side edge. The warp is of doubled S-2z thread (Fig. 2.20).

Cat. no. 14d (F.S. 3686) The left side border of the large cloak from Thorsberg is not preserved. However the contours of its presence can be partially ascertained, as the warp threads of the original band from the left side border are preserved, and these threads which serve as wefts of the finishing border are different in appearance from the main fabric. Thus, it is obvious that a border was there, although, it is only possible to ascertain its width. This is also why it is rather difficult to determine the precise number of tablets in the side border. Its width is approx. 16 cm and thus it must have used c. 178 tablets, i.e. over

700 threads. The excess of the warp threads from the borders meet in the corner and are braided into elaborated fringes. At the lower left corner of the fabric, only one loop from the fabric is preserved (see Fig. 2.21) which proves that the left side border was woven after the fabric was finished and that the loops of the selvedge were used to interlink with another weft thread to make the broad tablet-woven side border afterwards. This signifies that the right side border has the same characteristics as the left, and that the right side border could very well have been of the same size as the left one.

Cat. no. 15 (F.S. 3688) A rather coarse twill fabric of c. 100 × 72 cm with tablet-woven border and fringes. Most wefts of the tablet border consist of two z-spun loops from the fabric, in all 4 single threads. New fringes of approx. the same material and quality are linked to the loops 1.5 to 2 cm from the twill. In a few places, extra fringes are inserted and cut at the nexus between border and fabric (Fig. 2.22). This is surely done to keep the balance between the border and the tablet weave. The fringes seem rather worn, but in many places they are still hard twisted. The weft thread of the border consists of z-spun threads from the fabric. The fabric has z-spun threads in one direction and s-spun threads in the other direction. More of the twill fabrics from Thorsberg have z-spun warp and s-spun weft, e.g. cloak F.S. 3686. Thus it is most likely that the z-spun threads of the twill fabric (F.S.3688) constitute the warp. As seen on other finds from Thorsberg, finishing borders either have long fringes which are passed through the tablet (NM 24823 a and b) or fringes which are passed out through one shed of the tablet border and back in the next shed (as F.S. 3689 and the finishing border of F.S. 3686 (Cat. no. 14a). As the border of F.S. 3688 has z-spun weft, and it is made with loops and not long fringes, it is most likely that it is a border made where we would expect a starting border to be. However, it must have been woven to the edge of the fabric after the latter was finished because the fringes would be pulled out of the border by the weight of the loom weights, if a starting border for the warp weighted loom had been constructed in this way.

The border is made using at least 10 tablets twisted 3,3,3, and 1 in opposite directions. The border was at least 2.5 cm and the fringes exceeded the border by at least 3 cm. The tablet count is 4 per. cm. This is most likely a border woven to the edge, where a starting border is expected to be. This border could belong to the same textile as F.S. 3689 (Cat. no. 16a) + FHM 607 1a (Cat. no. 23) or to NM 24823 a + b (Cat. no. 10) (For a different interpretation of this find see Möller-Wiering, this volume) (Fig. 2.23).

Cat. no. 16a (F.S. 3689) A coarse twill fabric of c.19 cm × 92 cm edged with tablet-woven borders on two edges. This band is long, c. 90 cm. It is approx. 3 cm across and was woven using at least 20 tablets – the outer edge is not preserved. The tablets are threaded in alternately opposed pairs. From the fabric, 4–5 threads are used as weft in the tablet weave. They join in one weft, the tablets are turned and the same 4–5 threads are taken back in the next shed, the tablets are turned again, and the excess thread cut at the join between the fabric and the border. The weaving principle highly resembles the finishing border of the large cloak F.S. 3686, Cat. no. 14a (see Fig. 2.17) Thus, this is most likely a finishing border. The tablet count is appr. 7 tablets per cm. F.S. 3689 (Cat. no. 16a) could belong to the same textile and border as FHM 607–1a (Cat. no. 23), and to the same textile as F.S. 3688 (Cat. no. 15) (For a different interpretation of this find, see Möller-Wiering, this volume) (Fig. 2.24).

Cat. no. 16b (F.S. 3689) The other tablet border of the twill fabric. The border is preserved for a length of 9 cm and it is at least 2.5 cm across. This border was woven before border no. 16a, as the warp threads of this border were utilized as weft threads of no. 16a at the meeting point in the corner. It was woven using at least 14 tablets. As no. 16a is most likely a finishing border, this might be a side border. The tablet count is 7 tablets per cm (Fig. 2.25).

Cat. no. 17 (F.S. 3690) A fine, light-brown diamond twill fabric edged by a small, dark reddish-brown tablet border. The border is quite similar to the right border no. 13c of the large Thorsberg cloak. The border is woven onto the fabric. The outer edge is not preserved. The weft comprises short loops from the twill fabric with both weft threads in the same shed, which gives two possibilities concerning the original weave: either the loops were linked to another weft thread and the border (which could have been very wide across) was woven after the fabric was taken off the loom, or a locking thread was lost just outside the 4 tablets. As the weft of the border consists of z-spun loops of the fabric, and as z-spun yarn most likely constitutes the warp of the fabric, this might be a border woven to the fabric at the place where we would expect a starting border to be as in F.S. 3688. The border was made using at least 4 tablets threaded in alternately opposed pairs, and the tablet count is c. 8 per cm (Fig. 2.26).

Cat. no. 18 (F.S. 3691) A leg wrap in a twill fabric with tablet-woven borders along the two, long opposite sides. The item is mounted on a brown fabric with a thin netting placed over the surface of the fabric. This makes analysis very difficult and not as reliable.

There are 5 tablets on both sides and they are arranged in alternately opposed pairs. The length of the border on one side is 30.5 cm, and on the other 25 cm. The warp thread of the borders seems to be the same s-spun single thread as is the thread of the twill fabric. The weft of the border is two threads from the fabric. On the outer side of the border, a pearly edge of single threads is visible which makes it very likely that this is a side or starting border (Fig. 2.27). As they are placed opposite and seem identical, these must be side borders. Evidence of the tablets having changed their turning direction can be noted on both the left and the right sides of the fabric. The change occurs at the same height on both sides (Fig. 2.28).

Cat. no.19a, 19b, 19c (F.S. 3692) A leg wrap made in tabby and edged on three sides by a tablet border of 3 tablets threaded alternately opposed. The fourth side is missing. The fabric is 73 cm long and 12 cm across. The weft passes double through the shed. The weft is seen as a pearly edge on the outer side of the tablet border, signifying that there are two weft threads in each shed. One border goes around the corner.

The item is mounted on a brown fabric with a thin netting placed over the surface of the fabric. This makes analysis very difficult and not as reliable as could be hoped and makes it impossible to take photographs. It seems that the border on the short edge is the starting border and the two borders on the long sides are side borders. The twisting direction of the side borders are changed a few times, but not at the same height. There are c. 6 tablets per cm.

Cat. no. 20 (F.S. 3695) A fragment of a twill fabric edged by an integrated tablet-woven border. It seems to be a starting border as the weft threads lie two and two in the shed. The weft forms loops, and one loop has each leg in neighbouring sheds. As the weft of the border is the hardest twisted of the two systems of the fabric, it seems safe to conclude that this is a starting border. The details are very difficult to ascertain, but Schlabow says that the border was woven using 6 tablets, three threaded in one direction and three threaded in the opposite direction (Schlabow 1976, 81). The tablet count is c. 8 per cm (Fig. 2.29).

Fig. 2.20. Cat. no. 14c, Thorsberg. Remaining fringes of the large cloak which served as weft threads of the tablet-woven right side border. The warp threads of the border are not preserved at this spot, but note the different length of the weft loops (Photo: ©Lise Ræder Knudsen).

Fig. 2.21. Cat. no. 14d, Thorsberg. The tablet-woven left side border is only preserved as weft threads of the finishing border. And this is the lower left corner where originally 178 tablets formed the widest known tablet border of the Iron Age. The white arrow indicates the place where a single loop is preserved, which proves that this side border was woven to the edge of the fabric, and not woven at the same time as the fabric as previously thought (Photo: ©Roberto Fortuna, National Museum of Denmark).

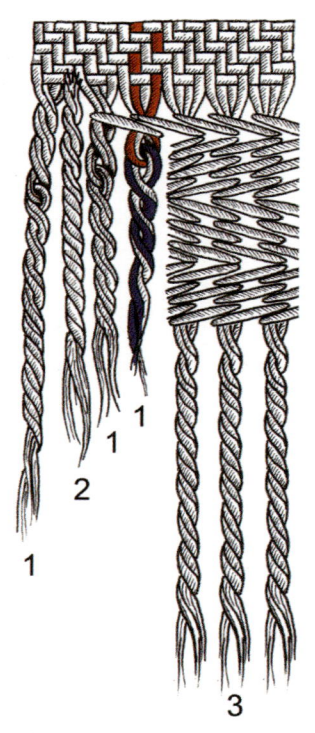

Fig. 2.22. Method of weaving border F.S. 3688. 1: two loops from the fabric are linked to two other threads inside the tablet border. 2: in a few places, an additional weft thread, which is not part of the fabric, is inserted. This is a very useful way of adjusting the balance between the border and fabric when a border is woven to the fabric after the ground weave has been completed. 3: Same as 1, but here the warp threads of the tablet weave are visible (Drawing: ©Lise Ræder Knudsen).

Cat. no. 21 (F.S. 3697) (Prachtmantel III) A fragment of a textile with a very broad and delicate tablet weaving and fringes. Only one edge with fringes of the border is preserved, but the fragment has all the characteristics of a fabric border, even though the fabric is missing. The border was woven using at least 79 tablets, each with 4 threads. The technique is the simple forward turning of alternately opposed pairs of tablets. The weft and the warp are of several different colours. The weft of the border comprises four single threads which make a loop of two threads each. This loop links to another thread at the outer edge of the tablet weaving and these threads are made into highly elaborate fringes (see Schlabow Abb. 120–123 and p. 65). As there are 4 single threads in each shed, this is most likely a finishing border. The tablet count is 16 tablets per cm. The border is woven in the same way as the finishing border of the large cloak F.S. 3686 (Cat. no. 14a and Fig. 2.17) (Fig. 2.30).

12. Tablet-Woven Textiles from 3rd to 4th-Century AD Weapon Deposits

Fig. 2.23. Cat. No. 15, Thorsberg. A tablet-woven border edging a twill fabric. The wefts of the border are loops from the fabric linked to another thread (Photo: ©Lise Ræder Knudsen).

Fig. 2.24. Cat. No. 16a, Thorsberg. A large twill fabric edged by a tablet-woven border of at least 20 tablets (Photo: ©Lise Ræder Knudsen).

Fig. 2.25. Cat. No. 16b, Thorsberg. The same twill fabric is edged by another tablet-woven border and the two borders meet in the corner. This border was woven first (Photo: ©Lise Ræder Knudsen).

Fig. 2.26. Cat. No. 17, Thorsberg. A fine, light brown, twill fabric edged by a tablet-woven border of at least 4 tablets (Photo: ©Lise Ræder Knudsen).

Fig. 2.27. Drawing showing the appearance of an edge of a border with one weft (left), and the edge which shows when two wefts are inserted in the shed from opposite sides leaving a pearly edge at the selvedge right (Drawing: ©Lise Ræder Knudsen).

Cat. no. 22 (F.S. 3706) Two fragments of a fine diamond twill, of which one has a small, integrated, tablet-woven border of 0.5 cm at one of the edges. The border is made using 3 tablets, one in one direction, the two others in the opposite direction. The weft consists of a loop of two threads from the fabric which goes through one shed and is locked by a double thread on the outer edge. The loops seem to be of various lengths, the difference being of up to 2 mm. The tablet count is about 6 tablets per cm. The spinning direction of the fabric is z in one direction and s in the other. The weft of the border is z-spun, which indicates that this is a border woven either to the end of the fabric, or to its starting point (Fig. 2.31).

Cat. no. 23 (FHM 607–1A) A fragment of a twill fabric with an integrated tablet-woven border of 3.5 cm made using 21 tablets. The tablets are threaded in alternately opposed pairs, and the warp is of single s-spun threads. The weft is 4 z-spun threads from the fabric which goes through one shed, the tablets are twisted, fringes of at least 2 cm are left on the outside of the border and the excess thread is used as weft of the next shed (see Fig. 2.32) and cut close to the nexus between fabric and border. This is a finishing border. Few remains of fringes are preserved, and the outer side of the fringes are mostly torn off. The tablet count is 6 tablets per cm.

Cat. no. 24 (FHM 607–1B) A fragment of a twill fabric with an integrated tablet-woven border of 12 tablets and 1.8 cm across. The tablets are threaded in alternately opposed pairs. The warp of the tablet border comprises z-spun single threads. The weft is two s-spun threads from the fabric. The outer edge is worn and it is not possible to see any details. The fabric is rather unbalanced. This might be a side border of the same fabric as no. 23 and the unbalanced twill might be a question of craftsmanship. Weaving experiments show that, unbalanced sides and narrowing of the weaving is a common irregularity (Anna Nørgaard, pers. comm.) (Fig. 2.33).

Vimose

From Vimose, five fragments of tablet borders are preserved. Most of the excavation took place very early and it is likely that, tiny fragments of textiles on metal were accidently removed during cleaning and thus not preserved. The width of the borders is between 0.5 cm and at least 3.2 cm and made using between at least 7 tablets and at least 43 tablets.

Cat. no. 25 (NM 24762) A lancehead of which the socket is missing. A tablet-woven border is wrapped 4 times around the lancehead. The border is made using at least 43 tablets threaded in alternately opposed pairs. The warp of the border is made of doubled S2z threads and the weft is probably 2 single s-spun threads. One edge of the border is preserved. It is a selvedge and the two outermost tablets are of a thicker thread than the others. The other edge is not preserved. This seems to be an independent band. The two single threads of the weft could indicate that it is a fabric border, but as much of the border remains, and no signs of a fabric can be discerned, and as it is very difficult to see the weft, it is most likely an independent band or perhaps an integrated band cut off from its fabric and used as an independent band. The tablet count is 14 tablets per cm (Fig. 2.34).

Cat. no. 26 (NM 24763) Spearhead with some fringes and a tiny fragment of tablet-woven border in the iron corrosion. The border has at least 7 tablets but no edges are preserved. The tablets are arranged with either one or two tablets twisted to one side, and then one or two tablets twisted to the other side (Fig. 2.35). It is not possible to see the weft of the border, but the relation between the thread count of the warp and weft indicates that, this was a border like many of the borders from the Thorsberg find where rather thick threads from the fabric are edged by rather thin threads of the tablet weave. The fringes are made Z2S4z. It is possible that the spearhead was originally wrapped in a cloak with fringes and that the tablet border is an integrated part of the fabric.

Cat. no. 27 (NM 24766) A shield boss with fringes and a fragment of tablet-woven border preserved in the iron corrosion. The border is at least 2.4 cm across and the preserved length is c. 3 cm. The border was woven using at least 25 tablets threaded in alternately opposed pairs. At one edge of the border, fringes are preserved. There are four fringes at a distance of 1.8 cm each. Some of the fringes can be described as Z3S6z, but they are different in size. The weft of the border is most likely 2 single s-spun threads, which indicates that the border was edging a fabric where one thread system was s-spun single threads. Most likely the shield boss was wrapped in a cloak with border and fringes (Fig. 2.36).

Cat. no. 28 (NM C9400) Very weak imprints of a tablet border on the blade of a lancehead. No further details can be ascertained.

Cat. no. 29 (NM UI160) A socket of a lancehead with tablet border preserved in the corrosion. The border is wrapped around the socket. The surface of the tablet border is only preserved in tiny fragments, but the border is mostly split and it is only the weft which is visible. The tablets are threaded in alternately opposed pairs, and there are 5 tablets at a distance of 3 mm each, which gives a tablet count of c. 17 tablets per cm. It is not possible to see further details (Fig. 2.37).

12.3. THE INTERPRETATION AND COMPARISON OF DIFFERENT TECHNICAL DETAILS CONCERNING TABLET-WOVEN BORDERS FOUND IN WEAPON DEPOSITS

Independent bands versus integrated bands

In the catalogue, tablet-woven bands are often referred to as "Integrated" or "Independent". By the word "Independent" we understand a band which was woven as a separate band not connected to another textile. When the weaving process was finished, it could be used as a band or be sewn onto a fabric. During the weaving process, an integrated band is connected to a fabric in such a manner that the weft thread of the border is part of the fabric. The weft threads of both kinds of bands are often hidden inside the border, and only the warp threads are seen. This makes a distinction between the techniques more difficult when only a little fragment is found, and it is not possible to see the nexus between tablet border and fabric.

The difference between tablet-woven borders used as independent bands and those made as an integrated part of a fabric is crucial as the bands serve different purposes and were made using different techniques. Furthermore, integrated bands seem to be closely connected to the looms used. Moreover, integrated borders can be woven before the fabric, at the same time as the fabric or they can be made after the fabric was removed from the loom, which makes it possible that the border was made at one place and the borders attached to the fabric at another geographical location.

This result includes a possible solution to a discussion held in the 1980s. Lise Bender Jørgensen argued that the uniform characteristics of the fabrics indicated a provincial Roman origin, possibly in a particular centre, which was automatically assumed for the borders as well (Bender Jørgensen and Wild 1988). John Peter Wild however, regarded the borders as Germanic and therefore suggested a non-Roman provenance of the cloaks in their entirety (ibid.). The possibility of weaving a border to

Fig. 2.28. Cat. no. 18. Thorsberg. A leg wrap edged by tablet-woven borders of 3 tablets (Photo: ©Lise Ræder Knudsen).

Fig. 2.29. Cat. no. 20, Thorsberg. A twill fabric edged by a tablet-woven border of approx. 6 tablets (Photo: ©Lise Ræder Knudsen).

Fig. 2.30. Cat. no. 21, Thorsberg. A very fine tablet-woven border of at least 79 tablets with elaborated fringes (Photo: ©Lise Ræder Knudsen).

Fig. 2.31. Cat. no. 22, Thorsberg. A diamond-twill fabric edged by a tablet-woven border of three tablets. Loops of the fabric form the weft of the border. The outermost loops are secured by a locking thread (Photo: ©Lise Ræder

Fig. 2.32. Cat. no. 23, Thorsberg. Finishing border of a twill fabric made using 21 tablets. At the nexus between the border and fabric remains of the cut threads can be detected (Photo: ©Lise Ræder Knudsen).

Fig. 2.33. Cat. no. 24, Thorsberg. Side border of 12 tablets, most likely the same textile as Cat. no. 23 (Photo: ©Lise Ræder Knudsen).

Fig. 2.34. Cat. no. 25, Vimose. A lancehead on which a long and very well preserved tablet-woven border is seen (Photo: ©Lise Ræder Knudsen).

Fig. 2.35. Cat. no. 26. Vimose. A tiny fragment of a tablet-woven border preserved in the corrosion of a spearhead (Photo: ©Lise Ræder Knudsen).

Fig. 2.36. Cat. no. 27, Vimose. A shield boss with fringes and a fragment of tablet-woven border preserved in the corrosion (Photo: Lise Ræder Knudsen).

Fig. 2.37. Cat. no. 29, Vimose. A weak imprint of a tablet border on the blade of a lancehead (Photo: Lise Ræder Knudsen).

Fig. 2.38. Warp from Tegle in Norway, where tablet-woven side borders are prepared (©Museum of Archaeology, University of Stavanger, Arkeologisk Museum i Stavanger).

Table 2.2. The distribution of integrated and independent borders from weapon deposits.

Band type	Characteristics	Cat. no.	Number of bands registered
Integrated	Starting border or border woven to the starting end of the fabric	14b, 15, 17, 19a	4
	Side border	14c, 14d, 16b, 18a, 18b, 19b, 19c, 24	8
	Starting- or finishing border	8, 12, 20	3
	Finishing border	10, 11, 14a, 16a, 21, 23	6
	Locking thread	13b, 22	2
	Edging of a fabric	2, 5, 6, 27	4
Independent	Simple straightforward tablet weaving	4, 7, 25	3
	Pattern weaving	3, 13a	2
Not ascertainable	Too little preserved to distinguish characteristics	1, 9, 26, 28, 29	5
			37

an already completed cloth, i.e. using interlinking between the loops of the fabric and the weft of the tablet border, eliminates the contradiction between these two positions (Ræder Knudsen 1998, 82). Thus, it is interesting to distinguish between independent bands and integrated bands in this study.

Previously, it has been demonstrated that, it is possible to distinguish with some certainty between independent bands and integrated bands by examining the amount of weft threads in each shed. One weft thread indicates an independent tablet-woven band, whereas more weft threads indicate an integrated tablet-woven band (Ræder Knudsen forthcoming a). When a fragment of a border is found, this detail might help to establish the band's original purpose.

Five bands from weapon deposits are too poorly preserved to form any conclusions concerning their original purpose. Out of 32 borders, which are preserved well enough to make conclusions, 27 borders are part of a fabric and 5 borders are independent bands. This signifies that 81% of the tablet-woven borders recorded from weapon deposits are borders integrated in a fabric and 19% are independent bands (Table 2.2).

Independent bands
Only 5 out of 32 bands are independent bands. They are distributed among the four different sites with one at each site and only Illerup having two samples. Four of these bands are preserved in the corrosion of iron objects. Out of these four samples, three are ordinary, forward tablet weaving preserved on the surface of lance- and arrowheads with the weaving being of a fineness of 6 to 16 tablets per cm (Cat. nos 4, 7 and 25).

When an army is on the march, it is necessary to tie up the soldiers' load on the back of each man, on horseback or onto a wagon. Bands for tying up the load would have been useful, and these strong and simple tablet-woven bands may very well have served this purpose before they were wrapped around weapons and thrown into the bog. One sample is preserved in the corrosion of a shield boss (Cat. no. 3), together with twill woven fabric and fringes. The band is wide, woven using at least 52 tablets, the quality is rather fine with 20 tablets per cm and the edges are made as forward tablet weaving with alternately opposed tablets, whereas the middle part is a pattern weaving based on ordinary double weave. As the band only has one weft thread in each shed, it is probably not an integrated band, but it might be a decorative band sewn onto a twill cloak with fringes.

Only one further independent band is preserved. It is the band of the sleeves of the incredibly well-preserved tunic from Thorsberg F.S. 3683 Cat. no. 13a. The bands of the two sleeves seem to be one band cut in two and therefore it is registered as one band in the catalogue.

The bands of the sleeves have edges of plain, forward tablet weaving and a central section of pattern weaving. The outer edge of the sleeve band is made in a special way where the threads of two tablets lie on top of each other instead of beside each other (see Fig. 2.15). On a tablet-woven tunic border from Evebö-Eide, Gloppen in Central Norway, a similar edge is found (Dedekam 1926,12, Raknes 1982, 77) and more tablet woven fabrics in this grave have the same detail as the border. In this case, the threads lying on the others are used for an invisible mounting of the border onto the garment. Scholars have convincingly suggested that this special mounting was done to make it possible to flip the border, so that one could choose which side to display – perhaps the border held some special significance (Nockert 1991, 31 and 105; Bender Jørgensen 2003, 61). From Snartemo in southern Norway, different tablet-woven borders with somewhat the same characteristic edge are found (Ræder Knudsen 1996, 70–71, 82, 100).

The sleeve borders from Thorsberg are mounted with the special detail at the outer edge of the sleeve, but the bands are not mounted with the threads from the tablet lying on top of each other as is the border from Evebö-Eide. However, the bands of the sleeves of the tunic might not *have* their original mounting. Information provided by the staff at the Museum of Schloss Gottorf indicates that, the mounting was done during conservation, and that the borders and the tunic had no sewing thread preserved when found (Ingrid Ulbricht, Schloss Gottorf, pers. comm.). The special detail of one tablet lying on top of the others on the outer edge of the border might serve two purposes: It could be for invisible mounting and it could be to reinforce the edge.

The only other registered tablet-woven edges of this kind so far are found in Norway and this could indicate a connection between Norway and the tunic from Thorsberg.

Integrated bands
Tablet-woven bands integrated with a fabric can have different purposes, such as:

1. Starting band for putting up the loom. The weft of the band is dragged out in very long fringes, which will serve as warp threads of the loom. The starting border is woven before the fabric.
2. Side borders, which can be woven along the sides of the fabric while it is woven on the loom. The side borders are woven at the same time as the fabric.
3. Finishing borders, which will use the excessive warp threads, when the fabric is finished, as the weft of a border. The finishing border fixes the threads in an aesthetically pleasing and solid way and often makes this border resemble the borders of the other three sides of the fabric. Finishing borders are made after the fabric was finished and removed from the loom.

It is possible to distinguish a finishing border, as it would generally have double the amount of weft threads as would the side- and starting border, and furthermore, it might be possible to see the place at the nexus between fabric and border where the excess fringes are cut. It can be impossible to distinguish between starting- and side borders when only a tiny fragment is preserved, as the threads can lie in just the same way, but as the warp threads of a fabric very often are twisted harder – and thus stronger – than the weft threads, it is sometimes possible to distinguish between them. Also a closer study of the threads in the nexus between the tablet-woven band and fabric is important. If the threads are snaggled, it must be a starting border, as it is only at the moment of putting up the warp that warp threads can become disordered. The threads of the side border are bound to lie in a special way. If the nexus is very regular, it is a side border, or a starting border made by a thoroughly skilled person.

However, recent research has demonstrated that, it can be more complicated than outlined above (Ræder Knudsen 1998, 79–84; forthcoming a). Borders can be attached in an invisible way to the edges of fabrics after the fabric is removed from the loom, and the appearance of the border is very similar to the above mentioned, which makes it difficult to distinguish the difference.

Below we will examine some of the more pertinent tablet borders mentioned in the catalogue, first the samples woven in the conventionally expected way and thereafter those woven in an unusual way.

Starting-, side- and finishing borders made in the conventional way
The starting border is made to hold the warp threads of the upright loom. A normal, simple tablet border is put up and the weft threads of the border are dragged out in long fringes to one side – this will form the warps of the weave. The border is mounted on the beam of the loom and the long fringes – the warp – are then arranged. When a textile with tablet-woven side borders is planned, the starting border has to be made with different amounts of warp threads per cm at the edges, where the borders should be, and in the middle, where the fabric will be woven. And this prior planning is seen in various well-preserved textiles with tablet-woven borders from the Iron Age, e.g., the Skærsø Blanket (see Ræder Knudsen forthcoming a) and the well-known warp from Tegle in Norway (Fig. 2.38). It was presumably a weaver's basket, full of materials including a fully prepared warp for an upright loom, which was thrown in a bog in the Roman Iron Age in mid Norway (Hoffmann 1974, 175). The Tegle find has recently been C^{14} dated to AD 445–545 (Halvorsen, 2009, 3).

This interpretation of starting borders is described by Hoffmann (1974, 151), Hald (1980, 164) and Schlabow (1976, 42).

A tablet-woven band on the short side of a leg wrapper (Cat. no. 19a, F.S. 3692) from Thorsberg is with high certainty its starting border. First, a tablet weaving of 3 tablets was put up and the warp for the loom prepared, the first 12 threads of the warp for the fabric are used in a new tablet weave of 3 tablets which would constitute one side border. On the other side, the 3 tablets of the starting border run along the corner of the fabric and continue as a side border (Fig. 2.39).

With a few tablets on each side of the loom, the production of a textile with tablet-woven side borders is quite easy. The tablets are normally twisted for every second weft which equalizes the tension between the tablet border and the fabric. Furthermore, it results in two wefts in each shed of the side border as is also the case of the starting border.

Finishing borders have the function of tidying up the excess thread of the fabric when it is taken off the loom. A common and aesthetically pleasing way to tidy up the edge and also render it solid is to make a tablet border using the fringes of the warps as the weft of the border. Generally, this is done as the finishing border of a large cloak, e.g. F.S. 3686 (Cat. no. 14a), where two warp threads are passed through a shed, the tablets are twisted and the two threads led into the next shed, and the excess fringes cut at the line between fabric and border (see Fig. 2.17). The cut would be almost impossible to discern and the result will be a very strong edge. If only some fragments of a tablet border are recovered, it may be possible to distinguish the finishing border as it is often thicker than the others. In the material from Thorsberg, finishing borders where the fringes pass straight through the shed too may be discerned (Cat. no. 11, NM 24823 a + NM 24823 b).

Starting- and side borders made in another way
The tunic from Thorsberg has a tablet-woven border of 4 tablets at the lower end at the back. This is normally seen as the starting border of the fabric (see Stettiner 1911, 43; Hoffmann 1974,

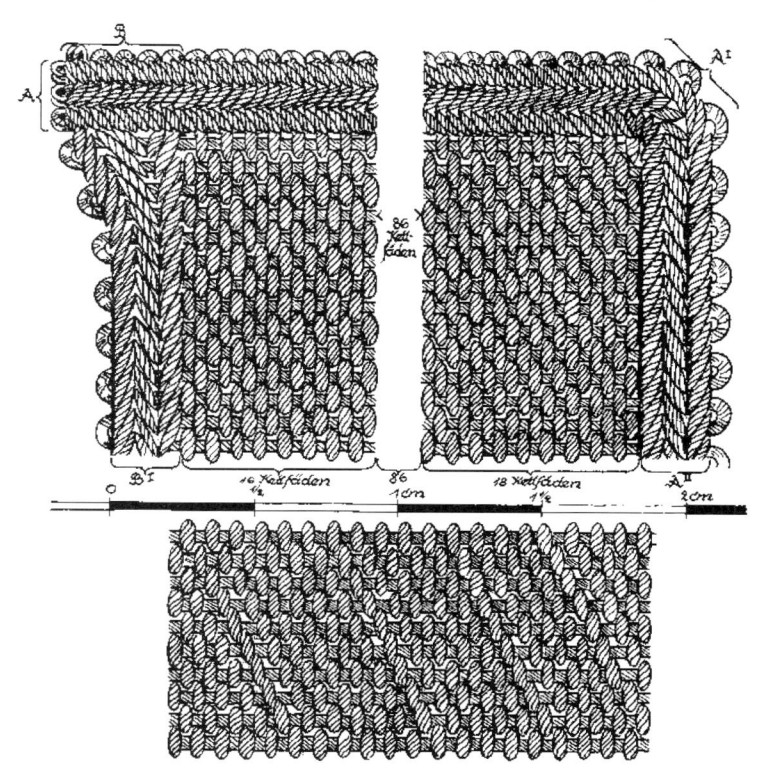

Fig. 2.39. A leg wrapper from Thorsberg with a normal starting border and the border continues down one side of the weaving (Drawing by Schlabow 1976 Abb. 231 – every effort was made to contact the copyright holder).

167–168; Schlabow 1976, 70). However, the border has a special detail: its weft is taken around a cord at the outermost edge of the border and back in same shed. This is termed an edging cord (see Fig. 2.14).

Schlabow illustrates some of the borders in his book: From Thorsberg: F.S. 3683 "Kittel", F.S. 3686 "Der Prachtmantel", F.S. 3690 "Geweberest", F.S. 3706 "Geweberest" (1976, Abb. 138, 117, 197b, 208c) all having an edging cord beyond the tablet-woven starting border.

In a meticulous examination of the tablet borders from Thorsberg, I found an edging cord only in the tunic (see Fig. 2.14) and in the textile F.S. 3706 (see Fig. 2.31). The large cloak and the other fragment of textiles have short loops and the tablet weave is badly preserved, but there is no evidence of an outer cord. The edging cord of the large cloak, F.S. 3686 and F.S. 3690, must be Schlabow's interpretation, although, no proof of this is evident in the archaeological material examined.

Hoffmann (1974, 167–168) describes a few finds which have tablet-woven edge borders, where the weft of the border is taken around a cord or twisted thread and then taken back through the same shed of the border. The finds she mentions are those from Thorsberg and based on Schlabow's argumentation concerning the starting border of the large cloak, she concludes that the tablet border of the tunic must also be a starting border. Furthermore, she mentions a cloth from Tegle in Norway with a tablet-woven border and outermost, an edging cord as a locking thread. Also the preserved stocking or sleeve in sprang from Tegle has this tablet-woven and corded edge at one end of the warp. Hoffmann believes that the sleeve or stocking was one of a pair made simultaneously and then separated in the middle. In the other end of the warp, she expects that there originally was a conventional starting border (Hoffmann 1974, 169). Here she argues that the border with edging cord might be the finishing border (Hoffmann 1974, 167, fig. 80).

In my examination of the two borders with edging cord from Thorsberg (F.S. 2683 and F.S. 3706), I have observed that the weft loops going around this outer cord are of a slightly different length (see Figs 2.14 and 2.31). Some lie close to the cord, while others are quite loose. If these borders were in fact starting borders, there would be so much tension on each of these loops – as they are the warp threads of the loom and hold the weight of the loom weights – that the surplus of thread would have been dragged down and the picture we would see would be of loops of the same length lying very close to the cord. As this is not the case, and we furthermore have the sprang textile from Tegle and no solid arguments concerning an edging cord of the starting border of the large cloak from Thorsberg, the tablet-woven borders with edging cord *are in fact borders made after the fabric was finished.*

This leaves us with yet another interesting conundrum: *Which loom would fabricate a textile which has little loops at the ends with just a few millimetres of difference in length?* (For a different interpretation, see Möller-Wiering this volume).

Another very interesting detail is that we again have a link between some of the textiles from Thorsberg, and Norway: The edging cord is only found in some of the textiles from Thorsberg (F.S. 3683 and F.S. 3706) and the Tegle find from southern Norway (see Bender Jørgensen 1986, 146–155 for further arguments on large cloaks with tablet-woven borders and the Thorsberg material).

To delve further into the question of the loom types, it is necessary to examine the tablet weavings of the large cloak from Thorsberg F.S. 3686.

12.4. THE LARGE CLOAK FROM THORSBERG F.S. 3686 "PRACHTMANTEL 1"

The large cloak from Thorsberg is mounted on a brown woollen cloth. As seen on the illustration, the cloak has been exhibited for many years and the mounting cloth is severely damaged by too much light. The cloak fabric is fragmentary, but rather well preserved. This picture shows the cloak with the finishing edge at the bottom, and what must be the starting point of the weaving at the top. To the right, the remaining warp threads of 4–5 tablets are seen, and to the left, only the lower corner is preserved, which shows that the left edge was a 16 cm wide tablet border. But this border is only preserved in the form of weft threads in the lower border.

The details numbered I–II–III–IV–V on the illustration are explained on the following pages (Fig. 2.40)

I: Finishing border of cloak no. F.S. 3686 from Thorsberg
The lower part of the cloak has a wide finishing border of about 136 tablets (see Fig. 2.18). When the fabric was removed from the loom, the remaining fringes were secured and tidied up in a tablet border. Two threads from the fabric emerge through the shed of the tablet border, a new thread is linked to the fringes made in a different colour and the two threads return in the next shed and the excess thread is cut in the line between the fabric and the border and thus invisibly secured (see

Fig. 2.17). The two threads of the fabric are firmly twisted to one thread in the shed of the tablet weave. There seems to be a contradiction in the fact that great effort is needed to secure and mend the fringes of the warp of the fabric in a strong and invisible way – and then new fringes are added to the edge of the tablet border. It would have been easier to use the fringes left from weaving the fabric and thus avoid the work of making the tablet border (Fig. 2.41).

II: Starting border of the cloak from Thorsberg F.S. 3686
The starting border of the cloak was considered by Schlabow to be a tablet-woven border using 9 tablets with an edging cord (Schlabow 1976, Abb. 117). However, there is no evidence in the material of an edging cord, and the neighbouring loops of the edge differ up to 0.5 cm in length which makes the idea of an edging cord impossible (Fig. 2.19). A normal, tablet-woven selvedge is not possible either, as the weft made of the shorter loops would not reach the edge.

A starting border made first to hold the warp of the fabric by using a method where two threads interlink seems a possibility, but as shown on the following pages, it is practically not feasible (Fig. 2.42).

A twist of the warp threads of the fabric at the time of making the border would have been possible if they hang freely. The warp from Tegle has shown us that the warp threads were kept in firm order by large knots (Hoffmann 1974, 153–154), and reconstructions of weavings also show us that keeping the warp threads of the upright loom in order before putting the warp up is essential. Furthermore, a freely hanging warp of hard twisted single threads would untwist and tangle up. This leaves one possible reason why the loops of the upper edge are twisted: The loops must have hung freely after the fabric was removed from the loom, and we can conclude that the fabric was woven first and the tablet-woven border was made after the fabric was woven. Previous work has indicated that an interlinking with the loops of the fabric and another thread was used to make the tablet-woven borders of a cloak from Vrangstrup in Denmark (Ræder Knudsen 1998, 81–83). This might also be the case of the cloak from Thorsberg (Fig. 2.43).

III: The right side border of the cloak from Thorsberg F.S. 3686
On the right side tablet border, loops are seen pretty much as the upper border (see no. III on the large picture of the Thorsberg cloak, Fig. 2.40). Also here the loops are of a different length and the weft of the tablet border must have been the loops interlinking to another thread, but this thread and much of the tablet weaving has not been preserved.

The main difference between the upper border and this side border is that these loops are not twisted. Why would that be?

At first we thought that it was a question of the warp of the fabric being made of a harder twisted yarn. If there was a solid difference between the twist of the warp and the twist of the weft of the fabric, that might be an answer. There seems to be a slight difference in the twisting angle of the warp and the weft, but not so much that it would explain hard twisted loops of the upper edge and no twist of the loops of the side border.

To find possible explanations, it must be remembered that the warp of the fabric is z-spun and the weft is s-spun. If a tablet border was woven after the fabric was removed from the loom using the interlinking method, and the yarn of the interlinking thread was composed of s-spun single threads, the s-spun loops of the side border and the s-spun interlinking thread would not twine. However,

Fig. 2.40. The large cloak from Thorsberg F.S. 3686. I: finishing border. II: The border on the opposite side of the finishing border normally seen as the starting border. III: Right edge border where mostly just small fringes remain. IV: Left side border, where the border is only seen as a "ghost" – the warp thread of it is used as weft threads of the finishing border at the corner of the cloak. V: A fragment mounted incorrectly during restoration and mounting on a brown supporting cloth. The circles with Roman numerals indicate areas with interesting details, and their close-ups with explanations are found below in the text (Photo: ©Roberto Fortuna).

if the same s-spun thread was used to interlink with the z-spun loops of the upper edge, the result would be an immediate and firm twist. This was the theory, and a test shows that it is correct (Figs 2.44–2.47). One would assume that the same method could be used to make a starting border for a warp using two threads: a z-spun long warp thread and an s-spun interlinking thread (see Fig. 2.42), but this is not possible in practice as the twist would tangle up the warp.

Another explanation is possible. Here, it is necessary to look at the twill fabric with tablet-woven

12. Tablet-Woven Textiles from 3rd to 4th-Century AD Weapon Deposits

Fig. 2.41. The lower edge of the finishing border of the large cloak F.S. 3686. The weft of the border consists of 2 single threads from the fabric, which twist naturally. Linked to the loops of the outer edge, traces of another thread are seen. This thread has surely been part of a fringe (©Lise Ræder Knudsen).

Fig. 2.42. Making a tablet-woven starting border with two balls of yarn. The yarn links inside the tablet border and thus the link is invisible (©Lise Ræder Knudsen).

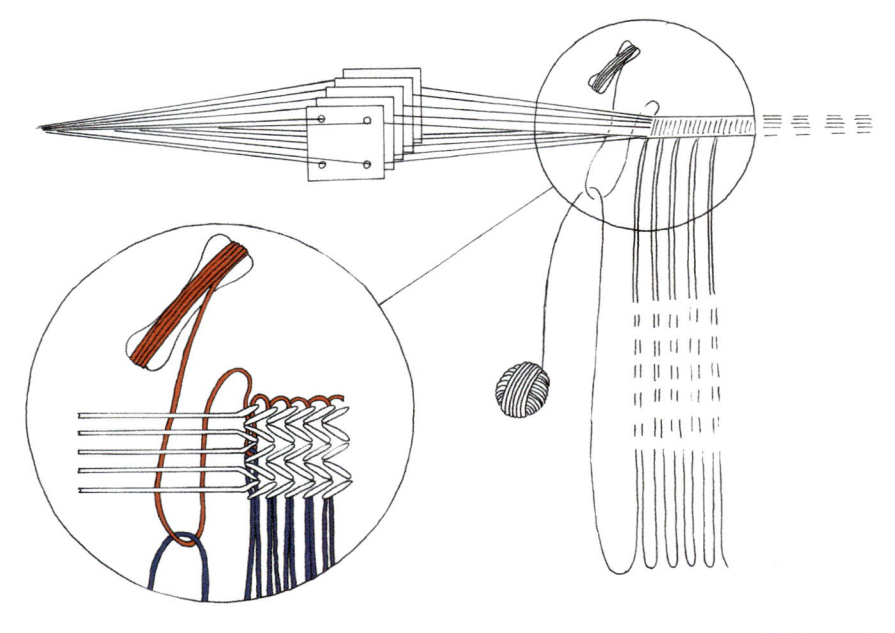

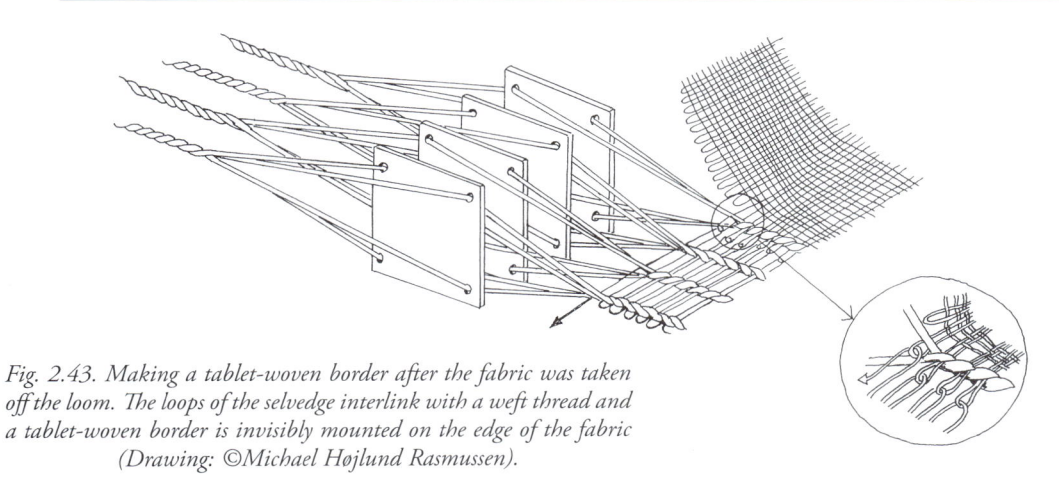

Fig. 2.43. Making a tablet-woven border after the fabric was taken off the loom. The loops of the selvedge interlink with a weft thread and a tablet-woven border is invisibly mounted on the edge of the fabric (Drawing: ©Michael Højlund Rasmussen).

border F.S. 3688 (Cat. no. 15) (see Fig. 2. 23). This fragment has one edge preserved in a similar fashion to the upper edge of the large cloak, but this border is better preserved. The border of F.S. 3688 is registered as a border woven onto the fabric where a starting border is expected to be, it has a simple tablet border which forms the edge of the fabric and beyond the border, twisted fringes are seen. As the border is rather worn, it is possible to see the weft inside the shed: two loops made of threads from the fabric link to two other threads, which in most places are hard twisted (see Fig. 2.22). The fringes of this fabric are longer than the tablet border by at least 3 cm. The most likely way to make these fringes would be to put up a tablet warp, and when inserting the weft, one would take two loops of the fabric, pass a double thread through the loop and twist it firmly with one's fingers, allow this weft of the border – which is also the fringe – to twist. Finally, one would turn the tablets, beat the weft in, and start all over again. This would result in twisted loops inside the shed of the tablet weave. Furthermore, if the fringe beyond the loops has disintegrated, the border of F.S. 3688 would be the same as the upper border of the large cloak. If it had been done in this manner, it may be concluded that as the loops of the side edges are not twisted, there might not have been fringes here.

Both explanations are possible, and it is highly interesting that both these explanations for why the loops of the upper edge of the large cloak are twisted involve weaving methods where the border is woven to the fabric only after the ground weave had first been woven. Therefore, the upper edge of the large cloak is most likely not a starting border, but a border woven to the fabric after it was removed from the loom.

IV: Left side border of the large cloak F.S. 3686 from Thorsberg
The left side border is only preserved as a ghost impression (Fig. 2.48). The warp threads of the left side border are used as the weft of the lower finishing border and thus it is possible to discern the colour of the left side border and the approximate amount of tablets used to make it. The border was about 16 cm wide. On the finishing border, the thread count of 50 tablets is about 4.5 cm. Thus the amount of tablets used to make the 16 cm of the left side border was approx. 178 tablets, which was also the number of tablets counted by Schlabow (Schlabow 1976, 64). The white arrow indicates a spot where a tiny bit of the twill fabric is preserved. This is the only preserved part where the tablet-woven left side border would meet the twill fabric, and if the left side border was made in the same way, as the right side border, the twill fabric would form small loops.

It was an amazing stroke of luck to find just one loop which proves that this large border was originally made using the interlinking method. It was formerly believed that this border of 178 tablets was woven together with the fabric (Schlabow 1976, 63–65) which would be very difficult and hardly rational. Schlabow had a reconstruction made, which needed the work of two skilled weavers for a year. One of the very difficult tasks for these weavers was the manufacture of the side borders. They had 178 tablets hanging at the left side of the loom and the wefts of the fabric and the wefts of the border were beaten in at the same time. Using the interlinking method would have been much easier, as it is woven after the fabric was taken off the loom. This weaving method needs much less work and uses the handicraft technique in a much more sensible way.

V: The incorrectly placed fragment at the upper edge of cloak F.S. 3686 from Thorsberg
At the upper edge of the cloak, a large fragment was placed incorrectly when it was being mounted on a brown woollen cloth. The fragment does not belong there as the s- and z-spinning of the threads

lie opposite the rest of the cloak (Schlabow 1976, p. 63). As the fragment has a small tablet border preserved, Schlabow argues that, the fragment belongs to the right edge border and as there is no room for it there, he argues that the cloak must have been more than 1.68m × 1.68 m which was the supposed size of the cloak. Schlabow changed the size of the cloak to 1.68 m × 2.36 m (Fig. 2.49).

However, as we now have proved that the left edge also had loops of the twill fabric linking to another thread, and as there is enough room for the fragment, it would in fact fit as shown in Fig. 2.50. Another way to prove the correct placing of the fragment is to compare the colour stripes of the fabric close to the tablet border. This was very difficult and no solid evidence can be found. However, dye analysis of the warp threads of the edge of the fabric close to the borders might provide the evidence.

The only possible weaving method of the large cloak from Thorsberg, F.S. 3686 seems to be that, the fabric was woven first and small loops were left at the upper edge and the side edges and long fringes at the lower edge. Afterwards, tablet-woven borders were attached and these borders may well have been very large on all sides.

The only other tablet weaving from weapon deposits which have tablet weaving and interlinking loops is also from Thorsberg. It is a rather coarse fabric F.S. 3688 (Figs 2.23 and 2.51).

But which loom produces a fabric with small loops at three sides?
On the basis of analysing a few textiles from Thorsberg belonging to the National Museum in Denmark, Margrethe Hald argued in 1950 that, these were probably woven on a tubular loom (Hald 1980, 70–71, 191, 222). However, she never had the opportunity to study the textiles from Thorsberg now in the Schloss Gottorf collection. On the basis of the new analysis of the tablet woven borders from Thorsberg we must conclude that some of the textiles were most likely woven on a tubular loom.

The finds from the other weapon deposits do not show interlinking. Where it is possible to see the threads, they are all made in the conventional way. However, as so little has survived compared to the textiles from Thorsberg, this might be a coincidence.

Both independent and integrated bands in the same find
In the material from the weapon deposits, we find a mixture of independent bands and integrated bands. However, there is no separation of the techniques. Both techniques are used in the same finds, at the same time and even on the same textiles. The Thorsberg tunic has an integrated tablet border as the finishing edge and independent bands sewn on the sleeves. In Vorbasse grave 4 (Ræder Knudsen forthcoming b), both an independent band and an integrated band were registered. In Corselitze too (Ræder Knudsen forthcoming a), both an independent and an integrated band were found together with a bog body.

Band with additional weft
A border found on a shield boss from Illerup, FHM 1880 UNK is with some certainty a border of a cloak with fringes woven onto a twill fabric. In a few places, it is possible to see that an additional weft was used. This additional weft could have had the function of securing the edge and the tablet border. As the fringes go from the twill fabric through the shed of the border and make fringes on the outer edge of the border, the warp threads of the border are not kept in place by the weft. An additional weft solves this problem. The only other known example of this technique is a well-

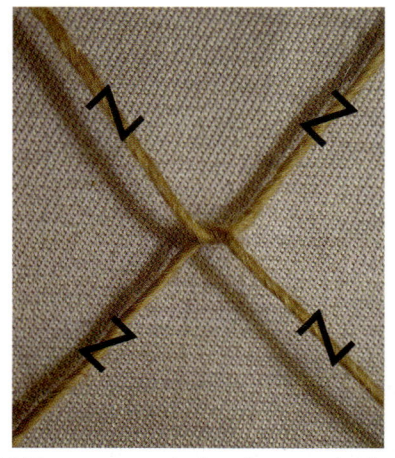

Fig. 2.44. Two z-spun single threads cross each other (©Lise Ræder Knudsen).

Fig. 2.45. When the threads are allowed to twist they refuse (©Lise Ræder Knudsen).

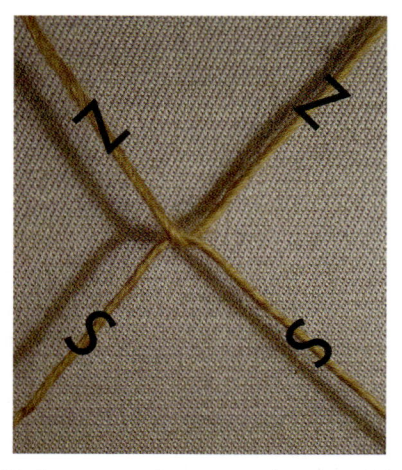

Fig. 2.46. A z-spun and an s-spun thread are joined in a cross (©Lise Ræder Knudsen).

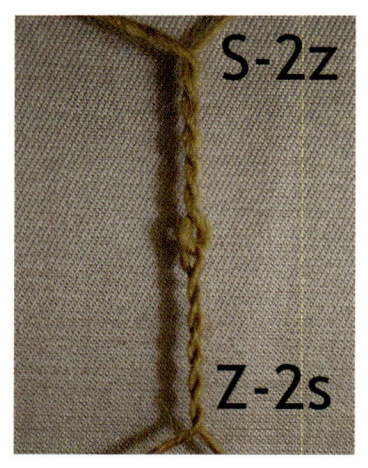

Fig. 2.47. When the threads are allowed to twist they do! (© Lise Ræder Knudsen).

Fig. 2.48. Left side border of the large cloak F.S. 3686 from Thorsberg. The arrow shows a single loop from the twill fabric indicating that also this side was originally made using the interlinking method (Photo: ©Roberto Fortuna, National Museum of Denmark).

preserved textile from Rovsbjerghøj (Ræder Knudsen forthcoming a). It is a very similar cloak with additional weft and was found in a burial urn.

Tablet borders on leg wrappers
A tabby leg wrap from Thorsberg, F.S. 3692 is preserved. The tablet border on the short side is the starting border of the fabric, as it has been woven first. The question of whether these long, leg wraps were woven with the long or the short side as the starting point is worth pondering. The border of F.S. 3692 proves that this was woven from the short side. This opens for the possibility of a small upright loom, a beginner's loom which was easier to handle than a wide loom for making large fabrics. It would be interesting to have this possibility in mind when loom weights are found.

Tablet-woven borders from weapon deposits compared to borders from bogs and burials
The tablet-woven borders found at weapon deposits are made in a great variety of single or combined methods. The most common method is conventional, forward tablet weaving of opposed tablets and woven as a part of a fabric. In weapon deposits, the find distribution is 81% integrated borders and 19% independent borders, while in grave and bog finds, the distribution is 15% independent borders and 85% integrated borders. These numbers are so close, that it is safe to say that no difference between the finds from weapon deposits and graves is detected.

A few very fine borders with pattern weaving too were found in both weapon deposits and graves. Narrow borders were predominantly found in both contexts, but wide borders sometimes occurred too. Moreover, the distribution of borders made of coarse thread and those made of very fine thread are somewhat the same, with the fine borders being rarer than the coarser borders. The use of single threads or double threads for tablet weaving also seems noteworthy. The use of double threads is often connected to the wide cloak borders in fine quality or independent bands with pattern weaving. We have a few samples from weapon deposits, and a few more from graves and bogs. This is not surprising as pattern weaving tends to untwist some of the threads while weaving, and single threads would thus break.

Both from Thorsberg and from a grave at Vrangstrup (see Ræder Knudsen forthcoming a) we have tablet-woven borders where the weaver has used warp threads of different spinning direction for tablets of different twist direction. This gives a special visual effect, but the twist of the tablets then has to correspond to the thread twist to avoid untwisting the yarn – which it does here.

12.5. CONCLUSIONS

The study of tablet-woven borders of 1st–4th century AD weapon deposits provides a comprehensive understanding of the existing material. The great variation in the use of the tablet-weaving technique seen in the material from bogs and graves (Ræder Knudsen forthcoming a) seems to be somewhat the same in the material from weapon deposits. The primary use of tablet weaving at this first stage of the technique in this geographical area is as a technique to help the making of fabrics on a loom. The amount of integrated bands versus the amount of independent bands are nearly the same (81% versus 85%) as in bogs and graves, and the great variation and combination of techniques seems alike in the context of graves and bogs as in the context of weapon deposits.

When the decision was made to treat the tablet weavings from weapon deposits as a separate study from those recovered from bogs and graves, it was assumed that the material from these contexts

Fig. 2.49. Schlabow's drawing of the cloak as it is mounted. For reasons unknown, Schlabow has drawn a mirror image of the cloak. Schlabow argues that fragment 3 in the upper left corner should be moved to the right edge of the fabric and that is why he enlarges the cloak and suggests that the original size was 1.68 m × 2.36 m (Drawing: Schlabow 1976 Abb. 116. Every effort was made to locate the copyright owner).

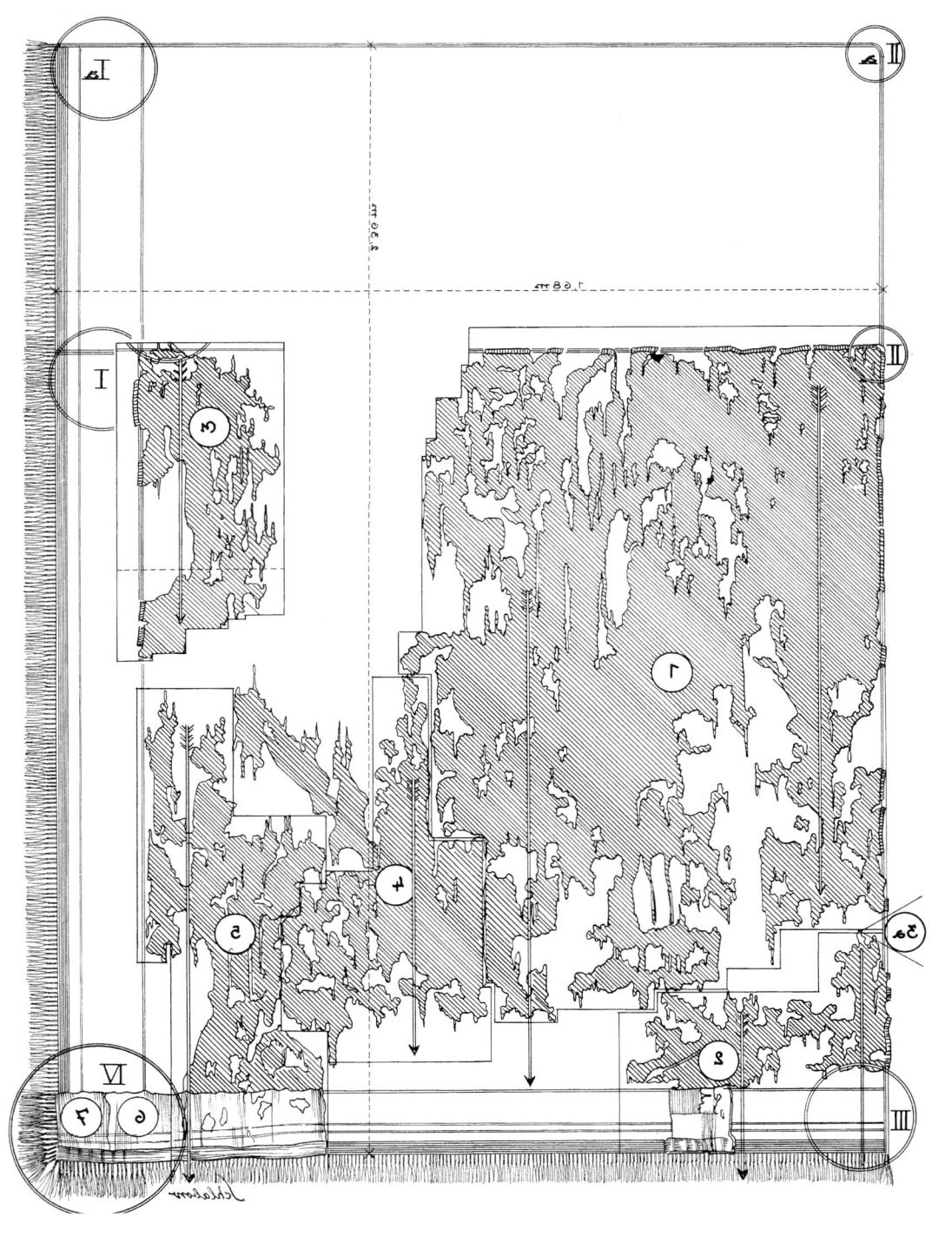

12. Tablet-Woven Textiles from 3rd to 4th-Century AD Weapon Deposits 193

Fig.2.50. Schlabow's drawing computer manipulated so that the fragment which must be moved is part of the left side edge and the loops of the fragment lie at the edge between the large border and the fabric (Drawing: Lise Ræder Knudsen. After Schlabow 1976 Abb. 116).

194 *War and Worship*

Fig.2.51. A coarse twill fabric from Thorsberg with interlinking loops at the edge (Photo: ©Roberto Fortuna, National Museum of Denmark). See also Fig. 2.22 for a close up of the interlinking loops.

could show clear differences. However, there seems to be somewhat the same distribution of various techniques. This leads to the conclusion that the tablet-weaving technique was on the same level of development in our geographical area as it was in the areas from which the defeated warriors originated.

The only find which seems to be somewhat of an exception is some of the textiles from Thorsberg, which have more unique details only seen in material found in Norway. Very recent research by Julia Gräf (2008, 216) where some of the leather artefacts from Thorsberg were analysed for strontium indicates that, some of the objects may have come from Norway or southern Sweden.

As the textiles from Thorsberg are so well preserved, it is possible to go much further into their manufacture than it is possible with the textiles from the other weapon deposits. The study of details concerning the tablet-woven borders have illustrated that, some of the scientific bases of this find must be reconsidered.

This study demonstrates that most likely the original size of the large cloak from Thorsberg (F.S. 3686) is square and not rectangular being around 1.68 m × 1.68 m. Furthermore, the large tablet-woven borders of this cloak, which are the widest tablet-woven borders integrated in a fabric found in the world hitherto, are, in fact, not woven together with the fabric, but woven onto the edges of the fabric after it was taken off the loom. This opens for the possibility that the fabric was woven in one geographical location and the borders woven onto the edges of the fabric elsewhere. Here a strontium analysis of the threads of the border and the fabric would be highly useful, but this has not been possible within the context of this work.

Also the huge time-consumption involved in the making of the cloak has to be reconsidered. Prior work has indicated that making such a cloak would take two skilled weavers a year. With the working method proposed here, using interlinking with an additional weft to the loops of the fabric, the work flow is much more rational.

A further point involves the edging cord on the outer side of some tablet-woven edges of some of the fine textiles from Thorsberg, for instance, the places where the tunic was studied. This has previously been considered as the starting border, but it might in fact be woven to either end of the fabric after it was removed from the loom. A main conclusion of this study is that, the large cloak

Table 2.3. Tablet-woven borders in weapon deposits.

Cat. No	Finding place	Museum number	*	Type of tablet border	Warp	Weft	Width, cm	Number of tablets	Number of tablets pr. cm
01	Illerup	FHM 1880 IXK	A	Cannot be determined	Single threads, spinding direction not possible to see	Cannot be determined	0,6 at least	11 at least	18
02	Illerup	FHM 1880 IXL	A	Edge of a fabric	Single threads slightly z-spun	2 wefts in each shed, spinning ?	1,5 at least	31 at least	22
03	Illerup	FHM 1880 IYF 1 og 2	A	Independent band with pattern	Double threads, S2z	Double threads S2z	3,0 at least	60 at least	20
04	Illerup	FHM 1880 QPC	A	Independent band	Cannot be determined	Cannot be determined	1,0 at least	20 at least	20
05	Illerup	FHM 1880 UNK	A	Edge of a fabric	Single threads z-spun	Two wefts in each shed ?	2,5	26 at least	10
06	Illerup	FHM 1880 VFD	A	Edge of a fabric	Single threads s- and z-spun	Single threads s- and z-spun	0,3 at least	2 at least	7
07	Nydam	1993 SL 217 x 6136	B	Independent band	Single threads s-spun	Z-spun, at least 2 single threads	1,3 at least	12 at least	9
08	Nydam	2860	B	Starting- or side border	Single threads z-spun	2 single threads z-spun	0,2 at least	2 at least	10
09	Nydam	5653 a	B	Cannot be determined	Cannot be determined	Cannot be determined	2,2 at least	29 at least	13
10	Thorsberg	24822 og F.S.3698	B+C	Finishing border	Single threads s- and z-spun	2–3 z- and s-spun single threads	7,0 at least	56 at least	8
11	Thorsberg	24823a og b	B	Finishing border	Single threads z-spun	3 single threads z-spun	4,6	12	2,6
12	Thorsberg	24824 c	B	Starting- or side border	Single threads s-spun	Single threads s-spun	0,7	4	6
13a	Thorsberg	F.S.3683	C	With edging cord, border woven to either end of the warp	Single threads s-spun	Single threads s- and z-spun	0,7	4	6

* A: Belongs to Moesgård Museum, B: Belongs to Stiftung Schleswig-Holsteinische Landesmuseen Schloss Gottorf, C: Belongs to The National Museum of Denmark.

Table 2.3. Tablet-woven borders in weapon deposits continued.

Cat. No	Finding place	Museum number	*	Type of tablet border	Warp	Weft	Width, cm	Number of tablets	Number of tablets pr. cm
14a	Thorsberg	F.S.3686	C	Finishing border	Double threads, S2z	2 single threads z-spun	13	136	10
14b	Thorsberg	F.S.3686	C	Starting border	Double threads S2z	2 single threads z-spun	0,8 at least	9	12
14c	Thorsberg	F.S.3686	C	Side border, right	Double threads S2z	2 single threads s-spun	0,5 at least	5	12
14d	Thorsberg	F.S.3686	C	Side border, left	Double threads S2z	2 single threads s-spun	16	178	12
15	Thorsberg	F.S.3688	C	Starting border	Single threads z-spun	4 single threads z-spun	2,5 appr.	9 at least	4
16a	Thorsberg	F.S.3689	C	Finishing border	Single threads s-spun	4–5 single threads z-spun	3,0 at least	20 at least	7
16b	Thorsberg	F.S.3689	C	Side border	Single threads s-spun	Single threads s-spun	2,5 at least	14 at least	7
17	Thorsberg	F.S.3690	C	Starting border	Single threads z-spun	Two wefts as a closed loop	0,5	4	8
18a	Thorsberg	F.S.3691	C	Side border	Single threads s-spun	Four threads from the fabric, twist ?	0,5	5	10
18b	Thorsberg	F.S.3691	C	Side border	Single threads s-spun	Four threads from the fabric, twist ?	0,5	5	10
19a	Thorsberg	F.S.3692	C	Starting border	Single threads z-spun	Threads from the fabric, twist ?	0,5	3	6
19b	Thorsberg	F.S.3692	C	Side border	Single threads z-spun	Threads from the fabric, twist ?	0,5	3	6
19c	Thorsberg	F.S.3692	C	Side border	Single threads z-spun	Threads from the fabric, twist ?	0,5	3	6
20	Thorsberg	F.S.3695	C	Starting- or side border	Single threads z-spun	2 single threads z-spun	0,8 appr.	6	8
21	Thorsberg	F.S.3697	C	Finishing border	Double threads S2z	Single threads s- and z-spun	6,3	79 at least	16
22	Thorsberg	F.S.3706	C	With edging cord, border woven to either end of the warp	Single threads z-spun	2 single threads z-spun	0,5	3	6
23	Thorsberg	FHM 607–1 a	A	Finishing border	Single threads s-spun	5 single threads z-spun	3,5	21	6
24	Thorsberg	FHM 607–1–b	A	Finishing border	Single threads z-spun	1–2 single threads s-spun	1,8	12	7
25	Viemose	24762	B	Independent band	Double threads S2z	2 single threads s-spun (?)	3,2 at least	43 at least	14

* A: Belongs to Moesgård Museum, B: Belongs to Stiftung Schleswig-Holsteinische Landesmuseen Schloss Gottorf, C: Belongs to The National Museum of Denmark.

(F.S. 3686), the tunic (F.S. 3683) and surely other textiles from Thorsberg might very well be woven on a tubular loom, which produces a fabric with short loops on 3 or 4 edges. Previously, the large cloak was seen as the ultimate product of the warp-weighted loom.

The study of the tablet-woven borders from weapon deposits shows us that there are many more possibilities and weaving methods involving tablet borders woven to the edges of fabric than previously believed. It opens up the possibility of new interpretations of the looms used to produce the fabrics, but this is a rather complex issue and many details of the weaving have to be taken into consideration. Further study of the tablet-woven borders woven to textiles in the extant material would be necessary in order to obtain more solid information (Table 2.3).

Acknowledgements

I would like to thank Susan Möller-Wiering very much for the opportunity to cooperate with her and for inspiring discussions, and Ingrid Ulbricht and conservator Gabriele Zink at Schloss Gottorf, Schleswig Germany for their kind help on several occasions. Also I am grateful to the staff at Moesgård Museum and the National Museum of Denmark for their kind help and the opportunity to study their material. A special thank you to Roberto Fortuna at the National Museum of Denmark who photographed the Thorsberg finds in the collections of both the National Museum of Denmark and Schloss Gottorf Museum and to Cherine Munkholt, who untiring worked on the language corrections.

Bibliography

Bender Jørgensen, L. 1980. Cloth of the Roman Iron Age in Denmark. 1–60. *Acta Archaeologica* 50 1979, Copenhagen.
Bender Jørgensen, L. 1986. Forhistoriske textiler i Skandinavien. Prehistoric Scandinavian Textiles, *Nordiske Fortidsminder*, Serie B, 9, København.
Bender Jørgensen, L. 2003. Krigerdragten I Folkevandringstiden. In P. Rolfsen and F.-A. Stylegar (eds) *Snartemofunnene i nytt lys.*, 53–79. Universitets kulturhistoriske museer. Skrifternr. 2, Oslo.
Collingwood, P. 1982. *The Techniques of Tablet Weaving.* London.
Dedekam, H. 1926. To tekstilfund fra folkevandringstiden. *Bergen Museums Årbok 1924–25*, 1–57, Bergen.
Hald, M. 1950. *Olddanske Tekstiler.* København.
Hald, M. 1980. *Ancient Danish Textiles from Bogs and Burials,* Copenhagen.
Halvorsen, S. W. 2009. Dates and Dyes – New test results from the finds from Tegle and Helgeland, Norway. *Archaeological Textiles Newsletter* 49, 2–6, Copenhagen.
Hansen, E. 1990. *Brikvævning, historie, teknik, farver, mønstre,* Højbjerg.
Hoffmann, M. 1974. *The Warp-weighted Loom.* 2nd ed., Oslo. First published 1964.
Jensen, J. 2003. *Danmarks Oldtid, Ældre jernalder 500 f.Kr.–400 e.Kr.,* København.
Mannering, U. and Gleba, M. (eds) forthcoming. *Designed for Life and Death,* National Museum of Denmark.
Nockert, M. 1991. The Högom Find and other Migration Period Textiles and Costumes in Scandinavia. *Högom Part. II. Archaeology and Environment* 9, Umeå.
Raknes, I. 1982. The textiles from the Migration period grave at Evebø/Eide, Gloppen, Sogn and Fjordane, Norway. *Studien zur Sachsenforschung* 4, 304–313, Hildesheim.
Ræder Knudsen, L. 1996. *Analyse og rekonstruktion af brikvævning.* Unpublished. 2. dels opgave. Det Kgl. Danske Kunstakademi, Konservatorskolen, København.
Ræder Knudsen, L. 1998. An Iron Age Cloak with Tablet-woven Border: a New Interpretation of the Method of Production. In L. Bender Jørgensen and C. Rinaldo (eds), *Textiles in European Archaeology. Report from the 6th NESAT Symposium 7–11th May 1996 in Borås*, 79–84. GOTARC Series A, Vol. 1. Göteborg, Göteborg University.

Ræder Knudsen, L. forthcoming a. Tablet-woven bands from bogs and burials of the Early Iron Age. In U. Mannering and M. Gleba (eds), *Designed for Life and Death,* National Museum of Denmark.

Ræder Knudsen, L. forthcoming b. Tablet-woven borders from Vorbasse (working title) in Ulla Lund Hansen *et al.*, *Late Roman Grave Fields of the Vorbasse Settlement. Grave Fields, Settlement, Environment and Textile Production. Late Roman Jutland reconsidered,* Nordiske Fortidsminder Series, National Museum of Denmark.

Schlabow, K. 1976. *Textilfunde der Eisenzeit in Norddeutschland,* Neumünster.

Stettiner, R. 1911. Brettchenwebereien in den Moorfunden von Damendorf, Daetgen und Torsberg, *Mitteilungen des Anthropologischen Vereins in Schleswig-Holstein* 19, 26–56.

Wild, J. P. and Bender Jørgensen, L. 1988. Clothes from the Roman Empire. Barbarians and Romans. In L. Bender Jørgensen and K. Tidow (eds), *Archaeological Textiles in Northern Europe. Report from the 2nd NESAT Symposium,* 65–98. Arkæologiske Skrifter 2, København.